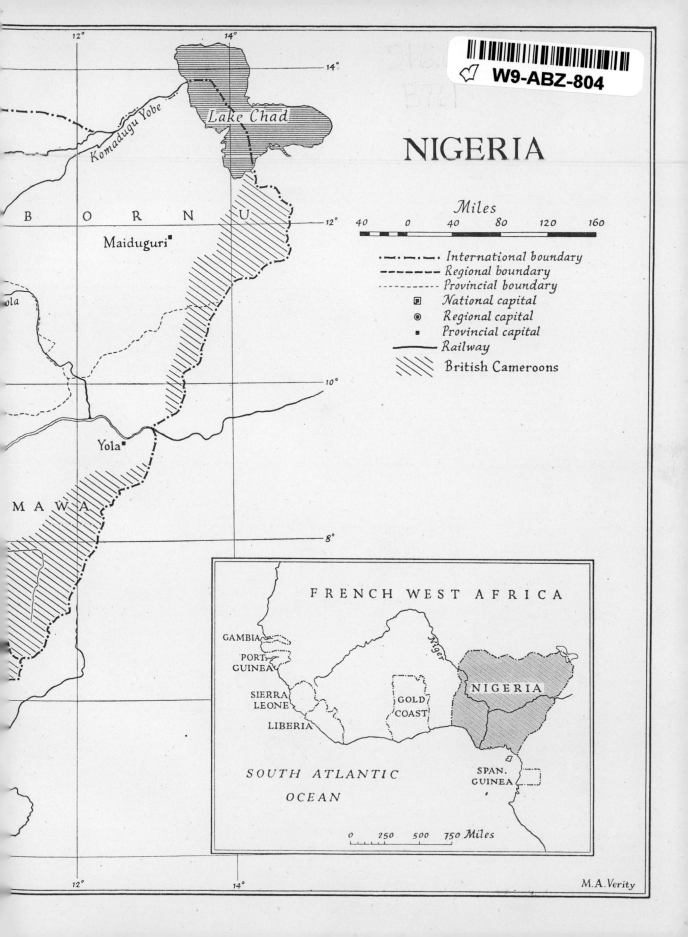

NIGERIA

12°   14°   14°

Komadugu Yobe

Lake Chad

B O R N U   12°

Maiduguri

ola

Yola

M A W A   8°

Miles

40   0   40   80   120   160

—·—··—·— International boundary
— — — — — Regional boundary
‑ ‑ ‑ ‑ ‑ Provincial boundary
▣ National capital
◉ Regional capital
▪ Provincial capital
——— Railway
//// British Cameroons

FRENCH WEST AFRICA

GAMBIA

PORT.
GUINEA

SIERRA
LEONE

LIBERIA

Niger

GOLD
COAST

NIGERIA

SPAN.
GUINEA

SOUTH ATLANTIC
OCEAN

0   250   500   750 Miles

12°   14°

M.A.Verity

LAND AND PEOPLE IN NIGERIA

To Ruth and Margaret
for their encouragement and their forbearance

LAND AND PEOPLE IN NIGERIA

The Human Geography of Nigeria and its Environmental Background

K. M. BUCHANAN, B.A.

Professor of Geography, Victoria University College, Wellington, N.Z.
Sometime Head of Department of Geography, University College, Ibadan

and

J. C. PUGH, M.A.

Lecturer in Geography, University College, Ibadan

With a contribution by

PROFESSOR A. BROWN, M.B., Ch.B., F.R.C.P.Ed.

Dean of the Faculty of Medicine, University College, Ibadan

and a foreword by

PROFESSOR L. DUDLEY STAMP, C.B.E., D.Litt., D.Sc.

Professor of Social Geography, University of London

UNIVERSITY OF LONDON PRESS LTD

WARWICK SQUARE, LONDON, E.C.4

AGENTS OVERSEAS

AUSTRALIA
(*and its Dependencies*)
W. S. SMART   P.O. Box 120, SYDNEY, N.S.W.
Showroom: 558, George Street.

CANADA
CLARKE, IRWIN & CO., LTD.,
103, St. Clair Avenue West, TORONTO, 5.

EGYPT AND THE SUDAN
DINO JUDAH NAHUM   P.O. Box 940, CAIRO.
Showroom: 44, Sharia Sherif Pasha.

FAR EAST
(*including China and Japan*)
DONALD MOORE   Oldham Hall, SINGAPORE, 9.

INDIA, PAKISTAN, BURMA AND CEYLON
ORIENT LONGMANS, LTD.,
BOMBAY: Nicol Road, Ballard Estate.
CALCUTTA: 17, Chittaranjan Ave.
MADRAS: 36A, MOUNT ROAD.

NEW ZEALAND
(*and its Dependencies*)
R. J. SARE   41, Shortland Street, AUCKLAND C.1.

SOUTH AFRICA
H. B. TIMMINS   P.O. Box 94, CAPE TOWN.
Showroom: 58–60, Long Street.

Printed & Bound in England for the UNIVERSITY OF LONDON PRESS LTD.,
by HAZELL WATSON & VINEY LTD., Aylesbury and London

FOREWORD

The old adage that a little knowledge is a dangerous thing conveys with it the implication that wide and accurate knowledge is the essential foundation for progress and development. At a time when planning for the future is a vital and urgent consideration, the need for a national stocktaking in every country of the world should be particularly apparent. It should surely be obvious that any planning and development for the future must start from the present position, and that where physical planning of land use and resources is concerned no country can be treated as if it were a blank sheet of paper. Every country does, in fact, present a complex pattern of natural factors—the varied relief of the land with its mountains, plateaux, valleys and plains; the hidden geological structure, with its control over the disposition of economic minerals; the varied climatic and weather conditions, with their influence on soil formation, plant growth and animal life. Further, every country exhibits the varied response of its human inhabitants, be they many or few, to this complicated environment, and so the surface exhibits a kaleidoscopic pattern of settlement and land use.

These things can be described, but they can only be shown accurately with the aid of maps. Accordingly, the authors have set out in this volume to do for Nigeria what is there, as elsewhere, badly needed. It surveys the present state of knowledge of the country's resources, accurately portrayed in a large series of maps, with a full explanation covering each. It thus combines an atlas of natural resources and of the factors governing development with a text which enables the reader to appreciate their significance and meaning.

For their task the authors are particularly well qualified. Towards the end of the last war, bomb-scarred Birmingham and the surrounding Midland counties began to look to the future, and it was Professor Buchanan who carried out for the West Midland Group on Planning and Reconstruction, under the chairmanship of the Vice-Chancellor of Birmingham University, the survey of the existing position. In addition, he studied in minute detail the agricultural geography of the productive County of Worcester for the Land Utilisation Survey of Britain. It was natural that when he moved to South Africa he should initiate similar studies, and when appointed to be Head of the Department of Geography at Ibadan, he turned his attention to almost untouched fields of study in Nigeria. It was there that he had the good fortune to meet one who shared with him an enthusiasm for getting things done and a passion for hard work. Mr. Pugh had already some years' experience in the Nigerian Survey Department before re-entering academic life, and his knowledge of the country was invaluable in the joint work.

This large collection of original maps, nearly all drawn personally by the authors and based on their own research in field, office and library, speaks for itself and is a work of intelligent national stocktaking. The text does not ignore those aspects of Nigerian life which lie outside the field of natural resources. It has often been said that disease is still the real ruler of Africa, and the lengthy section by Professor Brown is therefore very apposite, whilst the discussion of agricultural development problems and of social services is likewise of vital importance.

Considered as a whole, this is a work which has a special value at a time when Nigeria is on the threshold of great development and is showing what has been achieved by harmonious inter-racial co-operation.

v

Current political differences between the three Regions of the country emphasise the variations in background, culture and development which are outlined in this book.   It is to be hoped that this work will also help to indicate the interdependence of the Regions and the advantages to be gained by close inter-Regional co-operation.

L. DUDLEY STAMP.

June, 1955

CONTENTS

PLATES

facing page

MAPS AND DIAGRAMS

INTRODUCTION

In spite of the growing importance of Africa in university studies and in spite of the growing interest in problems of African development there exist few studies of the geography of the British African Territories sufficiently detailed to serve either as a text-book at university level or as a source of background material for those concerned, directly or indirectly, with development projects. This volume has been prepared as an attempt to overcome this deficiency as far as Nigeria is concerned. It is hoped that it will be of value not only to university students in West Africa and overseas but also to private individuals and individuals in Government service who wish for a general picture of the resources and problems of Britain's largest Colonial dependency. The work has been based on three major groups of sources:

(1) existing published material, notably the annual reports of various Government Departments but including also some periodical literature; of the periodicals used two, *Farm and Forest* and *Nigeria*, both published in the Territory, deserve special mention.

(2) unpublished statistical material furnished by various Government Departments and especially by the Departments of Agriculture and of Marketing and Exports.

(3) field observations; field work for those sections contributed by K. Buchanan was carried out during the period Nov. 1948–Dec. 1950, supplemented by a short period of work in the Northern Region during the early summer of 1952; that for the chapters by J. C. Pugh was carried out during the period 1948–52, and the chapters include also the fruits of the author's earlier experience as an officer in the Survey Department.

It was originally intended that the material should be presented in the form of an atlas with a short text commentary. It soon became clear, however, that such an undertaking presupposed the existence of a considerable volume of background material which could be used to supplement the necessarily brief text such a layout would have entailed, and in the absence of such material the authors were forced to recast the original layout and to work on the basis of a greatly expanded text. The maps remain, however, the most important part of the volume; they contain a considerable amount of material never before published and it is hoped that they will give the reader a clear and concise picture of our existing knowledge (and of the gaps in that knowledge) regarding the land and people of this vitally important African territory.

The writers owe a very great debt to the many members of various Government Departments who have furnished data and given freely the benefits of their experience of Nigerian problems. It would be invidious to single out any individual for special mention, and the opportunity is taken of expressing the authors' thanks to all those who gave so generously of their time and advice;* for opinions expressed in the text and for any errors of fact or interpretation the authors alone are responsible.

During their field work the authors found much kindness and hospitality; they owe a special debt of thanks to the following: D. W. H. Baker, Kaduna; Mr. and Mrs. Dudley, Bida; Malam Aba Gana, Kaduna; R. Lander, Keffi; Mr. and Mrs. Tasker, Vom.

Keith Buchanan
J. C. Pugh

* At Prof. Brown's request a special acknowledgment of help received during the preparation of the section on Health Problems is included overleaf.

ACKNOWLEDGMENTS

I am indebted to Dr. S. L. A. Manuwa, C.M.G., O.B.E., Inspector-General of Medical Services for his co-operation and help in allowing access to official records; to Dr. L. J. Bruce-Chwatt, Senior Malariologist to the Nigerian Government, on whose advice and published work the section on malaria largely depends; to Dr. T. F. Davey, O.B.E., Leprosy Adviser to the Nigerian Government, who furnished the principal data for the section on leprosy; and to Dr. P. B. Stones, lately Medical Officer at the Virus Research Institute, Yaba, who kindly made available the annual reports of the Yellow Fever Research Institute.

I wish to express gratitude to Dr. J. L. McLetchie, O.B.E., Adviser in Rural Health to the Inspector-General of Medical Services, without whose tireless help the bulk of the section on disease could not have been written, and who provided all of the data relating to Trypanosomiasis, Bilharzia and the work of the Medical Field Units.

Lastly I would like to express my thanks to the medical officers and others who gave me the benefit of their experience in Nigeria.

A. BROWN.

The authors and publisher are indebted to Aerofilms Limited for permission to reproduce Plates I–V and VIII–XVI, and to the Nigerian Electricity Supply Corporation for data and maps referring to electricity supplies on the Jos Plateau. The map of soil types (p. 37) is based on a detailed map by Dr. H. Vine and is reproduced by courtesy of Dr. Vine and the Inspector-General of Agriculture, Nigeria. The authors are also deeply grateful to Margaret Pugh for her help in the compilation of the index.

CHAPTER I

THE ENVIRONMENTAL SETTING

Recent development work in Nigeria has demonstrated convincingly the crucial importance of a full understanding of the various elements in the tropical environment. Modern technological and economic progress, far from diminishing the importance of environmental factors, rather enhances it, for such progress is accompanied by an increasing delicacy of adjustment to local environmental conditions. Over wide areas the old subsistence economy has been progressively replaced by specialised production of those crops most suited to local conditions. Imported skills and capital have made possible the fuller exploitation of resources such as coal, tin and columbite and the investigation of potential resources, such as the oil of the Delta or the water of the Chad Basin.

An understanding of the existing pattern of development and of Nigerian potentialities calls, therefore, for a full discussion of the physical environment—of the geological structure which controls the distribution of mineral and water resources and of soil types; of the topographical conditions limiting development of communications, of agricultural mechanisation or irrigation; of the character of the climate and its regional variations. It calls also for an understanding of the biological environment, of the vegetation which summates the influence of both physical and biotic factors and of the diseases and parasites which have had a major influence on the pattern and quality of human life in the Territory. Chapter I, which summarises the major features of the Nigerian environment, is intended to provide the basis for such an understanding.

GEOLOGY

Over the greater part of the country, surface rocks are those of the Pre-Cambrian Basement Complex, crystalline rocks forming part of the main African continental mass. Although younger rocks (sedimentary or volcanic) are exposed in many parts of the country, the Basement rocks underlie these at varying depths. These crystalline rocks include those carrying minerals, such as tinstone, columbite and gold, referred to in detail later; they also give rise to characteristic landforms, such as the rounded domes of bare rock (inselbergs) which are found not only in the different Basement areas of Nigeria but also in other parts of tropical Africa where similar rocks are exposed.

The sedimentary rocks are comparatively young; the earliest sedimentary formations reported in Nigeria were deposited in the Lower Cretaceous period, and there are probably no formations intermediary in age between the Pre-Cambrian and the Cretaceous, such as are found farther west in the Gold Coast. The Cretaceous rocks lie in the valleys of the Niger, Benue, Cross and Gongola Rivers, and underlie newer formations in the N.E. and extreme N.W. of Nigeria, and along the coastal margins. The sedimentary formations include the coal and lignite deposits, also the limestones and clays which may assume increasing importance in industrial development. The landforms, particularly the hill forms, developed on them are markedly different from those of the crystalline Basement rocks, and the crossing of the crystalline-sedimentary boundary zone is frequently apparent on the ground, even to the traveller with little or no geological knowledge, by a transition from inselbergs to low flat-topped hills.

In some areas, however, the boundary cannot be so readily identified, geological processes having reached a late stage where wide plains of little diversity transect crystalline and sedimentary rocks equally and without distinction.

Volcanic rocks are found in the centre and east of Nigeria, particularly in the Cameroons. These are marked on the map as Tertiary in age, but volcanic activity may have started as early as the Cretaceous.   In some areas cones and craters leave no doubt as to the origin of the present landforms; in others, lava flows over large areas have been subjected to erosive forces for a long enough period of time for plains to be cut across them, or even, as in the case of the Jos Plateau, for such plains to be further dissected to leave remnants standing as flat-topped hills similar in appearance to those characteristic of some of the sedimentary areas.

It must be stressed that over wide areas of the country no exposures of fresh rock are apparent. Where the processes of physical geology have advanced to a stage giving mature or old-age plains upon which forces of erosion operate very slowly, weathering has taken place to great depth and the rocks are decomposed to a degree which precludes identification of original type. The common end-product of such decomposition is the "laterite" characteristic of the tropics, developed on rocks of widely differing nature, and "laterites" and lateritic concretions may be found in all areas. Similar surface formations of this nature are therefore no indication of any similarity of underlying parent rocks, nor may they invariably be used to correlate erosion plains in different areas, since the geomorphological processes which have had the greatest effect in producing the present landforms appear to be those of backwearing by lateral scarp retreat rather than downwearing by general vertical corrasion. Consequently similar lateritic development occurs at the present time on plains which owe their origin to different cycles of erosion following successive changes of relative level between the sea and the land.

The main geological groups are treated below in more detail, in relation to original rock type and age and not in accordance with present surface exposures, as these may include—or may consist entirely of—decomposition products of the type mentioned.

The Pre-Cambrian Basement Complex

This includes a variety of igneous and metamorphic rocks, which have not yet been mapped in detail, and no major subdivision of the Basement has been attempted. Distinction can, however, be made between the Older and Younger Granites. The former merge into gneisses and migmatites, and may be found to include several major groups when they have been more fully investigated. The true Younger Granites are biotite and riebeckite granites, with considerable mineralisation; from them is derived most of the cassiterite (tinstone) exported from Nigeria. With syenites and other associated rocks they form the greater part of the high Jos Plateau (Fig. 4), with outlying masses to N.E., N.W. and S.W. The Younger Granites are particularly resistant to erosion, and have led to the preservation of the Jos Plateau and smaller highland areas, such as the Mada Hills between the Plateau and the railway to the south-west of it.

The Basement Complex also includes areas of schists and quartzites, as in parts of Sokoto and Oyo Provinces, and the principal gold deposits are associated with the schists. Pegmatite veins are widespread in the central areas, and also occur elsewhere. These are frequently mineralised to some extent, containing small quantities of cassiterite, columbite and tantalite.

The Cretaceous Sedimentaries

The earliest sedimentary rocks recorded in Nigeria are Lower Cretaceous (Albian), exposed in the middle basins of the Cross River and the Benue, and consisting of sandstones, shales and thin bands of limestone. These beds show folding, which is apparent west of Abakaliki on the road from Enugu, and continues eastward to the Basement rocks of Ogoja and the Cameroons. Folded beds were described by Falconer and Longbottom in the middle Benue,[1] and although originally thought to

[1] J. D. Falconer, *The Geology and Geography of Northern Nigeria*, London (1911), p. 147.

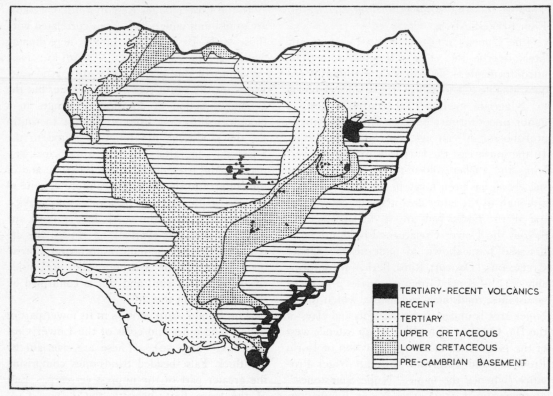

FIG. 1. GEOLOGY

The wide extent of the crystalline Basement is at once apparent, as is also the significant distribution of Cretaceous sedimentaries in the Niger and Benue Troughs. The Lower Cretaceous rocks pass beneath the Upper Cretaceous and later sediments in the N.E.: they do not lie beneath the Upper Cretaceous rocks of the Niger Trough, where warping has caused the partial stripping of the sedimentary cover.

The volcanic rocks include the Fluvio-volcanic Series of the Jos Plateau and the cones of the Benue Trough. In the latter, individual occurrences may each represent several cones. The N.E.–S.W. trend of the volcanics represents structural weakness in this direction, and the absence of volcanics from the Niger Trough may be structurally significant.

be Turonian (Upper Cretaceous) in age, these have more recently been relegated by Tattam to the Albian and correlated with the folded beds of this age in the south-east.[1] The Lower Cretaceous sediments throughout these eastern exposures contain scattered lead-zinc deposits and salt springs, and in the middle Benue are broken through by a number of small volcanic hills, to which reference will be made later.

The Lower Cretaceous deposits were laid down in a long arm of the sea following the line of the Benue valley, continuing northward through the present lower Gongola valley and curving N.W. and W. towards the middle Niger. In Nigeria most of the surviving areas of Lower Cretaceous deposition, other than those mentioned above, are now covered by newer rocks, but the early sediments are exposed in parts of Katsina and Sokoto provinces, as grits and clays of gentle inclination, lacking the marked folding of the contemporary beds of the east and south-east. The Gundumi Series of Sokoto has been identified by Brynmor Jones with the Grès de

[1] C. M. Tattam, "A Review of Nigerian Stratigraphy", *Geol. Surv. Nig.*, *Annual Report*, 1943. Appendix B, p. 38, para. 112.

Tegama of the *Continental Intercalaire* of French West Africa.[1]

The Upper Cretaceous beds (Turonian and later) overlie the older sediments, sometimes unconformably. (There is no mention of unquestionable Cenomanian rocks in references to Nigerian geology.) Tattam[2] suggests a major unconformity between the folded rocks, probably of Albian age, and later tilted beds. In the south-east the later beds are tilted, overlying the earlier folded rocks, and a similar succession has been noted in the middle Benue, although in the latter area it would appear that not all the folded beds are of Albian age. In Sokoto the Lower Cretaceous Gundumi Series has also been shown to underlie the Upper Cretaceous (Danian) Rima Series unconformably. The Rima Group comprises a series of sandstones, mudstones and shales, which in the Niger area is underlain by the grits and clays of the Illo Group. The Illo Group extends west of the Niger into the Borgu Division of Ilorin Province, and southward through Niger Province (whence the name " Nupe Sandstones " originated) to Lokoja at the Niger–Benue confluence apart from one break-through of the crystalline Basement rocks from which the younger cover has been stripped. Similar clayey sands form the base of Mount Patti at Lokoja, overlain by shales with carbonaceous clays, sands and a top capping of oolitic ironstone. East of the confluence the sands and oolitic ironstone reappear on a low escarpment in the Bassange country, with seams of poor coal outcropping near the foot of the scarp. Sands and clay shales lie beneath the coal. Tattam identified the sandstones above the coals with the False-bedded Sandstones of the south-east, mentioned later as lying between the Lower and Upper Coal Measures, and he therefore considers the Illo Group to be a basal horizon below the Lower Coal Measures, conformable with them and not older than the Turonian.[3]

In the Lower Niger Region south of Lokoja are sandstones which have been correlated with those of the Bassange escarpment, here dipping gently to the south-east. There are local variations of dip as the rocks are traced eastwards on the south side of the Benue, but the general direction of dip slowly changes in a clockwise direction from south-east to south. As the sandstones are followed round to the S.E., the dip alters in the same clockwise pattern; the irregular scarp of Bassange and of the country to the E. becomes more definite as it turns southward and passes east of Nsukka, until by the time the scarp has attained the height of the cliffs overlooking Enugu the dip is W.N.W. All the indications favour a broad open syncline in the Anambra valley area inside this surrounding rim, and this is confirmed by the succession in this area.

The Enugu scarp consists in its lower part of shales, sandstones and coals of the Lower Coal Measures (Fig. 50). These are overlain by the thick False-bedded Sandstones comprising the greater part of the impressive scarp. East of the scarp foot, beneath the Lower Coal Measures, lie clay shales tilted gently to the W.N.W., resting unconformably upon the folded Lower Cretaceous rocks which appear at the surface farther to the east. The area of shales to the east of the scarp is considerable in the north, but narrows progressively to the south until superseded by a sandstone facies, also unconformable on the folded Lower Cretaceous shales. The sandstones increase in thickness to form the Awgu escarpment, which overlaps and replaces the Enugu scarp in this southern section, and behind the Awgu scarp the False-bedded Sandstones prominent at Enugu rest directly on the Awgu sandstones and shales; the Lower Coal Measures and their underlying shales have thinned out and disappeared, either by change of facies or through a minor unconformity. (The Coal Measures also appear to thin out and disappear on the western side of the Anambra

[1] Brynmor Jones, "The Sedimentary Rocks of Sokoto Province", *Geol. Surv. Nig.*, Bulletin 18 (1948), p. 44.
[2] C. M. Tattam, *op. cit.*, p. 39, para. 120.
[3] C. M. Tattam, *op. cit.*, p. 37, para. 106.

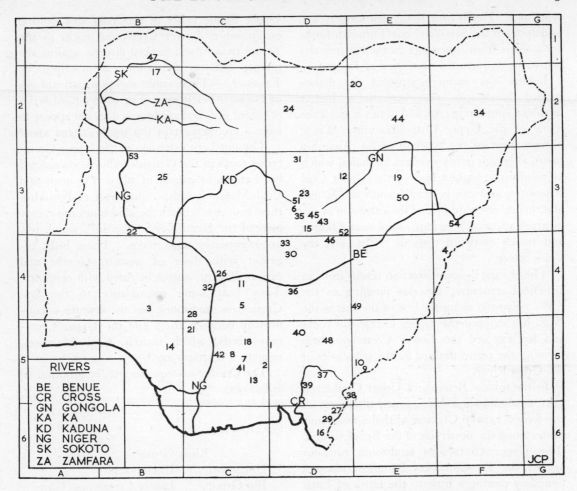

FIG. 2. LOCALITIES CITED IN THE CHAPTER ON GEOLOGY

1	Abakaliki	D5	19	Gombe	E3	37	Mamfe	D5
2	Afikpo	C5	20	Hadejia	E2	38	Manengouba Mts.	D5
3	Akure	B4	21	Ishan Plateau	C5	39	Oban Hills	D5
4	Alantika Mts.	F4	22	Jebba	B3	40	Ogoja	D5
5	Anambra valley	C4	23	Jos	D3	41	Okigwi	C5
6	Assob	D3	24	Kano	D2	42	Onitsha	C5
7	Awgu	C5	25	Kontagora	B3	43	Panyam	D3
8	Awka	C5	26	Koton Karifi	C4	44	Potiskum	E2
9	Bamboulo Mt.	E5	27	Koupe Mt.	D6	45	Ropp	D3
10	Bamenda	E5	28	Kukuruku	C4	46	Shendam	D4
11	Bassange scarp	C4	29	Kumba	D6	47	Sokoto	B1
12	Bauchi	D3	30	Lafia	D4	48	Sonkwala Hills	D5
13	Bende	C5	31	Liruein-Kano Hills	D3	49	Takum	E4
14	Benin	B5	32	Lokoja	C4	50	Tangale	E3
15	Bokkos	D3	33	Mada Hills	D4	51	Vom	D3
16	Cameroon Mt.	D6	34	Maiduguri	F2	52	Wase	D3
17	Dange scarp	B2	35	Makafo	D3	53	Yelwa	B3
18	Enugu	C5	36	Makurdi	D4	54	Yola	F3

syncline.) Fossils from the Awgu scarp appear to date from the Senonian, but Turonian forms are known from limestones in the tilted shales below the scarp to the north-east of Enugu.

Behind the main escarpment the False-bedded Sandstones pass beneath a higher sequence containing coal, and to this is given the name of the Upper Coal Measures. These occupy most of the syncline of the Anambra basin, although partly overlain by shales, which are really the highest beds of the Upper Coal Measures, and can be traced south to Okigwi and thence eastward behind the extension of the escarpment, which swings round near Okigwi and trends eastward towards Afikpo and the Cross River.

The change in scarp direction results from an anticlinal structure, the axis pitching to the S.W. Erosion along the line of the axis to the N.E. has stripped the Upper Cretaceous rocks and has exposed the Lower Cretaceous beds forming the plains drained by the tributaries of the Cross River.

In the middle Benue area Upper Cretaceous grits, sandstones and shales, gently tilted, rest on the folded Lower Cretaceous shales and sandstones along the north side of the Benue trough. The Upper Cretaceous sandstones run out against the Pre-Cambrian Basement along a boundary passing a little to the north of Lafia and Shendam. Poor coal is known a little south of Lafia, and this probably represents the Lower Coal Measures.[1] It is not yet clear whether these coals lie above or below the sandstones contacting the crystalline rocks to the north. If the former, these coarse sandstones represent the Nupe—Lokoja beds; if the latter, they would appear as a northward representative of the False-bedded Sandstones. Coals are also found in the Gombe Division west of the Lower Gongola River, and may be correlated with the general Coal Measures group.

Upper Cretaceous sandstones occur in the Upper Benue valley in the Yola area, resting on (possibly) Lower Cretaceous rocks in the Benue trough, and banked directly against the granite hills to the south, as described by Falconer.[2] These sandstones pass eastward out of Nigerian territory. The earlier basal series of folded grits and sandstones does not appear to have a counterpart in the south-eastern area.[3]

The northern extension of the Upper Cretaceous rocks in the Gongola valley is considered by Tattam to consist of tilted Turonian and Coal Measures beds. South-east of Potiskum these beds pass beneath the sandstones and clayey grits of the Kerri-Kerri "plateau", which rest unconformably upon them. These beds, together with those of western Gombe and eastern Bauchi, cannot be dated with certainty. They bear some resemblance to the late Cretaceous sandstones, but the definite unconformity between them and the Upper Cretaceous beds, which include Coal Measures, suggests a Tertiary age.[4]

The Cretaceous sequence may be summarised as follows:

NORTH-WEST

Rima Group
Unconformity　　Unconformity
Illo Group　　　Lower Cretaceous (Gundumi Group)

SOUTH-EAST

Anambra Shales
Upper Coal Measures
False-bedded Sandstones
Lower Coal Measures
Awgu Sandstones and Shales
Tilted Shales and Limestones
　　　Unconformity
Lower Cretaceous (Folded Shales, Sandstones, Limestones)

[1] C. M. Tattam, *op. cit.*, p. 38, para. 113.
[2] J. D. Falconer, *op. cit.*, p. 188 and Plate XVI.
[3] C. M. Tattam, *op. cit.*, p. 39, para. 116.
[4] C. M. Tattam, *op. cit.*, p. 39, para. 118.

GONGOLA-BENUE

Lower Coal Measures
Sandstones
Tilted Shales, etc.
    Unconformity?
Lower Cretaceous (Folded Sandstones, Grits,
    Shales, Limestones)

The Tertiary Deposits

The Kerri-Kerri beds of the north-east are considered to be Eocene. They form a succession at least 600 feet in thickness, horizontal or only slightly inclined. Raeburn and Brynmor Jones also refer to a group of beds, including loess (although this has not been confirmed), intervening between the Cretaceous and the Eocene in the Kerri-Kerri area, as further evidence of the unconformity with the underlying rocks, which is plain in some places.[1] The Eocene rocks form not only the Kerri-Kerri "plateau" itself, but stretch southward west of the Gongola valley (which is overlooked by a prominent escarpment) and into eastern Bauchi; they also pass eastward from Kerri-Kerri to southern Bornu, resting against the crystalline Basement. Northward they dip gently beneath the younger rocks (the Kerri-Kerri "plateau" has a well-marked southern edge where the Eocene rocks form the scarp above the Cretaceous, but an indeterminate northern limit) and do not reappear in Nigeria, although similar rocks occur in French territory to the north of Nigeria. Deep wells inside the sedimentary boundary of the Chad Group, e.g. to the north-east of Kano, have shown rocks possibly of Eocene age beneath the later cover and resting on the crystalline floor, and deep drilling at Maiduguri encountered Cretaceous mudstones at a depth of 2,000 feet.

The overlying sediments are known as the Chad Group, and comprise basal sands and gravels with greenish clays above, the latter containing some minor bands of sands. These sediments appear to have been laid down under water during a period of subsidence, and the included clays increase in importance with distance eastward from the landmass which remained unsubmerged to the west, and from which the sediments were probably derived. In central Bornu well borings show the clays to be over 200 feet in thickness. Diatomite has been noted from wells in a number of localities, and has also been found in the Upper Cretaceous beds north and north-east of the great bend in the Gongola River. No other fossils have been reported from the Chad Group apart from hippopotamus remains, probably of Lower Pleistocene age, found in one well at a depth of 190 feet.[2]

Throughout the basin the Chad Group rocks are concealed by an overlying mantle of drift, the depth to the top of the thick clay stratum being fairly constant at 70 feet. The basin suffered desiccation in Recent time, with dune formation in some areas, particularly near Chad, in central and north Bornu and in north Kano, but under the more humid conditions of the present day dune formation has ceased and there is an apparent tendency for the dune sands to disperse.

Calcareous sub-surface accumulations, usually of small individual extent, are found throughout the Chad Group.

The wells of the Chad basin, with a few exceptions which tap perched aquifers, draw water from beneath the thick clay bed. These supplies appear to rely on percolation of rain and river water on the western and southern margins of the basin, and the Lake Chad waters above the clays can have no effect on available supplies in the main aquifers. Even the possible drying out of Lake Chad, which may follow if the capture of the Logone by the Benue in French territory is not checked, will therefore not affect the well supplies. (In this connection Tilho has shown that of the lake waters, 76% are supplied by the Shari-Logone systems, 23%

---

[1] C. Raeburn and Brynmor Jones, "The Chad Basin—Geology and Water Supply", *Geol. Surv. Nig.*, Bulletin 15 (1934), p. 25.
[2] C. M. Tattam, *op. cit.*, p. 39, para. 119.

by direct rainfall and about 1–1½% by the Nigerian rivers. It should also be noted that there is probably a sub-surface flow from Chad towards the Bodele depression to the N.E., especially along the line of the Bahr-el-Ghazal.) The water supplies in the Nigerian part of the Chad basin can be described as subartesian, in that pressure is sufficient to carry water in some areas up to the level of the groundwater above the clays; with the unlined wells of this area there is seepage from the wells back into the permeable layers above the clays.[1]

Tertiary sediments also occur in the north-west of the country, in Sokoto Province, over-lying the Rima Group in the east, and the Illo Group farther west. The south-eastern edge of the Tertiaries (which stretch away into French territory) is marked by the Dange Scarp, running in a N.E.–S.W. direction and passing some 10 miles south-east of Sokoto and averag-ing some 150 feet in height. The scarp is com-posed of the Calcareous Group at the top, with the Clay-shale Group beneath, and overlooks the Mesozoic sediments. Some distance north-west of the line of the scarp, the Calcareous Group dips gently beneath the Post-Eocene Gwandu Group. There is an unconformity between the Gwandu Group and the rocks beneath it; the Clay-shales lie conformably on the Upper Cretaceous.

The Clay-shale Group attains a maximum thickness of only 68 feet at Sokoto, and thins out and disappears altogether to the S.W. The Calcareous Group displays the same thinning-out and disappearance to the S.W., but to the N.E. it increases in thickness, unlike the Clay Shales, which fade out in French territory, where limestones corresponding to the Cal-careous Group are up to 200 feet in thickness. The Group, to the north of Sokoto, is some 70 feet thick, but the outcrop shows marked con-trast with that of the Clay-shales; the latter appear on the Dange Scarp only, whereas the Calcareous Group outcrops over a width of 30 miles. This difference is due to the resistance

of the Calcareous rocks to erosion, and their characteristic development of a thick crust of lateritic ironstone when within reach of agents of atmospheric weathering. This crust forma-tion is general, even though practically the whole of the Calcareous outcrops are mantled by surface accumulations of drift.

The Gwandu Group comprises massive clays, clayey grits and sandstones; the clays being most prominent in the east. The Group over-lies in turn the Calcareous, Clay-shale, Rima and Illo beds, taken from E. to W., and finally, outside Nigeria, rests on the Basement Com-plex. Its maximum thickness in Nigeria is some 1,000 feet, near the N.W. frontier. Prior to its formation, the earlier beds were folded into a gentle syncline, centred outside Nigeria, and the Gwandu Group represents continental rocks, chiefly lacustrine in origin, laid down in this syncline.[2]

In the southern part of the country three main groups appear. Possibly separated by an unconformity from the Upper Cretaceous beds beneath it is the Bende-Ameki Group (Eocene-Lutecian), and lying above this are the Lignite Group and the Coastal Plains Sands. It is not yet clear whether the latter overlie the Bende-Ameki Group conformably. The Bende-Ameki Group is represented in the south-east by clayey sandstones, grey-green in colour, and by clays, and is locally highly fossiliferous. The group is thought to extend eastwards into Cala-bar Province. Westwards it has not been traced as a continuous belt, but it is likely that it may be found to extend beneath the younger sediments of north Benin and to join up with the green clays, clay-shales and sands, containing Eocene fossils, which are exposed in the south-west in Abeokuta, Ijebu–Ode and Ondo Pro-vinces. In Onitsha Province, in the Awka area, several hundred feet of sands lie above typical Bende-Ameki rocks, and pass beneath the Lignite Group farther west. Stream sec-tions have shown thin beds of uncompacted sandstone intercalated with the Bende-Ameki

[1] C. Raeburn and Brynmor Jones, op. cit., p. 45.
[2] Brynmor Jones, op. cit., p. 41.

beds, and the Awka exposures may represent a thickening of these beds.

The Coastal Plains Sands and the Lignite Group include the remaining Tertiary beds in the south, and stretch from Calabar Province in the south-east to the Dahomey border in the west. These beds appear to lie unconformably on the Bende-Ameki Group, and consist of clays, fine-grained sands, lignites and carbonaceous shaley clays. In the area of the Ishan Plateau, in northern Benin Province, there is an upper layer of some 200 feet of lignite facies, including massive clays, above several hundred feet of coarse sands, beneath which typical lignite facies are again found. Farther south are the red earth plains of Benin, similar to those extending east of the Niger to Calabar Province, and it is possible that in these areas the upper lignite series has been removed by erosion. The brown lignites are particularly well developed in Benin Province, but are not yet exploited commercially. The widespread occurrence of red earths and sands was earlier regarded as a late series lying unconformably on earlier beds, and the name of "Benin Sands" was given to this supposed series. It is now realised that the red sands of Benin form part of the Lignite Group, that those of the Awka area are Bende-Ameki deposits, and that those above the Enugu Scarp are the False-bedded Sandstones of Cretaceous age. The concept of the "Benin Sands" series has therefore disappeared.[1]

The Recent Deposits

These, apart from riverine alluvial deposits, are restricted to the south, and include the sandbars and creeks of the coast, the deposits of the Niger Delta area, and the estuarine areas of the Cross River, the Rio del Rey and the mouths of the Cameroons.

The Volcanic Rocks

Volcanic rocks occur in a number of areas in the centre and east of the country. The "Tertiary Volcanics" shown on the map (Fig. 1) are taken from the Provisional Geological Map of Nigeria produced by the Geological Survey Department, with the addition of the small volcanic cones of the Benue Trough, reported and mapped by Falconer.[2] They also include the Fluvio-volcanic Series of the Jos Plateau, of which the larger areas are marked on the official map as Tertiary deposits.

The largest occurrences of volcanic rocks are in the Cameroons, of which the Cameroon Mountain itself is the best known. These are dispersed along a N.E.–S.W. line, extended seawards by a line of islands. The following table, taken from Gèze,[3] indicates the magnitude of the volcanoes along this line and their diminishing relative size towards the N.E.

TABLE I

THE VOLCANOES OF WEST AFRICA

Name	Height above Sea-level	Altitude of Base	Approx. Altitude Relative to Base
	(Heights in metres)		
Annobon . .	990	− 4,000	5,000
Sao Thome .	2,140	− 3,100	5,200
Principe . .	930	− 3,000	3,900
Fernando Po:			
S. Cordillera .	2,660	− 1,000	3,700
Sta. Isabel Peak	2,850	− 500	3,300
Cameroon Peak .	4,070	− 70	4,100
Mount Koupe .	2,050	+ 250	1,800
Manengouba			
Mountains .	2,420	+ 800	1,600
Mount Bambouto .	2,679	+ 1,300	1,300

Comparative figures for size with well-known volcanoes elsewhere give:

Name	Kilometres	Approx. Altitude Relative to Base (metres)
Cameroon . .	50 × 35	4,100
Etna. . .	35 × 30	3,274
Kilimanjaro .	90 × 60	6,000

[1] C. M. Tattam, *op. cit.*, pp. 28–33.
[2] J. D. Falconer, *op. cit.*, map and text.
[3] B. Gèze, "Geographie Physique et Géologie du Cameroun Occidental", *Mém. de Mus. Nat. d'Hist. Nat., Nouv. Série*, Tome XVII (1942), p. 46.

Cameroon Peak is the only volcano in Nigeria which still shows signs of activity. Eruptions in this century occurred in 1909, 1922 and 1954. The Manengouba Mountains are some 25 kms. in diameter, and include the two calderas of Elengoum and Eboga, in diameter 8 kms. and 4–5 kms. respectively.

Only major areas of volcanic rocks in the Cameroons are shown, and of these the best known are those N.N.E. of Kumba, S.E. of Mamfe, and the extensive area centred on Bamenda. The Cameroons have yet to be mapped topographically and geologically, and therefore little can be said of the volcanic areas. Trachytes and rhyolites occur as well as basalts, and landforms range from old lava flows to steep cones; in the Eboga caldera alone there are 20 puys and 3 crater lakes. Such lakes, usually small, are not uncommon in the volcanic area of the Cameroons. Falconer has described a number of small cones and craters in Adamawa Province. The volcanic rocks of these regions are usually classed as Tertiary, but it has been suggested[1] that Cameroon Mountain may have originated in the Late Cretaceous period.

Towards the north-east of the country is the extensive basalt area of southern Bornu, known as the Biu Plateau or the Barbur Plateau. The degree of dissection of the surface suggests that the lava fields are not very recent although the area includes recent cones. The flows have been regarded as Eocene on the strength of a single exposure of included sandstone intercalated among the basalt flows; but the sandstones are not fossiliferous and the suggested Eocene age is therefore open to doubt. The lavas appear to have been extruded from a number of separate vents.

The Jos Plateau provides the third area of extensive lava flows. These have been studied in greater detail in connection with the exploitation of the tin-fields.[2] The earliest flows have weathered to give the Fluvio-volcanic Series, consisting of decomposed basalts overlying sands, grits and clays. Decomposition is far advanced to give clays varying in colour from pure white to red and purple, and these were at first mistakenly thought to be sedimentary deposits. The lavas flowed into the existing stream beds and buried the alluvium therein, which was frequently stanniferous. Hence these early flows are of economic significance in respect of the buried alluvial deposits. The name "Fluvio-volcanic" unfortunately tends to be shortened to "Fluvio", which is to be deplored; but the full name has now passed into accepted usage, and is adequate if correctly quoted. Much of these flows has been removed by erosion, leaving isolated flat-topped hills with an ironstone capping; the smooth outlines of these residuals contrast markedly with the typical forms of the granites. Individual flows rarely exceed 300 feet in thickness. Dixey's figure of a maximum thickness of 1,100 feet,[3] apparently based on differences in altitude of remnants, would seem excessive, for the original flows descending from higher to lower levels may not have been more than a few hundred feet thick. Not all the remnants form flat-topped hills; others blanket low watersheds, retaining the typical smooth outline. The upper surface across the series is erosional, as shown by its extension on to the neighbouring granite in a few places.

Later volcanic activity on the Jos Plateau is manifested by a number of small cones and basalt flows. That the scarp surrounding the Plateau was already in existence at the time is clear from places where the lavas can be seen descending the scarp, as at Assob, near the Jos–Kafanchan railway.

These later flows can be recognised as being of different periods of activity, and as a general rule the lavas became increasingly viscous

---

[1] B. Gèze, op. cit., p. 46.

[2] J. D. Falconer, "The Geology of the Plateau Tinfields", Geol. Surv. Nig., Bulletin 1 (1921), and "The Southern Plateau Tinfields", Geol. Surv. Nig., Bulletin 9 (1926).

[3] F. Dixey, "The Morphology of the Jos Plateau". Appendix to R. A. Mackay, R. Greenwood and J. E. Rockingham, "The Geology of the Plateau Tinfields—Resurvey 1945-48", Geol. Surv. Nig., Bulletin 19 (1949), p. 76.

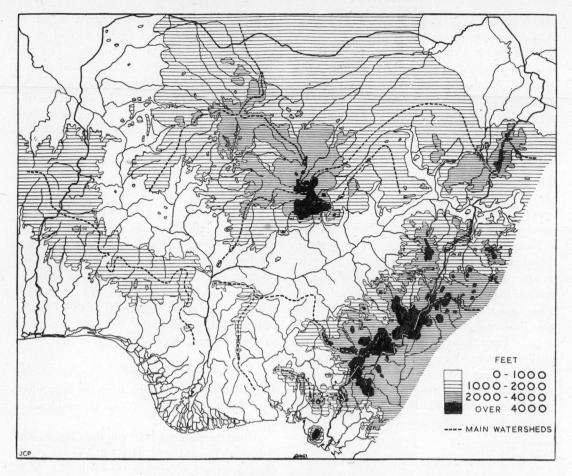

FIG. 3. RELIEF AND DRAINAGE

It will be seen that only a small part of the country lies above 4,000 feet above sea-level, namely the Jos Plateau and the eastern highlands. (Cameroon Mt., in the extreme S.E., rises to 13,358 feet.) A large part is, however, above 1,000 feet, particularly in the north, and much of it is above 2,000 feet. Reference is made in the text to the high level of the old-age plains characteristic of the north. Below 1,000 feet are the coastal areas and the delta, the valleys of the Cross, Niger and Benue Rivers, and the lower parts of the down-warped Chad Basin. Both the Niger and the Benue enter Nigerian territory at less than 600 feet above sea-level.

The pattern of major watersheds is interesting. The separation of major drainage basins by indeterminate watersheds on the old-age surface of the Jos Plateau is particularly noteworthy and the shape of the Gongola basin deserves further study. A considerable area in the N.E. does not drain to the sea, but much of the water in this basin is lost before reaching Lake Chad. The scale of the map (approximately 1 inch = 150 miles) should be kept in mind: Nigeria can claim many rivers which are well above the average length of European rivers.

towards the close of the volcanic period. Early flows, such as those from the insignificant Kassa focus between Jos and Ropp, spread across country at a low angle for as much as 15 miles; the last burst of activity, shown in the Kereng area south of Panyam, resulted in a line of steep cones several hundred feet in height, with com-

paratively short flows where these occurred. The majority of the small cones on the Plateau are breached, an example being that in which Vom Veterinary Station is sited. Only one crater, Dutsin Pedong in Kereng, carries a lake. The lavas vary slightly in composition: olivine is well displayed in many instances. In a few places, such as Makafo, the basalts are columnar. Although some of these later cones and flows on the Plateau are well preserved, erosion has considerably modified others and has destroyed the original continuity. With the progressive working-out of the exposed tin-bearing alluvial deposits of the Plateau, increasing attention is being paid to the "deep leads" beneath the basalt flows in the former stream courses.

The remaining area of volcanic activity is in the Benue Trough, from some little distance above Makurdi north-eastward towards the upper river.[1] A number of small cones pierce the Cretaceous rocks in this area, and although the majority of them are well-worn, they have been regarded as Tertiary to Recent in age on account of the presence of slightly thermal springs in the immediate neighbourhood. The most striking examples are those of Tangale Peak and the Wase Rock, both phonolite plugs. Lava flows from these Benue cones are small or absent altogether. No corresponding forms are found in the Niger valley, and suggested differences in the origin of the two great troughs are mentioned in the relative sections dealing with topographical units.

RELIEF AND DRAINAGE

To the traveller reaching Nigeria by sea, one major feature of the country's topography is at once apparent, i.e. the distinction between the sandbanks, lagoons and creeks of the coast and the mainland proper. This distinction is less clear at Lagos than farther east, but is, nevertheless, apparent; in the Niger delta area the creeks widen out to a maximum.

In the west the mainland rises steadily inland to some 2,000 feet at a distance varying from 120 to 200 miles from the coast (Fig. 3). Much of the country north of the great rivers of the Niger and the Benue is also at about 2,000 feet, but in the west the two areas are separated by the Niger valley, and farther east the great Benue trough similarly marks the southern limit of the high northern plains.

A considerable part of Nigeria could be classed as "lowland", taking this to include all areas below 1,000 feet in altitude. The two main lowland areas, that is, the coastal regions and the mainland margins, and the Niger–Benue troughs, run roughly W.–E. across the country in two curving belts, which merge into one another south of the Benue and east of its confluence with the Niger. It is worthy of note that the 600-foot contour (not shown on the map) passes out of Nigerian territory along both the Niger and the Benue valleys, even though in the latter case the frontier above Yola is over 700 miles from the sea, measured along the river course. Other areas below 1,000 feet are found both in the north-west and in the north-east; both can be explained in terms of geological history, the former in connection with the synclinal development of the Tertiary beds in Sokoto, and the latter by reference to the repeated down-warping of the Chad basin.

In the centre of the northern region lies the Jos Plateau, rising abruptly from the 2,000-foot high plains and with an average general level of some 4,000 feet.

Along the eastern border run the Cameroons–Adamawa mountains. Highest near the coast, they decrease in altitude towards the N.E. Broken by the Benue at Yola, the line of these highlands is continued by the Mandara Mountains before dying away into the Chad basin.

In the south-east, west of the mountains and east of the Niger, the land is generally lower than in the other major regions. Summit heights rise to a maximum of 1,700 feet west of the Enugu scarp, and most of the Cross River basin is of low altitude.

The major watersheds form an interesting pattern. In the south-west the major divide traces a fairly simple line from Dahomey to near the Niger, when it swings south. In the south-east the areas draining to the Niger and to the Cross are separated by the Awgu–Enugu scarp, and the continuation of this line follows

[1] J. D. Falconer, *The Geology and Geography of Northern Nigeria,* Chap. VIII.

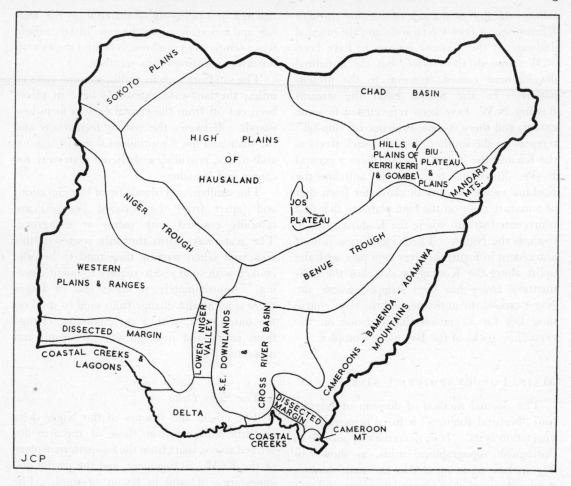

FIG. 4. TOPOGRAPHICAL UNITS

The individual regions shown are discussed in detail in the text.

The names suggested are arbitrary. It must be remembered that in order to produce a relatively simple sub-division of an area the size of Nigeria it is inevitable that any one unit should include a wide variety of landscape forms. The boundaries shown are therefore not clearly defined, except in a few cases, and the majority of the units plotted are capable of further sub-division.

round the northern side of the Anambra syncline. The Cross–Benue boundary is less well-defined, except where it turns into the mountains towards the eastern frontier. The Oban Hills mark the Cross–Sea watershed. The eastern frontier follows approximately the divide between the drainage basins of Nigeria and of the French Cameroons.

In the north the most interesting feature is the watershed pattern on the high plateau south of Jos, whence streams drain to the Kaduna (and

Niger), the Benue, the Gongola (and Benue) and to the inland basin of Chad. This hydrographical centre is insignificant on the ground, the various "branches" of the watershed lying on an almost level surface of great age. The shape of the Gongola basin is unorthodox and requires further study. The Chad basin is referred to elsewhere: in the north it lies against the basins of the Kaduna and the Sokoto rivers, both tributary to the Niger. The watershed between the Kaduna and the rivers of Sokoto follows the line of the axis of warping through Kontagora, of Post-Cretaceous age; the original drainage of the Kaduna appears to have been N.W. towards the Sokoto, but the anticlinal development caused diversion to the present pattern. In the Sokoto basin the streams flowing N.W. have been rejuvenated to some extent, and there is some evidence of "slip-off" terraces on the southern banks of such rivers as the Ka and the Zamfara, which have a general E.–W. direction. South of the anticline the Kaduna valley changes in character from that of a mature river on the high plains to that of a rejuvenated stream where the Kaduna turns S. towards the Niger. The Niger course is itself antecedent in form; the river kept pace with the uplift along the Kontagora axis, but the sedimentary cover has been stripped where the Niger crosses the anticline, and the river course now lies for a considerable distance on the crystalline rocks of the Basement Complex.

Main Topographical Units

The normal method of division of Nigeria into "Natural Regions" is based principally on vegetation belts. It is, nevertheless, possible to distinguish topographical units, as shown in Fig. 4, bearing in mind that the map shows a minimum number of physical divisions, and that widely differing landscapes can be found within some of the individual units.

1. *Coastal Creeks and Lagoons*

These form a belt of varying width from the western boundary eastward, until it is lost in the confusion of creeks and distributaries of the Niger delta. The sea coast runs as a straight or gently curving beach on which the Atlantic surf breaks continuously, and broken through in very few places, of which Lagos is one (Fig. 43). The beach material shifts eastward by longshore drift, and the quantities moved are considerable. Interference with the natural movement by the construction of the breakwaters at the entrance to Lagos harbour has resulted in a piling-up of material on the west side and serious scour on the east; in 1950 there was a temporary cut-through behind the eastern breakwater during heavy weather.

The sandbars vary in width, in some cases of miles; the landward extensions have in places been cut off from the coastal bars to form low islands. Between the coastal formations and the mainland lies a continuous series of lagoons and creeks, providing a sheltered waterway for canoes and launches.

The sandbars and islands are of low elevation, and (apart from the seaward beaches) are typically covered with palms or mangrove. The waterways form the only routes in this area, and when narrow they tend to become choked with sudd and to require frequent clearing. Approximately 70 miles east of Lagos there is an abrupt change from sand to mud on the outer coast, with a corresponding change from palms and undergrowth to swamp and mangrove.

2. *The Niger Delta*

The creeks and swamps of the Niger delta are little different from those of the area described above, apart from the fan-pattern in place of the E.–W. arrangement, and the partial disappearance of sand in favour of mud. The radial pattern of the distributaries provides outlets to the sea, of which the major examples are the Forcados and the Nun. The former has near the sea the ports of Burutu and Forcados; the latter Brass and Akassa, now of little importance compared with the past. The Forcados bar has shallowed in the last twenty years, and the Escravos bar is now usually used by ocean-going vessels destined for Burutu or Sapele. Burutu is a transhipment port for the Northern Provinces, goods passing by sternwheel vessels and lighters to the Niger. The distributaries show gradual changes in volume of discharge, as would be expected.

The vegetation changes from mangrove to forest towards the apex of the delta as the land becomes drier.

3. The Dissected Margins

These are the most southerly of the mainland units, and form the transition area between the coast and the higher regions inland. They represent in effect the dissected edge of the African continental mass, and show some evidence of down-warping towards the coast. Altitude varies from sea-level to some hundreds of feet, and landscape from the low scarps of North Benin and the Ishan Plateau, and areas marked by comparatively steep-sided valleys to areas which are no more than undulating. The red-earth plains of Benin are little different from those of western Calabar and Owerri, although the latter is included for simplicity in Region 5. In the extreme south-east this arbitrary division includes the narrow belt of coastal mangrove and the Tiko plains north of Cameroon Mountain. Most of these areas are under high forest, and views are rare, even from ridge crests, as shown by the fact that students from these regions are frequently unfamiliar with even the simple landforms of their home areas.

It is admitted that these marginal divisions are not altogether satisfactory, but they form a contrast with the regions to the north, and their internal variations—unless resort be made to detailed subdivision—are regarded collectively as those of a marginal and transitional area. The northern boundaries chosen are the sedimentary-crystalline contacts, since certain features typical of the areas of crystalline rocks are not found in the sedimentary areas.

4. The Western Plains and Ranges

These comprise all the area of crystalline rocks west of the Niger, and include varied landscape types. In the south-west, near Abeokuta, the landscape has much in common with the northern parts of the dissected marginal areas, and shows the common features of an area of active erosion, although with features typical of the rock types encountered—bare rock faces and boulder-strewn hills. Farther to the north lies a series of mature erosion surfaces with

FIG. 5. EXFOLIATION DOMES

Above. Near Kusheriki in Niger Province.
Below. North of Akure, in Ondo Province, rising abruptly above forest country.

scattered inselbergs (bare rock domes), typical of much of the crystalline basement of Africa, and well exemplified in western Oyo. In the Akure area of Ondo Province these residual erosion domes are particularly well seen, and the highest altitudes attained in this western region are found in the Idanre Hills, south-west of Akure, which surpass 3,000 feet. Such inselbergs are never encountered in the marginal areas of sedimentary rocks to the south. The different mature erosion surfaces are separated by areas of active erosion and youthful landscape forms; Ibadan lies in such an area.

This unit includes the Kukuruku Hills in the east, and also the features commonly referred to in Nigerian texts as the Yoruba Heights, a term loosely used and which the writer would prefer

FIG. 6. MASSED INSELBERGS NEAR BAUCHI

These rise abruptly from the "African" erosion surface.　View eastward from the Panshanu Pass.

to see discarded.　It also includes a wide range of vegetation types, from high forest to open parkland, partly a reflection of decreasing rainfall to north and west.

5. *The South-east Downlands and the Cross River Basin*

This is a composite unit, the western downlands being separated from the Cross River basin to the east by the scarp which passes behind Enugu.　It is throughout an area of sedimentary rocks; the downlands, including the Anambra syncline, are mainly on the Upper Cretaceous, and the Cross basin is mainly, but not entirely, on the Lower Cretaceous.　To the south are younger rocks giving a landscape similar to the red earth plains of Benin and western Calabar, grouped above in the "marginal" areas.

The downland area shows typical scarp and dip-slope features as successive beds are encountered dipping to the west.　Much of the higher part of this area between Enugu and Awka is open country largely "farmed-out", and gullying is apparent in many places. Individual gully systems, near Agulu, south of Awka, cover areas of some square miles with a difference in height of about 800 feet between top and bottom levels.　Grove has recently made reference to these elsewhere.[1]　The drainage of the downland area is partly westward to the Niger and partly southward to the Imo River.

East of the main scarp lie the lowlands of the Cross River basin, with a heavier vegetation, except in the northern part, where clearing has resulted in the open country of south-west Benue Province.　The extension of the upper Cross basin into the eastern highlands consists of much more broken country than is encountered anywhere else in this major unit.

6. *The Lower Niger Valley*

This unit marks the connection between the wide flood-plains of the Niger and Benue troughs above Lokoja and the delta already mentioned.　The river valley in this section is in marked contrast to the wide, mature valleys farther inland; here the Niger is largely restricted between its banks.　At low water the river channel is broken by low islands and sandbanks, but these disappear with the arrival of floodwater, when the water level may rise by over 30 feet.　In places the river is bounded by plain tracts, flooded at high water; in others the flood is confined within a comparatively narrow channel bounded by rocky hills.　The Niger, viewed at the road ferry at Onitsha, is disappointing compared with the Niger at Jebba or the Benue at Makurdi.

[1] A. T. Grove, "Land Use and Soil Conservation in Parts of Onitsha and Owerri Provinces," *Geol. Surv. Nig.*, Bulletin 21 (1951).

7. The Niger Trough

Above Lokoja the river valley itself varies in form, running through gorges above Koton Karifi and Jebba, and in wide flood-plains from Jebba eastward to the bend where the river turns south and again in the north-west. Between Jebba and Yelwa the river (here running on crystalline Basement rocks) is much broken by rapids, which make navigation impossible. Jebba is, therefore, the effective head of navigation for large river craft. The appearance of the channel naturally varies widely with the season, and high water is, on average, from July to October; at low water a considerable part of the river bed may be exposed as sandbanks in those sections with broad flood-plain features.

The "trough" is wider than the river and its immediate flood-plain. It includes the Upper Cretaceous sedimentaries in the Niger valley, and also the area of crystalline rocks across the Kontagora anticline from which the sedimentary cover has been stripped. The Cretaceous rocks in the lower half of the trough include distinctive flat-topped hills, which are remnants of a former erosion surface and very different from the bare rock domes or kopjes of the crystalline areas north and south of the trough. For some distance north of Lokoja these flat-topped hills run out close to the river on the west side, and later on both banks, confining it within a narrow channel.

It has been suggested elsewhere that the Niger trough represents a broad down-warped area of Upper Cretaceous age, in which sediments of that period were deposited. The bordering areas of Basement rocks probably remained above sea-level throughout, and the trough borders were marked by flexing and not by faulting.

8. The Benue Trough

This unit corresponds to that just described, but shows a number of differences in character and origin. The alternation of flood-plain and restricted channel seen in the Niger is absent in the case of the Benue, where the river flows in a broad flood-plain from the frontier to the confluence. The Benue flows over sedimentaries throughout, and has suffered no transverse movements such as that of the Kontagora anticline; the underlying Basement is therefore not exposed, nor has the progressive grading of the river been retarded, and rapids are absent. When the river is in flood shallow-draught steamers can pass up to Garua, outside British territory. Vertical down-cutting has largely ceased, but large quantities of material are transported by the river, with resultant shifting sandbanks.

Flat-topped hills of sedimentary origin occur in the lower parts of the trough, and again, with more varied outline, towards Yola; but the middle part of this region is characterised by small volcanic cones, considered to be Tertiary to Recent in age. These volcanic features are shown in Fig. 1, but it should be noted that the individual occurrences marked frequently represent as many as three or four neighbouring cones.

The hypothesis has been advanced that the Benue trough is an ancient rift valley of Lower Cretaceous age; that is, earlier than the Niger trough in origin, and bounded by faults instead of being down-warped. It must be admitted that bordering faults have not yet been reported, although faulting has been identified in the lower Gongola valley. The arguments in favour of a rift valley hypothesis include the known N.E.–S.W. lines of weakness in this area, the occurrence of volcanic activity frequently concomitant with rifting, the attitude of the Lower Cretaceous beds, and the disposition of the major erosion surfaces of Nigeria, correlated with those of other parts of Africa; the hypothesis also invokes the theory of continental drift, with separation of Africa from South America in Cretaceous time. Even if these suggestions regarding the origin of the Niger and Benue areas should be unacceptable, the "troughs" might still be considered, under that name, as major geomorphological units of greater extent than the actual river valleys.

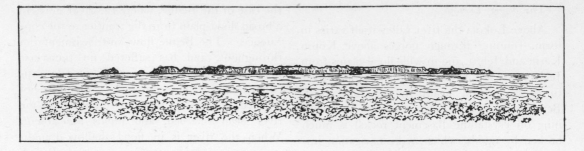

FIG. 7. THE SOUTH SCARP OF THE JOS PLATEAU

The south scarp of the Jos Plateau, viewed from a distance of about 60 miles. The scarp in this area averages about 2,000 feet in height, and separates the old-age surfaces of the Jos Plateau, at about 4,000 feet above sea-level and of the High Plains of Hausaland, which surround the Plateau. The upper surface has been correlated with the "Gondwana" surface identified in other parts of Africa, and the High Plains of Hausaland with the "African" surface widespread in other parts of the continent.

9. *The High Plains of Hausaland*

These represent the major exposure of crystalline rocks in the North (although the included Jos Plateau is regarded as a separate entity). The plains are not uniform throughout, and can be sub-divided into a number of erosion surfaces separated by scarps or by belts of youthful topography. The most widespread of these surfaces (referred to as the "African" surface in other parts of the continent) lies at 2,000–2,400 feet, with a lower section at 1,600–2,000 feet; younger surfaces lie at lower elevations. These surfaces give wide plains of little relief, crossed by mature streams; the latter flow in broad, shallow valleys separated by inconspicuous watersheds. Above the plains rise kopjes and inselbergs, some by over a thousand feet above the general level. Generally speaking, the size and number of these residuals decrease outwards from the Jos Plateau, with secondary decreases below the scarps separating different surfaces.

These plains, old-age in form over much of their extent but more broken towards the margins or in areas where they have been affected by local land movement, terminate abruptly against the scarps marking the Jos Plateau, and against outlying masses such as the Mada Hills and the Liruein–Kano Hills, which also rise to over 4,000 feet.

10. *The Jos Plateau*

This small area must be regarded as a distinct unit. It comprises high plains at about 4,000 feet above sea-level, with granite hills rising to over 5,800 feet in the Shere Hills east of Jos. On the west and south sides, the Plateau is bounded by a scarp 1,500–2,000 feet in height (Fig. 7); on the east side the scarp is more broken and the drop is in a stepped form; on the north the transition from higher to lower plains is less abrupt, and the surrounding lower plains extend up between the hill groups. Reference has already been made to the watershed pattern on the high Plateau surface, which has been identified with the "Gondwana" of other parts of Africa, and can be regarded as a remnant of the oldest surface found in the continent. The Plateau owes its survival to the resistance of the Younger Granites, of which it is largely composed; the impressive surrounding scarps are erosional forms, and are not fault features as originally supposed.

Mention has already been made of the occurrence of tinstone on the Plateau, and of the volcanic forms found there, both as the older Fluvio-volcanic Series now decomposed, and best seen as flat-topped residual hills, and as volcanic cones and lava flows.

The Plateau landscape forms a marked contrast to the rest of Nigeria. Forest cover is

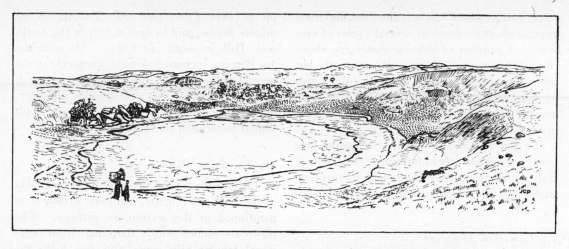

FIG. 8. CRATER LAKE SOUTH OF PANYAM, PLATEAU PROVINCE

The skyline shows remnants of the "post-Gondwana" surface across surviving occurrences of the Fluvio-volcanic Series.   Note the basin-listing on the lower slopes.

absent in favour of short grass and bare rock, with the scars of mining operations in many areas.   The southern part of the Plateau round Bokkos, where the general surface level rises to 4,400 feet, presents a landscape which is probably bleaker than anything else in the country.

It is important that the name Jos Plateau should replace the earlier title of the Bauchi Plateau, given before the creation of Plateau Province and when this area formed part of Bauchi Province.   Bauchi itself lies some 2,000 feet below Jos, on the "African" surface forming the high plains of Region 9.

11. *The Hills and Plains of Kerri-Kerri and Gombe*

This area has been classified as a single unit, although showing considerable variation in surface form; a more detailed study would permit subdivision into smaller contrasting areas.   The justification for the present grouping lies in contrast between the sedimentary rocks of this area and the crystalline Basement to east and west; the inselbergs and kopjes of the latter areas are naturally absent in the sedimentary belt.

The northern part of this unit covers the Kerri-Kerri "plateau", which is no higher than the plains of Bauchi to the west and is correctly

an inclined plane, passing gently beneath the younger sediments to the north.   The southern edge is marked by a broken and discontinuous escarpment, rising in places to sandstone cliffs over 500 feet high, overlooking the plains running south to the Gongola.   The streams flowing south from Kerri-Kerri, and also the Gongola itself west of Gombe, run in deep, narrow valleys bounded by flat-topped hills; but the lower Gongola valley widens out to broad plains with scattered flat-topped hills decreasing in number to the south and east.

12. *The Biu Plateau and Plains*

East of the Gongola, after its great bend southwards, lies a large area of basalt, to which the name Biu Plateau—or Barbur Plateau—has been given.   The summit level is between 2,000 and 3,000 feet, and the term "plateau" needs to be regarded, as in Kerri-Kerri, with some reservation, bearing in mind the wide plains of Hausaland at the same elevation.   The western limit is well-defined by a scarp some 600 feet high bordering the plains of the Gongola valley.   The southern margin is less clear, since altitudes decline by 1,500 feet over a distance of 20 miles to the Maio Hawal valley; a similar steady fall occurs to the north.   The upper surface of the basalts is dissected, and there appears to be evidence of several cycles of erosion. A number of volcanic cones rise above the plains; some appear well-preserved, but others are of sufficient age for their outer slopes to show the development of free face, talus slope and pediment characteristic of the back-wearing processes of normal erosion.

To the east and south-east the basalts give place to Basement rocks forming typical old-age plains similar to those of Hausaland, increasingly studded by inselbergs towards the mountains to the east.

13. *Cameroon Mountain*
14. *The Cameroons–Bamenda–Adamawa Highlands*
15. *The Mandara Mountains*

Although separated from one another, these regions may be discussed together, as forming the highlands of the eastern boundary. Regions 14 and 15 represent the reappearance of the crystalline rocks, which here give a mountain mass some 500 miles in length. In the Mandara Mountains north of the Benue trough the hills rise to between 4,000 and 5,000 feet, but greater altitudes are encountered southwards; the Shebshi Mountains exceed 6,000 feet, and summits surpass 8,000 feet in the volcanic area of Bamenda. Summits are not far below this figure farther south, and the great volcano of Cameroon Mountain, separated from the highlands to the north, rises to 13,350 feet.

The highland mass, some 15 miles in width of Nigerian territory in the Mandaras, widens southward to include nearly 100 miles of country W.N.W. of the frontier at Bamenda. It is broken by the upper Cross River basin at Mamfe, but extends westwards again as the Oban Hills between the upper Cross River and the sea. The mountain mass becomes increasingly dissected towards the Biu Plains and the Benue trough; westward extensions appear as isolated masses and then as groups of hills rising from the bordering plains. Generally speaking, summit heights decrease in the same direction to 2,500–4,000 feet in altitude, but run up to over 5,000 feet near Takum, in the middle Benue, and to over 6,000 in the Sonkwala Hills in south-east Ogoja. As with the Jos Plateau, increased altitude is reflected in the vegetation cover, and the Bamenda grasslands at about 6,000 feet are well known; the short-grassed open country carries Fulani herds similar to those of the southern Jos Plateau.

16. *The Sokoto Plains*

These comprise the area of sedimentary rocks in the N.W. of Nigeria, and have already been mentioned in the section on geology. The plains are monotonously flat, apart from occasional tabular hills some 100 feet high, the upper and lower plains being separated by the 150-foot-high Dange Scarp.

The Sokoto River, with its tributary the Rima, is seasonal in flow, and above Sokoto water runs in the rains only. The lower valleys take the form known as *dallols*, where they traverse the Gwandu Series, with floodplains a few miles wide lying in trenches below the plain level and bounded by steep sides 100–200 feet high. Similar trench-like valleys occupied by seasonal or diminutive streams occur to the north-west in French territory. The explanation lies in the development of ironstone surface capping on the Gwandu Series to an extent not seen on the older rocks to the south-east; the lower plains of the latter are graded to the river systems, and hence the valleys are shallow in their upper parts.

17. *The Chad Basin*

The area included under this title is co-extensive with the sedimentary rocks of the north-west, and does not include the areas of crystalline rocks which drain to the inland basin.

Most of the region consists of a vast featureless plain, quite unrelieved by hills. In the north-east, near Hadejia, are areas of rolling dune country, but the dunes are dead and are colonised by vegetation.

Gradients on all the rivers are low, and very little water ultimately reaches Lake Chad.

PLATE I. VEGETATION PATTERNS IN THE NIGER DELTA

Dense mangrove forest, diversified by isolated patches of high forest on "islands" of drier sandy soils, and traversed by a complex network of distributaries. An area of very low density of population.

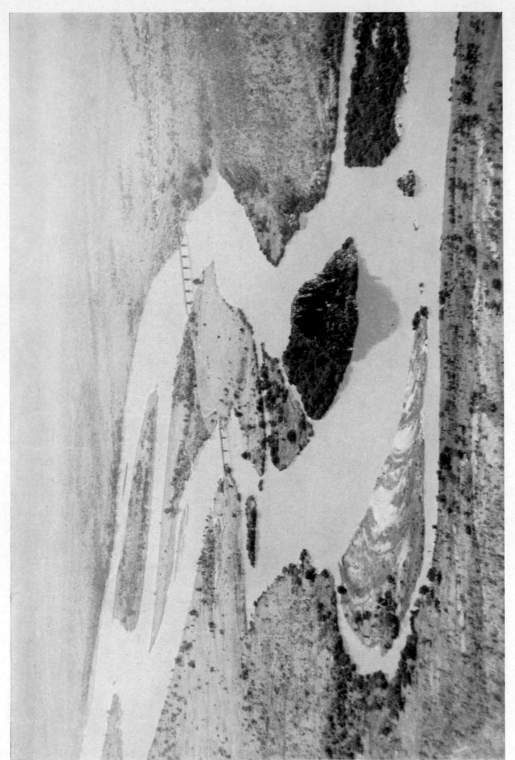

PLATE II. SAVANA LANDSCAPE IN THE MIDDLE BELT

View of the braided channel of the Niger at Jebba, looking downstream. Typical Guinea savana woodlands, much degraded by cultivation and felling for fuel. The river here forms a cultural divide between the Yoruba and Niger peoples; the modern settlement round the railway workshops on the west bank is predominantly Yoruba in character while the town on Jebba Island is typically Nupe. The combined road and rail bridges constitute the major link between the Northern and Western Regions.

PLATE III. THE SOUTHERN ESCARPMENT OF THE JOS PLATEAU

The general level of the Plateau is over 4,000 ft.; that of the plains in the foreground a little above 2,000 ft. The paler deforested tracts in the middle distance give an indication of the extent to which the original savana woodlands are being destroyed by shifting cultivation.

PLATE IV. THE SOUTHERN RAIN FOREST

Dense high forest on the rocky coast below Cameroon Mountain, with the port of Victoria in the middle distance. Ocean-going vessels lie offshore in the bay.

Most of it is lost by percolation or by evaporation from the swamp and marsh areas, in which many streams lose themselves altogether. Stream channels are ill-defined and subject to frequent change, and the grade is so low that Raeburn records that the setting of a fishtrap was once sufficient to divert the water of a river permanently from over 1,000 square miles in Bornu.

Lake Chad, of which only a part lies in Nigeria, varies considerably in area. In its "normal" state it has an area of 5,000–5,300 square miles, but in the period 1913–24 it declined to 4,600–4,800 square miles, with a mean depth of 3–4½ feet and a maximum depth of 10–13 feet. From 1850–90 it covered some 6,600–8,300 square miles, with an average depth of 13 feet. A single wet or dry summer is sufficient to cause wide variation.

CLIMATE

Damana mai ban samu.

(Rainy season, thou provider of livelihood.)
Northern Proverb.

The climate of Nigeria is normally explained in terms of the seasonal shifting of pressure belts in response to the movement of the overhead sun, with added "monsoonal" tendencies during the months of the northern summer. Recently it has been restated in terms of the now recognised Equatorial Maritime and Tropical Continental air masses. The boundary between these two is known as the Intertropical Front, and in this part of Africa, even in mid-winter, this front remains north of the Equator. The Equatorial Maritime air mass is characterised by south-westerly winds coming to the land off the Gulf of Guinea, and these are the main rain-bearing winds of the region. The Tropical Continental mass is that of the dry north-easterly winds known as the Harmattan.

The year can be broadly divided into two major seasons: the Wet Season or Rains of the northern summer months, when the Intertropical Front has retreated northwards into French territory and, in July and August, the whole country is traversed by south-westerly winds; and the Dry Season of the winter months, when north-easterly winds cover the whole of the northern part of the territory and may even break through to the coast on a few days during the height of the season.

Pressure

The surface position of the Intertropical Front is often considerably to the north of the equatorial low-pressure belt, which corresponds in a general way with the doldrum belt. It should be remembered that here is no symmetrical trough of low pressure with inflowing winds forming similar patterns to north and south. The boundary between the Equatorial Maritime and the Tropical Continental air masses is not vertical but decreases in altitude towards the north, the average slope of the contact surface being 1 in 300; the former mass is therefore in the shape of a thin wedge increasing in depth southward until a few miles thick, and overridden by the north-easterly winds in the contact zone and by the Equatorial Easterlies farther to the south. The intertropical Front lies approximately E.–W. across the country.

Winds

The surface winds, with local variations, conform to the main currents of the air masses, but local modifications of surface winds can be substantial; land and sea breezes and hill and valley winds exercise considerable influence, and will be mentioned below. Fig. 9 shows surface wind directions by months at Kano, Enugu and Ikeja (Lagos Airport), as percentages of total winds, read at three-hourly intervals.

The Kano winds show clearly the passage of the Intertropical Front across the city, northwards in April and southwards in October. Throughout the year the great majority of winds are either N.E. or S.W., or close to these directions. At Ikeja, surprisingly enough, the S.W. wind *sensu strictu* appears less clearly

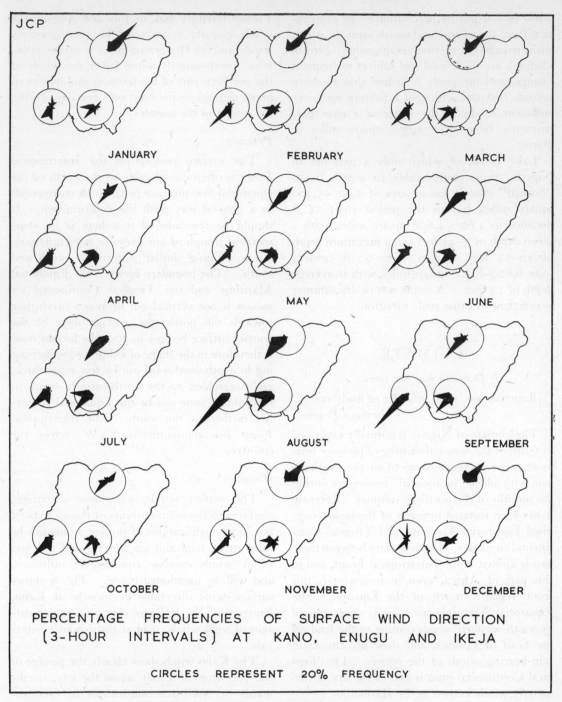

PERCENTAGE FREQUENCIES OF SURFACE WIND DIRECTION
(3-HOUR INTERVALS) AT KANO, ENUGU AND IKEJA

CIRCLES REPRESENT 20% FREQUENCY

FIG. 9. WINDS

Detailed comments on wind directions are in the text.
The most striking feature is the passage of the Intertropical Front across Kano northward in March–April and southward in October, with a resulting reversal of the prevailing winds. The approach of the I.T.F.

(continued on opposite page)

dominant than at Kano, during the summer months, except in August and September, but this is probably due to the effects of land and sea breezes. R. Miller cites June to September as months with a marked tendency to westerly winds at Lagos, which appears to be true at Ikeja, which is 13 miles inland. The statement does, however, require amplification, in that these are the months during which the truly S.W. wind is most strongly developed— the shift of direction is apparent in an increase of W. and W.S.W. winds by about 12% to 25–30% of the total, with a corresponding decrease of S. and S.S.W. winds from 20–28% of the total to as little as 4% in July. Ikeja shows over much of the year a definite southerly component, which may be the result of the sea breezes characteristic of the coastal area. The relative absence there from June to October of the northerly land breezes would be expected in an area with strong S.W. winds where the land and sea breezes are less powerful than the prevailing winds, as the sea breezes would give an increased southerly or south-westerly wind, while the land breezes would result only in a reduction of the strength of the winds from the S.W. The mid-winter months show more varied directions of surface winds at Ikeja, when the Intertropical Front lies much closer to this station, and the northerly component at this period represents land-breeze effects overcoming the weaker S.W. winds of this season.

Enugu shows S.W. winds throughout the whole year. The Intertropical Front does not lie regularly to the south of this station, and even in mid-winter the Harmattan fails to break through as a strong feature. Interest centres in the marked tendency to westerly and southerly winds at Enugu, the former in particular never completely absent and of greatest strength during the mid-summer months. Of the sixteen major points of the compass, Enugu shows three as each having over 10% of the annual total winds: South-west 24%, West 20% and South 12%. These winds from W. and S. at Enugu should not, however, be regarded as typical, and too much significance should not be placed upon them, as the data were recorded in Enugu town where local effects of the physical features shown in Fig. 50 may be expected. Nevertheless, observations of upper winds show that the south-westerly current can blow anywhere between S.E. and W. More work on wind direction is required to obtain a clearer picture of the general pattern over the country. R. Miller has suggested (from Lagos observations) that both the "little dry season" of the south-west and the mid-summer orographic rain on the western slopes of the Cameroons Highlands may be due to a mid-summer shift of wind direction towards the W. in the southern part of Nigeria. This would seem to be partly justifiable in the former case; future observations from a more reliable site at Enugu will possibly bring confirmation in the latter case, where the present figures show a marked veering from S. and S.S.W. to W. and W.S.W. in July and August, in fashion rather similar to that seen at Ikeja. The important and more certain cause of the "little dry season" is the existence of an inversion in the south-westerly current at a height of about 2 kms.

Rainfall

Mean annual totals, as shown in Fig. 12, are of little significance and wet- and dry-season maps (Figs. 10 and 11) indicate the seasonal nature of the precipitation. Even Debundscha, on the western side of Cameroon Mountain, and probably the second wettest place in the world, which for the five years 1944–8 had an average rainfall of over 425 inches (494 inches

towards Lagos in December–January is reflected by the increased percentages of northerly winds; these are not the Harmattan wind, but result from the ascendancy of the land breezes over a weakened S.W. wind during the winter months. The Enugu observations were taken at a poorly sited station, and are probably influenced by the scarp immediately west of the town. This would account for some of the westerly winds, as cold air currents descend the scarp, and for some of the southerly emphasis, as winds are deflected to a course parallel to the scarp.

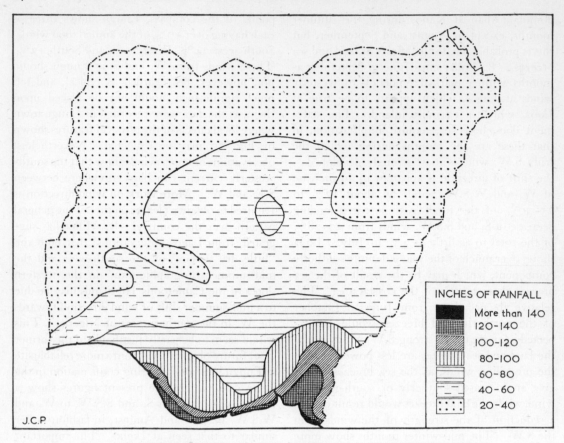

FIG. 10. RAINFALL—WET SEASON (APRIL TO OCTOBER INCLUSIVE)

Heavy rainfall is general over the country during the wet season (although it is possible that in the extreme N.E. the rainfall may be less than 20 inches). Orographic effects are marked on the Jos Plateau and in the Cameroons: in the latter area Debundscha, on the west side of Cameroon Mountain, receives nearly 400 inches. A rain-shadow effect is apparent in the Niger valley.

in 1946), may show January rainfall figures of under 5 inches. It is more satisfactory to show the wet-season rainfall for seven months than to show half-yearly totals, but further detail is required to indicate differences in intensity for stations with equal totals, and the wet-season map needs to be read in conjunction with maps showing the Dry Winter (Fig. 13) and the Winter Drought (Fig. 14). In the construction of the latter map "no rain" is taken to include any month with a mean of less than 0·10 inch, to avoid false impressions given by averaging any out-of-season storm over a number of years.

Fig. 13 reveals how near the coast the effects

of the Intertropical Front are felt during the winter months, since although the Harmattan may blow over Lagos Island for a few days only during the year, the area with two months of less than 1 inch of rain is only a short distance inland. It should, nevertheless, be remembered that rain occurs mainly when the depth of the south-westerly current is between 3,000 and 6,000 feet, and the surface position of the I.T.F. is therefore invariably well to the north of the edge of the rain-belt. Only over the delta and along the coastal area of the south-east is monthly rainfall consistently above 1 inch throughout the year. The isolated area of the Jos Plateau, and particularly of its south-western margin,

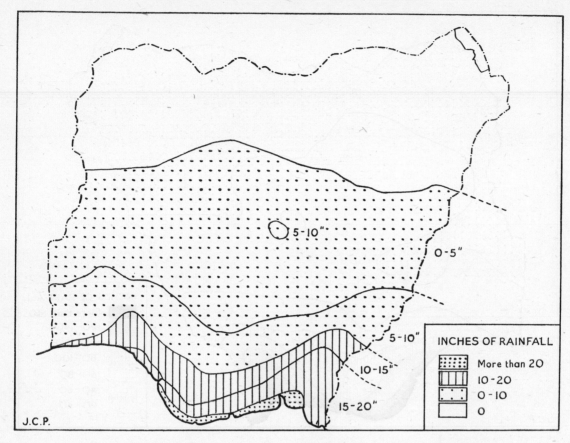

FIG. 11. RAINFALL—DRY SEASON (NOVEMBER TO MARCH INCLUSIVE)

The scale of tints used is the same as for Fig. 10, and reveals the marked contrast between the two main seasons. Only along the coastal areas of the delta and the S.E. does dry season rainfall exceed 20 inches. Orographic effects are similar to those of Fig. 10, but much subdued.

stands out clearly in the Northern Provinces. Conditions generally are emphasised by Fig. 14. These two figures, considered with the wet-season map, bring out the difference in rainfall regime between, for example, areas of 40–60 inches wet-season fall in some parts of the Western Region and to the north of the Jos Plateau: the former with no dry months and a corresponding "spread" of the total rainfall; the latter with a season of complete dryness and a heavier concentration in the mid-summer months.

It is customary in Nigerian climatology to refer to the difference between the "equatorial" type of rainfall regime, with monthly figures showing two peaks during the rains, representing the northward and southward traverses of the rain-belt, and the "tropical" type of regime, with monthly figures rising to a single peak and then falling away again as the rain-belt turns and moves south.

In mid-summer much of the southern part of Nigeria experiences a slight diminution in rainfall between the earlier and later peaks, although this does not necessarily imply months of low rainfall. Mean monthly figures for Onitsha, for example, show August as 9·9 inches, compared with 11·6 inches for July and 13 inches for September. Mean figures are not altogether satisfactory, however, even in the south:

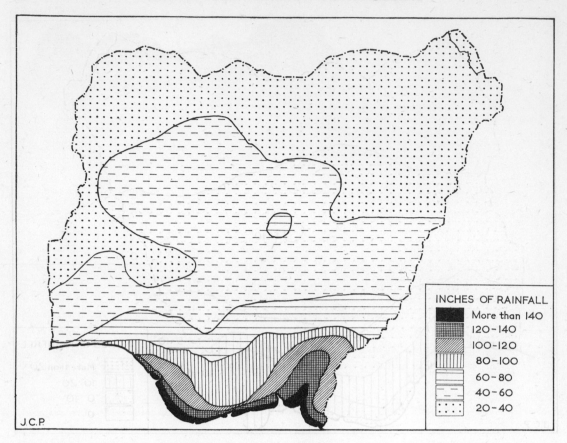

FIG. 12. RAINFALL—ANNUAL TOTAL

This map does not give a full picture, since it does not distinguish the season distribution of precipitation:
in particular it gives an incomplete impression of the north, and should be read in conjunction with Fig. 14.

a mean monthly graph for Aba over seventeen years showed a single-peak regime, but examination of individual years showed none with a single peak. Low mid-summer rainfall has been mentioned as a feature of the south-west, giving the "little dry season" of parts of the Western Region, with mean monthly figures below 4 inches.

Kendrew shows the boundary between the two types of rainfall regime as lying south of the great rivers of the Niger and the Benue, which is the impression to be gained from a study of plotted graphs of mean monthly values, all stations north of the rivers apparently having a single peak. Checking of individual years,

however, reveals that the boundary between the two types lies much farther north (Fig. 15), and runs approximately from north of Yola westward to the Jos Plateau and the area to the north-west, before continuing westward and passing out of Nigerian territory through southern Sokoto Province. In some years the boundary passes north beyond Nigerian territory, particularly in the north-west, but also in the Chad basin and along the north-eastern frontier. In some years a minor peak in May is apparent over wide areas, and even Maiduguri shows minor peaks in half the years recorded, although the mean annual figure is only 25 inches and the period from October to April

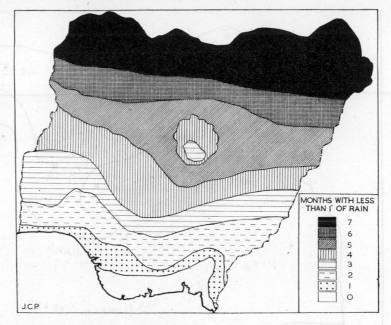

FIG. 13. THE DRY WINTER

This map should be used in conjunction with Fig. 10 to emphasise the greater intensity of the rains in the north compared with the west. The close approach of the two-month area to the coast in the S.W. is an indication of the extent of the southerly migration of the Intertropical Front during the dry season.

MONTHS WITH LESS THAN 1" OF RAIN

7
6
5
4
3
2
1
0

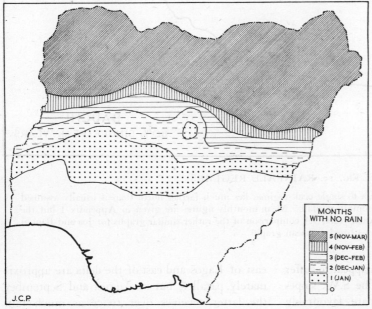

FIG. 14. THE WINTER DROUGHT

Mean values of less than 0·1 inch have been ignored as representing the result of averaging infrequent freak storms not characteristic of normal conditions. The months quoted are correct in most areas but are one month in error at a few stations.

The full extent of northern seasonal aridity is well shown and is an obvious major control in any scheme of agricultural development.

MONTHS WITH NO RAIN

5 (NOV-MAR)
4 (NOV-FEB)
3 (DEC-FEB)
2 (DEC-JAN)
1 (JAN)
0

inclusive has an average total of less than 1 inch.

Orographic effects are apparent in the distribution of rainfall. The southern part of the Cameroons Highlands receives high rainfall on its western and south-western slopes. In the Northern Region the Jos Plateau stands out as

above average for its latitude in the country, with similar emphasis on its S.W. side; Wamba, a few miles from the foot of the S.W. scarp of the plateau, receives a mean annual rainfall of 66 inches, the highest figure in the North. The south-facing slopes of the Niger and Benue troughs also benefit by comparison with the

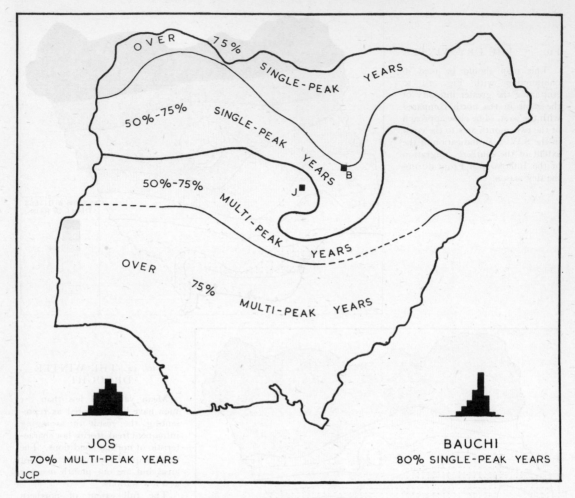

FIG. 15. RAINFALL REGIMES

The transition from double-peak to single-peak regimes lies much farther north than is usually assumed from a study of graphs of mean monthly rainfall. Mean monthly figures are given in Appendix I but the map is based on a study of individual years. A comparison of the rather similar graphs for Jos and Bauchi indicates the dangers of assumptions based on mean graphs.

slopes south of the rivers, which appear to suffer from a rain-shadow effect.   The S.W. slopes of the Western Region compare favourably with the area north of the watershed here and draining to the Niger.   Miller quotes the Biu Plateau as being of relatively higher rainfall of an orographic nature, and also refers to high totals on those parts of the coast which are crossed most obliquely by the rain-bearing winds.   The latter point is not at first apparent from a study of the map, in that the coasts east of Lagos and east of the delta are approximately parallel, but in August and September the latter receives over twice as much rain as the former. More detailed study of wind directions at coastal stations may reveal that the mid-summer westerly emphasis at Lagos, which would result in winds travelling roughly parallel to the coast, may not be matched by a similar tendency on the eastern margins of the delta, where the "funnelling" effect of the Gulf of Guinea induces increased divergence between wind and coast direction.

The difference between the short wet season of the North and the longer rains of the West is reflected in the crops grown—in the Western Region it is possible to grow both wet-season plants such as yams, which require a long growing season, and also short-season crops, such as maize, of which double sowings are possible in the Western Region but which necessarily provide only a single harvest in the north. In the Eastern Region station records normally show mean annual totals of 80 inches and upwards, largely concentrated in the wet season, and the high totals of high intensity have resulted in badly leached soils and severe erosion in places.

The early and late rains of the wet season come in the form of short, violent storms generally referred to locally as "tornadoes", a term which should be abandoned, as they are dissimilar from storms of that name in the New World, both in origin and intensity. These storms should properly be called line squalls; they are associated with belts of thunderstorm, and travel in a general south-westerly direction at a speed of some 30 miles per hour. They are frequently presaged by at least one day of high temperature and humidity. Such storms are heralded by very dark skies and masses of cumulo-nimbus cloud in the N.E., such cloud masses extending approximately from 1,000 feet to over 20,000 feet, accompanied by lightning flashes. As the cloud base passes overhead, there is a violent squall from the E. or N.E., sometimes of over 60 miles per hour in the Northern Provinces, followed by torrential rain. Both the squall and the rain give very audible warning of their approach. A marked drop in temperature accompanies the passage of the storm. Incessant thunder and lightning accompany the torrential rain, which eases to a downpour as the storm passes on. Falls frequently amount to as much as several inches in less than an hour, and even Lagos has known over 10 inches in one day of prolonged rain, as well as considerable damage from particularly heavy

storms. Line squalls continue throughout the rains, being more frequent in the north than in the south, but of less violence than the early- or late-season storms. Damage is a characteristic accompaniment, particularly in the form of beaten-down crops and broken roofing, and, less spectacularly but of greater seriousness, as damage to the land surface. Even with the first storm of the year bringing rain to completely dry soil, the fall may be so heavy and intense that the soil is unable to absorb anything like the quantity of water available; general sheet flow occurs across the surface, becoming turbulent, and therefore erosive, on encountering potential channels, however shallow. Tyre-tracks on a road may develop into parallel streams inches deep, and if unchecked such scars can rapidly destroy the road surface and lead to

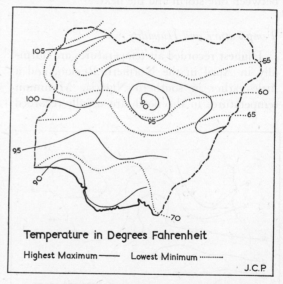

Temperature in Degrees Fahrenheit

Highest Maximum ——— Lowest Minimum ············

J.C.P.

FIG. 16. TEMPERATURE: MONTHLY MEANS

The hottest months of the year show high temperatures over the whole country. Only a narrow coastal belt has less than 90° F. as the mean temperature of the hottest month; much of the country experiences a mean of over 100° F., and the north-west exceeds 105° F.

Whereas highest mean temperatures increase inland, the coolest months of the year show mean temperatures increasing towards the south. The 75° F. isotherm does not appear even on the coast and in the N.E. lowest mean temperatures are only a little above 50° F.

gullying. Run-off percentage is notably high in some areas of crystalline rocks, and rivers may rise 10 feet or more in a few hours, falling again with equal rapidity if the catchment area is small. On the other hand, it appears that at least in some southern areas the soil absorption capacity is very high, and run-off virtually absent even during the heaviest storms.

The distribution of rain from these storms is markedly localised. Of two places a few miles apart, one may receive over an inch of rain from a storm while the other receives none. Irregularity of place may be matched by irregularity of time: intervals between storms are unpredictable, and an apparently high mean monthly rainfall, if distributed as three big storms, may do more harm than good if the storms are unevenly spaced, since young crops may wither between one storm and the next.

Temperature and Humidity

Highest recorded air temperatures are normally in April in the Northern Region, and a little earlier in southern Nigeria. Minimum temperatures in the north are usually recorded

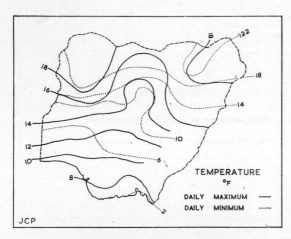

FIG. 17. TEMPERATURE: ANNUAL RANGE OF MONTHLY MEANS

The monotony of the coastal temperatures is well shown, particularly in the case of minimum temperatures. Range is greater in the north, but the Jos Plateau and the surrounding high plains modify ranges compared with the lower areas of the N.W. and N.E.

about December; in the south there is less difference between the December temperatures and the relatively low temperatures of the rainy season, and the lowest temperatures of the year may even be recorded during the latter season.

Mean maximum temperatures increase from the coast northward. Fig. 16 shows a highest monthly mean of 90° F. for the coastal regions, temperatures increasing inland to a monthly mean of over 105° F. in the extreme north. Mean minimum temperatures, on the other hand, decrease northward, the same map showing a lowest monthly mean of 70° F. on the coast, compared with less than 55° F. in the north. Altitude naturally modifies temperature, maximum figures falling by approximately 4° F. per 1,000 feet, and minimum figures by 1–2° F. per 1,000 feet. The map shows that Jos, at 4,000 feet above sea-level, has a highest monthly mean maximum of under 90° F., compared with over 100° F. on the surrounding plains 2,000 feet lower. Insufficient data prevent the continuation of the isotherms into the eastern highlands, but a similar reduction for altitude would result in a southward deflection of the isotherms in this area. It should be understood that the approximate reduction rates quoted cannot be too rigidly applied, since Cameroon Peak, over 13,000 feet above sea-level, is never snow-capped even in the coldest months; 16,000 feet is about the freezing level over Nigeria in free atmosphere.

The most striking contrasts between different parts of the country in respect of temperature are apparent when range is considered. Fig. 17 shows the annual range of mean monthly temperatures, and emphasises the extremely low range of the south-eastern coastal belt compared with the north-east. Calabar has mean monthly maximum figures ranging from 81·6° F. in July to 89·4° F. in February and March, and mean monthly minimum figures from 72·3° F. in August to 74·5° F. in March and May. Nguru, in the north-east, shows a mean maximum range from 87·3° F. in August to 103·6° F. in April, and mean minimum temperatures ranging from 53·8° F. in January

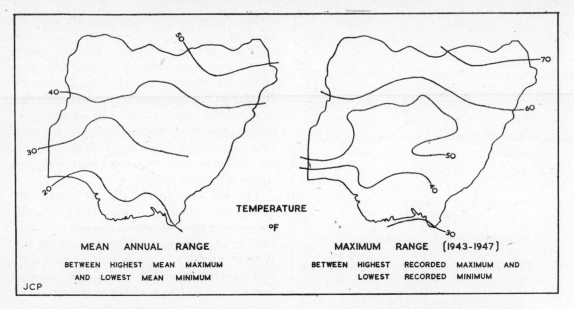

FIG. 18. TEMPERATURE: MEAN ANNUAL RANGE AND MAXIMUM RANGE

These maps show the contrast in the temperature regimes between north and south. A mean range of under 20° F. on the coast is a low figure, and considering the high temperatures experienced, this low range accentuates the enervating effect of the coastal climate. The northern mean range of over 50° F. is much greater than the ranges of western Europe, and although temperatures do not fall to freezing point, the contrast between hottest and coldest months places a strain on the inhabitants (effects are accentuated by humidity changes) and has a direct effect on the occurrence of disease (see p. 45).

to 74·3° F. in June. Fig. 18 shows the annual range between highest mean maximum and lowest mean minimum monthly temperatures, and the differences between south and north, which are further emphasised when record maximum and minimum observations are plotted. Apapa (the port of Lagos) has records of 96° and 59°, Calabar 97° and 55°; Benin, some distance inland, 100° and 56°; in the north, Maiduguri shows 112° and 43°, Nguru 111° and 40° and Katsina 115° and 40°. All these are dry-bulb screen Fahrenheit temperatures.

In considering the effect of temperature ranges on human beings, it is necessary to review not only annual ranges but also diurnal ranges, and Fig. 19 illustrates the maximum and minimum mean daily ranges experienced in any month of the year. The monotonous regularity of temperature in the coastal regions is clear, indicating the little relief by night com-

pared with the northern parts of the country. Maximum recorded ranges in any month have not been plotted, but in the north these are frequently not much less than the maximum annual ranges shown in Fig. 18. The strain of temperature variations on the inhabitants could probably be better assessed in terms of sun temperatures, but only in recent years have a few meteorological stations recorded such data, and there is, of course, a very great difference between a thermometer and the human body in respect of the nature of the exposed surface, among other factors, so that instrumental temperatures will not be the same as actual body surface temperatures. However, in the absence of data on the latter, instrumental readings can give some idea of the ranges involved. The writer has recorded over 145° F. on an ordinary thermometer laid in the sun, in early April south of the Jos Plateau, at an elevation of nearly 2,000 feet, when African labourers were

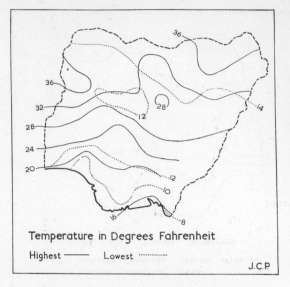

Temperature in Degrees Fahrenheit

Highest ———   Lowest ············

J.C.P.

FIG. 19. TEMPERATURE: MEAN
DAILY RANGE IN ANY MONTH

This map shows a feature of importance to the
inhabitants. The southern monotony is again
apparent, and the northern ranges may represent
both relief and discomfort. The maximum
ranges have not been plotted, but may be well
above the mean figures and not far short of the
maximum ranges shown in Fig. 18.

engaged in felling trees and clearing bush.
Probably in view of the higher night temperatures at this season, this appeared to be less of
a strain on the local people than November
recordings, at 4,000 feet on the north edge of
the Plateau, when night temperatures were
below 50° F. after sun temperatures by day of
the order of 120°. It is not surprising that
when left to himself the African farmer ceases
work from midday until the cooler evening.
The African appears to be more sensitive to
temperature changes than is the European; it is
quite common to hear people from Southern
Nigeria refer to the "bitter climate" of the Jos
Plateau, and even to comment on the strain of
the Kaduna climate during the railway journey
from south-east to south-west (Fig. 151).
Such comments may, however, be a reflection
of differences in humidity rather than in temperature, since the effects of the latter on human

beings depend very largely on the relative
humidity.

Much of the Northern Region obtains
some benefit from altitude, notably in the case
of the Jos Plateau, and also the Cameroons
Highlands; but temperatures are high notwithstanding this amelioration. By contrast the
troughs of the Niger and the Benue are extremely
fatiguing; altitude is low and both temperature
and humidity high by comparison with the
regions bordering them.

The low humidity in the north manifests
itself in the curling-up of papers and books, and
the warping even of seasoned wood; the latter
effect is also apparent well to the south in the
Western Region where furniture will split with
loud reports if made with inadequately seasoned
material. The effects of low humidity on the
human body are no less marked, and are particularly apparent in the drying and cracking of
the lips and skin, already coated with dust, and
the desiccation of the nasal passages. This is
very noticeable to the traveller by air from the
coast to the north and applies equally to both
African and European.

Humidity has to be considered in relation to
temperature. In the extreme north towards
the end of the dry season humidity may fall well
below 10% in the afternoon, and under 30%
at dawn. Potiskum has a mean relative humidity in March of 28% at 06.00 G.M.T. and
8% at 12.00 G.M.T., compared with August
values of 95% at 06.00 hours and 74% at
12.00 hours. This is in marked contrast with
the coastal regions, where during the year
Warri shows 95–99% at 06.00 hours and
65–82% at 12.00 hours. Fig. 20 shows mean
annual and lowest monthly mean values for
humidity at 12.00 G.M.T.

The persistently high humidity of the south
is extremely enervating for Europeans, and a
temperature of 85° F. on the coast may be much
more of a burden to the individual than a
temperature of over 100° F. in the low humidity
of the northern dry season. This generalisation presupposes an adequately large supply of
drinking water; if this is not available, the

FIG. 20. HUMIDITY

FIG. 20. HUMIDITY

Humidity must be regarded as of no less importance than temperature in effects on human activity in Nigeria. A mean humidity on the coast of over 70%, with a lowest monthly mean of over 60%, related to temperatures, speaks for itself. The northern figures reveal the extreme dryness of the winter months: the low humidity makes the great heat bearable, but accentuates the effects of lower night temperatures, and this latter fact, coupled with the dust of the dry season, can cause considerable discomfort.

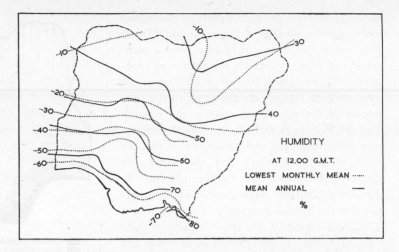

HUMIDITY

AT 12.00 G.M.T.

LOWEST MONTHLY MEAN ......

MEAN ANNUAL ——

%

effects on the human body are unpleasant. On the other hand, low humidity combined with low night temperatures, while to some extent a relief to the European, can give a sense of extreme cold to the indigenous population. Reference is made elsewhere to the relation between temperature and humidity and the incidence of disease.

VEGETATION

Fundamental to an understanding of the vegetation pattern of the Territory is an appreciation of the dynamic character of the vegetation in any given area.[1] Left to itself, the vegetation of a region tends to develop in a definite direction, from communities consisting of small and relatively simple plants to communities dominated by larger plants with a more complex structure; this change is known to ecologists as "succession", and various stages in succession may be observed on cultivated land which has been allowed to revert to fallow. As a result of these changes, each area tends to develop a stable vegetation in close equilibrium with the environment, and the vegetation undergoes no further change as long as environmental conditions remain constant. This stable type of vegetation is known as the climax vegetation, and each great climatic region tends to develop a characteristic climax vegetation; thus, in Nigeria closed forest represents the climax vegetation of the humid south, grassland appears to be the climax over the higher parts of the Cameroons and savana or parkland vegetation is the climax vegetation over much of the Middle Belt and north. Interference by man, in the form of cultivation, burning or grazing by domestic animals, may, however, arrest the development of this climax vegetation and maintain the vegetation at a lower level of development; such a vegetation, dependent for its character upon human factors, may be termed a "biotically determined sub-climax vegetation". Much of the vegetation of Nigeria appears to fall into this category, for long centuries of cultivation, burning and grazing have profoundly modified its original character; the open savana grasslands of the N. are thus almost certainly man-created while most of the high forest of the S. consists of secondary forest following cultivation.

Vegetation Zones[2]

Three major types of vegetation may be recognised in the Territory—the swamp forests

[1] For a general discussion of succession and related topics see A. G. Tansley and T. F. Chipp, *Aims and Methods in the Study of Vegetation*, London (1926).

[2] The most comprehensive study is *An Outline of Nigerian Vegetation*, by R. W. J. Keay, Lagos (1949).

of the coast-belt, the high forests of the humid
south and the savanas of the subhumid Middle
Belt and north.   As can be seen from a comparison of Figs. 21 and 10, the pattern of vegetation follows closely that of rainfall map; the
most striking features are the break in the continuity of the rain forest zone in the western
Yoruba Provinces and the southward penetration of savana grassland conditions in the dry
zone of Oyo Province and also along the
Cameroons upland belt in the extreme E.
These two features have been of some importance in the human geography of the Territory.
The replacement of rain forest by a more open
type of forest in the Provinces of Oyo and
Abeokuta provided an environment infinitely
more favourable to man than the rain-soaked
forests of the east, and it is no accident that the
highest forms of political organisation found in
the south—the Yoruba kingdoms—should have
arisen in this area.   The open savanas of Oyo
and the Cameroons represent extensions southwards of the great belt of savana grasslands of
Northern Nigeria and, like these latter, offered
no serious obstacle to the extension of military
power based on cavalry; in consequence, it
is in these two areas that Mohammedan and
Fulani influences achieved their greatest
southward penetration during the nineteenth
century.

Swamp Forests

The swamp forest zone comprises the mangrove and coastal vegetation developed under
brackish water conditions on the muddy banks
of coastal creeks, and the freshwater swamp
forest of the freshwater lagoons and estuaries.
The mangrove forest,[1] is present along the
greater length of the coast line, attaining its
maximum extension in the maze of anastomos-
ing creeks and inlets in the Niger delta.   The
forest is dominated by red mangrove; this,
under favourable conditions, may attain heights
of 150 feet, but for the most part the forest is

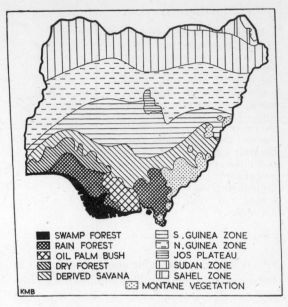

FIG. 21. VEGETATION ZONES
(Modified from a map by R. W. J. Keay)

Note the southward trend of vegetation boundaries in the dry belt of Oyo (cf. Fig. 10), the
marked recession of high forest suggested by the
broad belt of Derived Savana and the replacement
of Rain Forest by oil palm bush over much of
Iboland.

lower and in places is little more than a low-
growing tangle of mangrove shrubs.   The
freshwater swamp forest forms a more or less
continuous zone between the mangrove belt
and the rain forest.   It is perhaps best regarded
as an edaphic variant of the latter, and is
characterised by stilt-rooted trees with a dense
undergrowth of shrubs and lianes where the
canopy is more open; raphia and climbing palms
are very typical of this zone, and swards of
floating grass may occur on its periphery.
Owing to obvious difficulties of extraction, the
swamp forests are of limited importance in the
export lumber economy of the Territory,
though they play an important role in the local
economy as a source of pit-props and of fuel for
the coastal settlements.

[1] On mangrove swamps see D. R. Rosevear, "Mangrove Swamps", in *Farm and Forest*, Vol. VIII, No. 1 (1947).

High Forest [1]

High forest forms the climax vegetation over most of the humid south; as noted earlier, it has almost everywhere been extensively modified by man. Structurally, mature high forest shows three strata: an upper stratum of emergents, their crowns not in lateral contact, rising to heights of 120 feet or more and including many of the more valuable timber trees, such as the African mahogany; an intermediate stratum of trees some 50–120 feet high, with crowns in lateral contact; a lower stratum or under-storey of trees up to 50 feet high, with spreading crowns and often bound together by woody climbers; below this there is usually a shrub stratum. Over much of the high-forest belt the climate is not sufficiently humid for the development of true rain forest, and Keay has divided the belt into two zones: the true rain forest of the wetter south and east, and the dry forest of the lower rainfall areas; as boundary between the two he proposes the 64-inch annual isohyet. The two zones show a general similarity of structure, but there are marked contrasts in floral composition, while the dry forest is in general more open and contains a greater proportion of deciduous trees. The rain forest is the main source of Nigeria's export timbers; though less rich florally than the rain forests of other parts of the humid tropics, it contains a high proportion of the valuable mahogany timbers, and possesses the great advantage of relative accessibility by water. Today much of the zone has been constituted Forest Reserve, the biggest blocks of such reserves occupying the former 'no-man's-land' between the larger towns; here, as a result of insecurity in the pre-British period, occupation by man was intermittent, and the degree of modification by farming and felling was much less than in the politically more settled areas.

Taking the high forest zone as a whole, it is probably no exaggeration to say that little virgin forest remains; everywhere the prevalent system of shifting cultivation has left its mark on the vegetation. On more fertile soils and under conditions of high rainfall, abandoned fields are soon recolonised by trees, provided the period of cultivation is short. But on poorer soils and under less humid conditions abandoned fields tend, especially if over-cultivated, to be invaded by grasses; the inevitable grass fires kill off the younger trees which may attempt to establish themselves and high forest is replaced by "derived savana" dominated by grasses and fire-tolerant savana trees. In appearance this derived savana is very similar to the savanas of the Guinea zone farther N., though patches of relict forest on the poorer and agriculturally unattractive soils of the hills and on the humid soils of valley bottoms provide a clue to the character of the climax vegetation. Elsewhere in the heart of the rain forest belt, in the Provinces of Owerri and Calabar, human interference has destroyed the original forest and replaced it over hundreds of square miles by oil-palm bush (Fig. 21).

Savanas

The northern limit of the derived savana represents the probable climatic limit of high forest. Beyond this limit, over much of the Middle Belt and the North, the dry season is severe and protracted, annual rainfall totals drop below 45 inches and forest is replaced by savana as the climax vegetation. [2]

The Southern Guinea zone represents a transition zone between forest and savana with a form of "Transition Woodland" as its climax vegetation. Small patches of such woodland,

[1] A detailed study of the Rain Forest, which includes regional examples from West Africa, has been made by P. W. Richards, *The Tropical Rain Forest*, Cambridge (1952).
[2] Leo Waibel has recently expressed the view that the original climax vegetation of semi-humid tropical West Africa was Campo Cerrado (a vegetation type intermediate between forest and grassland and consisting of a dense cover of low twisted trees with a ground cover of tall grasses) and that the existing savana vegetation results from degradation of this formation. "Land Use in the Planalto Central of Brazil", *Geographical Review*, Vol. XXXVIII, No. 4 (1948), especially p. 554.

consisting of both fire-tolerant and fire-tender trees (many of the latter having high-forest affinities), can still be seen, but over large areas the vegetation has been degraded by fire and farming into open savana woodland with tussocky grasses 5–10 feet high and short-boled, broad-leaved trees up to 50 feet in height. This zone is swept annually by fierce grass fires; in consequence, though the typical trees possess remarkable powers of recuperation, fresh sucker growth is usually burned back, and the trees grow gnarled and crooked and are useless for timber. Local variations on this general pattern, due to local soil variations, may be recognised; thus, the occasional rocky hills which break the monotony of the plateau surface have an irregular, broken vegetation with abundant fire-tender climbers; while the more extensive flood plains support a tall grass vegetation with wide-spaced trees, especially fan palms.

The climax vegetation of the Northern Guinea zone consists of broad-leaved savana woodlands, representing a western extension of the great *miombo* woodlands of Eastern and Southern Africa. When well-developed, the tree cover may attain heights of 30–45 feet, forming a continuous cover which may be dense enough to suppress grass; more usually, as a result of cultivation and grazing, the vegetation is relatively open, and grass is dominant, though shorter than in the Southern Guinea zone. The larger flood-plains carry a distinctive vegetation of grass and raphia or fan palms, while relatively dense gallery forest occurs along some of the streams; in this gallery forest the dominant tree species have savana affinities and this contrasts sharply with the gallery forests of the Southern Guinea zone in which the trees are similar to those of the southern high forest. Human modification of the vegetation cover is very marked in this zone and, as Keay has pointed out, the vegetation around the larger settlements shows a marked zonation; each settlement is surrounded by a zone of more or less permanent cultivation within which the natural vegetation is com-

pletely suppressed. This gives place to a zone of regrowth savana which is cultivated for short periods and then grazed, and this in turn merges, on the outer fringe of the village territory, into savana woodlands, locally exploited for fuel but in remoter areas mature and relatively undisturbed in character.

Within the Guinea zone, the Jos Plateau merits mention as a distinctive region. Its climax vegetation appears to have been savana woodland, and the vegetation includes several species with South or East African affinities. It has, however, suffered extensive and severe degradation by man, with the result that today woodland is confined to the steep and less accessible plateau margins while most of the High Plateau consists of open, grassy plains. These are heavily farmed and grazed, and the only woody vegetation surviving consists of occasional scattered trees on rocky outcrops and occasional patches of coppiced shrubs.

With decreasing annual rainfall and increasing length and severity of the dry season, the Guinea savanas give place to Sudan savanas, the zone of transition between the two vegetation types running broadly E.–W. through northern Zaria Province. The typical Sudan vegetation is more open and favourable to man than the savanas to the south (though this openness is certainly in part man-induced) and consists of fine-leaved, thorny trees (especially acacias), often of Sahel affinities, mixed with broad-leaved species of Guinea affinities. There is a more or less continuous grass-cover, the grasses being short and feathery and contrasting with the tall, coarse, tussocky grasses typical of the Guinea zone, while many valleys carry a discontinuous belt of fringing forest. This consists of a dense tangle of dry-zone species with isolated larger trees and patches of tall grass, and is very different from the dense evergreen gallery forest of the Guinea zone. As elsewhere in the Territory, the vegetation has been extensively modified by man, the modification being most striking in the closely farmed areas around the larger towns; here, the original plant-cover has been more or less completely obliterated and replaced by continuous stretches of arable land dotted with farm trees, such as the shea butter tree, *Acacia albida*, and *Tamarindus indica*. In view of this profound alteration, it is difficult to decide with certainty what was the original climax vegetation. Keay, arguing from the general similarity of environmental conditions, suggests that it was probably similar to the *mutemwa* vegetation of Northern Rhodesia, consisting of "a dense understorey of deciduous shrubs, with larger emergent trees forming a rather open canopy, and grass absent or sparse". Relict vegetation of this type survives in isolated rocky areas throughout the Sudan zone.

Vegetation of the Sahel type is represented only in the extreme N.E. of the Territory, the boundary between the Sudan and Sahel savanas coinciding broadly with the 20-inch isohyet. Typically, the Sahel vegetation consists of open thorn savana some 15–30 feet high and with a sparse, short grass-cover; *Acacia seyal* forms almost pure stands in low-lying sites.

Montane Vegetation

Owing to the inaccessibility of the area, data on the vegetation of the Cameroons highland belt is extremely fragmentary. In the S., on Cameroon Mountain itself, there is a distinct altitudinal zonation of the vegetation. Between 3,500 and 6,000 feet humidities are high for much of the year, and the vegetation may conveniently be described as "mist forest"; it is characterised by an often broken and irregular tree canopy, and by a profusion of mosses, epiphytes and tree ferns. Above 6,000 feet the vegetation is drier and more stunted, tree ferns are absent and the mosses and epiphytes of the mist belt are replaced by lichens; this forest zone gives place to grasslands: at lower levels coarse and tussocky and dotted with stunted trees; at greater elevations (above approximately 10,000 feet) shorter and more compact with thick cushions of moss. This zone of rolling mountain grasslands extends northwards into Adamawa, and has played an important role in the diffusion of the Fulani and their pastoral economy (Fig. 72).

SOILS

The character of the underlying rocks has been of great importance in the evolution of the major soil groups of Nigeria, and many of the boundaries between the various groups follow closely the boundaries shown on the provisional geological map. The most important exception to this generalisation is to be found on the plains of Hausaland, where the underlying rocks have been veneered by sandy superficial deposits derived from the north during former southward encroachment of the desert; these "drift" deposits are not indicated on the geological maps, but they have exercised a profound influence on soil evolution in the northern section of the Territory.

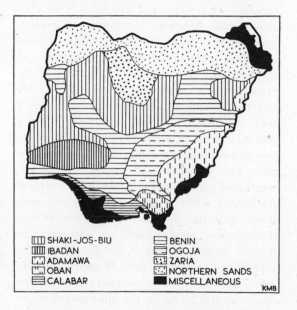

▥ SHAKI-JOS-BIU	▤ BENIN
▦ IBADAN	▣ OGOJA
▨ ADAMAWA	▥ ZARIA
▧ OBAN	⣿ NORTHERN SANDS
▤ CALABAR	■ MISCELLANEOUS
	KMB

FIG. 22. MAJOR SOIL GROUPS

(Modified from a map by H. Vine)

Soils derived from Basement rocks are shown by vertical shading; those derived from sedimentary rocks by horizontal shading; and those derived from the sandy drift deposits of the Sudan zone by stippling. The Northern Sands include the Kano, Zurmi and Damaturu Groups of Vine. The Miscellaneous category comprises the Swamp soils of the south, the poorly drained clays and dry sands of the Chad Basin, the high-level basalt-derived soils of Bamenda and the varied soils of the Kumba Complex.

H. Vine[1] has recently regrouped Nigerian soils into five main classes, further subdivided into sixteen groups, some of which are multiple. The main classes are briefly:

(1) Well-drained reddish-coloured soils, moderately to strongly leached, with low humus content.

(2) Well-drained soils, moderately leached, with high humus content.

(3) Well-drained yellowish-brown soils, excessively leached.

(4) Swamp soils.

(5) Poorly drained clays and dry sands.

The first of these classes is by far the most important in terms of area occupied, covering about nine-tenths of the country. The southern boundary of these soils can be regarded as a function of geology and rainfall. This class shows wide variations in reserves of fertility, covering as it does sedimentary rocks, areas of crystalline rocks of the Basement Complex and the northern areas of drift. The soils of the crystalline areas sometimes possess considerable reserves of fertility in the form of unweathered rock minerals in the profile; but this is not a general rule. In some localities the soils are thin and sandy over concretionary layers. The class also shows a wide range in texture, weathered gneisses giving a relatively heavy and fertile soil; while granites, quartzites and sandstones give rise to a coarser and poorer soil. Topographic factors exert an important influence on soil texture, as, for example, in the crystalline areas of the Western Region, where there are striking contrasts between fertile clays and clay loams on the hill tops and upper slopes and the sandy or concretionary soils of the lower slopes. This sequence of soil types is known as a catena, and is illustrated in Fig. 23; it constitutes a factor of some importance in the agricultural geography of the south-west, for cocoa will flourish on the heavier and moisture-retentive soils of the upper slopes, but frequently, although not invariably, makes only poor growth on the sandy soils of the lower slopes. Vine distinguishes hill-creep soils, generally sandy, loamy and gravelly without concretionary layers, as subdivisions of a number of the soil groups within his main classes, in the areas of Basement rocks.

The soils derived from the sedimentary rocks in this class tend to far lower fertility than those over the crystalline rocks, due to the sedimentary parent material being poor in minerals whose decomposition will provide a supply of plant nutrients, and also due to a general coarse-textured soil character favouring quick seepage and rapid leaching. These latter features are well illustrated by the soils above the Udi escarpment, south-west of Enugu, derived from the soft red sandstones of the Upper Cretaceous sequence, which are easy to work but are of only limited agricultural value owing to their poverty in plant nutrients, due to intense leaching and to their tendency to dry out during the dry season. The soils of the sedimentary zone of the southern forest area present one of the major agricultural problems of the country, on account of low fertility; they are derived from beds of age from Upper Cretaceous to post-Middle Eocene, particularly from sandstones, are heavily leached as a result of soil texture and high rainfall and are strongly acid in reaction. When freshly cleared from forest they may be very fertile, but this fertility is concentrated in the top few inches of the profile and is rapidly depleted by cropping, and long periods of bush fallowing are required for their regeneration. In emphasising the physical factors affecting these soils, it should be remembered that high population density is of very great importance in producing present characteristics; reduced fallowing leads to rapid degradation of the fragile soils, and this result of increasing population pressure is creating a situation of the utmost gravity in many parts of Iboland.

The position is less acute on the areas of sedimentary rocks in the Niger trough and the Benue–Cross basins. In the former lie the Nupe sands, typical of the western sector of the

FIG. 23. A SOIL CATENA IN
THE COCOA BELT

(After H. Vine)

Illustrating the characteristic
sequence of soil types found on
many valley slopes in the cocoa
belt. Owing to more favourable
moisture conditions, cocoa suc-
ceeds best on the sedentary clay
soils of the interfluves and the clay
loam of the upper slopes; the concretionary or sandy soils of the
lower slopes are unsuited to the
crop.

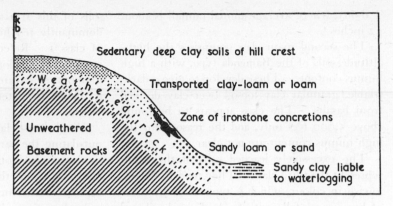

Sedentary deep clay soils of hill crest

Transported clay-loam or loam

Zone of ironstone concretions

Sandy loam or sand

Sandy clay liable
to waterlogging

Weathered rock

Unweathered
Basement rocks

Middle Belt, derived from Upper Cretaceous
sandstones. These soils are lighter in colour,
and although rainfall is still considerable
(Fig. 12), they are leached to a lesser extent,
longer fallow periods being possible with the
lower density of population (Fig. 35). Nevertheless, fertility in this area cannot be classed as
more than medium. The soils over the Lower
Cretaceous beds of the Benue–Cross area and
the western part of the eastern crystalline mass
are also of generally low fertility, even though
they are of varied nature, from light sands to
heavy clays.

Over the northern plains of Hausaland and
the Chad basin, the character of the soil depends
largely upon the nature of the drift deposits
which mantle the solid sedimentary and Basement rocks. These deposits derive from the
desert sands of the last arid period, and furnish
the most important groundnut soils of West
Africa. Depth of drift is variable and independent of latitude, but texture becomes finer
towards the southern margin. This southward
increase in fineness led to distinction of two
major soil types, the Zaria and the Northern
Drift soils, although further subdivisions can now
be recognised. The Zaria type represents the
southern part of the drifted area, where the
covering material, although up to 14 feet in
depth, is very fine in texture; the soils are, in
consequence, heavy and relatively difficult to
work, tending to become waterlogged with
heavy rain and to dry out and crack during the
dry season. Farther north the drift is coarser,

resulting in light sandy soils of buff or red-
dish colour, of low to medium fertility, easily
worked and well suited to crops such as
millet and groundnuts, which are less exacting in their requirements than cotton, the
latter being a characteristic crop on the Zaria
type of soil.

It need hardly be stated that this first class of
soils, covering so large a part of the country,
and including soils developed over crystalline,
volcanic and sedimentary rocks as well as over
drift-covered areas, with wide variations in rainfall totals and regimes, must necessarily be
extremely varied, and Vine subdivides it into
nine major groups, with further distinction
between sub-types. Local differences are to be
expected, as for instance on the Jos Plateau,
where shallow sandy soils over concretions may
border relatively deep clay loams over basalts.
The varying types can be grouped as one class
by virtue of the qualities which they have in
common: good drainage (normally), a tendency
to red colour rather than to yellow, low to
medium humus content and a moderate to
strong degree of leaching. That soils are
leached right up to the northern frontier is
worth recording, pH values being $5 \cdot 5$–$6 \cdot 5$ in
the surface layer and under $5 \cdot 0$ in the second
foot, and it is necessary to look to the lower rainfall areas to the north of the frontier before there
is apparent a tendency to soil profiles of normally low acidity. Tests of soils from French
territory to the north show pH values of
over $7 \cdot 0$ down to a depth of 20 inches at

Tahoua, where average annual rainfall is about 12 inches.[1]

The second main class comprises the high-altitude soils of the Bamenda type, with a high humus content. These develop to give a dark, friable, granular clay topsoil over clay derived from basalts. The class appears to be found above 5,000 feet only, and the reasons for the high humus content are not clear.

The excessively leached soils of the south represent the third class. They tend to be yellowish in colour, which is typical of the areas of heavier rainfall; with freely drained soils red predominates where annual totals are up to 90 inches and there is a marked dry season, but above this figure yellow soils can be expected.[1] Although this belt of soils is slight in width, in length it passes across sediments of varying age and across both Basement and volcanic rocks, and there is much internal variation within the class as a result. Across the more or less unconsolidated sedimentaries the soils are deep, porous, yellowish-brown and sandy, but in the higher eastern part of this belt there is marked local variation, but with a predominance of clays and loams. Soils at Calabar, even under high forest, show pH values for surface soil as low as 4·3, and the detailed pattern within this class would seem to depend more on rainfall than on geology.

The identification of swamp soils as class 4 needs no justification. Along the whole length of the coast the mangrove holds a dark saline mud between its tangled roots. A little inland from the coast in the area of the delta and the swamps westward, the soils are freshwater instead of saline, and the muds are replaced by sands and clays. Included in these areas are small patches of dry-land soils on which settlements are frequently sited, and which can usually be easily distinguished ecologically.

Lastly, there is the area of poorly drained clays and sands of the extreme north-east, marked as class 5. The black to grey-brown soils of this area stand in contrast to the predominantly red hue of the neighbouring soils of class 1. Reference has been made in the section on geology to the remarkably low gradients of stream channels in this area, which is liable to extensive flooding in the wet season.

Vine's latest classification may be regarded as out-dating the earlier systems, which laid particular emphasis on the soil groups known as the Ilepa soils and the Acid Sands. Both these types are now included in the area of class 1 soils, but finer distinctions have been made. The name "Acid Sands" has now disappeared (compare the disappearance of the geological group of the "Benin Sands"), and the name Ilepa has been relegated to a subdivision of one of the groups found in the Western Region and included in the main soil class.

The broad pattern of soils shown in Fig. 22 and outlined above provides an important key to the distribution of natural and cultivated vegetation in the Territory. A. F. A. Lamb, in a paper entitled "Different Soils make Different Forests",[2] has shown the close correlation existing in many areas between soil conditions, and especially soil moisture condition, and the characteristic plant association, and this is well exemplified in the case of cultivated crops. Cocoa, which is sensitive to soil acidity, flourishes on the better soils of the south-west, but is of negligible importance on the more acidic soils of the south-east. Reference has already been made to the emphasis on cotton on the Zaria type of soil and the preference of groundnuts for the Northern Drift soils. Soils alone do not account for crop distribution: the section on climate has shown the agricultural importance of varying rainfall regimes, but the soil character will itself be influenced by rainfall distribution. The relationship of crops to soils is described more fully in the sections dealing with individual crops; a visual impression of its importance may be obtained from a comparison

[1] H. Vine, "Nigerian Soils in Relation to Parent Materials", Comm. Bur. of Soil Science, Tech. Communication No. 46 (1949), p. 4.
[2] A. F. A. Lamb, "Different Soils make Different Forests", Farm and Forest, Vol. IX (1948).

of the soil map and the crop distribution maps (e.g. Figs. 108, 115, 121).

DISEASE AS AN ELEMENT IN THE NIGERIAN ENVIRONMENT

The Health Problem of Nigeria

In the year 1950 Nigeria, with its 373,000 square miles and with an estimated population of some 25 millions, had 344 medical practitioners (of whom 179 were in the Colonial Service) to care for the health of its inhabitants. The ratio of doctors to patients is extremely low by Western standards (compare England and Wales with 38,000 medical practitioners for a population of 44 millions), yet it should be stressed that never before had there been so many doctors and never before had a sum so large as £1,500,000 been voted from central funds for the health services of the country. It is, in consequence, less surprising that statistics as to health are neither abundant, nor, for the most part, very detailed, than that there are any statistics at all, and it is therefore inevitable that any account of the state of health of the Territory should be broad and bold, with islets of detail here and there and containing generalisations which future research may prove ill-founded.

The present account is based in part on hospital statistics, on the annual reports of the Medical Department and on discussions with those of long experience in the country. The more detailed sections lean heavily on the reports of the Malaria, Leprosy and Sleeping Sickness Services, of the Medical Field Units and on the rather scanty published literature.

The doctor coming from abroad will find much that is familiar to him in the wards of a Nigerian hospital; yet, taking the Territory as a whole, the problems which it poses are very different from those of more temperate and better-developed countries. The Nigerian inherits almost all the disorders of temperate climates and only escapes the others by dying relatively young. On top of these he may suffer from a multitude of other diseases to which his ignorance of their causes, his poor standards of hygiene and his geographical situation on the globe make him liable.

Disease of a type which, in the present state of knowledge, is not amenable to prevention is plentiful enough in Nigeria, and as the expectation of life increases, this type of disorder will appear with greater frequency. At the present time, however, the more massive hazards to life and health are preventable. Prevention is proverbially better than cure; it is also vastly cheaper, and its lessons once well learned are self-perpetuating. But even the cheapest of schemes is expensive in a country where the annual expenditure on health services from central and local funds is about 2s. per head. Poor resources, inadequate communications and scantiness of trained personnel make any bold frontal attack on disease impossible. Much ingenuity is required in selecting only those points of attack from which the maximum benefit can be derived to the exclusion of those of less promise. Moreover, there exist the problems of securing the co-operation of a conservative, often apathetic and largely illiterate community.

The diseases from which Nigerians suffer may be broadly divided into three groups:

Group I: This group comprises diseases common to mankind in any climate and in any state of prosperity. It includes such familiar names as measles, mumps, chicken-pox, tuberculosis, various types of heart disease, the venereal diseases, asthma, pneumonia, bronchitis, peptic ulcer and so forth; all conditions similar to those found in groups of like age composition in Europe or America. In discussing disease in the tropics, the fact is often overlooked that the inhabitants contend not only with so-called tropical diseases but with most other types of disease as well. Less dramatic, more readily overlooked, more expensive and difficult to diagnose and often not complained of till far advanced, they tend to be accepted with fatalism by the African as part of the general discomfort of existence. With increasing expectation of life and with improving standards of education and of life in general, sickness of this more universal character will undoubtedly receive more attention in the future than it has hitherto.

Group II: This group includes diseases common in more backward countries with low standards of living and of hygiene, and thus not essentially "tropical". It includes the fevers of the typhus group, relapsing fever, leprosy and some of the intestinal worms. The general problem of nutritional deficiencies is discussed separately.

Group III: This group consists of the truly tropical diseases, limited to those areas of the globe which provide the warm and humid climatic conditions necessary for the propagation of the disease agent or its vector. It includes malaria, yaws, sleeping sickness, the filarial diseases, bilharzia, guinea worm and yellow fever. Malaria is by no means limited to the tropics, but only there does the problem attain such massive proportions, with the majority of the population affected throughout the year.

Owing to limitations of space in a work such as this, any treatment of the topic of disease must be selective, and in the discussion which follows the major emphasis is on the diseases falling into Groups II and III. Such a selective treatment is, indeed, inevitable, since many of the diseases included in Group I pass unrecorded, and adequate statistical data on their incidence and distribution are very scanty.

Group I: Non-localised Diseases

Tuberculosis: It is impossible to say whether this disease was introduced by the European, or whether it has always existed in West Africa and been confined in its spread by the very restricted travel of earlier times. It is certain that it is now universal in its distribution and probably on the increase. All forms are seen, with a greater proportion of the more acute and florid types than is common in Europe. Extensive surveys at present in progress, together with mass radiography, will provide much-needed data on the infection and morbidity rates.

The majority of cases up to the present have been advanced and beyond treatment when first seen. This is partly due to the very rapid advance of the disease and partly to delay in seeking advice. All kinds of folk remedies are usually tried before the help of the hospital is sought; further, except in a few districts, there are no facilities for extended treatment, and even if these were available, the unsophisticated African is not only averse to the long hospital stay required but cannot afford to be laid up. Treatment of the disease on the scale common in Europe is beyond the present resources of the Territory and institutional care will have to be on a much simpler (but not necessarily less effective) scale.

The long-term solution is, as in the case of so many other diseases, bound up with improved standards of housing and of public hygiene.

Venereal Diseases: Venereal diseases are extremely widespread and the infection rate is high in most areas. Gonorrhœa is the most common, and is a frequent cause of sterility in both sexes; syphilis is widespread, but with a notably higher incidence in the north where, in Sokoto City, a survey showed that the infection rate was 592 per 1,000 in prostitutes and ranged from 431 to 294 per 1,000 in other groups of the population.

Group II: Diseases associated with Low Standards of Living and of Hygiene

Smallpox: This is endemic, with frequent epidemic outbursts, and affects all parts of the Territory. Epidemics occurred in Bauchi and Sokoto in 1946–7 and in the Eastern Ijaw, Owerri and Onitsha areas in 1948. In Bornu the epidemics are frequent and the disease severe in type. In the decade 1940–50 medical records show 66,000 cases to have occurred, with 10,000 deaths; but, for reasons obvious from the introduction to this section, the majority are never notified and therefore do not feature in any statistical accounts. That the disease is more common than the above statistics suggest is borne out by the large number of

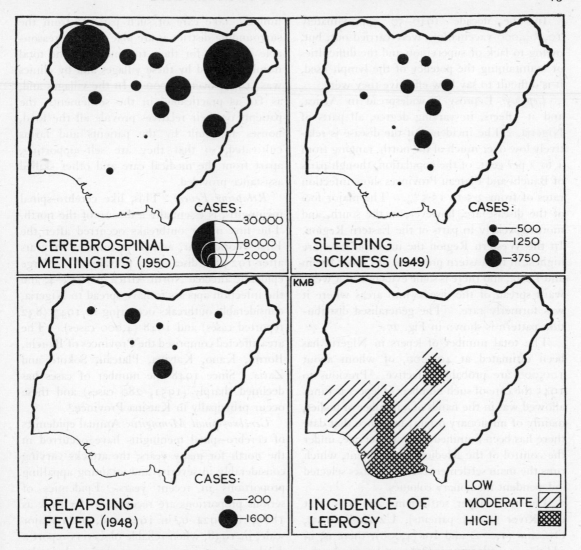

FIGS. 24–27. CONTRASTING PATTERNS OF DISEASE DISTRIBUTION

Note that cerebro-spinal meningitis is especially typical of the Sudan zone, while human sleeping sickness shows a marked localisation in the central sector of the Middle Belt. Relapsing fever is another typically "Sudan disease" though overlapping into Plateau Province. Leprosy, by contrast, is of major importance in the humid south, especially in the Eastern Region, though there is an important outlier of this belt in Plateau Province; the broad correlation with the areas of leached and impoverished soils is striking.

pock-marked individuals seen in any Nigerian village. In various districts carefully surveyed, proportions of the population ranging from 6 to 25% showed evidence of past smallpox, and in the north at least it is one of the major causes of blindness.

McLetchie states: "As an epidemic scourge smallpox ranks second to cerebro-spinal fever. From a steady level of 5,000 to 7,000 cases annually from 1943 to 1948 returns rose to 20,000 in 1949–51 and are continuing at that rate in 1952."[1]

[1] J. L. McLetchie, Lecture to World Health Organization, Malaria Course, Lagos (1952). (Unpublished.)

In the decade 1940–50 approximately 10,000,000 vaccinations were carried out, but, owing to lack of supervision and the difficulties of maintaining the potency of the lymph used, it is difficult to say how effective they were.

Leprosy: Leprosy is widespread in Africa, and it affects, in varying degree, all parts of Nigeria. The incidence of the disease is relatively low over much of the north, ranging from 1 to 2 per cent. of the population, though parts of Bauchi and Plateau Provinces show infection rates of from 3·5 to 15·5%. The major foci of the disease are, however, in the south, and more especially in parts of the Eastern Region. In the Western Region the infection rates are highest in the eastern provinces of Ondo, Benin and Delta, and there is some evidence of a westward spread of the disease into areas where it was formerly rare. The generalised distribution pattern is shown in Fig. 27.

The total number of lepers in Nigeria has been estimated at 400,000, of whom about 100,000 are probably infective. Previous to 1945 the care of such numbers of lepers as funds allowed was in the hands of a number of bodies, mainly of missionary origin; but since that date there has been a unified Leprosy Service, under the control of the Medical Department, which runs the main settlements and subsidises selected independent missionary colonies.

The main leper settlements are (1951) at Oji River (1,094 patients), Uzuakoli (935), Ossiomo (1,072) and Itu (4,000); there is, in addition, a settlement at Ogbomosho, run by the American Baptists and about nineteen in the Northern Region run by various denominations. These settlements segregate and treat infective cases, provide education, care for the children of the infected parents, and offer suitable employment for those whose condition allows them to work. The total number of in-patients in 1951 was nearly 28,000. In addition, there are segregation villages, visited at intervals by medical officers from the settlements. These villages, in addition to looking after their own inmates, take care of such patients from the surrounding district as are able to walk reasonable distances for their treatment. The total number treated by these villages and by clinics was (1951) over 26,000. In the villages and, as far as practicable, in the settlements, the patients or their relatives provide all the food, houses are built by the patients and farms cultivated, so that they are self-supporting, apart from the medical care and other skilled assistance provided.

Relapsing Fever: This, like cerebro-spinal meningitis, is essentially a disease of the north. The first major outbreaks occurred after the First World War, and for a number of years after 1923 the disease was prevalent. A large epidemic affected North Africa in 1943–4, and the infection appears to have spread to Nigeria, considerable outbreaks occurring in 1947 (832 reported cases) and 1948 (4,000 cases). The area affected comprised the Provinces of Bauchi, Bornu, Kano, Katsina, Plateau, Sokoto and Zaria. Since 1948 the number of cases has declined sharply (1951, 280 cases) and these occur principally in Katsina Province.[1]

Cerebro-spinal Meningitis: Annual epidemics of cerebro-spinal meningitis have occurred in the north for many years, the attacks varying considerably in severity and attaining appalling proportions in recent years. Epidemics of serious proportions are recorded as far back as 1885,[2] in 1924–6, in 1933 and, on a major scale, in 1938, when reliable observers report a death-rate running into many thousands in the Provinces of Katsina and Sokoto. Each of the years 1944 and 1945 saw epidemics exceeding 10,000 cases, but these were dwarfed by the epidemic of 1949, involving 53,000 people, and by the 1950 epidemic, which involved 93,000 people. The death-rate in these outbreaks has varied from 15 to 20%. These epidemics are not peculiar to Nigeria. Those recorded were parts of major outbreaks which have affected the whole of the savana belt of West Africa for at least the past thirty years. These epidemics

[1] J. L. McLetchie, Personal Communications.
[2] D. W. Horn, *Journal Roy. Sanitary Inst.* (1951), LXXI, p. 573.

PLATE V. THE HIGH-LEVEL GRASSLANDS OF THE JOS PLATEAU

The abrupt transition from the general Plateau surface to the steep granite residual hills can be clearly seen in the background. In the foreground a drag-line is excavating open-cast tin workings. Because of their fly-free character these grasslands play an important role in the grazing economy of the nomad Fulani.

PLATE VI. GRANITE INSELBERG IN SOKOTO PROVINCE

Acacia scrub grows on the talus slopes. Note the village on the pediment at the base of the inselberg and a patch of cultivated land in the left foreground.

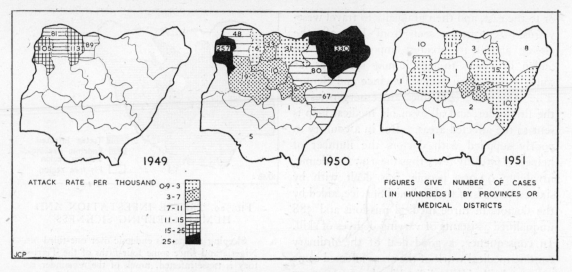

F IG. 28. CEREBRO-SPINAL FEVER

Incidence in recent years. The 1950 figures include the latter part of the epidemic of 1949–50 and the early part of the epidemic of 1950–51.

have tended to occur in cycles of about five to six years, with minor outbreaks intervening. Such a periodicity might be explicable in terms of climatic fluctuations, but experience elsewhere suggests that a more likely explanation is to be found in the development of a state of temporary immunity in a population following a major epidemic, this immunity lasting some five years. Further, the occurrence of the next outbreak appears to be determined in some degree by such factors as over-crowding and low standards of hygiene, and in countries with high standards of living the interval may be as long as twelve years. In areas which have not been severely affected for some years, the tendency is for an epidemic to affect mainly those under 5 years of age, but when a district is attacked in consecutive years the emphasis shifts to higher age groups.[1]

These epidemics show a markedly seasonal character. They invariably begin with the drier and colder weather towards the end of November, reach their peak in March and April and subside rapidly in May. It has been suggested that they are related to the dryness,

wind and dust so characteristic of the north at this season, but the meteorological parameter which most closely parallels them is the mean minimum temperature; this is at its lowest in December (c. 60° F.) when the epidemics begin, and rises steeply until May, following closely the curve of weekly notification of cases; in May the mean minimum temperature reaches 80° F., and the curve of notifications drops precipitously. A possible explanation of this may lie in the fact that during the colder weather the Northerners tend to crowd together indoors during the night, instead of sleeping outdoors as they do in the hotter season; for experience elsewhere has shown that proximity and over-crowding are cardinal factors in the transmission of the disease.[1] Some support is lent to the climatic hypothesis by the fact that throughout the northern hemisphere the disease occurs in annual waves with peaks in the period February to May, and that this periodicity is reversed in the southern hemisphere, while Uganda, on the Equator, has little seasonal variation.[2]

Broadly speaking, the waves of infection tend to enter the Territory in the vicinity of Katsina

[1] D. W. Horn, Jour. Roy. Sanitary Inst. (1951), LXXI, p. 573.
[2] M. J. Freyche, Epidemic and Vital Stat. Report, World Health Organization (1951), IV.

or to the east, and then gradually to travel westwards.   As can be seen from Fig. 28, the
disease attains its greatest importance in the
Sudan Provinces though it may spread as far
south as Northern Niger Province and Benue.
The large-scale epidemics are emergencies of
the first order, and all available medical help is
sent to the affected areas.   But in a country so
poorly supplied with doctors the number of
helpers is pitifully few; thus the 1950 epidemic,
involving 93,000 people, was dealt with by
sixteen doctors of the Colonial Service, aided by
the doctors in three medical missions and 588
unqualified assistants of varying degrees of skill.
In consequence, a good deal of the ordinary
routine medical work of the areas affected came
to a standstill.   The difficulties due to shortages
of staff are aggravated by poor transport, many
of the areas affected being accessible only by the
poorest of tracks or over open country.

Other Infections: Fevers of the *typhoid group*
occur, but recognised cases are surprisingly few,
having regard to the poor state of sanitation.
Cholera is unknown.   A few cases of *undulant
fever* are reported from the north annually,
while *louse-born typhus* occurs from time to
time—a small epidemic was reported in Kano
and Jos in 1946.   A small number of cases of
murine (*flea-borne*) *typhus* occur each year,
mainly in Lagos.

Intestinal disorders, such as *bacillary and
amœbic dysentery* and others of less clearly
understood origin, are very common throughout
the Territory.   *Tetanus* (lockjaw) is common
at all ages.

Group III: Tropical Diseases

Malaria[1]: This, like sleeping sickness, is
an excellent example of a tropical disease complex involving as essential elements a microbe,
an insect vector and an animal or human host.
In the case of malaria, the major parasite in
Nigeria is that of malignant tertian malaria,
which is responsible for 96% of all infections;

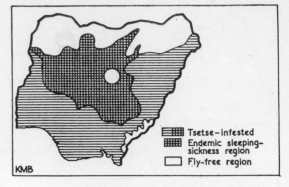

Tsetse-infested
Endemic sleeping-
sickness region
Fly-free region

KMB

FIG. 29. TSETSE INFESTATION AND
HUMAN SLEEPING SICKNESS

Sleeping sickness is endemic over one-third of
Nigeria and since some four-fifths of the Territory is tsetse-infested, much of the remainder is
potentially dangerous. The major fly-free areas
are the open savanas of the Sudan zone and the
higher parts of the Jos Plateau and the Cameroons; only in these areas can cattle be kept without
contracting trypanosomiasis. It should be emphasised that, except in the *Morsitans* belts, the
fly is confined to the watercourses and the intervening areas are usually fly-free.

eight species of anopheline mosquito are known
to act as vectors, but of these, two—*Anopheles
gambiæ* and *A. funestus*—far outweigh the
others in importance.   Along the coast *A.
gambiæ* var. *melas* is of importance in that it
breeds in brackish water.   Their range of distribution depends, among other factors, on the
presence of free-water surfaces and on suitable
temperature and humidity conditions.   These
latter are as yet ill-understood.   General
meteorological data are not necessarily a reliable
guide, as what is of importance for the insect is
the microclimates to which its habits expose it.
In general, however, it seems that malarial
transmission is inhibited by temperatures below
60° F. and above 100° F., and requires relative
humidities of 60% or greater.[2]

The breeding cycle of the mosquito follows
closely the annual rainfall curve, increasing
sharply with the onset of the rains and falling

[1] L. J. Bruce-Chwatt, *Bulletin World Health Organization* (1951), IV, p. 301.
[2] P. F. Russell, L. S. West and R. D. Manwell, *Practical Malariology* (1st ed.), Philadelphia and London (1946),
pp. 360–3.

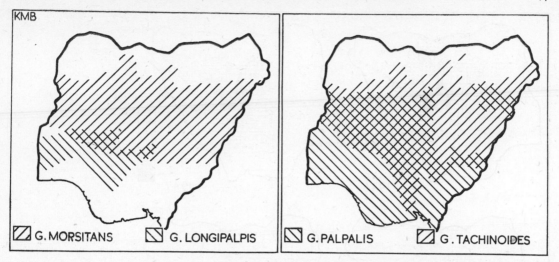

FIG. 30. CONTRASTS IN TSETSE DISTRIBUTION
(After T. A. M. Nash)

Each species of tsetse fly has distinct preferences with regard to habitat and this produces marked contrasts in distribution. *G. Morsitans* is absent from the high rainfall areas of the south and is essentially a savana species, being especially typical of thinly peopled game-infested areas. It is able to stand very hot and dry conditions and extends as far north as 13°, taking refuge in pockets of riverine vegetation during the dry season. *G. Longipalpis* is not found in areas with less than 45 inches of rain or more than four dry months; it is therefore the typical species in the Dry Forest zone. *G. Palpalis* possesses the ability to withstand a great range of climates and is the most widely diffused of all species. Towards its northern limit it is riverine in distribution and can be eradicated by streamside clearing; in the secondary forests of the south, however, clearing of the dense undergrowth creates conditions more favourable to the fly. *G. Tachinoides* can stand a dry season of up to seven months and, in consequence, extends farther north than any other species; it appears unable to tolerate dense vegetation and is absent from most of the south.

with the advent of the dry season; the minimum density of the mosquito is not reached until the middle of the dry season.

In the coastal belt, as a result of high year-round humidity and abundant water surfaces, the density of the mosquito population remains high throughout the year, and continuous transmission of the disease is possible. In the forest region the period of transmission is 8–9 months, dropping to 6–7 months in the Guinea savanas and to less than 5 months in the Sudan and Sahel zones, though even here man-created water surfaces, such as borrow pits, may allow of continuous breeding in even the driest regions. Of the mosquitoes capable of transmitting malaria, an average of 5% are actually infected, but this figure varies from almost nil to 20% at different seasons and in different localities.

Infection begins in the earliest months of a child's life; by the end of the first year two-thirds are infected, and the highest rates are reached between the ages of 3 and 7. Surveys have shown that between 65 and 90% of all children between the ages of 1 year and 10 years harbour malaria. In later childhood, however, a degree of partial immunity to the disease begins to be acquired, so that the number showing evidence of infection in the 11–15 age group is between 20 and 50% and in adults 11 to 28%. Malaria is a disastrous sapper of energy and initiative at all ages, but its most lethal effects are shown in the earlier years of childhood, when it is responsible for at least 10% of all recorded deaths; the number of unrecorded deaths is a matter for surmise.

Sleeping Sickness (Trypanosomiasis): In Ni-

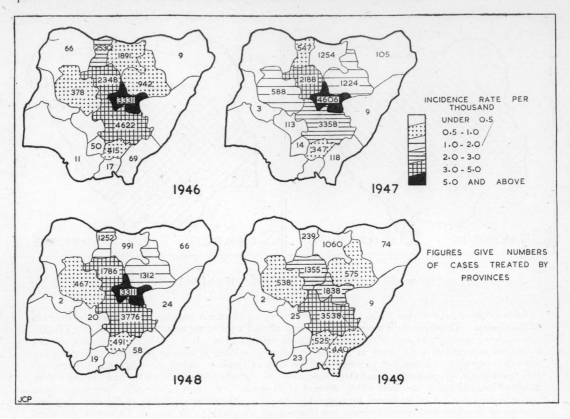

FIG. 31. TRYPANOSOMIASIS

Incidence in recent years. The Provinces most severely affected—Katsina, Zaria, Plateau and Benue—stand out clearly.

geria sleeping sickness is transmitted to the human population by the tsetse flies *Glossina palpalis* and *G. tachinoides*. Fig. 29 shows that the range of the fly extends from the coast to the open savanas of the Sudan zone, and that only the extreme north, parts of the Cameroons and the Jos Plateau are fly-free. With the exception of small foci in the south, however, sleeping sickness is confined to the north,[1] and more especially to the Middle Belt; this relative freedom from the disease in the south does not extend to the animal population, and over the whole of the high forest zone nagana (cattle trypanosomiasis) prohibits the rearing of horses and the larger zebu-type cattle.

The disease was recognised as being fairly common, especially in the Benue area, in the early years of the century, but in the decade 1920–30 a rapid rise in the number of reported cases occurred. This was due in part to the greater attention which the disease was attracting, but mainly to a real increase in its incidence. With the coming of the *pax Britannica*, the old pattern of defensive settlement in large villages surrounded by intensively cultivated and therefore tsetse free farmlands broke down; settlers drifted into hitherto unoccupied areas, setting up farms in the empty bush and exposing themselves to large-scale fly contact and infection; long-distance travel became safe and more

[1] The reasons for this virtual absence from the south are obscure; Nash suggests that it may be due to the fact that, in a more humid environment, the fly does not concentrate around the water-points as in the north, and that in consequence the degree of man-fly contact is less.

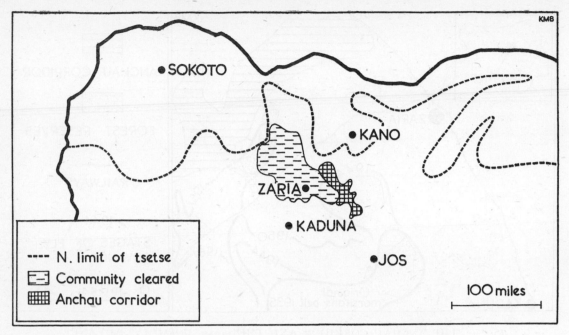

FIG. 32. THE NORTHERN FRONTIER OF THE TSETSE FLY

In the Anchau corridor the fly has been eradicated from 610 square miles and the policy of clearance has been accompanied by a considerable measure of population redistribution, involving the construction of sixteen villages and a new town and the resettlement within the corridor of the population of forty-two adjoining hamlets. In the community-cleared areas, which amount to 4,000 square miles, the aim has been to reduce man/fly contact by the clearing of tsetse-infested streams in the vicinity of settlements; this programme has given a large measure of protection to some 290,000 people in Zaria and southern Katsina.

frequent, and this, together with the large-scale displacement of labourers seeking work in the tin-mines, or in road or railway construction, was responsible for the large-scale diffusion of the disease from two endemic foci in the Benue area and northern Zaria.

The surveying in the field of the extent of the disease began in 1931 with the sending out of the first team of the Sleeping Sickness Service. This work has continued ever since. By 1940, 2,750,000 inhabitants had been examined and 300,000 cases of the disease found; by 1952 primary survey of another 926,000 had added further 8,500 cases, thus giving an average a incidence of 8·6%. The provinces most severely affected are the southern sector of Katsina, Zaria, Plateau and Benue, which together account for 70% of all cases in the North. The Provinces of Kano, Bauchi, Niger and Adamawa accounted for rather less

than 25%. There are no known foci of the disease in the Western Region, while in the East it is confined to small foci, including part of Ogoja and the Cameroons.

The problem was attacked by the clearing of vegetation along streams and around settlements with varying degrees of ruthlessness, and thus destroying the pockets of shade and humidity sought by the fly; by the setting up of dispensaries and by mass treatment; by large-scale resettlement, as at Anchau; and, more recently, by the prophylactic use of modern drugs in selected populations. Re-survey of the affected areas began in 1946, and up to 1952 over 5,000,000 people have been examined. The number of cases found was less than 16,000, an infection rate of 0·47%. This amazing reduction was achieved by a service whose qualified medical staff never exceeded twenty-five and fell at times to one-third that number, together

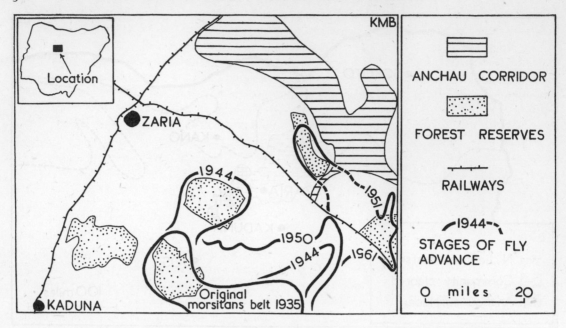

FIG. 33. THE ANCHAU CORRIDOR AND THE 1950–1 *MORSITANS* ADVANCE
IN EASTERN ZARIA

(Based on T. A. M. Nash)

This map serves to emphasise the extreme precariousness of the biological equilibrium in the tsetse-infested areas of the Territory. In the early 1940s the main *Morsitans* belt in eastern Zaria was in the immediate vicinity of the Kaduna River east of Kaduna itself. During the war years small advances were made by the fly to the east of the Galma River while in 1950–1 the fly advanced rapidly on a narrow front towards Anchau, taking advantage of several areas of thinly peopled game-infested forest reserves. This advance threatened to cut the Anchau corridor and, since *G.Morsitans* is the most serious vector of animal trypanosomiasis, threatened to render useless thousands of square miles of valuable grazing land. At the time of writing drastic counter-measures appear to have arrested the advance; the potential menace remains.

with one entomologist; the expenditure was no more than £380,000 in a decade.

Yellow Fever: The urban type of this disease is due to a virus transmitted by the mosquito *Ædes ægypti* and limited in Africa to the western and central sectors. Malaria and yellow fever were together responsible for the evil reputation of the Guinea Coast, and wrought havoc among the crews of trading vessels and slavers visiting the Coast during the eighteenth and nineteenth centuries; in recent years, however, complete protection against yellow fever has been afforded by immunisation. Lifelong immunity results from an attack, and the detection of the immune substances in the blood provides a method of mapping the distribution of populations which at one time or another

have been affected by the disease. This method has shown not only that the geographical area involved was much larger than previously thought, but also that the number of people within the area who had had yellow fever in the past was surprisingly large. Attention in the past has been focused on the more severe cases resulting from isolated outbreaks of the disease; these have been few in Nigeria, and the condition, in consequence, came to be thought of as uncommon. There is, however, excellent evidence that the infection is widespread throughout the south, extending as far north as Ilorin and possibly to the parallel 10° N. In an area containing an estimated number of 5,000,000 children under 15, a sample of 599, taken from widely scattered areas, showed that

10·9% had had the disease; the number of cases each year must thus run to many thousands.

Recent research has shown that the disease amongst Africans is for the most part a mild one, often lasting no more than a few days and with a mortality rate of less than 1%, a feature which explains why it has gone largely unnoticed in the past. From time to time, however, more virulent outbreaks do occur. Thus in 1946 an outbreak occurred at Ogbomosho; only eleven deaths were recorded, but since the area involved contained an urban population of some 100,000 people, and since proven cases wandered as far afield as Ilorin, Kafanchan and Gusau, the total number affected, if only in a mild form, must have been very much larger. In 1951–2 a much more serious outbreak occurred at Enugu, involving 5,000 cases and resulting in some 600 deaths. Another considerable, yet probably mild, outbreak was detected in retrospect along the north shore of the Lagos Lagoon. No case of yellow fever had been reported from the Lagos area between 1925 and the time of the investigation (1945), yet 17% of all children in the area had had the disease, the youngest being 5. An epidemic of some size must have taken place in the district about the year 1941, and yet passed quite unrecorded.[1]

There is considerable evidence that monkeys form a natural reservoir of the virus.

Yaws: There is very little exact information regarding the prevalence of yaws, but the disease is certainly extremely common and affects practically the whole country. Various surveys in Benue Province have shown that 17% have had the infection at one time or another and that in 10% it was in the active state. In Abeokuta active yaws was found in 15%, with another 22% giving a history suggestive of past infection. Surveys in the Eastern Region have given figures indicating infection in 12–18% of the population. In the Cameroons the average incidence is probably of the order of 10%, rising as high as 25–35% in parts of Mamfe and Bamenda.[2]

The disease responds very well to treatment with compounds of bismuth and arsenic and to penicillin, and mass treatment has begun.

Diseases due to Worms: There must be relatively few Nigerians whose intestines do not harbour worms of one sort or another. In routine examinations of 50,000 specimens of stools 3% were found to contain tapeworm (*T. saginata*), 20% the roundworm *Ascaris* and about 40% the hookworm *Ankylostoma*. The type and degree of infestation vary strikingly; thus in the North hookworm infestation rates range between 67 and 1·8%. The question of the exact part played by the roundworm as a producer of ill-health is unsettled. It certainly can produce a considerable amount of abdominal discomfort, and sometimes severe and often fatal intestinal obstruction; in most people, however, it is probably more or less harmless. The hookworm has a more sinister reputation. In most Nigerians the number of parasites harboured appears to be small and no harm results, but where the number is large, and particularly where the subject is undernourished, severe and frequently fatal degrees of anæmia can be produced.

Dependable data on *Guinea Worm* infestation are hard to come by, but, broadly speaking, it may be said to be very common in the North, moderately common in the West, much less common in the East and extremely rare in the Cameroons. The infestation tends to be patchy with areas of heavy infestation, surrounded by districts where the degree of infestation is low; for example, in one district in the North, of the 20 cases found in a survey, 16 occurred in one village of 100 people, and the remaining 4 amongst the 2,500 inhabitants of four adjacent villages. In the Western Region the infestation affects most severely those drawing their water from ponds and stagnant pools. Those having access to freely running streams are relatively exempt.[3] The condition is worst

[1] Yellow Fever Research Institute, Yaba: *Annual Reports*, 1945 *and* 1946.
[2] J. L. McLetchie, Personal communication.
[3] S. D. Onabamiro, *West African Med. Journal* (1952), I (new series), p. 2.

in the rainy season, and may be so widespread as to incapacitate most of the members of a community. The sores produced become infected, which may result in the destruction of much tissue, and occasionally lockjaw may supervene; in the absence of these secondary complications, the condition rarely results in death, but it produces a vast amount of invalidism and loss of working time, and that at the best season of the year for agriculture.

In the case of *bilharzia*, the incidence of the disease is heavy and its geographical distribution wide. Two types of the parasite occur in the Territory, one affecting the bowel (*Schistosoma mansoni*), and the other, much more common, affecting the bladder (*S. hæmatobium*).

The Eastern Region appears to be affected to only a mild degree and the Cameroons are free of the disease, with the exception of small foci around the crater-lakes. On the other hand, both the Western and Northern Regions are badly affected. The general impression is that the North suffers more than the West, but this may be due to the fact that very little in the way of organised field surveys has been carried out in the latter; wherever the condition has been sought, it has been found; thus Epe, in the lagoon zone, is notorious and 76% of its in-

habitants are affected, at Ilaro 14% were found to be affected and cases are common at Ibadan. Practically all the Northern Provinces are very badly affected with the exception of Plateau Province, where only small foci occur. Between 30 and 50% of all school children are affected, and in parts of Adamawa the figure reaches 90%.

In no other field do the hospital statistics show up to less advantage as an index of the prevalence of a disease than in the case of bilharzia. In Sokoto, for example, where the hospital incidence was 1·8%, field survey showed the actual incidence in the general population to be between 10 and 50%; similarly, in Bornu, Medical Field Units found the incidence in the general population to be nearly 20% and among school children 38%, whilst the hospitals report only 1·28%. This is mainly due to the fact that many have no symptoms and many who have never seek treatment. This, of course, applies to a greater or lesser degree to all the diseases discussed here.

The distribution pattern of *filariasis* is somewhat different from that of guinea worm or bilharzia, being very common in the Cameroons, in the adjacent parts of the Northern Region and in the Eastern Region; there are no reliable figures for the Western Region, but cases occur in the Ibadan district and loasis is common at Ilesha. In the Cameroons, 75% of the adult population and 20% of the children are

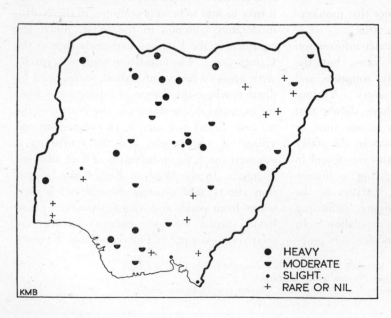

HEAVY
MODERATE
SLIGHT.
RARE OR NIL

KMB

FIG. 34. APPARENT GUINEA WORM INCIDENCE

Guinea worm shows a very patchy distribution pattern though it is especially important in the central sector of the Sudan zone and the Jos Plateau. Its incidence has been strikingly reduced in many areas by the provision of improved wells designed to prevent infection.

affected. This group of parasites gives rise to little hazard to life but causes a great deal of discomfort, and one parasite is responsible for a form of blindness and for distressing skin troubles. This latter form (onchocerciasis) is extremely common in the Cameroons where, around Victoria, 60% of the population were found to be affected, and in parts of the Eastern Region (85% in the Udi district). In the Northern Region the condition is widely distributed in Adamawa Province; it occurs also on the Jos Plateau and at Dass, south of Bauchi; it is second only to trachoma as a cause of eye disease, and is the commonest single cause of blindness.

A map showing the distribution in West Africa of filariasis due to loasis is to be found in a recent publication by Gordon *et al.*[1]

Malnutrition

Although it is a commonplace that states of malnutrition are widespread in Nigeria as in most of Tropical Africa, accurate data as to the forms they take, their distribution and intensity are very scanty. Apart from the scarcity of trained research workers, the size of the country and its environmental and cultural diversity make the problem of nutritional survey unusually massive and difficult. Accurate information is more or less limited to the work of McCulloch,[2] Nicol[3, 4] and the Medical Field Units.

The first superficial impression on the traveller arriving in Nigeria as to the state of nutrition of the people he sees is likely to be favourable. Only closer scrutiny and frequently only the scrutiny of the expert will reveal the stigmata of malnutrition, which are, in reality, so widespread.

Actual starvation occurs sporadically in the more northerly parts of the country in the periodic famines and in the hungry season, towards the end of the dry season and in the early rains, before the new crops have ripened. Most surveys have shown the subjects to be underweight to the extent of from one to one and a half stones, compared not only with European standards but also with well-nourished subjects of their own race. Yet, taking the country as a whole, deficiency of calories is less important than lack of specific nutrients such as protein. The African regarded as a human machine runs on a fuel more or less adequate as regards bulk and theoretical energy content but grossly unsatisfactory in composition.

It would probably be true to say that the inhabitants of the forest country of the humid south and of the river valleys are somewhat better nourished than those of the north with its protracted dry season and less varied agriculture. But in a country showing such a wide diversity of agricultural environments and so little investigated, even the widest of generalisations is dangerous.

Any catalogue of food consumed in a particular area of the country is likely to be formidable (see, for example, that of Bascom[5] for the Ife district), but in actual practice the diet of the majority of the people is remarkably restricted and monotonous. McCulloch,[2] speaking of the Kano-Sokoto area, says: "It has been shown that apparently a large variety of food is grown and used by the people, but inquiry elicits the fact that the vast majority of the population live on a porridge made from millet seed, adulterated sour milk and a soup which is composed very largely of leaves. . . . The various other foodstuffs listed need not be considered in a survey of the food of the Hausa, as they are used only occasionally and in such small quantities that they cannot enter into the nutritional problem of the people." With some variations, the same could be said of the Ibadan area.

[1] R. M. Gordon, W. E. Kershaw, W. Crewe and H. Oldroyd, *Tr. Roy. Soc. Med. and Hygiene* (1950), XLIV, p. 14.
[2] W. E. McCulloch, *An Enquiry into the Dietaries of the Hausas and Town Fulani of Northern Nigeria*, Lagos (1930), p. 25.
[3] B. M. Nicol, *Brit. Jour. Nutrit.* (1949), III, p. 25.
[4] B. M. Nicol, *Brit. Jour. Nutrit.* (1952), VI, p. 34.
[5] W. R. Bascom, *Africa* (1951), XXI, pp. 21–41.

Most diets contain an excess of carbohydrate. In the north this is derived from cereals, such as guinea corn, millet and maize, with a certain amount of cassava in addition. In the south, carbohydrate is derived from root crops, such as cassava, yams, and cocoyam with the addition of maize. For the most part, the starchy foods are eaten in the form of a paste or porridge, with a soup or sauce containing green leaves in varying amounts, onion and salt, the whole being very highly seasoned with red peppers. In the south, red-palm oil is added, in the north groundnut oil when obtainable. Meat may be added, in amounts rarely exceeding a few small lumps. To these foods may be added beans in the form of porridge or fried cakes. The most northerly part of the country is the cattle-raising area, but there is no animal industry to speak of over much of the Middle Belt and south. In these latter areas most of the meat consumed must be imported from the North, is expensive and of poor quality, and is eaten sparingly or not at all. The amount of meat obtained in the form of game is difficult to estimate, but in the south at least game, except of a very small type, seems remarkably scarce. Fresh fish is obtainable only along the sea coast and the rivers. Although a certain amount of dried fish finds its way inland from the coast or is imported from the Chad and Middle Niger areas, it keeps badly and is, again, expensive.

In most areas stews contain leafy vegetables often quite sparingly, and frequently giving the mixture a glairy consistency. The amounts used are quite small, and Nicol[1] records one group which does not consume them at all. Probably the most widely used of other vegetables is the okra, either fresh or dried. Habits as to the eating of fruit seem to vary greatly, contrary to what the stranger would expect in a tropical country. But fruits are neither as plentiful nor of such good quality as might be imagined. Villagers in the Ibadan area seem to eat remarkably little fruit, and in Warri Province Nicol[1] found that fruit was eaten hardly at all.

Despite the large-scale production of vegetable oils, fat is consumed on only a small scale. Groundnut oil is the most commonly used form in the north with red-palm oil and to a much lesser degree egusi (melon seed) oil in the southern forest zone. Even in the latter area, however, the quantity commonly consumed is only one-third of that in a good European diet.

There is evidence that most diets are seriously deficient in calcium and probably also in iron.

It is hardly appropriate in an account such as this to enter into the complex subject of vitamin deficiency. As might be expected, diets vary from area to area in their adequacy in this respect. The most general lack is of vitamins of the B complex; vitamin C is often present in borderline quantities and vitamin A tends to be deficient outside the palm belt. The existence of vitamin D deficiency is shown by the occurrence of rickets,[2] although the grosser forms are not frequently seen. In general, the more severe forms of vitamin deficiency are not often seen, but the milder yet still debilitating manifestations are very widespread.

The most damaging dietary deficiency is that of protein, and its effects show at all ages. No particular regard seems to be had for the dietary needs of an expectant mother; from her deficient diet she has to manufacture a child, to undergo the risks and blood loss consequent on primitive midwifery in giving it birth, and then to suckle it for a period of up to two years. It is not, therefore, surprising that she frequently suffers from some degree of anæmia throughout her reproductive period, and that her child often has a poor start in life. He may even show degenerative changes in his liver within a week or two of birth.[3] He probably receives breast milk deficient in quantity if not in quality, but, despite this, may maintain a reasonable gain in weight until, say, his sixth month; then

[1] B. M. Nicol, *Brit. Jour. Nutrit.* (1952), VI, p. 34.
[2] D. B. Jelliffe, *Tr. Roy. Soc. Trop. Med. and Hygiene* (1951), XLV, pp. 119–24.
[3] D. B. Jelliffe and W. D. Silvera, *Jour. Trop. Med.* (1952), LV, p. 73.

grappling with his poor supply of milk, with the low iron content of his diet and with his recently acquired malarial infection, he tends to become thin and anæmic. About this time he receives supplementary feeding, consisting almost exclusively of starchy gruel of maize and cassava flour. Lactation goes on until the end of his second year, long after he can walk, but the milk supply is scanty and not, by this time, a significant factor in his nutrition. Starchy feeding is now the rule until he grows older and can fend for himself. Many now begin to show in varying degree the effects of protein lack, with bleaching of the hair, changes in the skin and often dropsical swelling of the legs.

In later life a disproportionate number of older children and of adults of both sexes show liver enlargement, with consequences for health which need not be elaborated here. In some of his villages Nicol[1] found that up to 19% of the inhabitants showed signs of liver disease; in a well-nourished section of the population the figure was 3%.

As regards deficiency in general, Medical Field Unit Surveys in the North found anæmia in proportions of the population varying from 20 to 80%; evidence of vitamin lack in 40% and of general under-nutrition in 20%.[2]

From what has been said it will be seen that malnutrition in its various forms is a major hazard to health in Nigeria, ranking in this respect along with malaria. Medical research will define the problem and offer suggestions for its solution, but it cannot solve it. It is here that the physician must give place to the agriculturist.

Conclusion

Full assessment of the influence of climatic and related factors on the distribution in space and time of the various diseases must await fuller investigation. Nevertheless, in the case of certain diseases such as malaria and sleeping sickness, it is apparent that the distribution pattern is not entirely a fortuitous one, rather can it be explained in terms of specific climatic and vegetation conditions favourable to the existence of the disease organism or its vector. A general zonation of diseases is, in fact, discernible: thus the Sudan zone is essentially the zone of epidemic cerebro-spinal meningitis, relapsing fever, undulant fever and louse-borne typhus; the south the zone of yellow fever, malaria, leprosy and filariasis; the disease pattern of the Middle Belt includes both Southern and Sudan elements, but is dominated by endemic sleeping sickness. A more refined delimitation of these broad *nosological regions* and a full analysis of their environmental relationships must, however, await more detailed investigations into the distribution of disease in the Territory and into the climatic and social conditions which form the essential background to this distribution pattern.

Such investigations will also make possible a more complete assessment of the importance of disease as a factor in the development of Nigeria. Some indication of its importance has already been given. Thus, malaria, a preventable disease, has been seen to be responsible for at least one-tenth of the deaths among young children and for a vast amount of ill-health among the adult population; the outbreaks of cerebro-spinal meningitis in 1950 and 1951 involved 100,000 people, with a recorded mortality (excluding Bornu) of close on 10,000; infestation with intestinal worms strikes at the well-being of people in almost every sector of the country and, since infestation is heaviest during the rainy season, the period of greatest agricultural activity, it is responsible for a loss of productive efficiency whose economic consequences cannot be estimated. Some four-fifths of Nigeria is tsetse-infested, and sleeping sickness is probably a major factor explaining the scanty population and low degree of economic development of much of the Middle Belt. Here, however, it is relevant to emphasise that the relationship between man and disease is a two-way one, and that the spread

[1] B. M. Nicol, *Brit. Jour. Nutrit.* (1952), VI, p. 34.
[2] *Nigeria: Annual Reports on the Medical Services*, 1940 to 1950–51.

of the sleeping-sickness vector in some areas was undoubtedly favoured by historical circumstances, notably depopulation following slave-raiding. This led to densification of the vegetation and an increase in game population which provided conditions more favourable to the fly. Sleeping sickness has also an important indirect influence on human well-being and economic development. It prevents the rearing of the larger types of cattle over one-half of Nigeria (including some areas which are relatively free from human sleeping sickness), and this leads to multiple nutritional deficiencies among the population. It also results in an absence of animal manure and animal traction, which are important factors contributing to the low agricultural productivity of many areas.

Disease, malnutrition and low agricultural productivity form, in fact, a vicious circle in Nigeria as in the remainder of Tropical Africa; the peasant, because of the multiplicity of diseases to which he is exposed and which sap his energy, is often an inefficient agriculturist; because he is inefficient his output is low and he is undernourished; because he is undernourished he is more susceptible to the wide range of diseases to which he is exposed. The breaking of this vicious circle is one of the main problems facing the Territory; it is a problem which can be tackled from two angles—medical and agricultural. From the medical angle by prophylactic measures and by improved rural hygiene (which is largely dependent on improved education); from the agricultural angle by raising the level of nutrition by improved agricultural techniques. In this latter context schemes for increasing output by the use of fertilisers and of machinery are of major importance.

These last remarks draw attention to one fundamental point: that the problem of disease cannot be tackled solely on the medical front; advance must also be made on the educational, agricultural and social-service fronts. Further, the close integration of the efforts of the Medical Department with those of various other Departments concerned with rural de-velopment is increasingly important. This is well illustrated by the relationship between the Sleeping Sickness Service and the Agricultural and Forest Departments. Two examples will make this clear. The Agricultural Department has been interested in extending the fruit industry in the North and, as the remarks on nutrition made earlier will have made clear, this is of major importance on dietetic grounds. For such plantations the most suitable areas are the river valleys, but the establishment of tree plantations in these areas has the effect of creating artificial gallery forests along which the tsetse fly may extend its range into fly-free country. This, in fact, happened in the valleys of the Challowa and Kano Rivers south of Kano. A somewhat similar difficulty arises in the case of forestry. Extension of the present system of forest reserves is essential to safeguard the timber and fuel supplies of the country, but these reserves, especially if sheltering a large game population, may constitute reservoirs of *Glossina morsitans*, and thus become a serious potential menace to animal health. A judicious harmonising of the interests of the medical man and the forester is essential, and, in fact, recent discussions have resulted in a working compromise between the two Departments (see page 173). These remarks underline the need for a co-ordinated approach to the whole problem of rural development in Nigeria, and this in turn depends upon the collection of data upon all aspects of the physical and biological environment which will permit a balanced assessment of the various factors involved and make possible the optimum use of the Territory's limited funds and the highest possible degree of disease control. That such control will ultimately be achieved is clear; the striking success of the sleeping sickness control measures or of the guinea-worm control campaign are sufficient evidence in support of this view. At the same time the reduction of the heavy annual wastage of human life, especially among young children, will have marked effects on the demographic situation in Nigeria, and with the disease checks removed the population may well enter on a period of rapid expansion comparable to that experienced in more developed tropical territories such as Indonesia or India. Such an expansion will create new and critical problems in a territory whose population is at present far from being well-nourished, and where, in many areas, the population pressure is already extreme. It may necessitate a radical reorientation of the whole agricultural economy and the replacement of specialised cropping for the export market by food production to meet the needs of Nigeria's own population.

BIBLIOGRAPHY

Geology, Relief and Drainage

Cotton, C. A., *Climatic Accidents in Landscape-Making*, Whitcombe & Tombs, 1947.
Grove, A. T., "Land Use and Soil Conservation on the Jos Plateau", *Geol. Surv. Nig.*, Bulletin 22, 1951.
Nigeria Magazine, various articles.
Pugh, J.C., and King, Lester, "Outline of the Geomorphology of Nigeria", *S. Afr. Geog. Journal*, Vol. XXXIV, 1952.
See also the *Annual Report, Geol. Surv. Nig.* 1948, Appendix A, for a bibliography of the geology of Nigeria and of the Cameroons under British Trusteeship.

Climate

British West African Meteorological Services, *Preliminary Note on the Climate of Nigeria*, with maps and tables (cyclostyled), 1950.
Hamilton, R. A., and Archbold, J. W., "Meteorology of Nigeria and Adjacent Territory", *Q.J.R. Met. Soc.*, Vol. LXXI, 1945, pp. 231–66.
Miller, R., "The Climate of Nigeria", *Geography*, Vol. XXXVII, 1952.
Pugh, J. C., "Rainfall Reliability in Nigeria", *XVII Int. Geog. Cong.*, Washington, D.C., 1952.

Soils

Doyne, H. C., *et alia*, "Soil Types and Manurial Experiments in Nigeria", *Proc IIIrd W. Afr. Agric. Conf.*, 1938.
Lamb, A. F. A., "Different Soils Make Different Forests," *Farm and Forest*, Vol. IX, 1948.
Rowling, C. W., *A Study of Land Tenure in the Cameroons Province* (mimeographed), Lagos, 1948.
Vine, H., "A Soil Catena in the Nigerian Cacao Belt", *Farm and Forest*, Vol. II, 1941.
Vine, H., "Soil Work of the Chemical Section", *Farm and Forest*, Vol. V, 1944.
Vine, H., "Soil Resources for Increased Production", *Farm and Forest*, Vol. IX, 1948.
Vine, H., "Nigerian Soils in Relation to Parent Materials", *Comm. Bur. of Soil Science, Tech. Communication*, No. 46, 1949.

Vegetation

Rosevear, D. R., *Nigeria Handbook*, London, 1953, pp. 139–73.

Disease

Davey, T. H., *Trypanosomiasis in British West Africa*, London, 1948.
Nash, T. A. M., *Tsetse Flies in British West Africa*, London, 1948.
Onabamiro, S. D., *Food and Health*, London, 1953.
Taylor, S., and Gadsden, P., *Shadows in the Sun*, London, 1949.

CHAPTER II

THE HUMAN PATTERN

THE PATTERN OF POPULATION

General Features

Nigeria, with its twenty-three million people, is not only the most important territorial aggregate of population in the African continent, it is also one of the most densely peopled. Its population is almost twice as large as that of the combined British East African Territories or of the Union of South Africa, and is 50% larger than the population of the vast, thinly peopled territory of French West Africa. The mean density of population is seven times as great as the density in this latter territory; it is three and a half times the density of inter-tropical Africa as a whole.

This large population is distributed over a territory four times the size of the United Kingdom in an extremely uneven fashion. Great areas are almost devoid of population; elsewhere rural densities approach those of the Monsoon Lands or Egypt. It is a population whose settlement forms show a diversity rare in Tropical Africa; the characteristic form of settlement is the village, but in parts of central and southern Nigeria this is replaced by a more or less completely dispersed type of settlement, while the population of the south-west shows a degree of urbanisation rare in Black Africa. It is, finally, a population whose distribution pattern is "immature"; the close adjustment of densities to environmental conditions, which is typical of long-settled areas, is here lacking, and the process of land occupation and settlement is incomplete over much of the Territory.

Population Totals and Distribution

Population estimates made by the Nigerian Department of Census and Statistics give the 1948–9 population of the territory as 23,130,000. This is distributed between the major administrative units of the country as follows:

TABLE II

THE POPULATION OF NIGERIA, 1948–9

Unit	Estimated Population	Estimated Density per Square Mile
Northern Region .	13,500,000	50
Western Region .	4,000,000	90
Eastern Region .	5,200,000	110
Colony . . .	430,000	310
Total Nigeria .	23,130,000	60

The distribution of population by divisions, the smallest statistical unit available for the country as a whole, is summarised in Fig. 35.[1] There are three major nuclei of population: those of Yorubaland, Iboland and the Kano area, and these contain an aggregate population of some ten million, or over two-fifths of Nigeria's population, on one-seventh of the area of the Territory. Each of these concentrations coincides with a "key area" in the country's economic and cultural geography; thus the south-western concentration coincides with the highly developed Cocoa Belt of the western dry forest zone and with the heart of the Yoruba territory; the south-eastern concentration coincides with the most intensive sector of

[1] The population maps in this section and the density figures quoted in the text are based on estimates of population (on a divisional basis) made available by the Regional Secretariats. The fact that, except in the case of Lagos, all population figures are estimates rather than census counts in the true sense of the word should be stressed at the outset; even the 1931 Census was not a full count but was based partly on estimates. For a critique of the official figures see R. R. Kuczynski, *Demographic Survey of the British Colonial Empire*, Vol. I, and for results of 1952–3 Census see Appendix II.

Note the three major nuclei—
those of Yorubaland, Iboland
and Hausaland—and the thinly
peopled character of the Middle
Belt. Note that the map shows
mean densities by Divisions and
that these mean figures may conceal wide variations in density
within the Division. Cf. the complex pattern of population within
Tiv Division (Fig. 39).

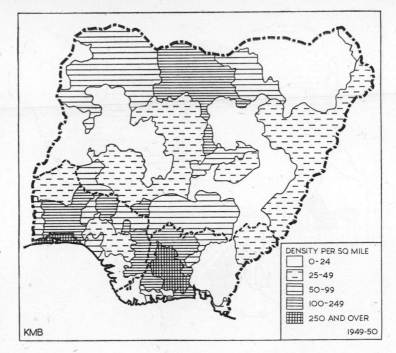

DENSITY PER SQ MILE
0 - 24
25 - 49
50 - 99
100 - 249
250 AND OVER

KMB   1949-50

the Palm Belt and the Ibo
home zone; the Kano nucleus
contains the major groundnut
and cotton producing zone of
the Northern Provinces and
represents the heart of Hausaland.

There are wide contrasts
between these areas. In the
northern area Katsina Emir-
ate shows a density of 127 per square mile, while
in Kano Emirate the average is 210; this latter
figure conceals wide variations within the
13,000-square-mile large statistical unit, for the
density in the intensely cultivated farmlands
around Kano City itself is certainly four or five
times the mean density for the Emirate, and this
is balanced by the relatively low density between
the city and the border of Zaria Province.[1]
This high density has undoubtedly been favoured by the physical environment; by the
advantageous position in relation to the trading
routes of the Sahara and its fringe; by the fly-
free grasslands and open savanas of the Sudan
zone; by the easy-working drift soils which, as
transport improved, showed themselves ideal
cotton or groundnut soils; and by the presence
of readily accessible ground-water supplies.[2]
Even more important, however, have been the
historical factors and, above all, the existence of
powerful states, such as the larger Hausa and

Fulani kingdoms, under whose protection trade
could flourish and the people prosper and
multiply.

Densities in Yorubaland range from 106 in
Ijebu Province to 220 in Ibadan Division.
Here a break in the continuity of the southern
rain forest, and the relative richness in plant foods
and the good water relations of the local soils,
have favoured the growth of a dense peasant
population drawing its sustenance from yams
and cassava and palm-oil and producing kola
nuts for sale to the North and cocoa for overseas
export. It is a population which has only
recently (in terms of human history) acquired
stability; many of the towns date back little
more than a century, and the wholesale depopulation of certain areas, which resulted from the
civil strife of the mid-nineteenth century, is
still reflected in the blank spaces of the modern
population map.

The south-eastern or Ibo nucleus represents

[1] See map in *Kano Survey* 1950 by B. E. Sharwood Smith, Zaria (1950).
[2] D. F. H. McBride has expressed the view that the two most important factors contributing to the development
of the Kano close-settled zone have been water supply and markets. See "Land Survey in Kano Emirate" in *Journal
of the Royal African Society* (Jan. 1938), p. 77.

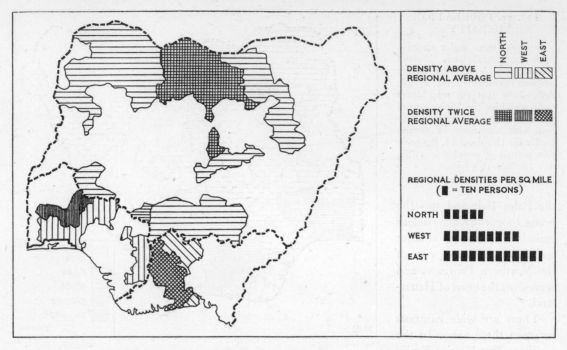

FIG. 36. THE REGIONAL PATTERN OF POPULATION

Emphasising the contrasts in density between the North and the South and the "dual make-up" of each Region (cf. page 58).

one of the most critical areas in West Africa. The mean density for the whole belt is 260 per square mile; in Owerri Province (3,870 square miles) the mean density is 410. Smaller areas show even higher densities: Abak Division of Calabar Province, 470; Okigwi Division of Owerri Province, 516; Orlu Division in the same Province, 760; while competent observers have estimated the density in certain overcrowded areas at well over 1,000 per square mile. Densities, in short, approach those of the crowded alluvial lands of the Nile Valley or Monsoon Asia, and like the populations of these latter areas, the population of Iboland is growing rapidly.[1] Environmental conditions in Iboland are very different, however. Here are no rich alluvial or volcanic soils. Instead, the sands which floor so much of Iboland rank among the poorest of Nigerian soils—highly

leached, extremely acid, suited only to a limited range of crops and eroding rapidly under conditions of overcropping. If it were not for the fortunate circumstance that the oil palm will tolerate these conditions the economic plight of the Ibo would be dire indeed. This overpopulated zone poses two problems to the human geographer. Firstly, how did such a high density of population originate in the first place, in an environment of dense rain forest and poor, heavily leached soils? Secondly, how can the problems of over-population be overcome and the vicious circle of over-population leading to over-cultivation and soil depletion and erosion be broken? This problem of over-population and some possible lines of solution are referred to later in this volume.

Population density is well below the average over much of the Middle Belt,[2] and in the north-

[1] The total population of the Eastern Region appears to have increased by 600,000 between 1931 and 1948–9; that of Owerri Province alone by 425,000.

[2] Provinces of Ilorin, Niger, Kabba, Plateau, Benue and Adamawa.

PLATE VII. VILLAGE IN THE COASTAL REGION OF THE SOUTH-WEST

Note the use of palm ribs in place of mud as a building material and the coconut groves in the background.

PLATE VIII. THE NUPE TOWN OF BIDA

Bida has a population of some 21,000. It is the economic and cultural centre of the Nupe people and possesses highly specialised craft industries. Note the relatively open urban pattern, with extensive areas of cultivated land separating the individual compounds; note, too, the complex pattern of footpaths offsetting the absence of a developed road network. The typical architecture consists of round huts with conical thatched roofs; thus the "Sudanese" type of house may be contrasted with the rectangular "Southern Forest" house found among the Yoruba (Plate IX) or the flat-roofed houses of the Northern cities (Plate XIII).

PLATE IX. A SECTION OF THE TOWN OF ILORIN

Though the ruler of Ilorin is a Moslem, the people of the Emirate are Yoruba and their city illustrates clearly the cell-like structure of the typical Yoruba town, an aggregate of family compounds, each consisting of a series of rectangular huts grouped around a central court. In many of these bigger towns the traditional thatched roof has been largely replaced by corrugated iron.

PLATE X. THE TRANSPORT AND ADMINISTRATIVE CENTRE OF MINNA

This centre has a population of some 10,000 and is an excellent example of a European-developed administrative and transport centre. Note the mechanistic gridded street pattern, typical of "colonial" town planning in all countries and at all periods and contrasting sharply with the organic pattern of the indigenous towns (Plates VIII and IX). Note, too, the admixture of housing styles reflecting the heterogeneity of population typical of the European-developed centres.

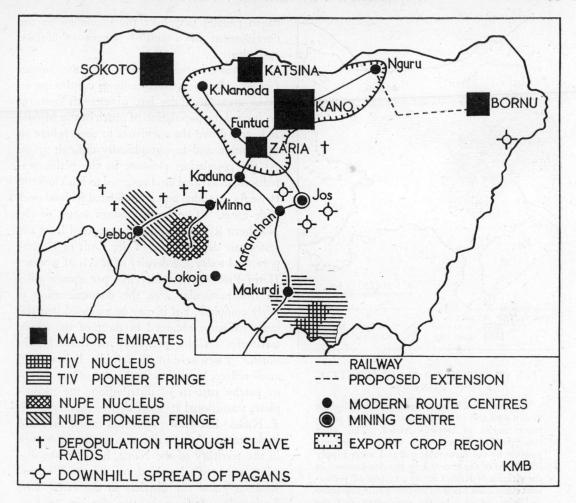

FIG. 37. SOME SOCIAL AND HISTORICAL FACTORS IN THE EVOLUTION OF THE
POPULATION MAP OF THE NORTHERN REGION

Showing: 1. The more important Northern emirates which, by reason of the security which they afforded
their populations, exercised a positive influence on population growth.   2. The two phases of settlement in
Nupe country and Tiv-land.   3. Areas depopulated by past slave-raiding; these were mainly Pagan territories on the periphery of the Mohammedan emirates of the Sudan zone.   4. Areas in which the *pax Britannica*
has encouraged a downhill movement of some of the Pagan peoples from their hill fastnesses.   5. The modern
rail system and the more important route centres which have developed thereon.   6. Areas where mining
development and the production of export crops have had an important influence on population distribution.

eastern Province of Bornu and in parts of the
dense rain forest zone of southern Benin and
Calabar.   These zones of low density are due
to a variety of factors.   The widespread absence of a permanent and dependable water
supply has been a factor of major importance
over much of the Middle Belt and Bornu;

especially in the latter province modern techniques of deep well sinking may completely
alter the carrying capacity of the area in terms
of both human beings and livestock.   It is also,
and surprisingly, a factor of importance in the
rain-sodden forests of South Benin, where the
extreme porosity of the Tertiary sands leads to an

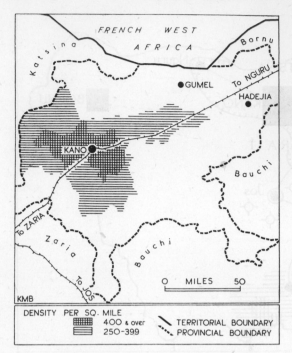

FIG. 38. THE KANO CLOSE-SETTLED
ZONE

The most densely peopled sector of the Nigerian
Sudan zone and one of the most important population nuclei of tropical Africa. This great
concentration of population has been rendered
possible by the favourable soil and water-supply
conditions of the area and by the development in
the vicinity of Kano City of a system of permanent cultivation based on the use of animal manure
and city wastes. In the peri-urban area the
proportion of land under cultivation locally
reaches 90% and the human transformation of
the landscape is perhaps more complete than in
any other part of Nigeria.

pagan peoples have met the challenge by the
development of a skilful system of terrace
agriculture.

Far more important have been the human
factors. Ruthless slave-raiding, continuing in
many areas until the late nineteenth century,
decimated the population of much of the Middle
Belt and drove the survivors to seek refuge in
the remote and topographically difficult areas.
As the population pressure in the plains was
reduced, cultivated land reverted to bush and the
tsetse fly extended and consolidated its hold over
wide areas. The south-western sector of the
Northern Region has never recovered from the
systematic depredations of the Emir of Kontagora, and today the density of much of western
Ilorin Province is under five per square mile.
In this particular area the documentation is
fairly complete, but it may be assumed that the
same situation obtained in most of the pagan
territories on the periphery of the Moslem
north. Elsewhere in the Middle Belt certain
areas reflect, by their low density of population
or patchy pattern of distribution, the incomplete, transitional stage of their settlement. S.
F. Nadel [1] has drawn attention to the historical
background of the striking contrasts in density
in the territory of the Nupe, between the districts west of the Kaduna River ("Trans-
Kaduna") and the districts to the east ("Cis-
Kaduna"). It was in the districts of Cis-
Kaduna that the Fulani conquerors of the Nupe
state, with their vast concourse of warriors and
dependants, settled, and today, five generations
later, Cis-Kaduna has a density three times as
great as that of the "pioneer fringe" west of the
Kaduna. A somewhat similar example of
"arrested occupance" is to be found in the
Tiv Division of Benue Province.[2] The Tiv
tribe is a relatively recent immigrant group,
which began migrating from the Cameroons
foothills to its present home in the plains of the
Benue during the eighteenth century. As the
migration progressed, the first clans to occupy

absence of surface water over much of the area
during the dry season and to a generally sparse
population. The influence of soil poverty can
easily be over-estimated; in the Middle Belt as
a whole, soil conditions are less favourable than
in Yorubaland or Hausaland, but soil poverty
cannot be said to be a limiting factor of major
importance, and in parts of the Jos Plateau,
where soils are rocky and skeletal, some of the

[1] *A Black Byzantium*, London (1946), p. 11.
[2] G. W. G. Briggs, "Soil Deterioration in the Southern Districts of Tiv Division" in *Farm and Forest*, Vol. II,
No. 1 (1941). The summary given here is based on this admirable article.

the plains were pushed by later immigrants to
the north-west, while later arrivals tended to
"pile up" in the southern districts on the margin
of the Benue plains. As a result of this process
the southern districts show very high densities
(locally over 200 per square mile) and severe
over-population; while the northern districts
are thinly peopled, with densities dropping
below that of 25 per square mile.   Meanwhile,
migration has, temporarily at least, ceased and
the population pattern results from the "freezing" of what was purely a transitional stage in
the Tiv occupation of the Benue lowland.

Neither in Tivland nor in the territory of
the Nupe can contrasts in population density be
explained solely in terms of climate, soil or any
other elements of the physical environment.

Urbanisation

It is difficult to discuss the degree of urbanisation in Nigeria.   In part the difficulty arises
from the deficiencies of the statistical material,
which have already been discussed; in part from
the character of the "towns" themselves. Many
of these lack the basic services and functions
which constitute the criteria of an urban area in
the West, and their population is often dominantly agricultural, working in the surrounding
countryside during part at least of the year.
They are, in short, more closely related to the
"urban villages" of the Spanish meseta or the
Hungarian plain, than to the normal Western
European urban area.   The qualification is
especially true in the Eastern Provinces—in
Iboland and the Cameroons—where settlements such as Otuocha-Aguleri or Bali are
scarcely more than five-figure clusters of population with little functional significance; it
applies even in the urban zones of Yorubaland
and Hausaland, with their long traditions of
compact settlement; and perhaps the only
exceptions are centres such as Lagos or Jos
which owe their development largely to
European influences.

If, however, the term "town" is defined
statistically and applied to all compact centres
of over 10,000 inhabitants, the Territory con-

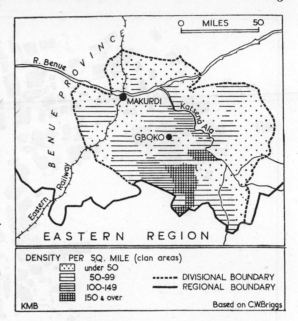

FIG. 39. THE POPULATION PATTERN
OF TIV DIVISION, BENUE PROVINCE

An excellent example of the extremely patchy
distribution of population found in many parts
of Nigeria. From the environmental and ethnic
standpoints the Division shows a high degree of
homogeneity and the present population pattern
is the product of social and historical factors.

tains a total of seventy-three towns, eleven of
which have populations of over 50,000 and one
of which, the great Yoruba centre of Ibadan,
ranks as the biggest city in Tropical Africa, with
a population variously estimated at between
335,000 and 450,000.   On this basis the
"urban" population of Nigeria totals some $2\frac{1}{2}$
million or one-ninth of the total population.
There are great contrasts between the Regions
in degree of urbanisation; thus in the Western
Region 35% of the population is town-dwelling
as against 7% in the Eastern Region and 4%
in the Northern.   The greater proportion of
the Western Region's town-dwelling population
—$1\frac{1}{4}$ million or one half of the total town-
dwelling population of Nigeria—is accounted
for by the greater cluster of towns in the Yoruba
Provinces.

Yorubaland has seven cities of over 50,000
inhabitants, and the high proportion of town-

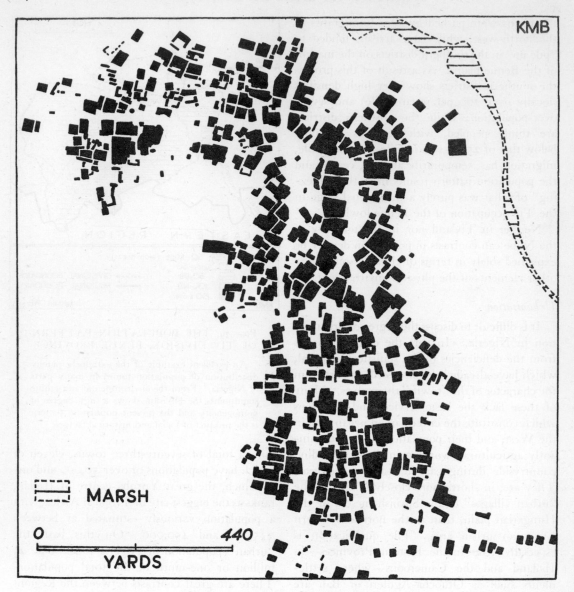

KMB

MARSH

0 ——————— 440
YARDS

FIG. 40. ILORA, OYO PROVINCE

Illustrating the irregularly nucleated layout typical of the small Yoruba town (based on a survey by J. C. Pugh).

dwellers to the total population is probably unequalled in Tropical Africa; in Ibadan Division the figure is 68%; in Oyo Division, 64%; in Ijebu Division, 40%.

Outside Yorubaland the degree of urban concentration is much lower; in the eastern provinces, if the anomalous Calabar Division is excluded, the highest proportion is 23% in Onitsha Division[1]; in the urban zone of Hausaland, classed by Leo Frobenius with

[1] Excluding the anomalous Calabar Division where the inclusion within one administrative unit of a large port and a thinly peopled "pioneer fringe" hinterland gives a figure of 54%.

Yorubaland among "the three great municipal territories of W. Africa", the proportion sinks to between 5 and 7·5%. Comparison of the Yoruba and Hausa municipal territories reveals clearly the unique position of the former; in a zone some 30,000 square miles in extent are to be found twenty-six towns with an aggregate population of one and a quarter million inhabitants; the Hausa centres, by contrast, contain only one-quarter of this population, but are disseminated over five times as large a territory.

From the broadest possible point of view the towns of Nigeria fall into two generic groups: those that are largely European-created, and those in which the urban nucleus is basically indigenous. The former are atypical and contain only a fraction of the country's urban population, though, since they include several important administrative centres such as Minna, Jos or Kaduna, they possess an importance out of proportion to either their numbers or their population. Their gridded street-pattern suggests their alien origin, but this external and visible design contrasts sharply with their formlessness from the human standpoint; only too often their populations consist of a loose aggregate of peoples drawn from a great diversity of tribes by the needs of administration or transport, and with the slenderest of ties with the neighbourhood. Nor, indeed, can it be said that the fullest use has always been made of the opportunity afforded by the development of these centres to raise the level of housing standards in the Territory. The corrugated-iron slums of Lagos or the more spacious drabness of Minna give a measure of the lost opportunities in this respect.

In contrast to the European-inspired centres are the older indigenous settlements, such as the Yoruba or Hausa towns, whose closely packed, closely peopled houses of red mud seem to spring organically from the landscape. Here, as in the tropical forest, is a perpetual cycle of decay and renewal, houses crumbling down into red laterite mud after a short, crowded life and others springing up incessantly to take their place. The complex

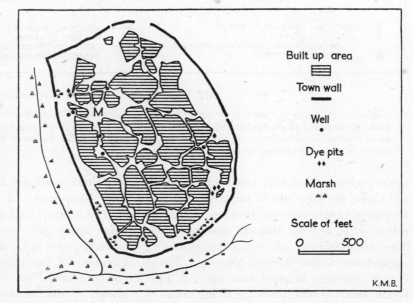

FIG. 41. OLD ANCHAU

The town of Anchau, in the northern part of Zaria Province, illustrates admirably the character of the smaller Northern settlements. Note the compact character of the settlement, closely confined within its sheltering walls and girdle of marsh; this defensive clustering of population is a legacy of the unsettled conditions of pre-British days and results in phenomenally high densities (Anchau, 21,000 people per square mile). Overcrowding, the absence of adequate wells and of sanitary facilities, and the prevalence of malarial mosquitoes in dyepits and surrounding marshes create major health problems. With the establishment of peaceful conditions in the north the need for such defensive nucleation passed away and in some areas the population is tending to diffuse outwards into the surrounding empty bush; since such vacant land is often tsetse-infested, this uncontrolled population movement creates a new set of health problems.

Built up area

Town wall

Well

Dye pits

Marsh

Scale of feet
0   500

K.M.B.

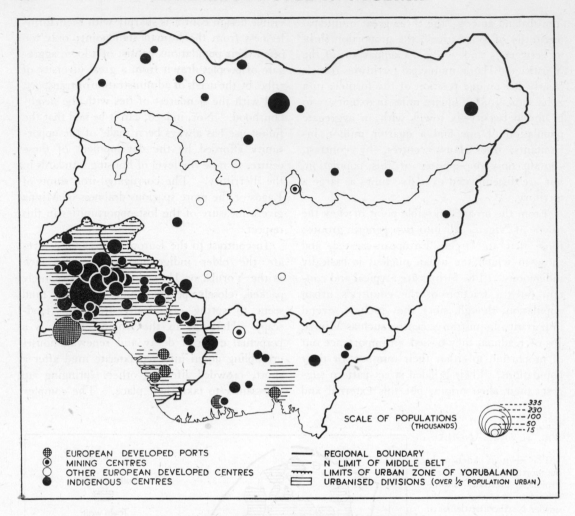

FIG. 42. THE URBAN CENTRES OF NIGERIA

Illustrating the great flowering of urban life in the south-west Yoruba Provinces and the very limited urban development of the Middle Belt; here the towns are to be attributed largely to outside influences. A broad fourfold classification of the towns is given; the category "Other European-developed centres" consists largely of route centres and administrative centres.

intermingling of housing, small-scale industry and shops, the labyrinth of unpaved roads and alleyways, closely confined between high compound walls, and the frequent absence of any dominating feature, convey an impression of shapelessness to the Western observer. But it is a shapelessness in appearance only; as Frobenius observed with reference to the towns of Yorubaland: "Every one of these towns resolves itself into a definite number of astonishingly large compounds, all of which are severally built on a clearly organised system, and in themselves again give expression to an extended, powerful, systematic and social ideal."[1] Half a century of European administration has not greatly modified the internal structure of these towns; it has, however, led to the grafting on to the indigenous nucleus of a new com-

[1] *The Voice of Africa* (English edition, London, 1913), Vol. I, p. 153.

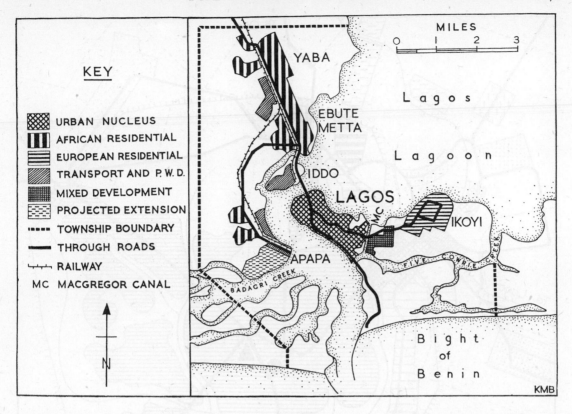

KEY

▨ URBAN NUCLEUS
▥ AFRICAN RESIDENTIAL
▤ EUROPEAN RESIDENTIAL
▨ TRANSPORT AND P.W.D.
▦ MIXED DEVELOPMENT
▨ PROJECTED EXTENSION
------- TOWNSHIP BOUNDARY
——— THROUGH ROADS
⊢⊣⊢⊣ RAILWAY
MC MACGREGOR CANAL

FIG. 43. LAGOS

The largest European-developed port on the West Coast and the second largest city of Nigeria. Note the fragmented character of the urban area: the original nucleus lay on the western tip of Lagos Island whence the urban area has expanded eastwards towards Ikoyi and northwards across Iddo Island to the mainland. Functionally the city falls into four clearly defined zones; the urban nucleus, with mixed commercial, residential and administrative development; the African residential areas of Ebute Metta and Yaba which have grown up along the main road and railway to the interior; the European residential area of Ikoyi; and the railway and harbour areas of Iddo and Apapa. Most of the city's large-scale industry is concentrated in Apapa; existing development plans, including ambitious extensions to harbour facilities, will firmly establish the supremacy of the area in the industrial economy, not merely of the Lagos area, but of the Territory as a whole.

The total population of the township is 230,000, giving an average density of 8,500 per square mile. There are striking contrasts in density between the urban nucleus and the peripheral areas; the density in the former attaining the fantastic figure of 88,000 per square mile as against 3,700 in the case of the peripheral areas.

mercial and administrative zone where the European trading concerns are established, along with the offices of various Government departments, the police-station, and, where present, the railway-station and the cinema.[1] This newer zone will also contain the new and better-class African housing and the settlements of non-native Africans, such as the Hausa and Nupe settlements in the southern city of Ibadan or the Yoruba settlement in the northern city of Zaria. Still farther out and isolated from the indigenous city by a broad belt of bush is the Government Reservation, where most of the European population and the higher rank African officials live.

[1] In some cases this dual personality is recognised by "twinned" place names, e.g. Yerwa-Maiduguri, Yola-Jimeta, the first referring to the indigenous city, the second to the later European development.

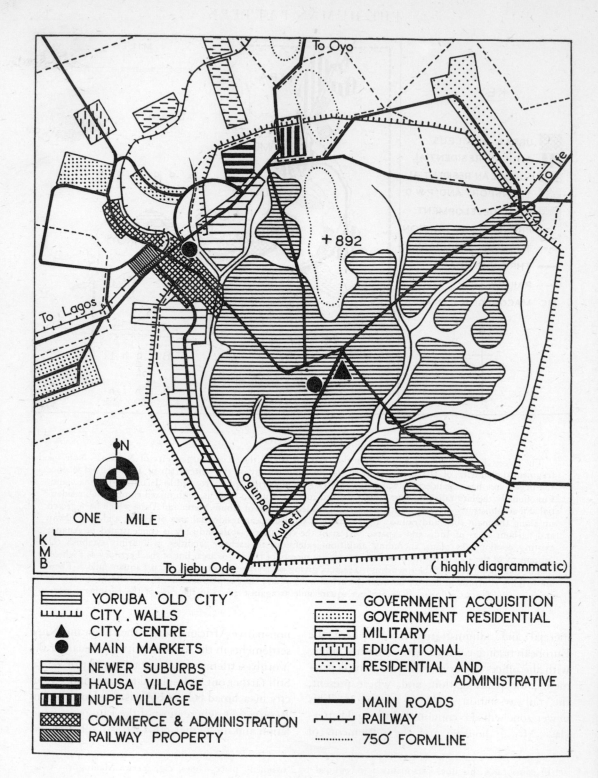

To Oyo

To Ife

+ 892

To Lagos

Ogunpa

Kudeti

N

ONE MILE

K
M
B

To Ijebu Ode

(highly diagrammatic)

YORUBA 'OLD CITY'		GOVERNMENT ACQUISITION	
CITY . WALLS		GOVERNMENT RESIDENTIAL	
▲ CITY CENTRE		MILITARY	
● MAIN MARKETS		EDUCATIONAL	
NEWER SUBURBS		RESIDENTIAL AND	
HAUSA VILLAGE		ADMINISTRATIVE	
NUPE VILLAGE		MAIN ROADS	
COMMERCE & ADMINISTRATION		RAILWAY	
RAILWAY PROPERTY		750' FORMLINE	

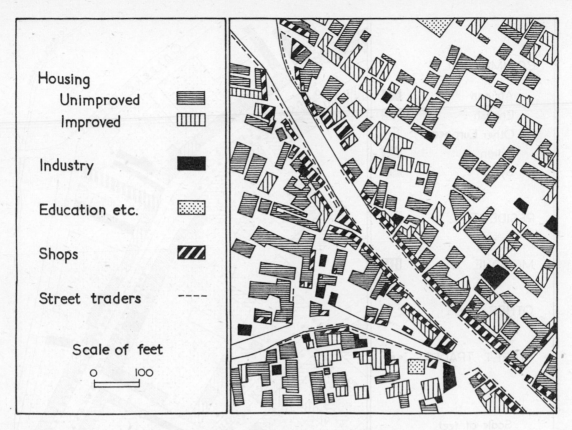

Housing
   Unimproved
   Improved

Industry

Education etc.

Shops

Street traders

Scale of feet

0   100

FIG. 45. PART OF THE OLD CITY, IBADAN

Here, in contrast to the commercial-administrative zone (Fig. 46) where foreign influences are dominant, the indigenous urban pattern is preserved with little modification. Note the poorly developed road network; the great majority of compounds are accessible only by narrow tortuous footpaths. Note too, the intermingling of housing and industry and the almost continuous line of small shops and street trading sites along the main thoroughfare. The term "unimproved" is applied to the normal single-storied dwelling of lateritic mud, roofed usually with corrugated iron; "improved" dwellings consist of newer dwellings, laid out on more spacious lines and often double-storied, and utilising brick or mud with concrete facing in their construction.

Left   FIG. 44. THE YORUBA METROPOLIS OF IBADAN

Illustrating the composite character typical of the larger Nigerian towns. Note the Yoruba Old City, disposed around the southern extremity of a long quartzite ridge, and surrounded by walls (now largely disappeared); the newer suburbs and the commercial-administrative zone which has developed in the north-west in proximity to the railway and the main Lagos road; the Outer Ring containing the government residential area, together with administrative, military and educational development.

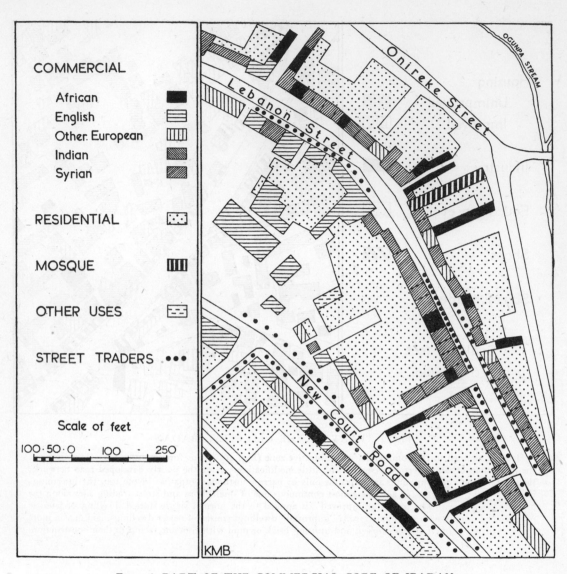

COMMERCIAL

African
English
Other European
Indian
Syrian

RESIDENTIAL

MOSQUE

OTHER USES

STREET TRADERS ...

Scale of feet

100·50·0 · 100 · 250

KMB

FIG. 46. PART OF THE COMMERCIAL CORE OF IBADAN

Based on a land use and housing survey carried out in 1948–50. Note the limited role of large-scale African enterprise in the main commercial core and the dominant role of foreign enterprise—European, Indian, and especially Syrian. The widespread distribution of street traders, usually women and often selling on a commission basis on behalf of the foreign firms, is very typical. Residential accommodation is behind or above the shops, though the majority of the more wealthy European and Syrian traders live in the government residential area on the fringe of the city (Fig. 44).

---

cont. from opposite page

Zaria road some thirteen miles from Kaduna and the road to Lagos is via Zaria; a new road is under construction to connect westward from Kaduna to the existing road to Lagos and this will effect a very considerable shortening of road distance. Kaduna was at one time regarded as a suitable choice for a national capital—it is much more central than is generally appreciated and suffers from no space restrictions—but Lagos has retained its position as national capital.

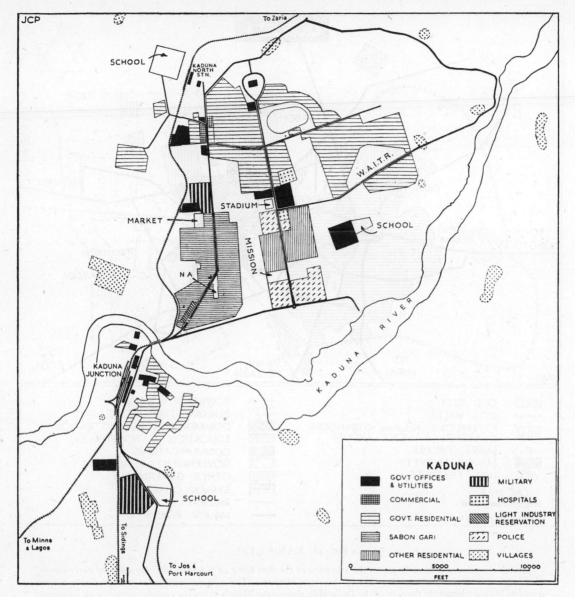

FIG. 47. KADUNA

Kaduna is an example of an administrative centre with secondary functions as a railway junction. As Headquarters of the Northern Region its population includes a large number of government employees, the balance of the population being largely dependent for their livelihood on this administrative group. Kaduna has always been an important military centre and, with the growth of the town and the provision of services, bodies such as the West African Institute of Trypanosomiasis Research have established themselves here. It is hoped in the future to establish light industries which will give the town a more balanced economy; in this connection the hydro-electric potentialities of the Shiroro Gorge may be decisive.

Kaduna Junction remains to some extent a separate entity, containing the railway yards, the power station and a few technical departments. The long-distance train time-tables are organised so that trains on the N.E. and S.W. lines are scheduled to unite at Kaduna Junction to form the train to Lagos. There is at present (1952) only one main road out of Kaduna, that to the north. The Jos-Enugu road branches from the

[cont. on opposite page

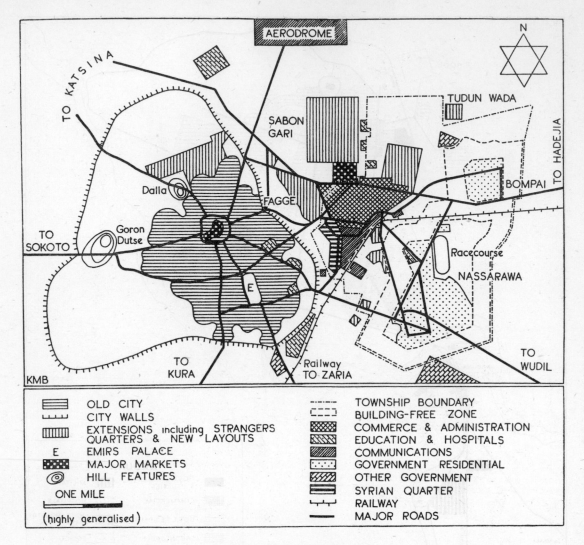

FIG. 48. KANO CITY

Though the Kano Chronicle places the accession of the first King of Kano in the year 999, the early history of this great Sudanese metropolis is lost in the mists of time. The original settlement was probably a small iron-smelting settlement at the foot of the Dalla Hill; during the Middle Ages the city developed as an important industrial and commercial centre at the southern extremity of the trans-Saharan caravan routes; today, with a population of 102,000, it is the largest and most flourishing city of the West African Sudan zone, the centre of the Nigerian groundnut belt and the economic and cultural heart of Hausaland.

Note, as in the case of Ibadan, the composite character of the city; the old Hausa city, incompletely occupying the space within the twelve-mile circuit of walls and centring upon the great market-place which has replaced the sacrificial grove of pre-Islamic days; the Strangers Settlement outside the walls occupied by immigrants from the south such as Yorubas and Ibos; the commercial-administrative zone in proximity to the station; and the government residential area insulated by its building-free zone.

72

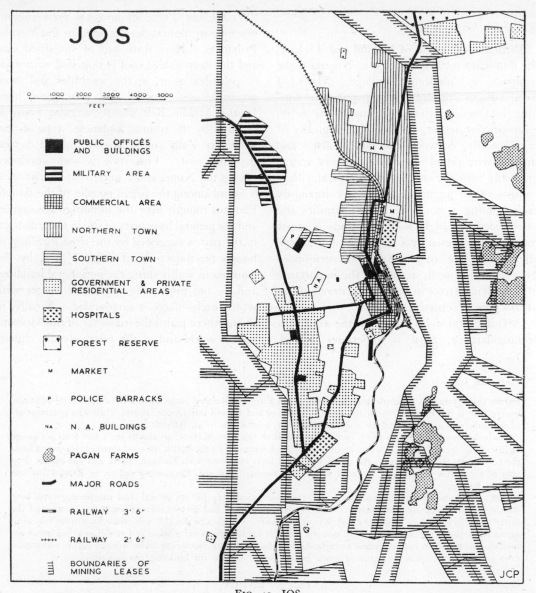

JOS

■	PUBLIC OFFICES AND BUILDINGS
▤	MILITARY AREA
▦	COMMERCIAL AREA
▥	NORTHERN TOWN
▤	SOUTHERN TOWN
⋮	GOVERNMENT & PRIVATE RESIDENTIAL AREAS
⋮	HOSPITALS
⬦	FOREST RESERVE
M	MARKET
P	POLICE BARRACKS
NA	N. A. BUILDINGS
⬮	PAGAN FARMS
▬	MAJOR ROADS
▭	RAILWAY 3' 6"
+++	RAILWAY 2' 6"
⊟	BOUNDARIES OF MINING LEASES

FIG. 49. JOS

Jos is an example of a European-created settlement whose development has from the beginning been bound up with the development of the Plateau tin deposits. As in the case of most mining centres it has attracted a cosmopolitan population and this is reflected in the triple make-up of the town with its northern quarter, dominantly Hausa, its southern quarter, more complex, with Yoruba, Ibo, Ijaw and Kalabari elements together with non-European immigrant groups such as the Lebanese, and its European quarter. In detail, however, these lines of cultural cleavage are not rigid: thus, the northern town includes many examples of southern architecture while the government reservation (the European reservation of pre-war days) houses both European and African members of the administration. The fourth element in the human pattern of the Jos area, the indigenous Pagan groups, are settled on small euphorbia-girt farms on the outskirts of the town, and find in the supply of firewood to the town a useful supplementary source of income. Note the central position of the commercial and business area; this is in marked contrast to the indigenous towns such as Kano or Ibadan where the commercial-administrative zone occupies a peripheral position. More than any other

[cont. overleaf

Rural Settlement Types

With the exception of Iboland and Tivland, the dominant settlement form in Nigeria is the compact or "nucleated" village. Many of these villages are large, with populations running into several thousands, and there is no clear-cut distinction, either morphologically or economically, between the large village and small town; rather does one category merge gradually into the other. The typical village consists of an aggregate of large compounds, each housing a group of related families and surrounded by high walls of mud or straw matting, intersected by a labyrinth of lanes and alleyways. Each in the old days was surrounded by a high mud wall, suggesting the importance of the defence factor in the original development of this type of settlement.

Architectural styles vary. In the south, the rectangular, or, as it is sometimes termed, "West Coast", type of house is predominant, reaching its highest development in the Yoruba Provinces. Here walls are of sun-dried clay and the steep gabled roof is thatched with grass or palm-leaves or, in the wealthier and more accessible areas, roofed with corrugated iron. In the Middle Belt the rectangular house is replaced by the round "Sudanese" type of hut, with clay walls and a steeply pitched conical thatched roof. This style is well developed among the Nupe, and a somewhat similar style is found among the pagan peoples of the Bauchi Plateau, though here the buildings are smaller and the general insecurity of life in these districts in the past is suggested by the close huddling of houses on the crests of isolated hills, by the continuous wall joining the peripheral buildings and by the impassable euphorbia hedges with which each village is surrounded. Finally, in the northern plains the influence of the Mohammedan world and of the relatively dry climate

cont. from page 73

feature this symbolises the contrast between the newer European-created centres where the commercial-administrative core is the *raison d'être* of the town's existence, and the old indigenous centres where the commercial-administrative zone represents an alien development, grafted on to an African base.

Jos is the terminus of the 3 feet 6 inches gauge branch line from Kafanchan and of the 2 feet 6 inches gauge light railway from Zaria. It is also an important road centre. To the north, the road through Naraguta links the town with the Chad Basin, the north-west road links the town with Kaduna, Zaria and the export crop area of the Kano region, and the road south runs through Bukuru, the mining centre, to Enugu and the Eastern Region.

Not only does Jos owe its existence to the tin-mining industry but its growth and morphology has been strikingly influenced by the industry. The boundaries of past and present mining leases are shown and the restrictive effects of these leases on urban layout are clear. Whether or not this will create long-term planning problems depends on the future of the mining industry; if the mines are worked out and if new industries are introduced, the town may continue to expand, though some of the bordering leases worked before restoration laws existed will require preparatory work before being suitable for building development.

Opposite   FIG. 50. ENUGU

The original settlement was the village of Enugu Ngwo, but the modern town dates from the development of the coal mines (coal was discovered in 1909). The area is composed of Upper Cretaceous rocks dipping gently to the west and the coal seams, of which five have been identified, occur near the base of the scarp. The original workings were those of the Udi Mine, originally opened up in 1913 but now exhausted; present workings are concentrated in the deep valleys of the Iva and Obwetti streams.

The original impetus was thus given by mining development, but in recent years the establishment of the Eastern Regional Headquarters at Enugu has been an important factor in the development of the town. This has led to a considerable increase in the administrative population and to an expansion of the residential and administrative sectors. Enugu has considerable industrial potentialities, especially for such industries as bricks and pottery, using local raw materials and coal, and possibly also for plastic industries based on coal.

The road north-eastwards is to Abakaliki, Ogoja, Makurdi and the north; a shorter route to Makurdi branches from the Onitsha road nine miles west of Enugu. The road to Onitsha and thence to the Western Region via the Asaba ferry ascends the scarp by the steep winding road known as Milliken Hill.

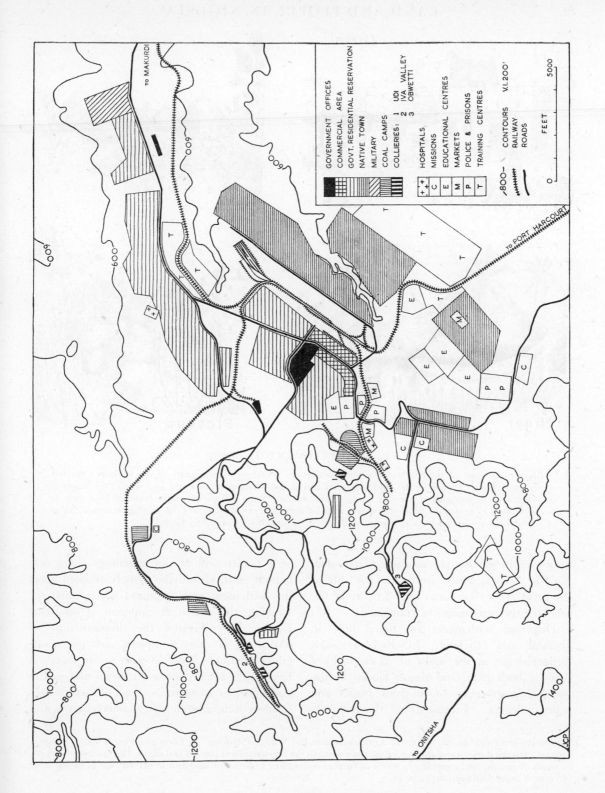

GOVERNMENT OFFICES
COMMERCIAL AREA
GOVT. RESIDENTIAL RESERVATION
NATIVE TOWN
MILITARY
COAL CAMPS
COLLIERIES: 1   UDI
               2   IVA VALLEY
               3   OBWETTI

HOSPITALS
MISSIONS
EDUCATIONAL CENTRES
MARKETS
POLICE & PRISONS
TRAINING CENTRES

+ HOSPITALS
C MISSIONS
E EDUCATIONAL CENTRES
M MARKETS
P POLICE & PRISONS
T TRAINING CENTRES

800─ CONTOURS   V.I. 200'
      RAILWAY
      ROADS

0   FEET   5000

TO MAKURDI

TO PORT HARCOURT

TO ONITSHA

FIG. 51. SETTLEMENT TYPES

Illustrating some of the characteristic settlement styles found in various parts of the territory: the flat-roofed mud houses typical of the Northern cities and of the Mohammedan world as a whole; the dispersed deep-thatched homesteads of the Tiv people; the compact Nupe village of round thatched-roof huts set in the midst of its fields; and finally the closely huddled defensively sited villages of the Jos Pagans whose clusters of round huts are linked by a protective wall and set behind thick euphorbia hedges.

shows itself in the characteristic flat-roofed, box-like houses, which are typical not only of the great cities like Kano but of many of the smaller rural settlements of Hausaland.

Dispersed settlements are found only in Iboland and Tivland. In Iboland[1] each farmstead lies in the midst of its crops, by a road or bush path, and almost hidden by the interlacing greenery of oil-palm fronds and plantain leaves. Frequently all the members of a family will occupy dwellings along one branch path, and in the densely peopled areas the settlement web is almost continuous, resembling the ribbon development of suburban Europe. In Tivland the dissemination of settlement is more complete, and the open, grassy landscape is dotted with neatly thatched farmsteads, usually set within trees and in the midst of their farmlands. Each of these homesteads is occupied by a man and his relatives, and

[1] On Ibo settlement see G. I. Jones, "Agriculture and Ibo Village Planning" in *Farm and Forest*, Vol. VI, No. 1 (1945). On the difficulty of applying European terms to the Ibo settlement pattern and on the Ibo tendency to think in terms of people, and especially in terms of family, rather than in terms of land and settlement, see S. Leith-Ross, *African Women*, London (1939), p. 49.

PLATE XI. THE SETTLEMENT OF BUKURU ON THE JOS PLATEAU

Illustrating some characteristic elements in the Plateau landscape: the level Plateau surface under shifting cultivation or scarred by opencast tin-workings; the compact mining villages housing workers drawn from all corners of Nigeria; the occasional European houses with their eucalypt girdles; and the relatively highly developed transport network called into existence by the needs of mining.

76]

PLATE XII. VIEW ACROSS CENTRAL LAGOS, LOOKING SOUTH

Two of the major functional zones are shown: the fringing commercial-administrative zone lying along the Marina (the coastal road) and the mixed residential-commercial core. The former comprises Government offices, banks, churches and commercial premises and is characterised by substantial multi-storied stone buildings. Much of the core area (see Fig. 43) consists of unsubstantial and grossly overcrowded buildings of mud or tin; the replacement of this congested area by planned multistoried housing is one of the major tasks facing the city.

PLATE XIII. KANO CITY

This view across the old city illustrates the characteristic features of the Northern Nigerian town—the absence, by western standards, of planned layout, the closely congested pattern of compounds, each surrounded by high mud walls, the labyrinth of alleyways and paths. The flat-roofed mud-housing and the presence of the date palm emphasise the affinities between these Northern cities and the cities of the Middle East. The zone of newer development, including Government residential areas, lies beyond the line of the old wall.

PLATE XIV. KAFANCHAN JUNCTION, NORTHERN NIGERIA

This settlement is located where the branch railway to Jos leaves the Kaduna–Port Harcourt main line, and is the best example of a European-created transport centre. Note the gridded layout of the main African settlement and the more open European (or Government) settlement close to the station. Note, too, the extensive destruction of the savana woodlands in the vicinity of the settlement. The old-age surface is typical of the High Plains of Hausaland.

it is occupied until the surrounding farmlands are exhausted by cropping, when the group shifts, or until the head of the family dies, when the sons disperse and set up their homesteads in adjoining land.[1]

The contrast between the closely nucleated Nupe village and the dispersed pattern of Tiv settlement, both found in the Middle Belt under not greatly dissimilar environmental conditions, draws attention to the importance of cultural and social factors in the evolution of the country's settlement pattern.

Over-population and Under-population

It is somewhat of a paradox that a territory with an average population density of 60 per square mile should be confronted with a problem of over-population, even on a local scale. Yet in at least two, possibly three, areas of Nigeria, population is pressing dangerously upon resources.

Reference has already been made to the extremely high density of population in parts of Iboland, and here over-farming has led to the replacement of the original rain forest by a grass vegetation and to severe and widespread gulley erosion. In the most crowded areas some redistribution of population seems inevitable, and in this connection it is noteworthy that densities drop sharply towards the Province of Ogoja and Eastern Calabar. It has, however, to be demonstrated that these empty areas have an adequate carrying capacity, and that population transfer on a large scale is feasible in the present social context.[2] In this respect the history of the pioneer Cross River–Calabar scheme is not encouraging, and it may be that in the long run an extensive policy of industrial-isation based on local coal will prove the only satisfactory solution to the problem of conges-tion in these districts. In the areas of moderate population density replacement of existing farm-ing methods by a system which will maintain fertility is imperative, but such a development is rendered difficult by the intractable and im-poverished character of the soil. It is now clear that green manuring alone is no solution, and the most promising line of approach appears to lie in a combination of green manuring and mixed farming with wider use of artificial fertilisers to increase yields on land still in pro-duction; long fallows under soil-restoring shrubs, such as *tephrosia* or *acoia*, seem the most promising means of restoring fertility to exhausted land.[3] Unfortunately, the whole area lies well within the tsetse belt, so that the introduction of a mixed farming economy depends on the development of cattle strains which are resistant to trypanosomiasis [4] and the inculcation of a livestock technique among a people utterly unused to cattle. There is no doubt that, given time, both of these problems can be solved—but time is short and the deterioration rapid and progressive.

Tiv Division shows an average density of only 65 per square mile, but as a result of the migration history of the tribe, population is extremely unevenly distributed, and in the southern sectors densities of 175–200 per square mile are recorded. This density is not excessive but the farming system of the Tiv is, however, extensive and with the expansion of cash-cropping has become more land-demanding. Fallows have in consequence been reduced in duration, the original savana vegetation does not regenerate and is replaced by grass, and soil deterioration in these more densely peopled dis-

[1] See *Akigas Story: the Tiv Tribe as seen by one of its Members*, edited R. East, London (1939), especially p. 15.

[2] For a brief discussion of the emotional, magical and religious aspects of Ibo land-attachment see J. Harris, "Human Relationship to the Land in S. Nigeria" in *Rural Sociology*, Vol. VII, No. 1 (March 1942), especially pp. 91–2.

[3] *Annual Report of the Department of Agriculture*, 1938, pp. 6–9.

[4] "Fly infection is so severe that cattle multiplication is extremely difficult. Even with the dwarf indigenous cattle, a breed credited with considerable tolerance, increase is barely sufficient to maintain the herd." T. A. M. Nash, *Tsetse Flies in British West Africa*, London (1948), p. 15.

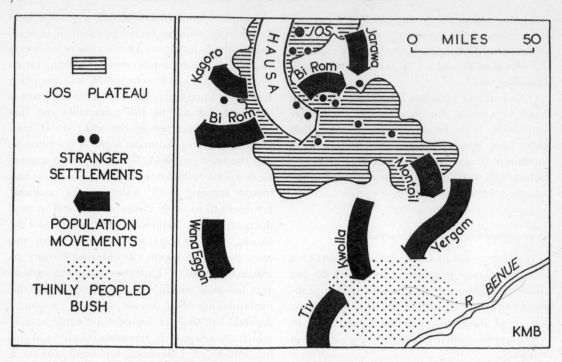

FIG. 52. SOME RECENT POPULATION MOVEMENTS IN THE JOS PLATEAU

Illustrating the dynamic character of the present-day tribal and density patterns. Three important types of population movement are illustrated: the downhill movement of Pagan peoples such as the Bi Rom or Jarawa in response to the more settled conditions following the establishment of British control; the drift of small farming groups from the fringes of the Plateau and from the Tiv country across the Benue towards the empty bush country on the north bank of the Benue; and the influx of Hausas and other "strangers" attracted by the development of the Plateau mining industry.

These movements, and especially the infiltration of relatively advanced groups such as the Hausa or the Ibo into areas inhabited by less advanced Pagan peoples, create complex sociological and land-tenure problems. These are not peculiar to the Middle Belt but are found also in the southern Cameroons and on the northern and eastern periphery of the Ibo territory; without some measure of control of migration and settlement in favour of already-established groups it is difficult to see how they can be avoided.

tricts has become as serious as in Iboland. The control measures are obvious: redistribution of the population and intensification of farming methods by the development of green manuring and mixed farming. Yet, as Briggs has shown, any redistribution of population, even within the tribal territory, appears "unacceptable . . . on account of their social and religious organisation;"[1] while the Agricultural Department's policy of intensification of farming has met a formidable difficulty in the reluctance of the men to increase their share of the farm work.[2]

Here, as in Iboland, the problem is not insoluble, but the time factor is critical.

In the third area, the densely peopled zone around Kano City, heavy manuring appears to be maintaining the soil in a rather precarious state of balance.

That the excessive concentration of human or livestock populations upon restricted areas may lead eventually to vegetation and soil degradation is readily appreciated; it is less readily appreciated that reduction of population below a certain level may create problems no less

[1] G. W. G. Briggs, op. cit., p. 11.
[2] See, for example, Annual Report of the Agricultural Department, 1936, p. 22.

serious, though of a different character. It has already been suggested that one of the consequences of the depopulation of parts of the Middle Belt by slave-raiding was the spread of the tsetse fly—in other words, a deterioration of the biological environment for man and beast—and recent work, in Nigeria and elsewhere, has shown that tsetse control is possible only if the population is sufficiently dense to maintain a certain level of bush clearing; if population drops below this level, and man's pressure is reduced, the bush becomes more dense, an increase in the game population follows, and the fly, taking advantage of the more favourable conditions, extends its domain. This minimum density of population probably varies with the density of the stream network (stream-side bush being one of the main strongholds of the fly); in the Anchau area, near Zaria, Nash estimated the critical density at 70 per square mile.[1] It is significant that over much of the Nigerian Middle Belt, the main endemic area for sleeping sickness, densities are well below this minimum (Fig. 35).

RACIAL AND CULTURAL GROUPS

Kome kyaun tafarnuwa, ba ta yi kamar albasa ba. ("However fine the garlic may be, it is never like the onion.")

Northern Proverb.

General Features

One of the most widespread and deep-seated beliefs regarding the Tropical African territories is the belief in their racial and cultural uniformity. In reality, nothing could be farther from the truth than this dangerous and misleading generalisation. The work of physical anthropologists, though still in its infancy as far as much of Africa is concerned, has

already drawn attention to the great diversity of racial elements which have contributed to the physical make-up of the peoples of Tropical Africa, while the studies of social anthropologists have revealed a pattern of civilisation and culture as complex as that of any part of the globe.[2]

Nigeria is no exception to the general picture. Its location athwart the great transcontinental migration route provided by the grasslands of the Sudan has meant that from earliest times it has been exposed to a great diversity of cultural and racial influences. Within the territory a great variety of environments, ranging from dense rain and swamp forests to open semi-arid grasslands, had encouraged a wide measure of cultural differentiation and linguistic fragmentation. As a consequence, the present-day racial and cultural pattern of the territory shows a richness and diversity paralleled in few African territories, and one which is of fundamental importance in its constitutional development.

Racial Elements in the Population

Racially, using the term "race" in its strict biological sense,[3] Nigeria lies in the zone of contact between two strikingly contrasted regions. To the south and south-east, the humid savanas and forests represent the "home zone" of the Negro race, one of the most distinctive and specialised of human races. Though the range of individual variation within the Negro race is great, certainly as great as within the White race, there are certain physical features, such as broadness of nose, a tendency to prognathism or forward-jutting jaw, woolly hair and dark skin colour, which serve to distinguish the group as a whole from the other great primary groups of mankind. To the north the semi-arid grasslands and the deserts represent the southern periphery of the "White" home zone. Here the distinguishing features of the population are relatively fair skin, narrow

[1] "The Anchau Settlement Scheme" in *Farm and Forest*, Vol. II, No. 2 (1941), p. 77.
[2] *Les Peuples et les Civilisations de l'Afrique* by H. Baumann and D. Westermann (French trans., Paris 1948) gives the most complete picture of the cultural pattern of Africa.
[3] As referring to "groups of mankind possessing well-developed and primarily heritable physical differences from other groups". See *What is Race?* Evidence from Scientists. Unesco (1952), p. 83.

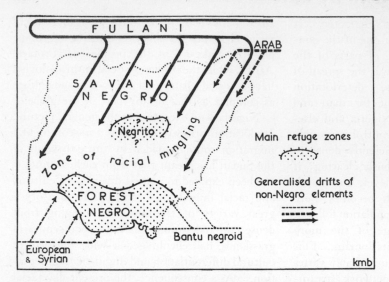

FIG. 53. SOME ELEMENTS IN THE RACIAL MAKE-UP OF NIGERIA

Illustrating, in diagrammatic fashion, some of the elements which have contributed to the racial make-up of the people of Nigeria. Note the role of the rain forest and the broken terrain of the Middle Belt as refuges for the Forest Negro and Negrito groups respectively; the infiltration of White (Caucasoid) elements by way of the open grasslands of the Sudan zone; and the zone of racial mingling extending across the centre of the country. No attempt has been made to show very early folk-movements such as the Yoruba migrations.

nose and thin lips, and wavy rather than woolly hair, features which may be observed among some of the Fulani and the immigrant Arabs resident in the northern cities. Within these two primary groups—Negro and White—it is possible to recognise a number of subdivisions, distinguished by slight variations in physical appearance; thus, the Negro group in West Africa is conveniently divided on the basis of build into two subdivisions—the tall Savana Negro of the northern plains and the shorter, stockier Forest Negro of the south. The picture is further complicated by large-scale hybridisation which over many centuries has tended to make the racial division between Black and White in the Sudan zone hazy in the extreme.

Today the racial picture,[1] greatly simplified, is somewhat as follows: in the southern forests the dominant racial type is the relatively stocky Forest Negro type, though the frequency of relatively finely cut features and fair complexions among many of the southern peoples, such as the Yoruba and Jekri, suggests a considerable measure of hybridisation in the past with non-Negro groups of problematic origin; this hybridisation may have antedated their arrival in their present homes, as is almost certainly the case with the Yoruba. In the northern plains

the Savana Negro type forms the dominant element in the Provinces of Sokoto, Katsina, Kano and Zaria. Farther east, however, in the Chad basin, this type has undergone a considerable degree of dilution with Arab, i.e. "White", elements, and the Shuwa Arab and Kanuri peoples are best regarded as of mixed Negro-White origin. The purest example in Nigeria of a group of "White" racial origins is provided by the nomad Fulani, whose affinities are with the olive-skinned, wavy-haired peoples of the Mediterranean basin; the settled Fulani, however, are fast losing their racial identity by inter-marriage with their Negro neighbours. The relationship of the primitive pagan peoples of the Jos Plateau to their neighbours is obscure; certainly the rocky recesses of the plateau have throughout history afforded refuge to the shattered fragments of peoples displaced from the surrounding lowlands by stronger neighbours, while observation suggests the presence among some of the plateau groups of a Negrito or dwarf Negro element akin to the Negrito peoples of the Congo Forest.

It will be evident from the above summary that the importance of race as a dividing factor in modern Nigeria is negligible; the great human groups, such as the Yoruba, the Ibo or

[1] Based largely upon field observations.

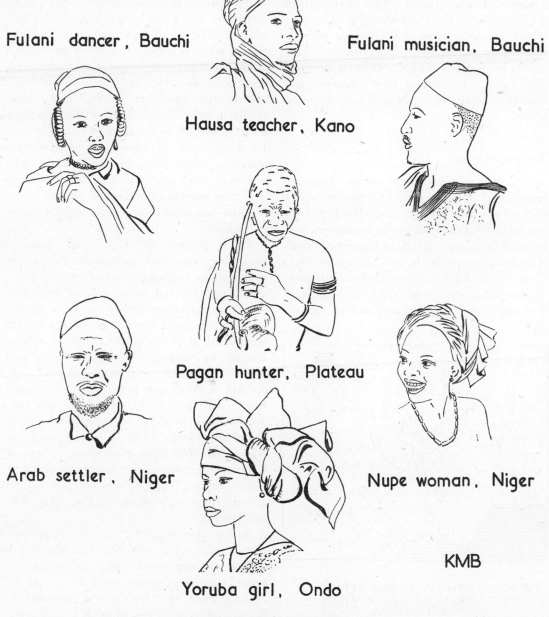

Fulani dancer, Bauchi

Fulani musician, Bauchi

Hausa teacher, Kano

Pagan hunter, Plateau

Arab settler, Niger

Nupe woman, Niger

KMB

Yoruba girl, Ondo

FIG. 54. RACIAL TYPES

A very great diversity of physical types is found among the peoples of Nigeria. The Yoruba, Nupe and Hausa are peoples of hybrid racial origin, though with a predominance of negroid features; the Fulani and Arab groups, by contrast, show a predominance of Caucasoid (White) features, with relatively fair complexion, straight narrow nose and straight or wavy hair. Negrito or dwarf negro traits are found among some of the Pagan peoples of the Jos Plateau.

the Hausa, are linguistic and cultural rather than racial groups, and indeed each may contain a variety of racial strains. This situation is in no way different from that obtaining in Europe, where the boundaries of the various national states cut across the major racial boundaries and follow lines of linguistic and cultural cleavage. The more important of these linguistic and cultural boundaries in Nigeria are discussed below.

Linguistic Groups

Nigeria lies at one of the major "linguistic cross-roads" of Africa (Fig. 55); representatives of three of the six great language families of the continent are found within its boundaries, and in detail the complexity of the linguistic pattern is probably unequalled in any African territory. Considerable differences of opinion exist regarding the classification of many African languages; the classification followed here and in Fig. 56

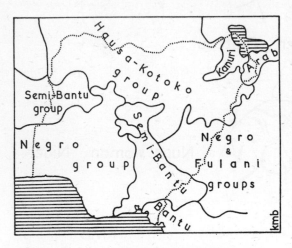

FIG. 55. NIGERIA IN RELATION TO THE MAJOR LINGUISTIC GROUPS OF WEST AFRICA

The frontiers of Nigeria, like those of most African territories, show a supreme disregard of linguistic and cultural boundaries; this is in striking contrast to Europe where frontiers frequently follow lines of linguistic cleavage.

is that established by the German scholars, H. Baumann and D. Westermann.[1]

The major families represented are the Sudanic family to which the great majority of languages spoken in Nigeria belong; the Bantu family, which is dominant over the greater part of the southern sub-continent and which extends north-west into the Nigerian Cameroons; and the Hamito-Semitic family, the dominant family in the Saharan zone, which penetrates south into the Chad area of Bornu Province. In detail, each of these families comprises numerous subdivisions, and these in turn may be broken down into language groups consisting of a great number of languages; further, many Nigerian languages show a wide range of dialectal variation.

Three divisions of the Sudanic language family are commonly recognised: Negro, including Kwa languages; Semi-Bantu or Sudan class-languages; and Inner Sudanic languages. Negro languages are widely spoken along the northern fringe of the Congo basin, and are represented in the Central Cameroons area of Nigeria by languages such as Camba and Takum. On the west coast a distinct subdivision of the Negro languages, the so-called Kwa subdivision, is recognised; to this subdivision many of the most important Nigerian languages belong. The Kwa languages in Nigeria fall into three geographical groups: a Cameroons group; a northern group including Jukun, Idoma, Nupe, Gwari and Igbirra; and a southern group comprising Ibo, Ijaw, Edo and Yoruba.

As the name suggests, the Semi-Bantu languages show some affinities with the Bantu languages of Southern Africa. In Nigeria they occur in an irregular arc, stretching across the country from the Southern Cameroons to Borgu, and, as in the case of the Kwa languages, it is convenient to adopt a broad geographic grouping. In the Cameroons they are represented by numerous small groups, such as Bali, Banso, Bamenda. Farther west, in the Cross

[1] H. Baumann and D. Westermann, *op. cit.*, pp. 449–68. Paris (1941).   See also L. Homburger, *Les Langues negro-africaines*,

FIG. 56. THE LANGUAGE
FAMILIES OF NIGERIA

Note the extension of the Bantu
and Semitic families into the
south-eastern and north-eastern
sectors of the Territory; the extension of the semi-Bantu languages
across the Middle Belt; and the
wide scatter of Fulfulde-speakers
over the open savanas of the north
and the Cameroons.

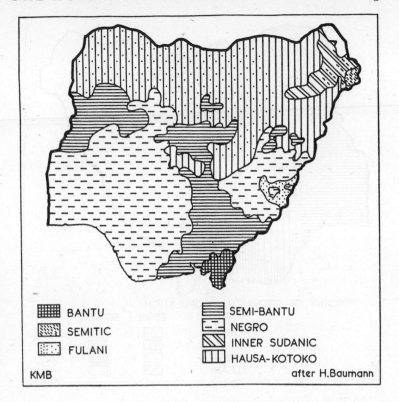

BANTU   SEMI-BANTU

SEMITIC   NEGRO

FULANI   INNER SUDANIC

HAUSA-KOTOKO

KMB   after H.Baumann

River–Niger Delta area features transitional to the Kwa
languages occur; here among
the Semi-Bantu languages
may be listed Efik, Ibibio
and Ekoi. In the Middle
Belt the continuity of the
Semi-Bantu languages is broken by a tongue of Kwa-
speakers in the Minna-Birnin
Gwari area; the eastern group
includes Tiv and many of the small linguistic
groups of the Jos Plateau, such as Jarawa,
Rukuba, Birom and Katab-Kagoro; the western group, mainly in Niger Province, includes
Kamuku, Bassa and Kamberi. The Fulani
language is also grouped by Baumann and
Westermann with the Semi-Bantu languages,
though a wide diversity of opinion exists on this,
some earlier writers claiming for it Indian or
Gypsy affinities.

The Inner Sudanic languages are spoken
over a wide area between the Anglo-Egyptian
Sudan and the Niger. Inadequate data pre-
cludes a completely satisfactory subdivision, but
in Nigeria two main groups are recognised: the
Kanuri group and the Hausa-Kotoko group.
Languages of the first group are confined to
North-east Bornu and include Kanuri and
Kanembu; the Hausa-Kotoko group (the
Hamito-Chad group of some writers) is much
more widely distributed, extending from Sokoto
in the north-west to the Benue in the south-

east. The dominant language in the group is
Hausa, while, on the eastern and southern
fringes of the Hausa linguistic area, a great
diversity of smaller languages are classed in this
group; examples are Madala (South Bornu),
Kerekere (West Bornu), Bolewa (Fika District), and some of the languages of the
Jos Plateau, such as Angas, Ankwe and
Kanam.

Languages belonging to the Bantu and
Hamito-Semitic families are found only on the
periphery of the Territory. The Bantu family
is represented in the extreme south of the
Cameroons by languages such as Ngolo, Lundu
or Kweli; while the languages of the Shuwa
Arabs of Bornu and of the Tuareg of the
northern desert fringe belong to the Hamito-
Semitic group.

It is not possible to discuss with any accuracy
the numerical importance of the various language groups, owing to the scanty data available;
the following table gives an estimate of the

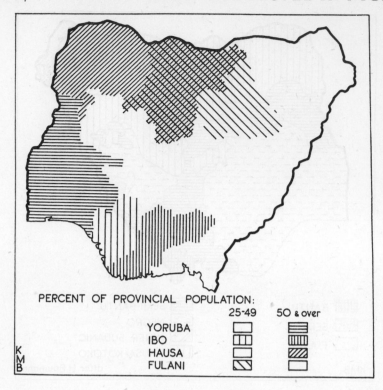

PERCENT OF PROVINCIAL POPULATION:

	25-49	50 & over
YORUBA		
IBO		
HAUSA		
FULANI		

FIG. 57. MAJOR TRIBAL NUCLEI

Dominance of Yoruba peoples in the south-west of the Territory, extending across the boundary of the Western Region into Ilorin Province, of Ibo peoples in the south-central Provinces and of the Hausa and Fulani peoples in the North. Together, these four groups make up two-thirds of the total population of the Territory.

inasmuch as most of the groups on which it is commonly conferred lack both self-consciousness and political focus as such, and often include a considerable diversity of ancestral stocks."[1] In the past, however, the majority of writers on the peoples of the Territory have tended to treat the terms "tribe" and "linguistic group" or "ethnic group" as synonymous and, though the qualification made in the above quotation is important, no useful purpose would be served by departing from this established usage.

approximate order of magnitude of the various groups.

According to the 1931 Census, the major tribal groups were as follows:

TABLE III

THE LANGUAGE GROUPS OF NIGERIA

Language Group	Per cent. of Total
Kwa languages	40
Hausa-Kotoko group	28
Semi-Bantu languages	25
Kanuri group	5
Hamito-Semitic	1
Bantu	0.2

TABLE IV

TRIBAL GROUPS

Hausa	3,630,000
Ibo	3,185,000
Yoruba	3,166,000
Fulani	2,027,000
Kanuri	931,000
Ibibio	750,000
Tiv	577,000
Edo	508,000
Others	5,122,000

Tribal Groups

A broad picture of the pattern of tribal distribution in the Territory is given by the volumes of the 1931 Census. It is important at the outset to stress that the term "tribe" is used somewhat more loosely in Nigeria than in many African territories. To quote the official Colonial Report: "The term 'tribe' is highly misleading as applied to the peoples of Nigeria,

The general distribution of the major groups is summarised in Figs. 57 and 58.

The Hausa are widely distributed throughout the Northern Provinces and attain their greatest

[1] See *Colonial Reports: Nigeria* 1949, London (1950), especially pp. 16–19.

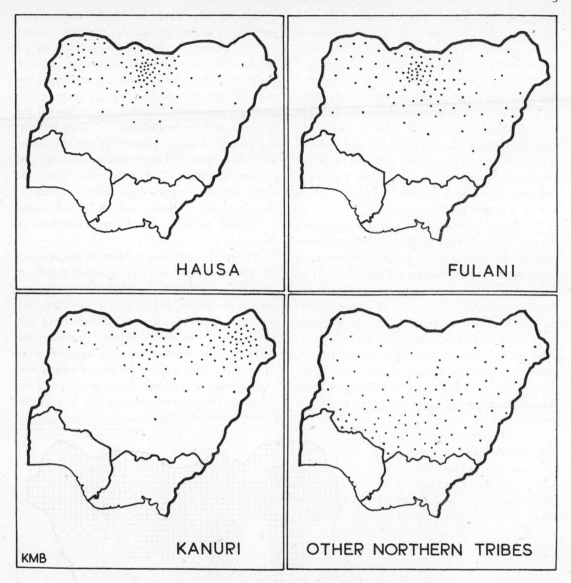

FIG. 58. DISTRIBUTION OF SOME NORTHERN TRIBES

Each dot represents 1% of the total population belonging to the group concerned. Note the concentration of the Hausa in the central and north-western sectors of the Sudan zone; the wider diffusion of the Fulani and their extension into Adamawa; the concentration of the Kanuri in the Chad Basin and its vicinity; and the contrast in tribal distribution between the Middle Belt and the remainder of the Northern Region.

importance in the Provinces of Kano, Sokoto and Zaria (the latter Province including Katsina in 1931), where they represent 62%, 61% and 50% of the respective provincial populations. The boundary between the Hausa and Fulani groups has become much blurred through inter-marriage and, according to the Census, many of those listed as Fulani actually speak Hausa as their home language. As a group the Fulani are more evenly dispersed than the Hausa, and attain their greatest relative importance in the open savana country of the North, representing over one-third of the population of Bauchi Province, and over one-fifth of the population of Adamawa, Kano and Zaria. The only other Northern tribes which exceed half a million are the Kanuri and the Tiv. The former are the dominant group in Bornu, where they make up 43% of the population, and are also found in the adjoining Provinces of Bauchi and Kano and, in smaller groups, in Zaria and Sokoto. The Tiv are more narrowly localised in Benue Province, representing 58% of the provincial population and outside Benue Province there are no Tiv groups of any size.

The tribal pattern of the South is dominated by the Ibo and Yoruba peoples, who together account for almost three-quarters of the entire population of the Southern Provinces. The Ibo group is of overwhelming importance in the Provinces fringing the east bank of the Niger; in Onitsha they make up 98% of the total population; in Owerri (including Rivers), 90%; they are the dominant group in Ogoja (57%), and they constitute substantial minorities in the Western Region Provinces of Benin and Delta (approximately one-third of the provincial populations in each case). In the Western Provinces the Yoruba occupy a position of even greater predomin-ance. In the Provinces of Abeokuta, Oyo and Ijebu there are no non-Yoruba

groups of any size; in Ondo they repre-sent 89% of the population, in the Colony 83%. Beyond the Regional boundary they are the dominant element in the population of Ilorin Province (76%) and constitute an important minority group in Kabba (13%); there are, in addition, important Yoruba groups beyond the Nigerian frontier in Dahomey. Two remain-ing groups of major importance are the Ibibio and Edo peoples. The former are concentrated almost entirely in Calabar Province, while the latter are the largest single ethnic group in the Provinces of Benin and Delta and possess a political focus in the former kingdom of Benin.

The total population included in the category of "Other groups" in 1931 exceeded 5 million. This figure includes some relatively large groups, such as the Nupe (326,000) or Ijaw (156,000), but consists mainly of a great diversity of tiny tribal units. In the Northern Provinces the 1931 Census listed over 150 separate tribal units of less than 10,000 people, of which one-third contained less than 1,000 people, and this linguistic fragmentation is repeated in a smaller

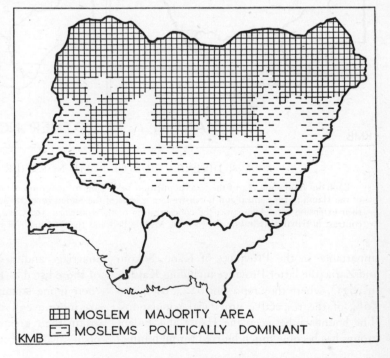

FIG. 59. ISLAM IN NIGERIA

Illustrating the dominance of Islam in the Sudan zone of the north and the extension of Moham-medan influence, in the form of ruling dynasties established by the Fulani "Jihad" at the beginning of the last century, over much of the Middle Belt. Note the Pagan "islands" of the Middle Belt where inaccessibility and rugged topo-graphy made possible the survival of the old ways of life.

MOSLEM MAJORITY AREA
MOSLEMS POLITICALLY DOMINANT

KMB

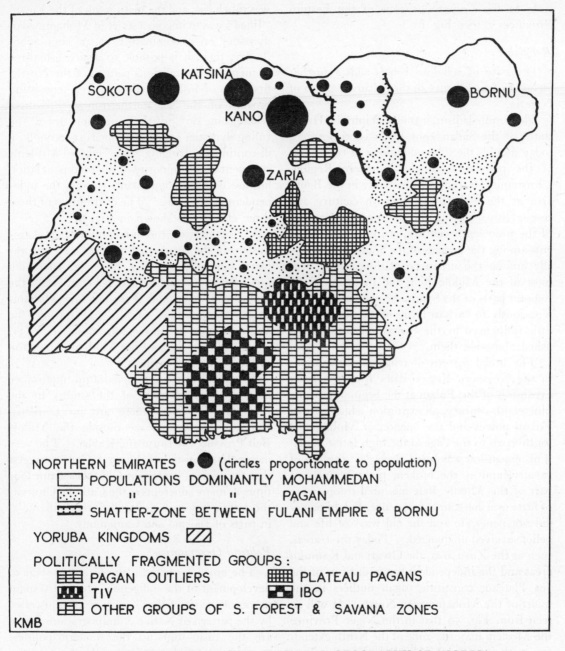

NORTHERN EMIRATES • ● (circles proportionate to population)

       ☐ POPULATIONS DOMINANTLY MOHAMMEDAN

       ⫶   "   "   PAGAN

       ▦ SHATTER-ZONE BETWEEN FULANI EMPIRE & BORNU

YORUBA KINGDOMS ▨

POLITICALLY FRAGMENTED GROUPS :

       ▦ PAGAN OUTLIERS   ▦ PLATEAU PAGANS

       ▨ TIV   ▦ IBO

       ▦ OTHER GROUPS OF S. FOREST & SAVANA ZONES

KMB

FIG. 60. MAJOR UNITS IN THE CULTURAL GEOGRAPHY OF NIGERIA

The three major types of society, the highly organised Mohammedan emirates of the north, the Yoruba kingdoms of the south-west and the politically fragmented peoples of the Middle Belt and the southern rain forest. The historical and social evolution of each of these groups and their mutual interaction have exercised an important influence on the present-day population pattern (cf. p. 62).

scale in the Cameroons zone of the Eastern Provinces. (See Fig. 65.)

Religion

Diversity of religious beliefs adds a further element of complexity to the cultural pattern of Nigeria.

Mohammedanism, introduced into the Hausa states of the Sudan zone seven centuries ago, today moulds the life and outlook of two-thirds of the population of the Northern Region. Christianity, introduced abortively in the Benin area at the end of the fifteenth century and re-established during the missionary expansion of the nineteenth century, claims many adherents among the peoples of the South and especially among the urban population. And over most of the Middle Belt, and in many of the remoter parts of the South, the population clings tenaciously to various forms of animistic belief, little influenced by the two world faiths established alongside them.

The broad pattern of religious distributions in the Northern Region dates from the great expansion of the Fulani at the beginning of the nineteenth century, an expansion which carried Fulani power and the religion of Mohammed southwards to the edge of the high forest zone.[1] This expansion was based largely on the use of cavalry, and in the broken, rocky country of part of the Middle Belt mounted troops were of little use; here, in consequence, Fulani power did not penetrate and the old ways of life and belief survived unchanged. Today these areas, such as the Zuru area, the Gwari and Kamuku areas and the independent pagan districts of the Jos Plateau, constitute pagan outliers in the midst of the Mohammedan North. It will be seen from Fig. 59 that in the Niger Province the Moslem majority zone of the North extends far south into the Middle Belt, broadly along the line of the modern main road between North and South. Elsewhere in the Middle Belt, however, the degree of penetration by Islam

was much less, and the main result of the Fulani "Jihad" was to impose a series of Mohammedan dynasties on a dominantly pagan population. Today, then, it is possible to distinguish three elements in the religious pattern of the North: firstly, a Moslem majority area consisting broadly of the six northern-most Provinces where some 90% of the population and all the ruling dynasties are Mohammedan; secondly, a discontinuous fringing zone where Moslems represent only a minority of the total population but are politically dominant; thirdly, the independent pagan areas. The distribution of these three elements is shown in Fig. 60.

Census data on the distribution of Mohammedans in the Southern Provinces were incomplete; generally speaking, however, Islam did not achieve any substantial penetration of the high-forest zone, and there are few Mohammedan communities of any size outside the Western Yoruba Provinces; these, in 1931, contained four-fifths of the Moslem population of the Southern Provinces.

Christianity attains its maximum importance in the coastal districts of the south; in the Northern Provinces there are no Christian communities of any size outside the Middle Belt Provinces of Ilorin and Kabba. The very incomplete statistics of the 1931 Census suggest that the various Protestant Churches claim four times as many adherents as the Catholic Church; the latter, however, is locally predominant, as in parts of Iboland and Cameroons.

Political Organisation [2]

The broad contrasts in the scale and stage of development of the indigenous political systems in various parts of the Territory are illustrated by the pattern of Native Administrations; these are the basic units in the modern political organisation of the country. In 1946–7 the twenty-four Provinces of Nigeria were split up into some 1,300 Native Administrations or subordinate Native Administrations ranging in

[1] On the Fulani "Jihad", see A. C. Burns, *History of Nigeria*, London (1948), pp. 44 *et seq.*
[2] M. Perham, *Native Administration in Nigeria*, London (1937); C. R. Niven, *How Nigeria is Governed*, London (1950).

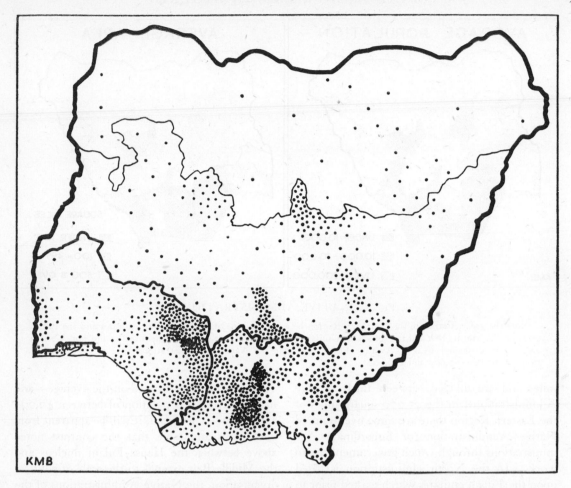

FIG. 61. THE DISTRIBUTION OF NATIVE ADMINISTRATIONS

Each dot represents one Native Administration or Subordinate Native Administration. Note the clustering of tiny units of local administration in the Ibo Provinces, in eastern Benue and in the pagan districts of the Middle Belt. Note, too, the "shatter zone" of smaller emirates along the western boundary of Bornu. The thin line represents the northern limit of the Middle Belt. (1946–7 data.)

character from the powerful Emirates of the Mohammedan North to the village units and clan units of parts of the South. They vary in size from Kano Emirate, one-quarter the size of England with a population of 2·6 million, to the tiny units of the Mamfe Division of Cameroons, with an average area of 20 square miles and a mean population of 1,100.

The distribution of Native Administrations, their mean size and population (by Divisions)

are shown in Figs. 61 and 62[1]; Table V summarises the main contrasts between the Regions and gives additional data illustrating the contrasts *within* the Northern and Western Regions.

It will be evident that the problems of administration are far greater in the South, and especially in the non-Yoruba areas of the South, than in the North. Thus the six most northerly Provinces (referred to conveniently as "Hausaland"), comprise an area of 150,000 square

[1] A list of Native Administrations is given in *Laws of Nigeria*, Vol. VIII, cap. 140.

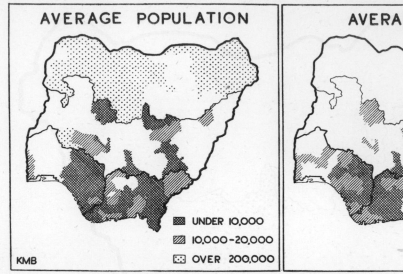
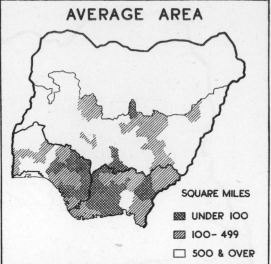

FIG. 62. NATIVE ADMINISTRATIONS

Note the great contrast in the Northern Region between the zone of Mohammedan emirates and the Pagan areas of the Middle Belt and the somewhat similar contrast in the south between the Yoruba and non-Yoruba areas. (In unshaded areas of Average Population map the Native Administrations have average populations of between 20,000 and 200,000.

miles and are divided between thirty Native Administrations; in the 45,000 square miles of the Eastern Region there are some five hundred Native Administrations or Subordinate Administrations through which government has to work. In the North administration is based upon the Fulani emirates which existed prior to the arrival of the British; they are large—almost

1,000 square miles in area on the average—and have an average population of between 40,000 and 50,000. In detail, it will be apparent from both maps and table that the contrast noted above between the Hausa-Fulani nucleus and the Middle Belt extends to the scale of political organisation, the Native Administrations of the six most northerly Provinces showing an average

TABLE V

AVERAGE SIZE, POPULATION AND REVENUE
OF NATIVE ADMINISTRATIONS IN THE REGIONS OF NIGERIA

	Area (sq. miles)	Population	Revenue (£)
NORTHERN REGION	921	44,000	10,000
Hausaland	5,030	300,000	70,300
Middle Belt	474	16,000	3,500
EASTERN REGION	87	10,000	1,350
WESTERN REGION	111	10,000	3,100
Yorubaland	196	19,500	6,700
Warri-Benin	61	4,500	1,000
(All figures rounded)			

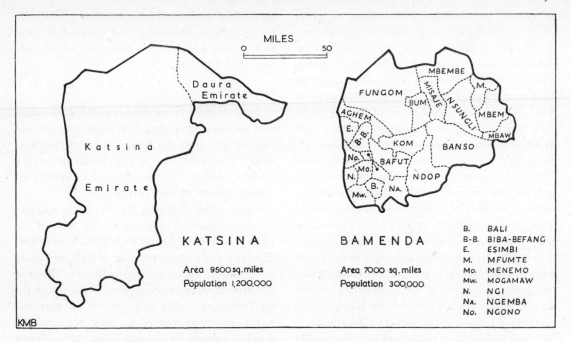

FIG. 63. CONTRASTS IN POLITICAL ORGANISATION BETWEEN THE PROVINCES
OF KATSINA AND BAMENDA

Katsina Province, which may be taken as typical of the Mohammedan north, has an area of 9,500 square miles and a population of 1,250,000; it comprises only two Native Administrations—the Emirates of Katsina and Daura. Bamenda Province, by contrast, has an area of 7,000 square miles and a population of only 300,000 but includes no fewer than twenty-three Native Administrations.

population of some 300,000 as against the average for the Middle Belt of 16,000. In this latter area, and especially in the pagan districts of Plateau Province and the northern sector of Niger Province, the development of local self-government has been based on administrations deliberately modelled upon the pattern of the Islamic North.

In the South, it is only in the Yoruba country that any approach to the strong indigenous political units of the Mohammedan North is found. Here the comparatively well-organised Yoruba chiefdoms had maintained their traditional forms of organisation, and a system of indirect rule through Native Administrations based upon these chiefdoms was built up in the early nineteen-twenties. In the remainder of the South political organisation is fragmentary in the extreme, and traditional authority frequently

does not extend beyond the family or clan area. The extension of the system of indirect rule to these areas is, in consequence, relatively recent (after 1928), and has necessitated the sedulous development by European administrative officers of Native Administrations based as far as possible on existing institutions.

Changing social and economic conditions are bringing about a gradual modification of the pattern shown in Fig. 61. This process of modification (or evolution) has been most marked in the Western Region, administratively perhaps the most advanced of the Regions, and has been prompted by the growing realisation that it is essential to have "units of local government large enough to ensure the maintenance of efficient services yet not so large that they become completely out of touch with the people they serve".[1] To achieve this, a twofold

[1] See *Local Government in the W. Provinces*, Lagos (1950).

policy has been pursued in the West in recent years. Firstly, in areas such as eastern and north-eastern Benin, where the typical Native Administration is small and lacking in resources, a policy of federation has been pursued, aiming at the creation of larger and stronger units of local government. As a result of this policy the total number of Native Administrations in the West has been reduced from 137 to 47. Secondly, for the larger centrally controlled Native Administrations a policy of decentralisation has been initiated, resulting in the establishment of subordinate Native Administrations in closer touch with the people; thus the million people of Ibadan Province are now organised into eleven Native Administrations as compared with five fifteen years ago. This twofold policy has been accompanied by a widening of the representation on all councils by the inclusion of more elected commoners and literate men, and by a widening of the sphere of responsibility of the Native Administration. These develop-

ments will go far towards establishing a broadly based pattern of strong and responsible local authorities, which is the essential basis for the new Constitution.

Revenue

Each Native Administration has a considerable measure of control over local taxation and expenditure, and the figures for their income, when related to area or population, provide a useful index to the wealth and prosperity of various sectors of the Territory.

Among the Regions, the Western occupies the most favoured position; on the basis of the 1949–50 revenue figures its Native Administrations enjoyed a mean revenue of £28 per square mile, almost twice the figure for the Eastern and almost three times as great as the figure for the Northern. Far more significant than the broad Regional contrasts, however, is the detailed pattern of revenue distribution (on a Divisional basis) shown in Fig. 64. It will be evident that the three Regions show a general similarity of pattern, each consisting of a block of relatively wealthy Native Administrations flanked by a peripheral zone within which revenue per square mile is but a fraction of that in the "core" area. It will further be apparent that the relatively wealthy Native Administrations are those in the major cash-crop zones of the Territory (compare Figs. 64 and 97). Thus, in the Western Region revenues are highest

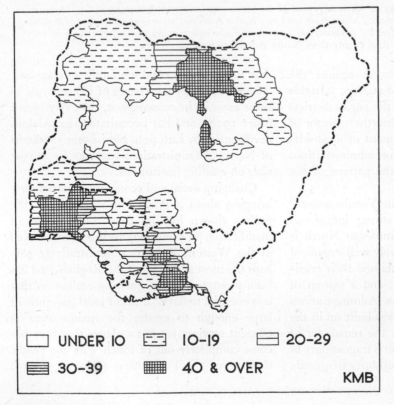

LEGEND:
UNDER 10   10–19   20–29
30–39   40 & OVER
KMB

FIG. 64. REVENUE (£ PER SQUARE MILE)

This map emphasises the duality in the economic and cultural make-up of each of the three Regions (cf. Figs. 36 and 57).

PLATE XV. THE TOWN OF IFE, WESTERN REGION

Ife is not only an important spiritual centre of the Yoruba people but also a flourishing commercial centre in the heart of the Cocoa Belt. Note the characteristic sprawling layout and the predominance of the rectangular, Southern Forest, style of architecture. Note, too, the relatively open character of the dry forest, resulting from heavy farming, and the level peneplain typical of the old-age surfaces of much of Nigeria.

PLATE XVI. PAGAN VILLAGE, JOS PLATEAU

The boulder-littered crests of isolated granite hills are favourite sites for settlement among the Pagan peoples of the Jos Plateau. Note the closely nucleated village surrounded by cactus hedge and half hidden among the boulders on the hill top. Pockets of deeper soil on the hillsides are cultivated but most of the farmland is found in the plain below. The euphorbia-hedged fields are kept in permanent cultivation, the open land beyond is farmed under a grass-fallow system.

**FIG. 65. ETHNIC COMPOSI-
TION OF THE REGIONS OF
NIGERIA**

None of the Regions is ethnically homogeneous and the ethnic
or linguistic contrast between the
Middle Belt and Hausaland is
reinforced by religious contrasts.

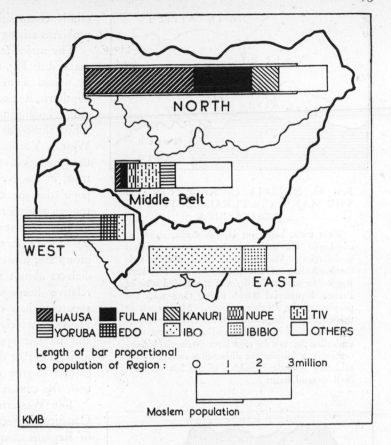

in the Cocoa Belt (Egba £82
per square mile, Ibadan £69)
and drop markedly in the
subsistence-crop areas of the
north-west (Oyo £10) and
north-east (Kukuruku £15).
In the Eastern Region the
main Palm Belt shows rev-
enues above £25 (Abak £81,
Ikot Ekpene £68), while in
the "pioneer fringe" of Ogoja
and eastern Calabar and in
the Cameroons revenues drop
well below £10 (Ikom £3,
Mamfe £3). In the North-
ern Region the high rev-
enue "core" is relatively
small; it comprises the Provinces of Kano (£50) and Katsina (with
an outlier in Jos Division), and coincides
with the major area of cotton and groundnut
production. Revenues over most of the remainder of the North and especially in the
Middle Belt are very low, dropping to £2·6 in
Lafia Division and £1 in Borgu.[1]

These contrasts in revenue form the essential
background to development policy in the
Territory. As can be seen from Fig. 64, over
much of Nigeria local revenues are very low
and are certainly inadequate to support those
ambitious schemes of social and economic
development which are essential if the potentialities of the Territory's "Empty Quarter"
are to be realised to the full. This is notably
the case in the Middle Belt. In these relatively
impoverished areas, development, at least in its

initial stages, must be dependent upon considerable injections of capital from outside if the
vicious circle of poverty breeding more poverty
is to be broken. The activities of the Regional
Production boards represent a promising step in
this direction.

Ethnic Composition of the Regions of Nigeria

In preceding paragraphs attention has been
confined to the racial and cultural pattern of the
Territory as a whole, and no attempt has been
made to discuss the detailed pattern of each
Region. Recent constitutional changes, however, and subsequent discussions, in the Press
and elsewhere, on the question of inter-Regional
boundaries have focused attention on this
regional pattern, and it is appropriate to con-
clude this section with a brief comment on the

---

[1] Based on revenue figures (by Divisions) supplied by the Regional Secretariats.

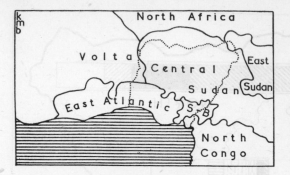

FIG. 66. NIGERIA IN RELATION TO THE MAJOR CULTURAL REGIONS OF WEST AFRICA

This map, based on H. Baumann, serves to emphasise the artificial character of political boundaries in West Africa. Note that the cultural affinities of the people of the Northern Region lie with the peoples of the Sudan zone of French Equatorial Africa rather than with the peoples of the southern forests. Maps such as this emphasise the wisdom of the recent policy of regionalisation in Nigeria and at the same time underline the need for close inter-territorial collaboration to minimise the dislocation caused by the arbitrary boundary-making of the last century. (S–B = semi-Bantu)

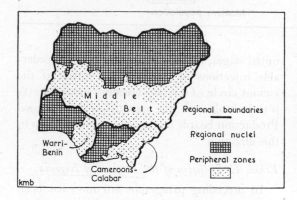

FIG. 67. THE DUAL MAKE-UP OF THE THREE REGIONS

Each Region consists of a core area, characterised by an advanced degree of economic development, by a high density of population and a high degree of ethnic homogeneity, and a peripheral zone with a lower degree of economic development, a thinner population and a more varied ethnic composition.

ethnic composition of the three Regions and problems arising therefrom.

The major features of the Regions are summarised in Fig. 65, based on the 1931 Census. It would seem at first glance that the two Southern Regions possess a greater degree of ethnic homogeneity than the Northern Region. Thus three-quarters of the population of the West is Yoruba-speaking, while two-thirds of the population of the East speak Ibo. By contrast, in the North, less than one-third of the population speak Hausa as their mother tongue, though together the Hausa and Fulani groups make up almost one half of the Region's population. Dialectal differences within the Ibo group are, however, so great as to make of the dialects almost separate languages so that the relative homogeneity of the East is more apparent than real. Further, in the North, Hausa is widely spoken as a second language and its use appears to have been spreading rapidly, so that the Region possesses a somewhat greater degree of cohesion and homogeneity than the census data would suggest.

The Western Regional Conference on the Constitution recommended that the three states or Regions comprising the federal unit should be formed "on an ethnic and/or linguistic basis"[1]; the difficulties inherent in such a suggestion will be apparent from Figs. 57 and 60, which, it should be stressed, give a highly simplified picture. Not one of the existing Regions approaches the ideal of an ethnic or linguistic unit; rather does each present a dual personality, consisting in each case of a "regional nucleus" occupied more or less compactly by a dominant group—Yoruba in the West, Ibo in the East, Hausa-Fulani in the North—with a peripheral zone occupied by minority groups. This duality has long been recognised in the case of the Northern Region,[2] where the contrast between the "Middle Belt" and the six northernmost Provinces constitutes the major feature of the Region's human geography; here the

---

[1] *Review of the Constitution: Regional Recommendations*, Lagos (1949), p. 19.
[2] On the contrast between the Middle Belt and the "Sudan Provinces" see K. Buchanan, "The Northern Region of Nigeria: the Geographic Basis of its Political Duality" in *Geographical Review* (October 1953).

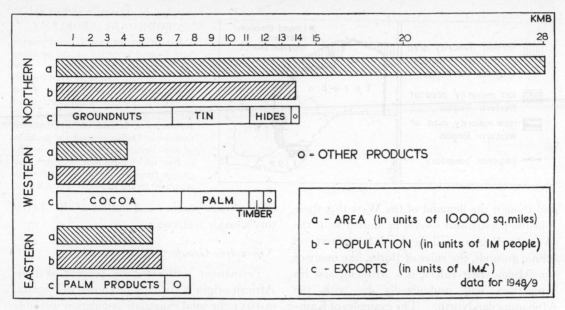

FIG. 68. AREA, POPULATION AND RESOURCES OF THE REGIONS

Emphasising the great contrasts in area and resources between the Regions, the highly developed character of the Western Region and the precarious over-specialisation of the Eastern Region.

linguistic contrast (Figs. 56, 65) is reinforced by religious factors (Fig. 59). It is no less important, though less widely appreciated, in the case of the Western and Eastern Regions. In the West the four Yoruba Provinces are clearly differentiated from Warri-Benin, and in the East, the physical, cultural and economic contrasts between Iboland and the Calabar-Cameroons zone are at least as great as the contrasts between "Hausaland" and "Middle Belt" (see, for instance, Figs. 57, 60–62, 64–65). Rigid application of the ethnic principle in boundary drawing in Nigeria is, in fact, impossible. It is impossible because, in many parts of Nigeria, the process of land occupation is far from complete and tribal movement is still in progress; the ethnic pattern is not static but dynamic (Fig. 52).[1] It is impossible because, even where today some measure of population stability appears to have been attained, past migrations and wars have left a legacy of complexly intermingled ethnic

groups, and without mass population transfers clearly defined ethnic boundaries cannot be drawn. And if these difficulties could be overcome it would be undesirable on economic grounds; the thinly peopled non-Ibo Provinces of Calabar and Cameroons are economically complementary to the over-crowded Ibo territories; the thinly peopled pagan Middle Belt with its great mineral wealth and water power is economically complementary to the more closely settled and dominantly agricultural territories of Moslem Hausaland.

In consequence, in spite of the recommendation quoted above, extensive modification of the existing pattern of Regional boundaries is unlikely, and application of the ethnic principle is likely to be limited to cases of minor boundary adjustment. For the moment, attention is directed to the northern and eastern boundaries of the Western Region. Beyond the northern boundary, the Provinces of Ilorin and Kabba contain an aggregate of half a million Yoruba,

[1] See, for example, C. W. Rowling, *Report on Land Tenure: Plateau Province*, Kaduna (1949), especially pp. 23–33, for an account of population movements in the Plateau area and of the social and economic problems which have arisen from such movements.

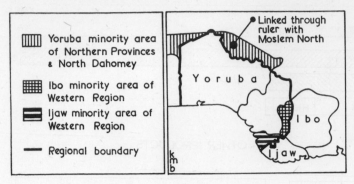

[IIII] Yoruba minority area of Northern Provinces & North Dahomey	
[####] Ibo minority area of Western Region	
[===] Ijaw minority area of Western Region	
——— Regional boundary	

FIG. 69. SOME NIGERIAN BOUNDARY PROBLEMS

Recent constitutional developments have focused attention on the problem of inter-Regional boundaries. The major problems arise in the West and fall under two heads: the problem of the substantial Yoruba minorities beyond the Regional boundary in Ilorin and Kabba (and beyond the international frontier in Dahomey) and the problem of non-Yoruba groups such as the Ibo or Ijaw which form part of larger tribal groups from which they are arbitrarily separated by the Regional boundary.

and though the demand of the West that these Yoruba populations should be united with the Western Region will be hard to gainsay on ethnic grounds, the ruler of Ilorin, like many of the Middle Belt rulers, is a Moslem, and his sympathies will undoubtedly be with the Mohammedan North. The examples of Kashmir and Hyderabad suggest the difficulties of finding a solution under these conditions. Along the eastern frontier of the Region, the Provinces of Benin and Delta contain an Ibo minority totalling 250,000 and, to the south of this group, an Ijaw minority of some 30–40,000. The Western Ibo group occupies a compact area along the western bank of the Niger, and their territory represents an extension of the Ibo nucleus of the Eastern Provinces; it is noteworthy that the economic links of the group, notwithstanding the water-barrier of the Niger, are with the East, rather than with the Western Region (Fig. 155). The Ijaw people present a somewhat similar problem, though as yet their political consciousness is less highly developed than among their Ibo neighbours. The Ijaw of Delta Province represent approximately one-fifth of the total Ijaw population of the South, and there is little in the physical or human geography of this part of the delta to justify the geometrical frontier which cuts them off from the main mass of Ijaw in Rivers Province. Boundary adjustment in these areas in conformity with ethnic principles would increase the population of the Eastern Region by some 300,000 and firmly establish the East in control

of the lower reaches and outlets of the Territory's major waterway.

Non-native Groups [1]

Permanent settlement by peoples of non-African origin is virtually unknown in Nigeria; in 1951 the total expatriate population was only 15,000 or some 0·06% of the total population, and of these the overwhelming proportion were transients, settling on retirement in the temperate zone. This is in striking contrast to the British East African Territories, where the highlands of Kenya and Tanganyika, with their more favourable climate and more responsive soils, have offered scope for large-scale and permanent settlement by Europeans. The non-African population of Nigeria may conveniently be considered under the two heads of (a) European and (b) other non-native groups.

(a) European Elements: European commercial and missionary contacts with Nigeria go back as far as the late fifteenth century, though these early contacts were confined to the immediate vicinity of the coast and were intermittent in character. Systematic commercial and political penetration of the interior, by contrast, did not begin until the closing years of the nineteenth century, and the existing pattern of European distribution has taken shape largely within the last generation.

The most striking feature of what for want of a better term may be termed the European occupation of the Territory is its thinness. In 1951 the total number of Europeans resident

[1] Based on unpublished estimates made available by the Regional Secretariats.

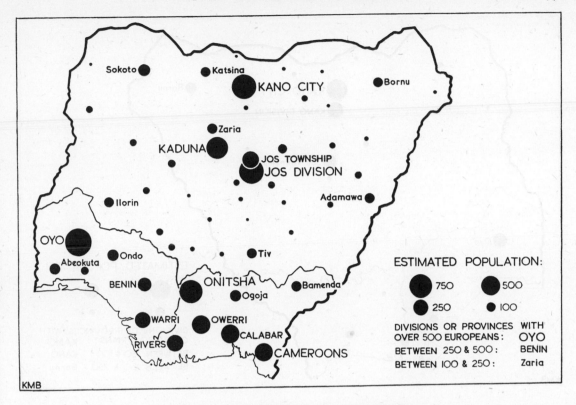

FIG. 70. DISTRIBUTION OF EUROPEANS

Major concentration is in the Cocoa Belt and Palm Belt of the South and in the commercial and administrative centres of the North. Numbers are insignificant in the Middle Belt and in the eastern and western sectors of the Sudan zone and consist largely of administrative personnel. At the end of 1952 the European population of the Lagos area was 4,200. Recently, Oyo Province has been sub-divided into Ibadan Province and Oyo Province; the greater proportion of the European population is resident in Ibadan Province.

in the Territory, and inclusive of wives and families, was 12,600. The significance of this figure is better appreciated if it is related, on a

TABLE VI

ESTIMATED EUROPEAN POPULATION IN THE THREE REGIONS[1]

Region	Europeans per Thousand Square Miles	Europeans per Million of Total Population
North	14·4	296
Middle Belt	6·5	209
West	39·5	452
East	55·7	421

[1] Excluding the Colony.

Regional basis, to area and total population.

The "dilution of effort in space" suggested by these figures constitutes one of the major problems of political and economic development in Nigeria.

A second striking feature is the extremely uneven distribution pattern, reflecting in part the uneven economic development of the Territory. The commercial and administrative significance of the Colony of Lagos is suggested by the size of its European community—4,200 in 1951. Outside the Colony the largest European community is that of Plateau Province; here, in a climatic environment unique in West Africa, mining, commerce and

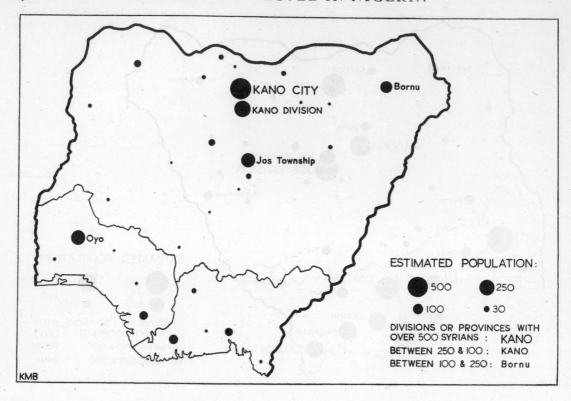

FIG. 71. DISTRIBUTION OF NON-EUROPEAN IMMIGRANT GROUPS

This category consists largely of Syrians with small numbers of Indians and Arabs. Major concentration is in the commercial centres of Ibadan, Jos and Kano, with a secondary concentration in the oil palm areas of the south. The 1952 Census gave a total of 100 Indians and some 500 Syrians and Lebanese in the Lagos area.

administration support a total of 1,200 Europeans. The Europeans of Kano Province (810) are largely concerned with administration or commerce, while the total for Zaria (660) includes the administrative and military personnel at the Regional capital, Kaduna. These three Provinces—Plateau, Kano and Zaria— together contain two-thirds of the Northern Region's European population.

In the South the largest totals are in the Provinces of Oyo (830), Onitsha (610) and Cameroons (500). In Oyo the city of Ibadan is the administrative centre of the Western Region and an important commercial and educational centre; Enugu, in Onitsha Province, is the headquarters of the Eastern Region and the centre of Nigeria's European-directed coal industry; the European population in the

Cameroons is concerned primarily with plantation development and to a smaller extent with missionary work.

The population figures quoted above give no indication of the national origins of the members of the immigrant community, nor do they throw any light upon the sex and age composition of the group. Brief comment on these two topics is, however, relevant. In terms of national origin the European group is dominantly British, the greater proportion of the immigrants being of United Kingdom origin with small numbers from most of the Commonwealth countries. There is, in addition, an important American element (6% of the European population of the South), while French, Swiss, and Italian enterprises have brought a small infusion of Continental

European elements. As in other parts of West Africa, significant changes in the sex and age composition of the European immigrant group have taken place in the last two decades. In the early stages of penetration few European women and fewer children came to the Coast, but with the establishment of settled conditions, with improved communications and health conditions during the inter-war years, it became increasingly common for wives to accompany their husbands to Nigeria for at least part of the tour. This tendency has increased during the last decade, while, at the same time, there is a growing tendency for younger children to spend their early years in Nigeria with their parents instead of, as of old, with relatives in Europe. This transformation of the expatriate way of life has had important consequences. Under its influence housing styles have tended to evolve in the direction of greater privacy and comfort, specialised shopping facilities in centres such as Lagos or Jos have expanded and a minor educational problem has been created. Even more important, taking the long-term point of view, has been the evolution of a self-contained European colonial way of life, nurtured by frequent leaves in the homeland and having relatively few social or cultural contacts with the African population. At the present stage of the Territory's development, when the very closest co-operation and understanding between Black and White is imperative, this is a development fraught with danger.

(b) *Other Non-native Groups:* The most important group in this category are the Syrians, though small numbers of North African Arabs (in Bornu) and Indians (in Lagos and Ibadan) are also included. These groups are dominantly traders and middlemen. They occupy a position analogous to that of the Jews in Eastern Europe, the Chinese in South-east Asia or the Indians and Arab communities of the East African littoral, and have played an important role in the economic development of parts of the Territory. Whether they will succeed in retaining their present commercial predominance in the face of growing competition from the African trader is problematical; it should, however, be stressed that they are unlikely to give rise to a problem of the magnitude of the East African Indian problem, for their numbers are small and they have shown no great interest in politics.

In 1951 "other non-natives" are estimated to have totalled 2,600. Of these, almost 1,500 resided in the Northern Region, 600 in the Colony, 350 in the Western Region and less than 200 in the Eastern Region. Regional figures, however, give an inadequate picture of their highly localised distribution (Fig. 71). Thus in the Northern Region almost four-fifths of the total are concentrated in the Provinces of Kano (860) and Plateau (280); the only other Province with a significant Syrian or Arab community being Bornu (150). The Middle Belt (excluding Plateau Province) has a total "other non-native" population of only 25, a significant index of its under-developed character. In the Western Region seven-tenths of the population in this category is to be found in Oyo Province (notably in the city of Ibadan), while the East Syrian activity in the palm produce trade results in a marked concentration in the southern coastal area.

In most administrative areas the "other non-native" population is very much smaller than the European population; in Kano Province and in Bornu Division, however, Syrians and related groups outnumber Europeans, while in Jos township they are only slightly inferior in numbers.

Possibly because of the absence of marked occupational cleavages within the group, the Syrian community is much more cohesive than its European counterpart; it is also more strongly rooted, for the regular leave abroad and the frequent transfers which tend to give the European a "footloose" character are less common in the Syrian community.

CHAPTER III

THE AGRICULTURAL ECONOMY

General Features[1]

The background to the agricultural economy of the Territory is provided by the "fundamental doctrine" to which Great Britain was committed by Sir Hugh Clifford in the nineteen-twenties. "Land policy should aim primarily, mainly and eventually at the development of the agricultural resources of these countries through the agency of their indigenous inhabitants." As a result, agriculture is based upon African peasant production, carried on by hand under traditional forms of land tenure, and, in contrast to the East African Territories, the role played by estate agriculture is relatively small. With the establishment of law and order in the country, and with the improvement of communications, production for internal trade expanded and a stimulus was given to the production of crops for export. Today it is possible to distinguish four elements in the agricultural economy of the country:

(a) *A Basic Subsistence Economy:* This is everywhere present, though its relative importance varies greatly from region to region. It attains its greatest relative importance in the inaccessible sectors of the Middle Belt and the Cameroons, and is of least importance in the cocoa-growing areas of Yorubaland, which are becoming dangerously dependent on food grown elsewhere in Nigeria. Because of the absence of statistical material, it is not possible to discuss in detail the contrasting distribution patterns of the major subsistence crops grown in the Territory; a general summary of the basic contrasts in the subsistence economies of Northern and Southern Nigeria is given below (pp. 105–115 and Fig. 82).

(b) *An Internal Exchange Economy:* The contrasting environments of North and South, each producing a characteristic assemblage of agricultural products, and the great variations in population density (and pressure upon food resources) between various areas, have encouraged the development of a flourishing internal exchange economy. The very great improvement in transport facilities during recent years, and the gradual rise of a land-divorced class in the larger towns and mining centres of the country, have resulted in a marked expansion of this branch of production. This trend has been favoured also by the relatively high prices and the greater stability of demand which the internal market offered. Commodities produced for this trade fall into two broad groups: basic foodstuffs, including guinea corn and cattle in the North, yams in the Middle Belt and palm-oil in the South, and more specialised crops, such as rice, fruit, sugar or kola nuts. The general area over which this type of production plays an important part in the local economy is illustrated in Fig. 72; production of some of the more specialised crops is discussed on pp. 116 et seq.

[1] The best account of the physical and social environment of the W. African peasant is given in H. Labouret's study *Paysans d'Afrique Occidentale*, Paris (1941). See also *West African Agriculture* by O. T. Faulkner and J. R. Mackie, Cambridge (1933) and *A Text-book of West African Agriculture* by F. R. Irvine, London (1944).

Farm and Forest, a quarterly published jointly by the Departments of Agriculture and Forestry at Ibadan, contains a wide range of articles on Nigerian land use. The progress of agriculture in each of the Regions is described in the *Annual Report of the Department of Agriculture*, Lagos.

The sociological background is provided by the series of reports on land tenure in various parts of the Territory published by the Nigerian Government Printer. The following have been published: Kano (1949); Niger (1949); Plateau (1949); Zaria (1949); Benue (1938); Ondo (1951).

In many areas local prosperity depends entirely upon this production for the internal market, and attempts to expand export production in such areas have failed completely. An outstanding example of this is afforded by Ilorin Province, which occupies an advantageous position with regard to the food-deficit areas of the Cocoa Belt, and which has a relatively favourable man/land ratio. Here attempts by the Agricultural Department to build up an export trade in groundnuts during the late nineteen-twenties proved unsuccessful; the output of yams, beans and onions for the internal market has, in contrast, expanded greatly, and in 1948 some 3,000 tons of miscellaneous agricultural products and 1,000 tons of yams were railed from stations in the Province, the yam tonnage representing a sevenfold increase over pre-war figures.

(c) *A Peasant Export-production Economy:* A detailed picture of the degree of development of this type of production is given in Fig. 72. Two main export crop regions may be distinguished: a northern zone, centring on Kano City and characterised by production of annual crops such as cotton and groundnuts and with an outlier in the benniseed and soya bean producing region of Benue Province, and a southern zone, extending across the high-forest region and characterised by the production of perennial tree crops, such as cocoa, palm produce and rubber. The pattern of production of these major export crops, based upon export gradings or export purchases, is illustrated in Figs. 100–127.

It should be stressed that, except in the case of cocoa and rubber, there is no hard-and-fast division between production for export and production for subsistence or local trade; thus, in years when guinea-corn production is low, groundnuts which would normally have entered the export trade are diverted to local consumption, while normally the amount of cotton sold for export depends on the relative price levels of the export and local markets and on the availability of imported goods, especially textiles.

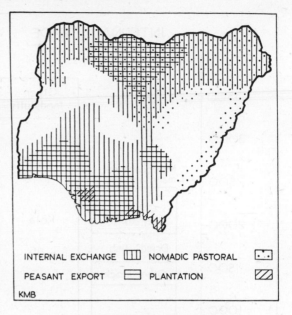

INTERNAL EXCHANGE |||| NOMADIC PASTORAL [·:·]

PEASANT EXPORT ⊟ PLANTATION ⧄

KMB

FIG. 72. DOMINANT TYPES OF ECONOMY

Production for subsistence is found in all areas and still represents the sole type of economy over much of the Middle Belt. Compare the distribution of cash (internal exchange and export) economies with the communications map (Fig. 154) and note the southward extension of pastoralism in the area of the Jos Plateau and the Cameroons Highlands.

(d) *A Plantation Economy:* This is of minor importance and is developed only in the coastal districts. The major development of this type of production is found in the former German territory of Cameroons; in addition, a small number of estates, owned by Nigerians or by European trading companies, are scattered through the palm- and rubber-producing areas of the South.

As shown in Fig. 72, all degrees of combination between these various economies are to be found in the Territory.

SUBSISTENCE AND INTERNAL EXCHANGE ECONOMIES

SYSTEMS OF CULTIVATION

The cultivation system of an area represents an equilibrium established by man, usually after

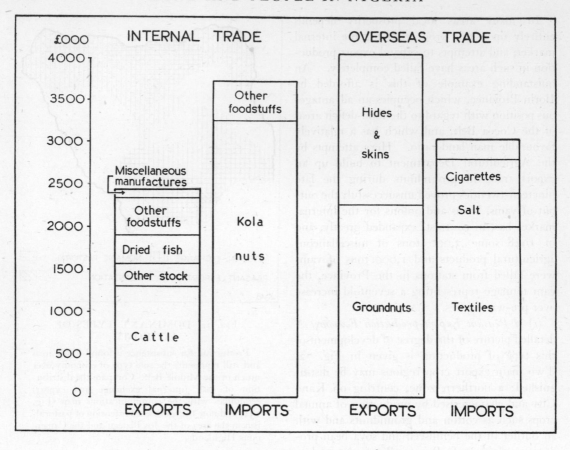

FIG. 73. THE TRADE OF KANO PROVINCE

The importance of internal trade in the economy of the Territory is strikingly illustrated by the fact that even in Kano Province, with its long tradition of production for overseas markets, the volume of trade with other parts of Nigeria is almost as great as the entire overseas trade.   Note the massive imports of kola nuts from the Western Provinces; a considerable proportion of these are in transit to other parts of the Sudan zone. Note also the important role of livestock in both the internal and overseas export trade.   (Based on figures given by B. E. Sharwood Smith "Kano Survey 1950".)

long centuries of trial and error, between himself, the physical environment (climate and soil) and what may be termed his "biological auxiliaries" (plants, animals and microfauna), and upon which his survival and progress depend.   Owing to the great variety of environmental conditions within the Territory, it is clear that a great variety of agricultural systems may be expected; the system of cultivation and the association of crops which will provide a dependable living in the rain-soaked forests of the south are unsuited to the drier areas of the Middle Belt, the cultivation practices

and crops suited to the more favoured parts of the Sudan Zone will fail on the skeletal soils of the Jos Plateau and the uplands of Adamawa. At the same time, it should be emphasised that the agricultural system of an area is rarely static, fixed for all time; it represents a state of equilibrium in a dynamic process of adjustment between man and his environment, and with change in one or more factors in the equation, modification of the system is inevitable.   The impulse for such a change may come from within the system itself or from without. Within the agricultural system, increasing pressure of population as a result of a more favourable ratio between births and deaths may necessitate important changes in cultivation practices; from without, the pressure of stronger people, the introduction of a new plant disease or of a new crop may lead to radical readjustments in the agricultural economy. Examples of all these processes may be found in Nigeria.

The distribution of land-use systems is thus not a fortuitous distribution; rather is it to be regarded as a definite pattern, a pattern which is closely related to, and explicable in terms of, the environmental background and historical experience of the area studied. In Western Europe, where a vast body of cartographic and statistical material is available, and where, over wide areas, a state of equilibrium has been reached, mapping of these patterns of land use and their interpretation offers no major difficulties, and a growing body of regional studies is available. In Nigeria, in contrast, owing partly to the inadequacy of the map coverage (see pp. 238–9) and of statistical material (especially relating to the major subsistence crops), and owing to the very size of the Territory, such a full discussion is not possible. All that can be attempted is to indicate the broad regional contrasts in systems of land use and to give an approximate and highly generalised picture of their distribution (Fig. 82).

As a basis for discussion, the following agricultural systems may be distinguished:

(a) Systems of shifting cultivation or bush fallowing; an infinite number of subdivisions may be distinguished within this general category.

(b) Systems of more or less stabilised terrace agriculture.

(c) Systems of permanent cultivation based on manuring and rudimentary crop rotation.

(d) Systems of rudimentary mixed farming.

(e) Intensive irrigated cultivation.

Systems of Shifting Cultivation or Bush Fallowing

Shifting cultivation may be defined as an economy of which the major features are rotation of fields rather than of crops; clearing by fire; absence in most cases of draught animals and larger types of stock; employment of the hoe, with the plough only exceptionally important; short periods of land occupancy and long periods of fallow. It is sometimes, and more accurately, termed "bush fallowing" or "field-forest economy" and in various forms is typical of the greater part of the Territory.[1]

The essential features of the system may be briefly outlined. The agricultural cycle commences with the selection of a plot of forest or savana woodland for clearing, areas with a dense tree-cover and therefore a thinner undergrowth and more humus-rich soil being generally preferred. Towards the end of the rains or at the beginning of the dry season this is cleared, the bigger trees are destroyed by ring-barking or firing at the base, the smaller trees, which provide the basis for the ultimate regeneration of the vegetation cover, are cut off some 3 feet above the ground. Economically valuable trees, such as the oil palm, the shea-butter tree, the locust-bean tree and the bigger timber trees, are left standing. After a few weeks the leaves and branches of the felled vegetation are thoroughly dry and they are then fired. Preliminary cultivation involves the throwing up of mounds or ridges on which the crop is sown,[2] though in some areas crops are sown on the flat and here preliminary cultivation is of

[1] On dearth of information regarding average size of farm holdings, see M. D. W. Jeffreys in *Farm and Forest*, Vol. VIII, No. 1 (1947), pp. 32–5. Scattered data assembled by Dr. Jeffreys shows a range of from 0·6 acres in parts of Calabar Province to 5 acres in the N. sector of Kano Province. Reassessment reports show a cultivated area of 5–8 acres in the Dan Zamo area of Gumel Emirate and in the Bomo area of Zaria, while Buxton found an average of 15 acres of cultivated land per household in the hamlet of Gata, N. Zaria. *The Anchau Rural Development and Settlement Scheme*, by T. A. M. Nash, London (1948), p. 8.

[2] Experimental work in both Nigeria and Tanganyika has demonstrated that ridge or mound cultivation gives striking increases in yields as compared with "flat" cultivation. See *Tropical Agriculture*, Vol. XXI, No. 9 (1944), pp. 177–8.

the scantiest. In regions with a markedly seasonal rainfall planting is timed so as to take maximum advantage of the rains and bring the harvest at the beginning of the dry season. During the period of growth an occasional cutlassing of weeds and of new shrub-growth is essential. The virgin soil is usually free from weeds and grasses, has a moderate humus content in its superficial layers, and receives additional fertilisation from the ash of the burned vegetation. In consequence, the cultivator obtains a good harvest in his first year, but with the depletion of humus and soil nutrients yields drop in the second year; further, weeds and bush invade the clearing. Under these conditions the plot is usually abandoned and a fresh clearing is made, while the old clearing reverts to second-growth vegetation and remains fallow for a period of from two to twenty years, depending on population pressure.

The area cultivated varies greatly according to climatic and soil conditions, from about 1 acre in the humid forest belt of the south to 10–15 acres in the subhumid north. To get a broad indication of the actual area cultivated over a period of years, the cropped area must be multiplied by a factor varying from 2 to 20, depending on the duration of the fallow period.

The typical plot is more appropriately termed a garden than a farm. Especially in the high-forest zone intercropping is usual and the plot presents a tangled and chaotic appearance; yams straggle over cotton bushes, maize rears its head above the tangled greenery, and gourds and pumpkins occupy the ground level. In the southern forest areas the basic crops are tubers, especially yams and cassava, grown usually on mounds or ridges and interplanted with maize, rice, peppers, vegetables and other crops. In the drier areas of the North grain crops, and especially guinea corn and millet, become the staples with oilseeds (groundnuts and, locally, benniseed) as important subsidiary crops. These shifting or rotational plots are supplemented by small garden areas in close proximity to the settlements (Fig. 77), which are kept in more or less permanent cultivation by manuring with waste products; these produce vegetables and a wide range of minor crops.

This system of cultivation is admirably suited to the environmental conditions of a Territory whose soils, over wide areas, are of only moderate fertility and liable to rapid exhaustion under crops. In spite of this, it has been so frequently criticised that a brief recapitulation of its many advantages is essential: it cashes in on the temporary fertility of forest or savana soils, supplemented by fertilising wood ash; it reduces liability to erosion by working the soil as little as possible and by preserving the natural vegetation intact around the cultivated plot; by its long

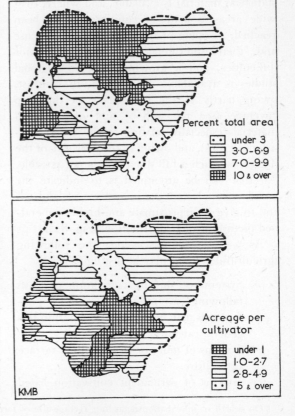

FIG. 74. CULTIVATED LAND

Data from 1931 Census. Note that the figures refer to Provincial units and that the Provincial average may conceal a wide range of variation within the statistical unit; an excellent example of this is provided by Kano Province (cf. Fig. 38).

fallow period it causes the minimum disturbance of the slow and delicate processes by which a certain measure of fertility is built up under the difficult conditions of the tropical environment; finally, in spite of the criticisms levelled against it by the European agriculturist, the latter has so far failed to find a satisfactory alternative form of land use for the poorer soils of the humid tropics. One important reservation must, however, be made: the system works admirably as long as the man/land ratio remains low, but breaks down under conditions of rapidly expanding population and rising densities; such a breakdown has begun in several parts of the Territory, notably in the high-density areas of Iboland and in the southern sector of Tiv Division.

Within the area dominated by this system of cultivation there are, as might be expected, variations in technique which can be used as a basis for distinguishing agricultural sub-types. It is thus possible to distinguish between bush fallowing based on hoe cultivation and the bush fallowing with plough cultivation of the central part of the Sudan zone; on the basis of rotation into field-forest cultivation and field-grass cultivation; on the basis of crops into bush fallowing based on root crops and bush fallowing based on cereals. For present purposes this latter distinction is the most useful, and the contrast between the Southern Root Economy and the Northern Grain Economy is of fundamental importance in the agricultural geography of the Territory.

(a) *The Southern Root Economy:* This is characterised by the cultivation, on a bush fallow system, of yams and cassava, with maize, rice and beans as subsidiary food crops. It extends, in an attenuated form, to somewhat north of latitude 10° N., but attains its most characteristic development in the high-forest country of the south; here the oil palm is an important element in both the subsistence and cash-crop economies, and the collection of sylvan products plays a subsidiary role of some significance. On the basis of cultivation tech-

niques, it may be subdivided into areas with a medium to long fallow period (5–15 years), and areas where, because of population pressure, the fallow period has been reduced to dangerously small proportions.

Except in the immediate vicinity of towns, much of the Yoruba country is farmed under a system of medium-length fallows. A fairly typical rotation (in Ondo Province) has been described by Allison[1]: "The area is cleared in February and the slash is burned soon after. . . . The main crops of yams and corn are planted with the first rains, together with pumpkins, melons and calabashes. When the first corn is harvested about June, beans, cassava, okra and cocoyams may be planted. A second crop of corn is planted in August and harvested in October or November; yams are harvested in September or October. If the ground has proved fertile a third corn crop may be planted in the following rains and the farmer may return for a year, or even two, to dig his cassava and cocoyams . . . the land is thus cropped intensively for one year while certain parts of the farm may be tended rather casually for a second year." The duration of the fallow in this area varies from 8 to 14 years according to soil conditions.

In Iboland, by contrast, population densities are, as has been pointed out elsewhere (p. 60), very high, and over much of the area the duration of the fallow period is dangerously short. On the outer farmlands the usual crop sequence is a year under yams or, less often, beans or cassava, followed by 3–4 years fallow. Under these conditions the natural vegetation has no opportunity to regenerate, and there has been a progressive degeneration, resulting in the replacement of high forest by barren grassland over wide areas. Such grasslands are of little use except as rough grazing, and their protective value is reduced by their tussock character and by annual grass fires, which lay bare the soil to erosion by the heavy rains of summer. The beginning of large-scale gulley erosion in parts of this area is an indication of the final collapse

[1] P. A. Allinson, "From Farm to Forest", *Farm and Forest*, Vol. II, No. 2 (1941), pp. 95–6.

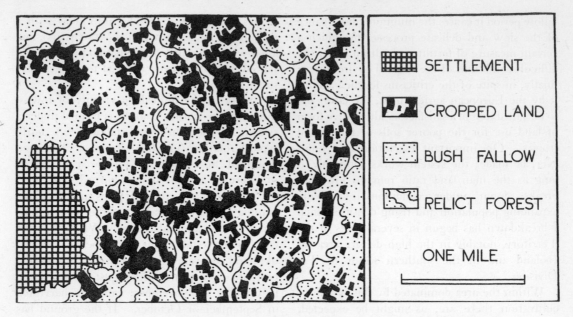

FIG. 75. LAND USE IN THE DRY FOREST ZONE OF IBADAN PROVINCE

A typical agricultural landscape in an area of relatively high population density. Complex pattern of small plots in a setting of secondary bush and occupying approximately one-third of the area. Relics of the original high forest survive only along the valleys; on the farmland the fallow period is too short to allow the regeneration of the high forest.

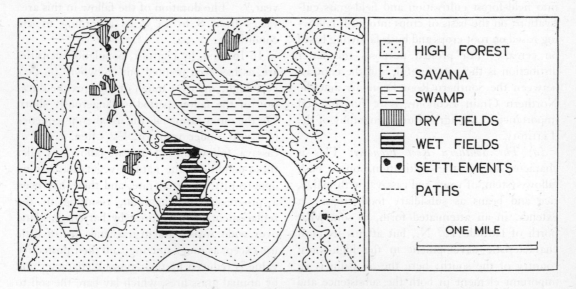

FIG. 76. LAND USE IN THE FOREST ZONE OF KABBA PROVINCE

This is an area of relatively low population density and in consequence tracts of high forest still survive, in a setting of secondary bush and riverside swamp. Note the small and scattered settlements, the isolated patches of dry-field cultivation, the extensive areas of open bush resulting from cultivation and abandonment and the compact area of wet-field cultivation in the swampy area to the south of the main settlement.

of the system of bush fallowing as a result of increasing pressure of population.

(b) *The Northern Grain Economy:* This is dominated by guinea corn and millets, with groundnuts as a subsidiary crop on the lighter soils. It attains its most characteristic development in the Sudan zone of the extreme N., but extends as far south as latitude 7° north, overlapping the Southern Root Economy in the Middle Belt. As in the case of the Southern Root Economy, a twofold subdivision is possible into areas with a generally adequate fallow period and areas where the fallow period is too short to permit the restoration of fertility; because of the much lower pressure of population over most of the North, these latter areas are of only limited extent.

Buxton's survey of the hamlet of Gata,[1] in the northern part of Zaria Province, illustrates admirably the general features of the farming system under conditions of medium density of population. As in the southern forest, a broad distinction must be drawn between compound and/or garden land and the outer farmlands proper. The former, which in Gata amounted to one-quarter of the total cultivated area, is kept under permanent cultivation by means of heavy manuring; household waste and ashes are used, together with the dung of goats and donkeys and the manure of nomadic Fulani cattle which visit the village during their dry-season migrations. The outer farmland, by contrast, is rarely manured; it is worked on a rotation of 4 years under cultivation (with cotton and guinea corn alternating), followed by a variable fallow period, ranging from 4 to as much as 30 years. All cultivation is by hand and the land is not stumped, so that rapid regeneration of the savana woodland is possible. The average area cultivated by each family is as high as 15 acres. Of this, 7 acres are under guinea corn, the main food crop, 7 acres under cotton and the remaining acre under minor crops such as cassava, beans, millet, maize, groundnuts and peppers; of these, millet, maize

or beans are also occasionally grown as an inter-crop between the guinea corn or the cotton. With the minimum fallow period, and assuming one-tenth of the village area is needed as a fuel reserve, the maximum density of population which this system can support may be estimated at 130 per square mile; such an estimate is based on the assumption, rarely realised, that all the land outside the fuel reserve is cultivable, and it serves to underline the limited carrying capacity of this system of cultivation in areas of medium fertility.

The disintegration of the system under the combined influences of population increase and outside pressures is well illustrated by conditions in the closely settled pagan areas of the Jos Plateau. In this area, over long periods of time, the shattered fragments of weak and primitive tribes sought refuge from the slave-raiders of the Sudan zone, dwelling in cactus-hedged villages on the hilltops and practising a system of bush fallowing centring on millet and the poverty-tolerant cereals *acha* and *tamba*. Soils are often poor and skeletal, yields are low and the area needed to support a family is large (4·2 acres per adult); consequently, with increasing population during recent decades, an ever-increasing proportion of the total area has been brought into cultivation, fallow periods have been reduced, and with the extinction of the original savana vegetation, the system of bush fallowing has been replaced by a system of grass fallows. Outside factors, notably the development of tin-mining which has diverted considerable areas from agricultural production (one-seventh of the Gyel village land), have aggravated the pressure of population and today the agricultural economy of the more closely settled areas is on the verge of collapse.

The Gyel Farm Survey, carried out by J. G. Davies,[2] provides the statistical background to this general picture. Arable land, in the Gyel district, represents 60% of the total area, the remainder being lost to agriculture through mining or useless on account of its rocky or

[1] T. A. M. Nash, *Anchau Rural Development and Settlement Scheme*, London (1948).
[2] J. G. Davies, "The Gyel Farm Survey in Jos Division", *Farm and Forest*, Vol. VII, No. 1 (1946), pp. 110–13.

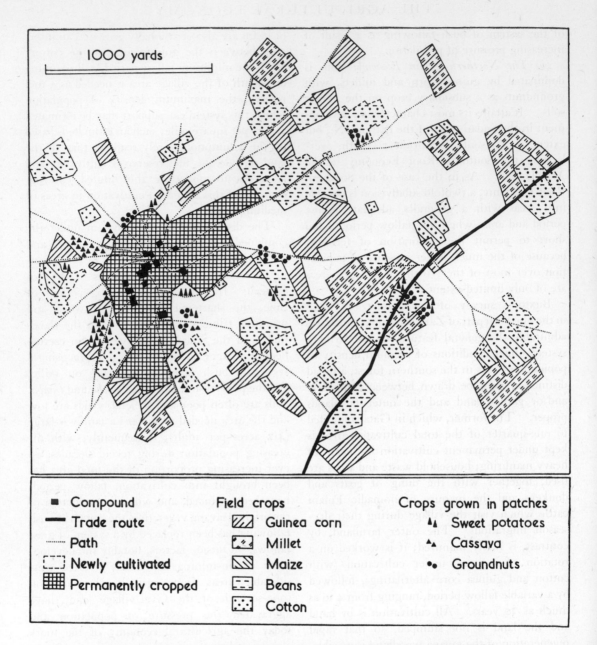

Key

Compound

■ Compound
▬ Trade route
⋯ Path
⌐ ⌐ Newly cultivated
▦ Permanently cropped

Field crops

▨ Guinea corn
⋰ Millet
▧ Maize
⊟ Beans
⋰⋰ Cotton

Crops grown in patches

◢◣ Sweet potatoes
▲ Cassava
•• Groundnuts

FIG. 77. LAND USE AROUND GATA VILLAGE, ZARIA PROVINCE

Illustrating the typical features of land use under a system of bush fallow. Land under cultivation totals 15 acres per household; of this, 7 acres are in cotton, 7 acres in guinea corn and the remainder in miscellaneous crops which are also interplanted with the guinea corn and cotton. In addition, each household has 15 acres of fallow. Note the zone of permanent cultivation in the immediate vicinity of the settlement; this is manured with household refuse and animal manure, including the manure from Fulani cattle; it represents about a quarter of the total cultivated area. The remainder is periodically fallowed, the usual period of cultivation being four years, followed by a fallow period usually three to six years but extending to as much as forty years on poorer soils. (Map and details based on T. A. M. Nash.)

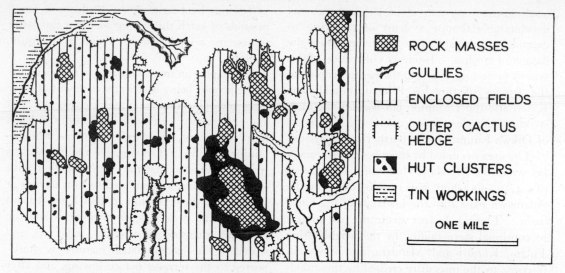

ROCK MASSES

GULLIES

ENCLOSED FIELDS

OUTER CACTUS HEDGE

HUT CLUSTERS

TIN WORKINGS

ONE MILE

FIG. 78. THE LAND USE PATTERN OF A PAGAN VILLAGE, JOS PLATEAU

Note the main settlement clustering around the edge of a series of broken granite hills (defence motive) with later settlement dispersed amid the farmlands around the village. The hatched area is the household land of the village; it is divided into tiny fields by a network of euphorbia hedges (not shown here but see Plate XVI) and is kept in permanent cultivation by the use of household waste and manure. The whole settlement is bounded by a thick outer hedge of euphorbia. Beyond the settlement proper (and outside the limits of the map) are the bush farmlands where the staple crops (acha, dauro, tamba, yams) are grown under a system of bush fallowing.

barren character; further, of the land actually cultivated some was "so poor that the Kano surveyors said Kano farmers would consider it barren land", and one-tenth was classed as "unprofitable" in that it gave very poor yields and was susceptible to erosion. Of the arable area, fallow land occupied 28%, *acha* 40%, millet 16% and other crops 10%. As is evident from these figures, the fallow period has been reduced to negligible proportions, and is now represented by an odd year or two under grass at the end of 4–6 years of cultivation; its role in restoring the soil's depleted fertility is reduced by over-grazing by immigrant Fulani herds and by the practice of using for fuel (in the absence of wood) both the cattle droppings and the grass itself. Only on the household lands is productivity being maintained; these represent one-tenth of the total agricultural area, are cactus-hedged and are kept in permanent cultivation by the use of livestock manure and household wastes. This is an area which supports one of the densest cattle popula-

tions in Nigeria and where the possibilities for the development of intensive mixed farming are greater than in any area outside the central sector of the Sudan zone; that so little progress has been made in this direction serves to underline the importance of the human factor (here the antagonism between the nomad Fulani and the pagan cultivator) in the agricultural development of the Territory.

Terrace Agriculture

Skilful and well-developed farms of terrace agriculture are to be found among the pagan peoples in many parts of the Territory; they are invariably associated with a defensive hill-top concentration of settlement, and represent a natural adjustment to the difficulties of an upland environment. Faced with the difficulty of getting a living from limited areas of often thin and skeletal hill soils, the hill dweller develops systems of intensive cultivation, using organic wastes of all types to build up the soil's fertility and to eliminate as far as possible the

L.A.P.—9

land-expensive system of bush fallowing, and developing elaborate systems of terracing to extend his cultivable area and to minimise the danger of erosion. Intensive cultivation of this type is to be found among the pagan peoples on the fringes of the Jos Plateau, notably the Kaleri and the Dimmuk, but possibly the most striking example is found among the hill pagans of Dikwa Emirate in the northern Cameroons.[1]

The area occupied by these peoples is usually known as the Mandara Mountains, and consists of a 4,500-foot-high spur running out from the Adamawa mass into the lowlands of the Chad basin. The whole area was in the past subject to continual slave-raiding by the neighbouring Fulani, Kanuri and Mandara, and it was in response to the insecurity created by these raids that the present pattern of hill settlement evolved. It is a tribute to the ingenuity and labour of the pagan farmer that the rocky hill-sides and grudging soils of the area were able to support a population whose density, at the beginning of British occupation in 1919, has been estimated at over 130 per square mile. This intensive system of land use was based on four major principles: prevention of erosion by terracing; heavy use of animal and human waste to build up the nutrient status of the soil; a simple rotation of crops to minimise depletion of fertility; and the planting and protection of trees to provide supplementary animal and human food. Except where topographic conditions make it quite impossible, the hill slopes are girdled with an elaborate system of drystone terraces. The terrace walls range in height from a few inches to as much as 10 feet, and they extend around every spur and re-entrant; according to Stanhope White, their aggregate length is of the order of 20,000 miles. The width of the plots thus created is usually between 5 and 10 feet, though occasionally they may be so narrow as to permit the sowing of only one line of corn. On gentler slopes less elaborate systems of erosion control are used, notably lines of fascines held in place by boulders or small mounds of earth thrown up by hoes; this latter represents a rudimentary form of contour-banking.

Cattle play an important role in the social life of the people, being used in the payment of bride price and of blood money; they are also sacrificed and eaten on ceremonial occasions. Even more important, however, is their role in maintaining fertility. Grazing on the terraces is strictly limited so that the cattle, together with sheep and goats, are confined to huts during at least part of the year; they are then hand-fed and watered, and bedded down with grass and the resultant manure is carefully collected and stored. The accumulated manure is transported to the terraces before sowing, and after the crop has appeared above ground is carefully scattered around the plants. Human excreta and ashes and other household waste are also utilised, and weeds are collected and composted down for later use.

Cropping is based on a simple three-year rotation: guinea-corn, beans (often with a little *tamba* sown on the edge of the terraces); bulrush millet with some beans. With such a rotation and manuring on the lines described above, plots can be cropped for ten successive years; while more distant plots which receive little manure may be used for two years only, then fallowed for a similar period. When a plot has been exhausted it is fallowed, usually for two years; it is then manured with grass, wood ash and household sweepings, and tiger-nut (*Cyperus esculentus*) is planted. Crops of this are taken for two to three years, by which time the land is usually sufficiently fertile to be brought back into rotational cropping. In addition to the crops listed above, Bambara groundnuts, sweet potatoes and maize are grown on a small scale, together with onions if suitable irrigable land is available.

Finally, as among some of the mountain peoples of Europe, trees play an important part

---

[1] S. White, "Agricultural Economy of the Hill Pagans of Dikwa Emirate", *Empire Journal of Experimental Agriculture*, Vol. IX, No. 35 (1941), and H. D. Tupper-Carey, "Fattening of Cattle at Gwoza", *Farm and Forest*, Vol. V, No. 4 (1944).

in the pagan economy, supplying leaves, seeds and oil for human consumption, seeds and leaves for fodder, and wood for building and for fuel. Especially important in these respects are the desert date, the fan palm, the acacia (Gawo or *Acacia albida*) and the African mahogany.

This highly specialised agricultural economy developed in response to special historical circumstances, viz. past insecurity due to slave-raiding; and as these circumstances have changed, the old pattern of settlement and land use is tending to break down and the hill dwellers are gravitating towards the more easily cultivated plains. This is a trend which is not peculiar to this north-eastern corner of Nigeria, for the same circumstances are found to a greater or lesser degree among many of the pagan hill dwellers of the Middle Belt. Administratively it is perhaps advantageous, but from the land-use standpoint it is fraught with danger, involving in the majority of cases the abandonment of

old conservational systems of farming in favour of land-expensive systems of shifting cultivation, which are destructive of both vegetation and soil. Only by careful planning and guidance can these dangers be avoided; the possibilities of such controlled population redistribution are suggested by the Shendam Settlement Scheme, which offers a pattern for planned rural development in the more backward areas of the Territory.

Permanent Cultivation

Continuous cultivation, based upon simple crop rotations and the use of manure on permanent and well-defined holdings, is developed chiefly in the vicinity of the bigger towns of the Sudan zone, where the light, easy-working soils lend themselves to intensive cultivation, and where the absence of the tsetse fly makes possible the keeping of larger types of stock. Cultivation of this type, often with

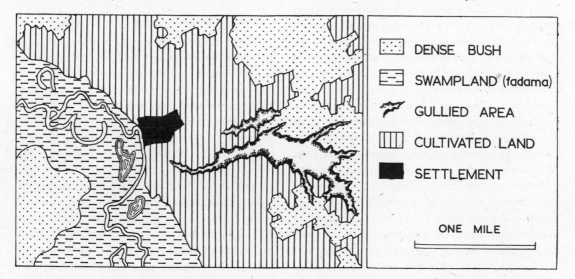

DENSE BUSH

SWAMPLAND (fadama)

GULLIED AREA

CULTIVATED LAND

SETTLEMENT

ONE MILE

FIG. 79. LAND USE IN A SECTION OF THE ZAMFARA VALLEY, SOKOTO PROVINCE

Note the extensive zone of cultivated land surrounding the town; this close-farmed zone, kept in continuous cultivation by the use of animal manure and household wastes, is a typical feature of the agricultural landscape of the Nigerian Sudan zone, and is seen at its most striking in the Kano area.

The threefold sequence of land use types illustrated here—alluvial swamp (*fadama*), cultivated sand slopes and bush-covered upper slopes (often ironstone-capped)—is very characteristic of much of Sokoto Province. Since any extension of the cultivated area on the higher land is rendered difficult by the infertility of the soil and by the need for maintaining around each settlement a considerable area of bush as a fuel reserve, the main hope for expanding agricultural production lies in the utilisation of the fadamas for crops such as rice; this is being done in the Birnin Kebbi-Argungu area but elsewhere the main role of the fadamas is still that of dry-season grazing grounds for Fulani cattle.

subsidiary irrigated cultivation along streams (see below), is found around Sokoto, Zaria, Katsina and Maiduguri, and attains its highest degree of development in the Kano close-farmed zone. Conditions in this latter area illustrate the general characteristics of the system.[1]

The Kano close-farmed zone occupies an area of some 2,000 square miles, forming an irregular ellipse with Kano City as its centre. The density of rural population is extremely high by African standards—taking the zone as a whole it is between 400 and 500 per square mile—and this has been made possible by a favourable combination of historical and physical factors; by the security afforded by the Kutumbawa state and its Fulani successor; by the presence of easily accessible ground-water supplies; and by the easy-working sandy soils which lend themselves to intensive cultivation. Of the total area, some 90% is under cultivation; even so, as a result of population pressure, holdings are small (3–4 acres), and to produce an adequate supply of basic foodstuffs and of the export crops upon which the local economy is coming increasingly to depend, the Hausa cultivator has developed a skilful system of intensive land-use. Cropping is based on the food grains, millets and sorghums, which occupy 57% of the cropped area, and groundnuts, which occupy 31%. In addition, minor crops, such as cassava, sugar-cane, cocoyams and sweet potatoes, are produced, often on the heavier soils beside streams or on the floor of small marshy depressions. Every available type of manure is utilised: the droppings of sheep, goats and donkeys and of migrant cattle, ashes and household waste. Further, many of the farmsteads are insubstantially built of corn stalks thatched with mud, and these are periodically dismantled, and the site, enriched with household refuse, is cultivated while a new dwelling

is built elsewhere on the farm. An additional source of nitrogen is provided by the leaf fall of the various farm trees (notably various species of acacia) which are dotted about the holdings. By these means, the farmer maintains a reasonable level of fertility in soils which have inherently a relatively low nutrient status, and has succeeded in eliminating the need for long periods of fallow.

The cultural landscape of these close-farmed areas is unique in Nigeria; except for the numerous farm trees, the natural vegetation has been obliterated over wide areas, and the land is parcelled out into small fields, bordered by boundary hedges of henna, euphorbia or *jema* grass, and closely dotted with small thatched farmsteads. It is a landscape contrasting strikingly with the landscape of irregular shrub-invaded clearings typical of the Guinea zone or the forest-girt plots of the southern high-forest zone.

Systems of Rudimentary Mixed Farming[2]

Mixed farming, involving a balance of crops and stock on individual holdings, the use of the plough and of animal manure to obviate the need for fallowing, is a relatively recent development, introduced from without by the Agricultural Department. Nevertheless, the shadowy beginnings of such a system (though without the plough) can be traced among farming groups in many parts of the Territory. The intensive agriculture of the Kano close-farmed zone, the more primitive farming systems of groups such as the Mumuye of Adamawa, are based, in part at least, upon the use of animal manure; while the practice among many cultivators of arranging for the kraaling of Fulani cattle on their land illustrates how widespread is the appreciation of the value of animal excreta in producing better crops and maintaining fertility. One of the major obstacles to the development of an

[1] D. F. H. McBride in *Journal Royal African Society*, Jan. 1938, p. 77. See also *Annual Report on the Department of Agriculture*, 1932 and 1933.
[2] E. R. Russell, "Primitive Farming in Nigeria: the Mumuye Tribe", *Empire Journal of Experimental Agriculture* (1940), and S. White, "Mixed Farming as Practised by some Shuwa Arabs in Dikwa Emirate", *Farm and Forest*, Vol. II, No. 1 (1941), pp. 24–6.

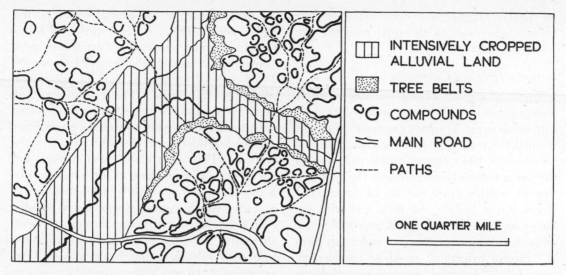

FIG. 80. LAND USE ON THE OUTSKIRTS OF BIDA, NIGER PROVINCE

One of the most striking features of the agricultural geography of the North is the intensive utilisation of alluvial areas lying within or close to the major population centres. Such land lends itself admirably to the production of specialised crops such as sugar-cane or rice or to dry-season crops such as vegetables, in which case it may be irrigated by a simple "shaduf". The alluvial land on the fringes of Bida is devoted largely to cassava, sweet potatoes and rice and will produce two crops of maize per annum; elsewhere in Nupe onions are widely grown on such land. Note the characteristic open irregular layout of Nupe settlement; note too, that the scale of this sketch is four times the scale of the preceding sketches.

indigenous system of mixed farming has in the past been the concentration of virtually the entire cattle population in the hands of a nomadic group—the Fulani—who have shown little interest in crop production, and the consequent difficulty experienced by the settled cultivator in obtaining cattle. Stanhope White has, however, described the beginnings of a system of mixed farming among the Shuwa Arabs, a dominantly pastoral group inhabiting the Chad basin. Here, during the rainy season, part of the herds migrate to wet-season grazings, but the remainder are kept in the village and, to escape the attacks of blood-sucking flies, are kept penned in huts (tumtums) during the hottest part of the day. The accumulated manure is removed daily and either spread on the maize or millet crop or is stored in a communal heap in the middle of the settlement. At the beginning and the end of the rains, before the fly attacks become severe, the cattle may be kraaled on the surrounding fields. Periodically, as the huts on the old site

collapse, a new settlement is built some distance away and new fields of maize and millet are laid out; the old site is meanwhile levelled, the accumulated manure is spread and the land brought into cultivation. Such a system does not do away completely with the need for shifting, for the Shuwa still shifts, but less often, and within a relatively restricted area.

The tentative beginnings of production of farmyard manure by bedding down the cattle on grass and other roughage has been described in the account of the hill pagans of Dikwa Emirate; this, however, is exceptional and as a broad generalisation it may be said that the systematic production of farmyard manure as an essential and major element in the agricultural economy, together with the growing of crops solely for livestock consumption and the use of the plough (all features of the mixed farming system of Western Europe), had no place in the Territory's indigenous cultivation systems; they are "exotic", introduced by Western agriculturists, accepted hesitantly by the peasant farmer and even today of only limited importance in the rural economy (see below, pp. 123–5).

Intensive Irrigated Cultivation

Partly as a result of unfavourable environmental conditions, the contribution of irrigated cultivation to the Territory's agricultural output is small. Crops such as sugar-cane, rice and various vegetables are grown on seasonally flooded riverine or *fadama* land throughout the Northern Region, notably in the vicinity of the cities of Kano, Zaria, Sokoto and Bida, and with the use of modern machinery and improved water utilisation techniques, the area under this form of "natural irrigation" could be considerably expanded. "Artificial" or man-controlled irrigation, as opposed to natural or flood irrigation, for the purposes of dry-season cropping occupies a more restricted area. The use of handscoops for watering the onion crops on the drier parts of Oyo and Ilorin Provinces represents a rudimentary form of irrigation, while a more developed technique is represented by the *shaduf* irrigation of the central sector of the Sudan zone. Here, in the vicinity of Kano City and Zaria, a wide range of dry-season crops—onions, carrots and other vegetables—is produced on small streamside plots for sale in the adjoining urban areas. The great majority of northern streams, however, carry little water over the winter months, so that the possibilities of extending this type of cultivation are extremely limited. This is particularly unfortunate, for one of the major problems of agriculture in the Kano–Katsina–Zaria area is its highly seasonal character which, combined with heavy population pressure, forces many farmers to seek alternative forms of employment, often away from their villages, during the dry season. An extension of the area under irrigated dry-season crops would reduce this necessity and would add greatly to local wealth. The alternative of irrigation from wells using bullock lifts (as practised in parts of the Middle East) does not appear to hold out any great promise, at least in the Kano area, for though water in small quantities is easily accessible by shallow wells,

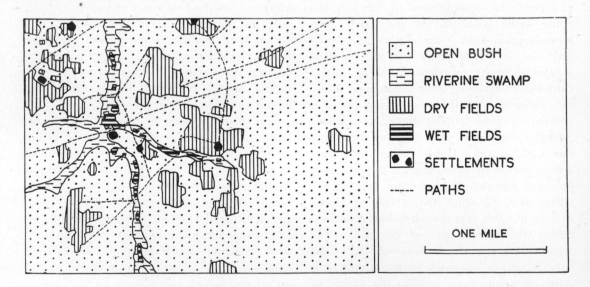

KEY:
- OPEN BUSH
- RIVERINE SWAMP
- DRY FIELDS
- WET FIELDS
- SETTLEMENTS
- PATHS

ONE MILE

FIG. 81. LAND USE IN THE VICINITY OF THE GBAKO RIVER, NIGER PROVINCE

Two contrasting types of land use; dry-field cultivation, based upon a system of bush-fallowing and producing crops such as millets, sorghums or maize; and more specialised wet cultivation of small alluvial plots on the valley floors. These latter plots may be kept under continuous cropping and produce more exacting crops such as rice, sugar cane or onions.

it has proved virtually impossible to find wells which would yield water in quantities sufficient to make such a development practicable. Only in certain geologically favoured areas, such as the Chad basin, where more plentiful supplies of underground water appear to exist, does any significant development along these lines seem likely.

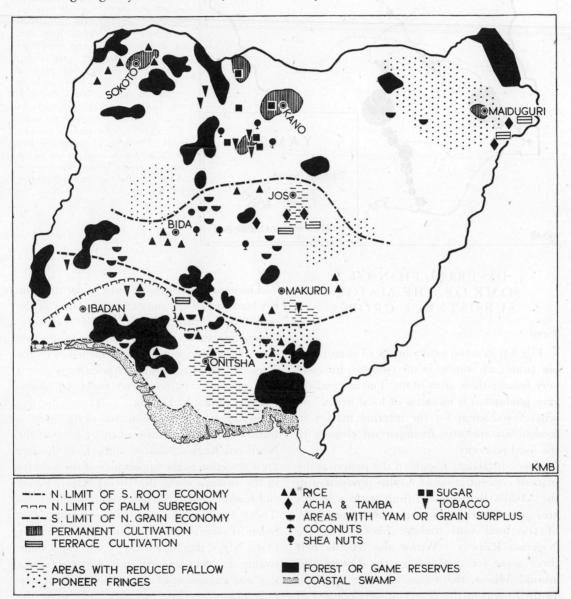

FIG. 82. SOME FEATURES OF THE SUBSISTENCE CROP ECONOMY IN NIGERIA

Note the distribution of the two major economies: the South Root Economy and the Northern Grain Economy; the Middle Belt is an area of overlap between these two economies. The major areas of permanent cultivation are found round the bigger towns of the Sudan zone; note that their aggregate area is, however, relatively small. Areas of agricultural over-population (areas with reduced fallow) are indicated, also the "pioneer fringes" where the man/land ratio is far below the optimum; for agricultural development schemes in these latter areas see Fig. 129.

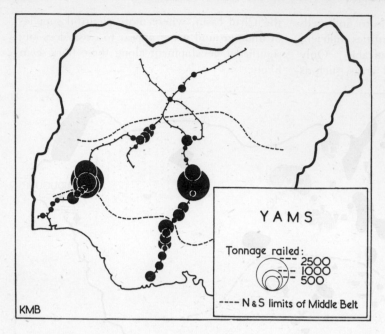

FIG. 83. YAMS

This map, showing yam tonnage railed out from various stations, suggests one of the important functions of the Middle Belt—that of a food-surplus area supplying food-deficit areas such as the mining areas of the Plateau and parts of the cocoa belt. Note the three major centres of export: Ilorin Province, the Gwari country and parts of Benue Province. No data are available regarding movement of yams by road. The limits of the Middle Belt as shown on the map do not follow administrative boundaries but are those of the agricultural region (cf. Fig. 82).

DISTRIBUTION OF SOME OF THE MAJOR SUBSISTENCE CROPS

Yams

Fig. 83, showing total tonnage of yams railed out from each station in the country, indicates very broadly those areas of the Territory where yam production is in excess of local needs, and where production for the internal market in foodstuffs constitutes an important element in the local economy.

The outstanding feature of the pattern is the marked concentration of surplus production in the Middle Belt, railings from stations in this area (as delimited in Fig. 61) representing 85% of the total yam tonnage handled by the Nigerian Railway. Within the Middle Belt three areas are outstanding: the Gwari area around Minna, the Lafia-Agyaragu area and Ilorin Province; the degree of development of food-export production in this latter Province is indicated by the fact that 50% of the total yam tonnage handled by the railway originates from stations within the Province.

Rice

The expansion of the acreage under this crop has been one of the outstanding features of the recent agricultural history of the Territory. Complete data on either acreage or production are not available, but estimates furnished by the Regional Departments of Agriculture give a total of some 165,000 acres for 1949, distributed as shown in Fig. 84.

Swamp-rice production has long been a feature of the agriculture of many parts of the Northern Region, and in 1904 Lord Lugard drew attention to the importance of the industry in the swamps along the Rivers Niger, Benue and Kaduna and to the potentialities of the crop. Today the major centre of production is in Sokoto Province where, in the valleys draining to the Niger, there are some 75,000 acres under swamp rice, and an active policy of mechanisation and expansion of acreage is being successfully pursued. The swampy areas along the Rivers Niger, Kaduna and Gbako in the Provinces of Niger and Ilorin constitute a second important producing area.[1] Here the industry, which caters largely for the Eastern

[1] A. W. Lines, "The Bida Rice Industry" in *Farm and Forest*, Vol. IV, No. 2 (1943), pp. 89–91.

FIG. 84. RICE

Major concentration in the valleys of the Rivers Sokoto and Rima in the north-west; wide scatter of production in small streamside swamps in the Southern Provinces; negligible production in zone of Delta and coast alluvium.

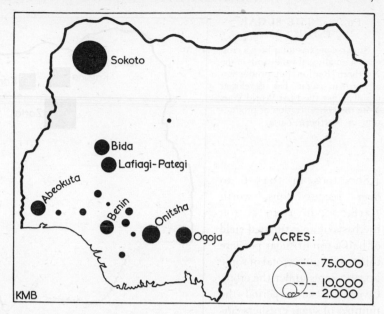

Provinces' market, expanded considerably during the recent war and, with the projected development of the very extensive areas of potential rice-land in this area, this upward trend may be expected to continue.

In the Eastern Region the major producing areas are in the Provinces of Onitsha and Ogoja, where it is widely grown in small streamside swamps. Here the rice acreage has shown a considerable expansion in recent years, the 1949 total of 30,000 acres representing a 50% increase over the 1948 figure.

In the Western Region some 35,000 acres are devoted to rice. The crop attains its maximum importance in the Provinces of Benin, Delta and Abeokuta. Especially in the western sector of the region the crop is mainly of the upland type, and is frequently grown interplanted with maize.

The successful development of swamp-rice cultivation in Sierra Leone and adjoining territories has led in Nigeria to a growing interest in the potentialities of the Territory's extensive coastal swamps for rice production. Experiments in Delta Province have shown that soil conditions are less favourable, and rice yields correspondingly lower, than in Sierra Leone; further, soil loss through tidal scour may be a problem.[1] In spite of these difficulties, however, a steady yield of 900 lb. per acre was

attained in the Warri Swamp, and with growing population pressure and soil depletion in many parts of the South, the coastal swamps may be expected to play an increasingly important role in the country's food economy.

Sugar

Sugar-cane is a characteristic crop of alluvial valley lands in the Northern Region, and is expecially important in the Provinces of Zaria, Kano, Katsina and the eastern part of Sokoto Province. The sugar is extracted by crushers in the cane-producing areas and the preparation of *gur* or brown sugar is an important and expanding rural industry.[2] There is also an important trade in raw cane (consumed as a sweetmeat); in the Maigana area of Zaria this absorbed one-third of the local cane output, the remaining two-thirds being made into sugar.[3]

No data are available on the acreage under cane, but the expansion of the industry may be judged from the graph on p. 118. It will be seen that the output of sugar has risen from

[1] *Annual Report of the Department of Agriculture* (1937), p. 29; *ibid.* (1938), pp. 34–5.
[2] Methods of extraction are dealt with by W. A. Watson, "Zaria Brown Sugar", in *Farm and Forest*, Vol. III, No. 2 (1942), pp. 92–4.
[3] J. W. Goodban, *Report on Sugar-cane Production in the Maigana Area* (1944). (Unpublished report in the Department of Agriculture, Kaduna.)

FIG. 85. THE SUGAR
        INDUSTRY

Sugar-cane has long been a crop
grown on alluvial valley soils in the
Northern Region but production
of brown sugar has been developed
mainly since the First World War.
Note the concentration of production in Northern Zaria.

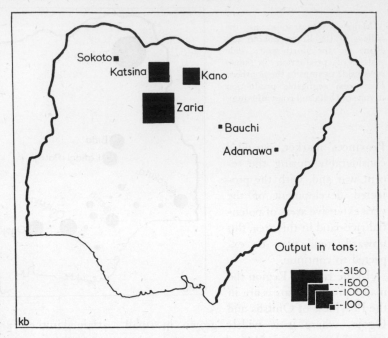

1,800 tons in 1945–6 to
over 10,000 tons, worth
£318,000, in 1949–50 (on
the basis of an estimated yield
of half a ton of sugar per acre
this would give a total of some
20,000 acres under the crop).
Over the same period the
number of sugar crushers employed in the North rose from
172 to 655. The recent
arrival of forty-six new crushers in the North
suggests a continuation of the upward trend in
the country's sugar production.

In 1949–50 Zaria Province, with 45% of

the crushers, accounted for 63% of the total
sugar output of the North; Katsina, with 16%
of the crushers and 17% of the sugar output,
was a poor second.

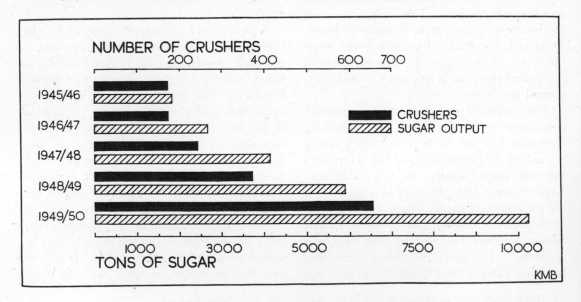

FIG. 86. THE EXPANSION OF THE SUGAR INDUSTRY

Illustrating the marked upward trend in sugar production in the Northern Provinces since the end of
World War II. Total output in the last five years has increased fivefold while a greater level of efficiency in
the industry is suggested by the fact that output per crusher has increased 50%.

FIG. 87. KOLA NUTS

As a result of encouragement by the Department of Agriculture, production of kola expanded greatly in south-west Nigeria during the inter-war years, the ability of the tree to flourish on the light sandy soils of the area (Fig. 22) making it especially valuable. Note that this map shows merely tonnage handled by rail and that no data are available covering kola nuts exported by road or consumed locally.

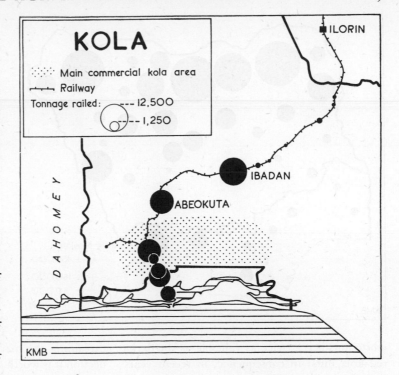

Kola

The use of the kola nut as a stimulant is universal among the peoples of Western Africa, and the trade in this commodity between the forest lands of Guinea littoral and the Sudan and desert regions of the north goes back far into antiquity. For centuries, indeed, the kola nut ranked with slaves and livestock as one of the most valuable items of commerce in the Guinea lands.[1]

The tree appears indigenous to West Africa, and the major centres of production lie in the Gold Coast, Sierra Leone and adjoining parts of French West Africa.[2] Large-scale production in Nigeria is a relatively recent development, and owes much to the policy of the Department of Agriculture in encouraging plantings during the years following the First World War. As a result of these plantings, kola has replaced cocoa over much of the extreme south-west of the Cocoa Belt, the formerly heavy imports from the Gold Coast and Sierra Leone have been reduced to a negligible figure, and a flourishing trade has grown up between the producing areas of Yorubaland and Northern Nigeria. In 1932, 11,000 tons

of kola nuts were railed to the North; five years later this figure had doubled and in 1948 railings amounted to over 47,000 tons.

The major producing area overlaps the south-western sector of the Cocoa Belt, the area of greatest intensity of production lying south of a line joining Ilaro and the northern boundary of Ijebu Province. The tree possesses the ability to flourish on the light soils of sedimentary origin, which are unsuited to cocoa, but appears to be very sensitive to climate for yields drop markedly with decreased rainfall and Harmattan conditions, and even at Ibadan the climate is no longer ideal for kola.

Two main types are grown, the *kola abata*, which is grown on a small scale for local consumption, and the *Gbanja* type, which is not popular in Yorubaland and which makes up the bulk of the exports to the Northern Provinces. Some trees yield both white and red nuts, the

[1] See M. H. Lelong, "La Route du Kola" in *Revue de Géographie Humaine et d'Ethnologie*, No. 4 (Oct. 1948–9), pp. 35–40.
[2] For a map of the main producing areas in W. Africa see *Afrique Occidentale Française*, by J. Richard-Molard, Paris (1949), p. 67.

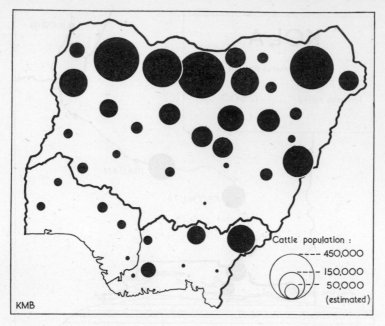

FIG. 88. CATTLE

Distribution by Divisions. Figures are derived from the *jangali* (cattle tax) returns; these almost certainly are underestimates and actual numbers may be as much as 50% above the totals mapped (it may be assumed that the error is evenly distributed over the Territory and that the general pattern of distribution as shown is fundamentally correct). Note the concentration in open Sudan savanas of the north and in the fly-free areas of Jos Plateau and Cameroons (and cf. Fig. 29). Cattle are of negligible importance in the south and in much of the Middle Belt.

Cattle population :

- - - - 450,000

- - - 150,000

- 50,000

(estimated)

KMB

white nuts being twice as valuable as the dark-red kola nuts; in consequence, in recent years the Agricultural Department has given its attention to the selection of trees bearing a high proportion of white nuts and to the possibility of developing kola strains yielding white nuts only.

THE LIVESTOCK ECONOMY

Distribution of Cattle

In spite of the importance of cattle in the Nigerian economy (in 1948–9 exports of hides alone were worth £1,000,000), the existing data on cattle population is extremely unreliable. Official statistics show a cattle population of some $3\frac{3}{4}$ million, but this, based largely upon *jangali* (cattle tax) returns, is certainly an underestimate (it is, for example, insufficient to maintain the country's hide exports at their existing level), and a recent study suggests that a figure of 7 or 8 million is nearer the truth. The concentration of the cattle population in the hands of a nomadic people, the Fulani, scattered over some 200,000 square miles of Tropical

Africa, and the inevitable widespread evasion of the cattle tax go far towards explaining the margin of error. In this connection it is worth stressing that the considerable recent increase in the Territory's herds suggested by the official returns is probably more apparent than real, being due largely to improved methods of *jangali* collection.

The general distribution of cattle according to the *jangali* returns is summarised in Figs. 88 to 90.[1] Some nine-tenths of the Territory's cattle are concentrated in the Northern Region, the Provinces of Kano, Sokoto and Bornu together containing one-half the total. This concentration in the north, and especially in the extreme north, is governed by climatic conditions; the sub-humid climate of the northern plains, with its wide range of temperature and its low humidities, is unfavourable to the tsetse fly, and there is, in consequence, little danger of the trypanosomiasis which precludes the successful rearing of the larger types of stock over three-quarters of Nigeria. The importance of the tsetse fly as a factor in the pastoral economy of the country may be judged from a comparison of Figs. 29 and 88.

The Territory possesses several important

---

[1] *Jangali* is normally collected during the months July to October so that the maps show *wet season* distribution.

FIG. 89. CATTLE DENSITY

Highest densities in Provinces of Katsina and Kano and in adjoining Katagum Division; outlier of high density in Jos Division of Plateau Province and, less marked, in Bamenda Province. Note that even in high density areas the intensity of stocking is relatively low by temperate zone standards; thus the comparable density for cattle in the United Kingdom is 112.

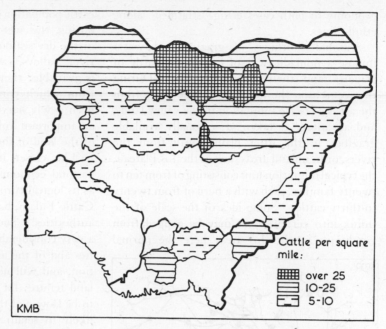

Cattle per square mile:
- over 25
- 10-25
- 5-10

breeds of cattle, some of which show a relatively restricted geographical range. The great majority are of the humped Asiatic or Zebu type; this includes the White and Red Fulani breeds which are widely distributed throughout the North, the Gudali breed of Sokoto and the Shuwa Arab breed of Bornu. Humpless types are less important economically; they include the Chad, or Kuri, type, whose geographic area is suggested by its name, and the dwarf shorthorn or Muturu. The latter appears to possess a considerable degree of tolerance to trypano-somiasis, and most of the cattle of the Middle Belt and the Southern Provinces are of Muturu stock.

Some 90% of Nigeria's cattle are to be found in the Northern Region, and of this total probably 95% are in the hands of the Cattle Fulani. The problem of Fulani origins has been alluded to earlier; the relationship of the pastoral Fula of Nigeria to the Hausa cultivator is somewhat similar to the relationship existing in the East African cattle area between the Masai and their Bantu neighbours, the

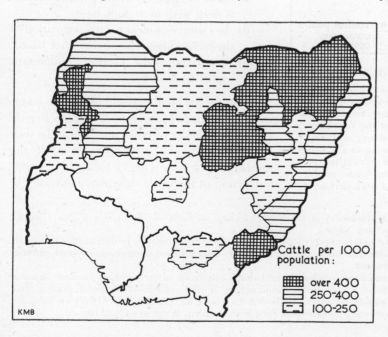

Cattle per 1000 population:
- over 400
- 250-400
- 100-250

FIG. 90. THE RATIO OF CATTLE TO POPULATION

The ratio is relatively low in closely settled areas such as Kano Province and highest in thinly peopled north-eastern and north-western sectors of Nigeria; southward extension of area with high cattle/man ratio along mountain grasslands of Cameroons.

economy in both cases being "stratified" along ethnic lines.

Seasonal shortages of grazing and water impose a nomadic way of life on the cattle of Nigeria and their Fulani owners.[1] During the wet season the herds are moved away from the areas of tsetse infestation in the valley lands, and advantage is taken of seasonally available grazings in the drier plains away from the rivers, or in upland areas such as the Jos Plateau, the typical migration unit consisting of from ten to twenty families, each with a herd of from twenty to thirty cattle. Some idea of the scale of the influx into certain areas may be gauged from conditions in the Jos area; here the normal cattle population of 30,000 is swollen to 100,000 during the wet season.[2] At the beginning of the dry season the animals are moved to the river valleys,[3] and other areas where water is available; they are grazed *en route* on fields from which corn, beans or other crops have been newly harvested, and their droppings play an important role in maintaining the fertility of the land of the settled cultivator.

The closer integration of the arable and pastoral economies of Northern Nigeria with, as its logical corollary, the sedentarisation of the Cattle Fulani, has been long advocated by many authorities. Such a development will demand a very considerable expansion of watering facilities and of the area under fodder-crop production, and will necessitate important changes in land tenure; for these reasons alone it is likely to be slow and the cattle economy of Nigeria is likely to retain its nomad character for many years to come.

Apart from their importance as a source of meat and milk products for the population of the northern pastoral zone, the Territory's herds have a threefold importance:

(i) As a source of dairy produce to meet the needs of Nigeria's urban population; this is dealt with more fully later.

(ii) As a source of meat for the population of the tsetse-infested southern forest lands.

(iii) As a source of the Territory's important export trade in hides.

Cattle on the hoof represent one of the major items in the trade between the Northern Region and the remainder of Nigeria. As can be seen from map 88, the cattle population of the southern forest zone is negligible and the greater proportion of the cattle slaughtered annually in

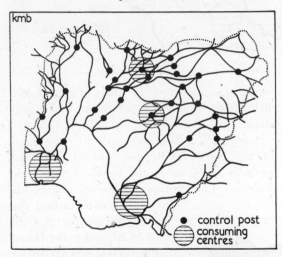

FIG. 91. CATTLE TRADE ROUTES

Showing existing network of routes along which cattle are driven from the cattle-rearing districts of the North to the meat-deficient South. Also indicated are the control posts of the Veterinary Department and the main consuming centres—Kano Province and Plateau mining area in the north, Iboland and the towns of Yorubaland in the south. Note the numerous trade routes entering Nigeria from adjoining French territory.

[1] F. W. de St. Croix, "The Cattle Husbandry of the Nomad Fulani" in *Farm and Forest*, Vol. V, No. 1 (1944), pp. 29–33; *idem* "The Fulani of Northern Nigeria".

[2] Though recently a limitation of numbers to prevent over-grazing has been instituted. In the absence of adequate data on the grazing potentialities of the Territory's pastures, however, determination of optimum livestock densities must be a matter of enlightened guesswork.

[3] In this connection it may be stressed that schemes of mechanised cultivation in the Northern *fadamas* (seasonal swamps), such as the Sokoto Rice scheme, which involve the ploughing of extensive areas of dry-season grazing, may cause serious dislocation of the local pastoral economy. In the Sokoto scheme an Administrative Officer was seconded to the area to watch over Fulani interests and to harmonise these with the needs of the settled cultivators.

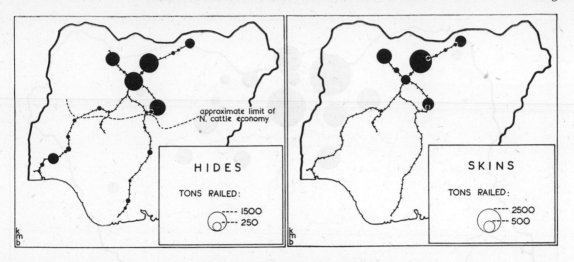

FIGS. 92–93. HIDES AND SKINS

Cattle hides, goat-skins and sheep-skins form items of major importance in the Nigerian economy. In addition to the quantities used within the country by the leather-working industry some £4,000,000 worth were exported in 1949. Major collecting centres for export are Gusau, Nguru, Kano, Zaria and Jos.

the south (135,000 in 1947) are of northern origin. These animals are derived mainly from the Provinces of Sokoto and Bornu, though considerable numbers enter Nigeria from adjoining French territories. The general direction of cattle movement is shown in Fig. 91.

Hides to the value of £1 million were exported in 1948, and the commodity ranks eighth in order of value among Nigeria's exports. The average number of hides exported in recent years has averaged 700,000, of which some 100,000 represented transit trade from French territories. Exports of goat-skins, for comparison, were worth £2 million in 1948, the number of skins exported averaging 6 million annually during the last decade.

Mixed Farming

For many generations the agricultural economy of Western Europe has been based on mixed farming, involving a close integration of arable and livestock farming on individual holdings. Such an integration has not been achieved in Nigeria, where virtually the entire cattle population is in the hands of one ethnic group—the Fulani—and where over wide areas arable farming is carried on as if cattle did not exist. It has long been recognised by agricultural experts that this cleavage constitutes a serious element of weakness in the country's agricultural system, and a recent official report[1] goes so far as to declare: "There can be no solution to Northern Nigeria's agricultural problem so long as the cattle population remains divorced from its soil." This is certainly an over-statement; nevertheless, the advantages to be derived from a system of mixed farming are many: the replacement of human labour by that of draught animals; the maintenance of the soil nutrient status by farmyard manure, and the eventual replacement of the land-prodigal system of shifting cultivation by permanent rotational farming; the extension of the cultivated area and the diversification of cropping; finally, the expansion of the output of those livestock products which are essential to overcome the low protein intake typical of most Nigerian diets. Under this system a holding of, say, twelve acres, would support two draught animals which, properly kraaled, would supply

[1] *Report of the Nigerian Livestock Mission*, Colonial No. 266, London (1950), p. 36.

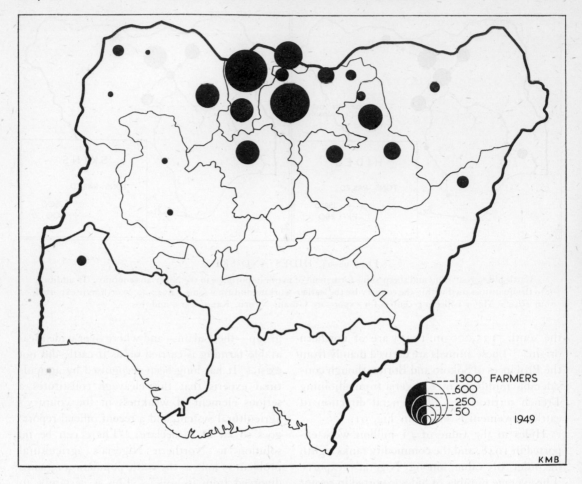

1300 FARMERS
600
250
50

1949

KMB

FIG. 94. THE DISTRIBUTION OF MIXED FARMERS

The development of mixed farming is one answer to the problem of maintaining fertility on the lighter
northern soils and the number of mixed farmers in the Northern Provinces has showed a marked and gratifying increase in recent years.   Even so, as the map suggests, mixed farming is confined largely to the central
sector of the Sudan zone and is of very minor importance in the peripheral Provinces of Bornu and Sokoto.
Heavy fly infestation at present prevents the extension of mixed farming to the Middle Belt and the south.

enough manure to dress four acres each year;
these four acres would be planted to the main
food crop (millet or guinea corn) and the remaining acreage devoted to cash crops. With a
simple rotation, the whole plot will receive a
dressing of farmyard manure every three years.
This is a simplified example; it will be obvious
that the size of the holding and the balance

between food crops (including fodder crops) and
cash crops will show considerable regional
variation.[1]

The system was introduced into the Northern
Provinces in 1928; the number of mixed
farmers first exceeded a thousand in 1936, and
by 1949 had reached a total of 5,763.   This is
a steady and gratifying increase; even so, it

[1] See D. H. L. Corby, "Changes being brought about by the Introduction of Mixed Farming" in *Farm and
Forest*, Vol. II, No. 3 (1941), pp. 106–9.   On an indigenous system of mixed farming see S. White, "Mixed Farming as practised by the Shuwa Arabs of Dikwa Emirate" in *Farm and Forest*, Vol. II, No. 1.

should be borne in mind that the number of mixed farmers represents only an infinitesimal fraction of the total number of farmers in the Northern Provinces (in Kano Emirate, for example, out of a population of 2·6 million the number of mixed farmers is only 1,062), and that there are several problems, such as the excessively small size of many holdings and difficulties in obtaining both cattle and ploughs, which must be surmounted before any great expansion can be expected.

Fig. 94 shows that the greatest development of mixed farming has taken place in the Provinces of Kano and Katsina and in the adjoining areas of Zaria and Bauchi Provinces, i.e. in the main cash-crop producing region of the north. Development in the peripheral Provinces of Bornu and Sokoto has been small; especially in the drier parts of the latter Province soil poverty makes difficult the introduction of the normal type of mixed farming, and future development may be based on goats (which already constitute an important element in the Sokoto economy) rather than on cattle.

Heavy tsetse infestation at present limits the development of mixed farming in the Middle Belt and the southern forest regions. It has, nevertheless, been shown that farmyard manure will maintain a high level of fertility under intensive cropping even on the poor soils of Iboland, and it seems clear that the solution to the problems of maintaining soil fertility in these areas, no less than in the Sudan zone of the North, lies in a system of mixed farming. Under these conditions the development of trypanosomiasis-resistant livestock strains becomes a matter of vital concern to the well-being of some two-thirds of the Territory's population.

Dairying

The development of the dairying industry on the Jos Plateau and in the adjoining area dates from the beginning of the Second World War,[1] when large-scale supplies of imported dairy produce were cut off, and today the industry is an important element in the agricultural economy of the Middle Belt, with an output in 1949–50 of 273,500 lb. of butter, 112,000 lb. of clarified butter fat (C.B.F.) and 81,000 lb. of cheese. The industry is based entirely on milk purchased from the local Cattle Fulani, the sales of milk representing a very considerable addition to the cash income of these pastoral people.

The butter is manufactured on the Plateau in a central dairy at Vom, to which the cream is delivered by lorry from some two score separator units scattered over the southern sector of the Plateau. A second dairy, which receives the bulk of its cream supplies by rail, is in operation at Kano; this, however, is of much smaller importance. To justify its existence a separator unit must deal with the 150–200 gallons of milk daily and, since the distance over which the Fulani will deliver milk is rarely more than five miles, the units are located approximately ten miles apart. During the early stages of dairying development butter was given priority, and cheese production tended to be experimental in character and dependent upon supplies of surplus milk. Today, however, there are three cheese units operating on the Plateau, and Vom cheese, a hard, processed variety of the Cheddar type, is firmly established on the local market. The difficulties of maturing cheese under conditions of tropical climate have been overcome through the more favourable temperature and humidity conditions of the wet season, and the pronounced drop in milk supplies during the dry season imparts a marked seasonal rhythm to output. C.B.F. was first produced commercially in 1940 at Vodni in Pankshin Division; today, as Fig. 95 shows, there are nine C.B.F. units operating in the Middle Belt, and output has doubled over the last two seasons,

[1] R. S. Marshall, "Wartime Activities of the Veterinary Department" in *Farm and Forest*, Vol. III, No. 3 (1942), pp. 103–9. A. J. Knott, "C. B. F. Production on the Plateau", *ibid.*, Vol. III, No. 2 (1942), pp. 57–60. For recent developments see *Annual Report of the Commerce and Industries Department* 1949–50, Kaduna (1951), pp. 19–20; *Report of N. Regional Production Development Board* (1951).

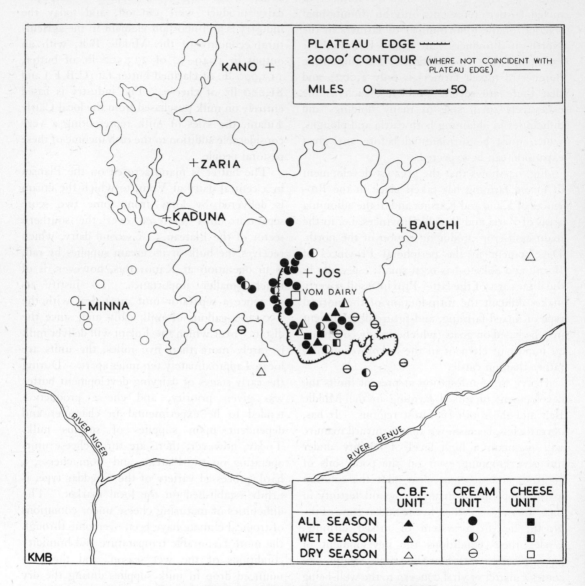

FIG. 95. THE PLATEAU DAIRYING INDUSTRY

During the last decade the Department of Commerce and Industries has built up a flourishing dairy industry on the high-level grasslands of Jos Plateau. Favouring factors in this area include the relatively long grazing season, the concentration on the Plateau of a considerable cattle-keeping Fulani population and the existence of a well-developed road system which facilitates the transport of the butterfat to the central creameries. Note the central dairy at Vom, the concentration of cream units in the vicinity of Jos, the clarified butterfat and cheese units on the southern fringe of the Plateau and the outlier of the main region in the vicinity of Minna. In the latter area the units are operated usually in the wet season but the cattle population is extremely fluid and in some years (e.g. 1951) the units do not operate; such units are indicated by hollow circles.

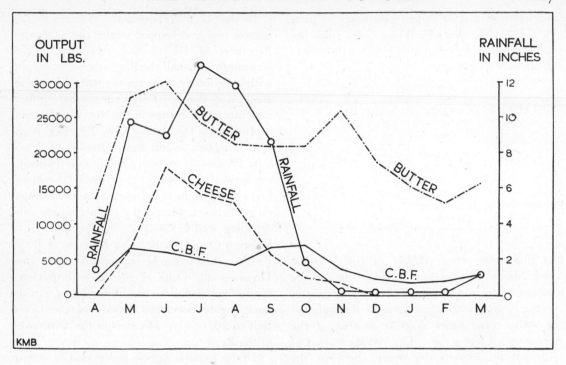

OUTPUT IN LBS.

RAINFALL IN INCHES

FIG. 96. SEASONAL VARIATIONS IN THE PLATEAU DAIRY INDUSTRY

Note the pronounced early summer peak in output coinciding with the beginning of the rains and the first flush of grass. The late summer decline and the secondary peak in October–November appear to be due to the fact that at the height of the rains the Fulani cannot or will not get their milk to the buying units owing to flooded streams and interrupted communications. (C.B.F. = clarified butter fat.)

showing that the product is more than holding its own with imported cooking fats.

The successful development of a flourishing dairy industry in a nomadic pastoral area within 9° of the Equator is a substantial achievement and reflects the greatest credit on those concerned with the project. It also serves to focus attention on the uniqueness of the Plateau environment. Here, and nowhere else in West Africa, is to be found the requisite combination of well-watered upland grazings, a high density of cattle in the hands of a skilled pastoral people, and a well-developed transport network permitting the rapid assembling of the highly perishable raw material and the distribution of the finished product. Thus favoured, the Plateau may well become a major source of dairy produce for the whole of tropical West Africa.

PEASANT EXPORT PRODUCTION

Distribution of Export Production

A broad picture of the importance of export crop production in the agricultural economy of various sectors of the Territory may be obtained from the analysis, on a value basis, of the grading statistics for major export crops. The maps and data presented here are based on estimates of the value of the export output in the crop year 1948–9. It should be emphasised that the maps refer to crop production only and exclude pastoral products (hides, skins), for which no detailed data are available; in consequence, they do not give an adequate picture of the rural prosperity of the pastoral districts of the Northern Region. Further, no account is taken of production for internal trade which, as already noted, is of major importance in parts of the Middle Belt and Bornu. In 1948 the agricultural export output of the Territory was distributed as follows:

TABLE VII

ESTIMATED VALUE OF AGRICULTURAL EXPORT PRODUCTION 1948

Region	Total Export Production	Value per Head	Value per Square Mile
Western	£11,400,000	£2·8	£249
Eastern	£7,300,000	£1·4	£159
Northern	£9,750,000	£0·72	£34

The dominating position of the Western Region is obvious; almost two-fifths of the export trade in agricultural products originates in the Region, and output per head of population is some three times as great as that of the remainder of Nigeria. The average output of agricultural exports per square mile in the Northern Region is, even including livestock products, barely one-eighth that of the Western; on a *per capita* basis it is one-half that of the Eastern Region and one-quarter that of the Western.

The detailed pattern of export crop production is shown in Figs. 97–99.[1] It will be evident that there are three major zones of relatively intensive production, coinciding broadly with the Northern Cotton and Groundnut Belt, the Eastern Palm Belt and the Cocoa Belt.

Within the northern export crop region highest values are recorded in Katsina Province (£290 per square mile) and Kano Province (£175 per square mile). This nucleus, with the adjoining Sokoto Division, occupies only one-sixth the area of Northern Provinces, but produces nine-tenths of the output in terms of value. Outside this nucleus production for export is of negligible importance in the North, and over much of the Middle Belt figures of output are below £1 per square mile.

Production for export in the Western Region is most highly developed in the cocoa-growing Provinces of Ibadan and Abeokuta, which account for one-half the Region's export output, with a secondary centre in the palm-oil zone of Benin and Warri. Output per square mile is very much higher than in the Northern Region; in Ife-Ilesha Division of Oyo Province it approaches £600 and in Egba Division of Abeokuta Province it exceeds £750 (cocoa representing between 70 and 90% of the total output). Over much of the remainder of the West output ranges between £150 and £300 per square mile, dropping well below £100 in the dry belt of Western Oyo, in Kukuruku Division of Benin Province, and in the Urhobo and Western Ijaw Divisions of Delta Province. Output per head of population ranges from £5 to £6 in the most highly developed sectors of the Cocoa Belt to 7d. in Oyo Division in the north-west of the Region.

In the Eastern Region production for export attains its greatest importance in the Provinces of Owerri and Calabar, which together account for three-fifths of the Region's export output. Highest values (over £1,000 per square mile) are recorded in the south-east in Aba, Abak, Eket and Opobo Divisions, and a secondary centre of production is located in the Divisions of Onitsha, Owerri and Bende. Lowest values per unit-area are recorded in the over-farmed Udi–Okigwi zone and in the Kumba and Mamfe Divisions of Cameroons. In spite of the high figures for total production in some divisions, the very great concentration of population per unit-area in much of the Eastern Palm Belt results in relatively low values in terms of output per head. Highest *per capita* values occur, as Fig. 99 shows, in peripheral Divisions, such as Degema, Brass and Calabar, where population density is below the average and where the volume of locally grown crops graded is augmented by supplies moving coastwards from interior districts. Lowest *per capita* values occur in the over-farmed zones of

---

[1] Based upon unpublished statistics (by buying stations) supplied by Department of Agriculture and Department of Marketing and Exports.

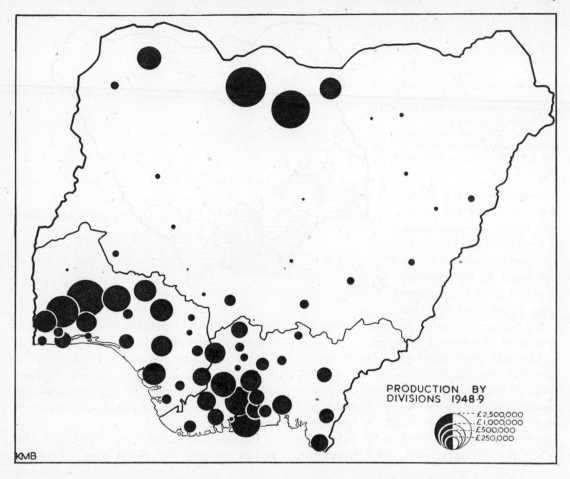

FIG. 97. AGRICULTURAL EXPORT PRODUCTION (I)

Showing the estimated value of production, at Nigerian price levels, for each Division in the Territory. Note the three major nuclei—those of Hausaland, Iboland and Yorubaland—and the negative character of much of the Middle Belt. Note, too, that since only overseas exports are shown the map does not give a complete index to the agricultural prosperity of various parts of the Territory; thus in both Bornu and Ilorin Provinces production for export to other parts of Nigeria makes an important contribution to local prosperity.

Onitsha and Owerri Provinces and in the under-developed sectors of Ogoja and Cameroons. Except in the case of the Cameroons, where cocoa, rubber and bananas are of some importance, virtually the entire agricultural export of the Region consists of palm produce.

Export Crop Regions

A generalised picture of the pattern of export crop production in Nigeria is given in Fig. 100,[1] which is compiled from the export purchase statistics for the major crops and from field traverses. The essential physical background to this map is provided by the maps showing climatic and soil conditions (pp. 22–39); some features of the human and economic background are shown in the population density map (p. 59) and the traffic-flow map (p. 213).

Two major features stand out clearly from the map: firstly, the absence, save for soya and

[1] Compiled from maps (Figs. 101–24) and from field traverses.

FIG. 98. AGRICULTURAL EXPORT PRODUCTION (II)

The data in Fig. 97 are here expressed in terms of £s per square mile. Note the much more highly developed export production of the southern provinces and the negligible importance of export production in the dry belt of Oyo Province. The dual character of each of the Regions (cf. Figs. 64 and 67) is very evident from this map.

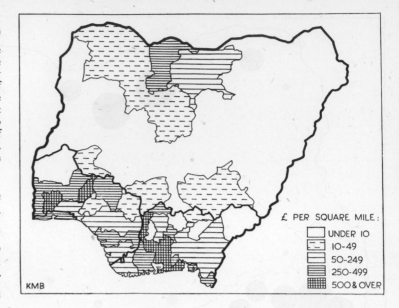

benniseed production in the Tiv country, of any signifi-cant export crop production in the Middle Belt; secondly, the contrasts between North and South in the character of export crops, the northern crops being essentially an-nuals, whilst the southern export regions are dominated by perennial tree crops.

The main export crop region of the Northern Provinces extends from the centre of Zaria Province towards the north-western and north-eastern rail termini of Kaura Namoda and Nguru respectively. It consists of two zones, a groundnut zone, developed on the light sandy soils of the subhumid north, and a cotton belt, developed on the somewhat heavier Zaria soils to the south. These zones overlap in Southern Katsina and Eastern Sokoto. To the south of the Jos Plateau and extending towards the foot-hills of the Cameroons, the Tiv benniseed and soya zone constitutes an export crop region of secondary importance.

The southern export crop region coincides broadly with the high-forest zone. Like the Northern Region, it falls into two major crop zones, deter-mined largely by soil con-ditions, and overlapping in the Western Yoruba Pro-

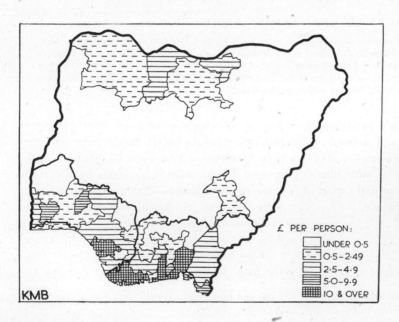

FIG. 99. AGRICULTURAL EXPORT PRODUCTION (III)

This map emphasises the fact that though many Divisions show a relatively large output of export crops, in terms of absolute figures, production per head, owing to high density of population, may be relatively low. Excellent ex-amples of this are afforded by the high density areas of Kano Province and the Yoruba country. The reasons for the concentration of high *per capita* values in parts of the coastal belt are commented on in the text.

FIG. 100. EXPORT CROPS

Generalised areas of production for major export crops are shown. Note the overlap of cotton and groundnut belts in the Provinces of Katsina and Sokoto and of the palm and cocoa belts in the Western Yoruba Provinces.

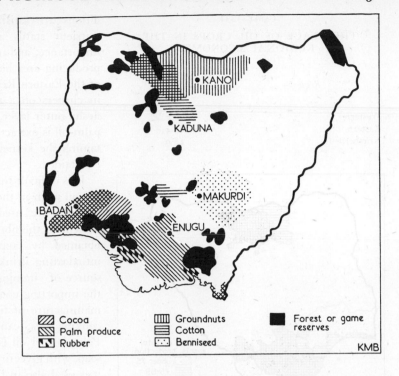

Cocoa
Palm produce
Rubber
Groundnuts
Cotton
Benniseed
Forest or game reserves

KMB

vinces. The oil-palm zone is more or less continuous from the Cameroons westwards to the Dahomey frontier though, as seen later, the greatest intensity of production is on soils of the Benin and Calabar groups in the central and eastern sectors (Figs. 102, 104). In the West, cocoa is the dominant element in the export economy, the main producing area lying on soils of the Ibadan group (Fig. 22) and extending across the dry-forest zone from Idogo in the south-west to the Ondo–Benin boundary in the north-east. Rubber production in the Benin–Warri area and, on a smaller scale, in the Calabar area constitutes a third element in the export economy, while on the volcanic soils of the southern Cameroons bananas, palm produce, rubber and cocoa are produced under plantation conditions.

Oil Crops

Oil crops—groundnuts, palm produce and benniseed or sesame—are of outstanding importance in the agricultural economy of Nigeria, and have accounted in recent years for approximately three-fifths of the agricultural exports of the Territory (in terms of value). Since the Second World War, Nigeria has dominated the world trade in these crops, and according to statistics compiled by the Commonwealth Economic Committee,[1] the Territory in 1949 was the leading exporter of palm produce, groundnuts and benniseed, accounting for 52% of the world's palm-kernel exports, 40% of the exports of groundnuts and benniseed and 34% of the exports of palm-oil.

The general distribution of production of these crops has already been briefly described; the relative importance of oil crops in the agricultural export output of various parts of the Territory is shown in Fig. 101. Within the export crop sector (comprising those Divisions where the value of export production exceeds £50 per square mile), the only Divisions where oil crops represent less than three-quarters of the total export output are those of the Cocoa Belt, the Benin rubber area and the southern Cameroons. Over most of the Eastern Region and in the main Northern export crop region around Kano, oil crops account for over 90% of the agricultural export output. Their importance in the export economy of the three regions is set out overleaf.

[1] See *Vegetable Oils and Oilseeds*, Commonwealth Economic Committee, London (1950).

TABLE VIII
THE PLACE OF OIL CROPS IN THE REGIONAL ECONOMY

Region	Oil Crops as % Total Exports (value)
Western . . .	30·7
Eastern . . .	82.4
Northern . . .	48·9

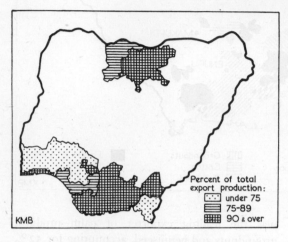

FIG. 101. OIL CROPS

Illustrating the dominant role of oil crops (palm-oil and groundnuts) in the export economy of the Kano area and the Eastern Region. Only those Divisions where the total export production is over £50 per square mile are shown.

Palm Produce

In 1948–9 palm products accounted for almost 30% of the Territory's exports by value. Production for export is confined to the south, and attains its maximum importance in the Eastern Region, where palm products make up over four-fifths of the exports. The oil palm is very sensitive to drought, and does not flourish in regions experiencing a pronounced dry season, even if the total annual precipitation may be abundant; given a well-distributed rainfall, it will thrive with totals as low as 50 inches or as high as 250 inches. It dislikes heavy or swampy soils, and grows best in damp, moist, yet well-drained soils; provided moisture conditions are satisfactory, the question of soil nutrient status appears to be of secondary importance, and in Nigeria the most important producing area lies on the heavily leached soils of the Eastern Region. The palm fruit grows in clusters on a thick stalk. It consists of a fleshy outer layer, or pericarp, from which the palm-oil is extracted; this encloses the nut containing the kernel from which palm-kernel oil is obtained.

It is difficult to exaggerate the importance of the oil palm in the forest lands of the south: its leaf-ribs are used in building, the leaves in thatching, the fibre in rope-making; palm-wine obtained by tapping the tree is a pleasant, intoxicating drink; the palm-oil is a valuable source of vitamins in the indigenous diet. In the importing countries palm-oil is used in the manufacture of tin-plate, soap, margarine and cooking fats, candles and lubricating greases. Palm-kernel oil is used in the manufacture of soap, with glycerine as an important by-product; it is used also in the manufacture of margarine and candy, pharmaceutical products and toilet preparations, while the residual kernel cake is a valuable livestock food.[1]

The plantation output of palm produce is relatively small, and virtually the entire output of oil and kernels comes from wild or semi-wild trees. These occur either scattered on farmlands, in which case the trees are usually individually owned, or in groves, which are usually communal property.

Figs. 102–103, showing purchase by grading stations, summarise the main features of the production pattern; it will be apparent that the producing area coincides closely with the southern high-forest region, though there is a notable break in the continuity of the dense Palm Belt in the thinly peopled upland country of North Calabar and Ogoja. Within the Palm Belt the greatest intensity of production is found on the heavily leached sands of Iboland; this is separated from a secondary concentration in the western Yoruba Provinces by a zone of lower intensity of production in Ondo Province.

[1] D. S. Correl, "The African Oil Palm" in *Lloydia*, 7 (1944), p. 103.

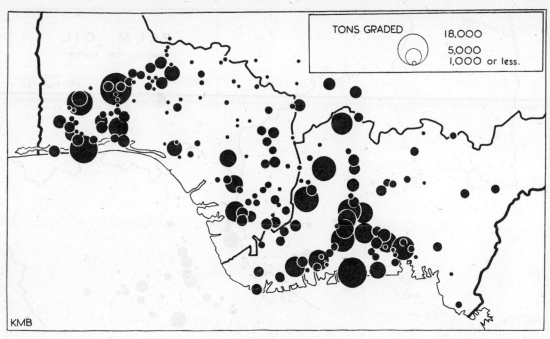

FIG. 102. PALM KERNELS

Concentration of production is in the high forest zone of the south with greatest intensity of production in the Ibo Provinces. Note the secondary centre of production in the western Yoruba Provinces and the break in continuity of the palm belt in Ondo Province.

Fig. 103 shows that the greater proportion of the territory's palm-oil exports (85% over the period 1947–9)[1] is derived from the Eastern Provinces, the exports of the Western Provinces consisting largely of kernels. This appears to be due to two factors: firstly, to the superior attractions of cocoa as an export crop on the better soils of the West; secondly, to the fact that the bulk of the oil produced in the West is relatively high-grade oil, which is absorbed locally or elsewhere in Nigeria.

At present, some 85% of the palm-oil is produced by hand. Methods of extraction are very variable, but may be grouped broadly into "hard-oil" and "soft-oil" methods. In the former the fruit is softened by fermentation and mashing, and the oil partly runs out and is partly squeezed out of the softened mass. In the soft-oil process the fruit is softened by pounding and boiling (this arrests the develop-

ment of the free fatty acid whose presence makes the oil "hard"), and the oil is separated by working the softened mass in water from which the oil is skimmed off. The "hard-oil" method gives a higher extraction rate and demands less labour, but the resultant oil is less valuable to the overseas manufacturer and commands a lower price than soft oil.[2]

It has been estimated that hand methods give a mean extraction rate of only 55%, and with the use of simple machinery a very great improvement on this figure can be obtained; thus, the simple hand-press gives a 65% extraction, and the oil-mill will give an 85% extraction with a much lower free fatty acid content. The small hand-press will deal with up to $1\frac{1}{4}$ cwt. of fruit at a time, and during the last twenty years its use has spread widely in the Palm Belt (Fig. 106); even so, it is estimated that only 15% of the output of oil is produced by

[1] *Nigerian Oil Palm Marketing Board: First Annual Report* 1949, Lagos (1950).
[2] On methods of extraction see *Annual Bulletin of the Agricultural Department*, Vol. I (1922), pp. 30–2.

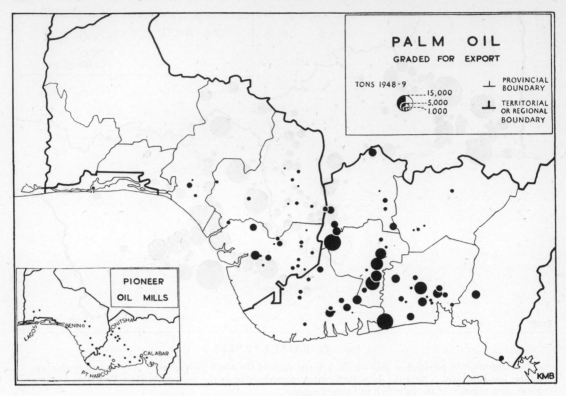

FIG. 103. PALM-OIL

Note the dominating role of the Eastern Region in the production of palm-oil for export; in the Western Region palm-oil is produced on a considerable scale but except in the Provinces of Benin and Delta the entire production is absorbed by the local market. In the Eastern Region the apparent break in the continuity of the producing area in the central sector of Onitsha and Owerri Provinces is due to the absence of grading stations in this belt, the oil being conveyed to grading stations on the Niger to the west or on the railway to the east.

hand-presses. During the last decade the Government has been giving increasing attention to the provision of oil-mills, especially in the Eastern Provinces. These "Pioneer Oil-mills" can handle some 5 tons of fruit per 8-hour shift, and have a production capacity of 350 tons of oil per annum. They use palm fibre and shell for fuel, and hence are self-sufficient in this respect, but are economic only in those areas where the tree density is adequate to provide a regular supply of fruit; it is obvious that in this respect plantation production,[1] with its regular and easily controlled output of fruit, possesses very definite advantages over the present system of production by a multitude of small units. Unfortunately, the introduction of mechanisation along these lines has been rendered difficult by the opposition of those who see in the oil-mill a threat to their livelihood.

No palm-kernel oil is extracted in Nigeria, and the preparation of the kernel for export involves only the extraction of the nut from the fibrous mass left after the extraction of the palm-oil and its subsequent cracking to extract the kernel; as described above, both of these processes are done by hand. The kernels are packed for export in standard bags containing $182\frac{1}{2}$ lb.

[1] The difficulties in the way of plantation development are discussed in *Annual Report of the Department of Agriculture*, 1938, pp. 21–3.

FIG. 104. THE GEOGRAPHIC SETTING OF THE EASTERN PALM BELT

Note the concentration of production on the sandy soils of Iboland. Note that most of the Belt has a rainfall of over 60 inches, though somewhat lower figures are typical of the palm belt of Yorubaland. The extensive tracts of forest reserve in the Oban Hills and South Benin effectively delimit the major producing area to east and west.

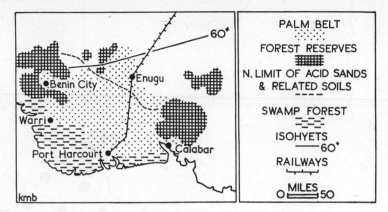

The export of palm produce is in the hands of some two dozen European, Syrian and African firms, who act as buying agents under the Oil Palm Produce Marketing Board. These undertake the assembling of palm kernels and palm-oil from the grading stations scattered throughout the Palm Belt, and the evacuation of these commodities to the ports. During recent years substantial economies both in time and expense have been achieved by the bulking of the oil for export and the use of oil-tankers; the distribution of the seven bulk oil plants is shown in Fig. 107. As a result of an agreement signed in June 1949, the Palm Produce Marketing Board agreed to sell to the British Ministry of Food the entire exportable surplus of palm-oil and kernels for the years 1950, 1951 and 1952.[1]

TABLE IX

PALM PRODUCE

(a) PALM-KERNELS

	1938	1947	1948	1949
Tons exported (000) .	312	316	327	379
Value (M.£) . .	2·2	6·2	6·3	12·3
Per cent of Nigerian exports, by value . .	23·4	16·7	17·5	21·2
Per cent. of total world exports . . .	46	58	52	52

(b) PALM-OIL

	1938	1947	1948	1949
Tons exported (000) .	110	121	139	159
Value (M.£) . .	1·0	3·2	3·9	7·2
Per cent. of Nigerian exports, by value .	10·6	8·7	10·9	12·4
Per cent. of total world exports . . .	22	43	38	34

The local and world significance of Nigerian palm products during recent years is summarised in the Tables IX(a) and (b).

Groundnuts

The groundnut, introduced to West Africa from the New World by the Portuguese, has long been grown as a food crop in many parts of Nigeria. The development of production for export is, however, more recent, and dates back little more than a generation. It was made possible by two technical developments: firstly, the perfecting of the hydrogenation process, which made possible the large-scale utilisation of the oil in the food industries (1903); secondly, the extension of rail transport into the Northern Provinces, which decisively linked this formerly inaccessible area with the world trade network (the railway reached Kano in 1912).[2] The striking expansion of export production which

[1] An excellent account of the economics of the palm industry is given in *United Africa Company Statistical and Economic Review*, No. 7 (March 1951).
[2] On these developments see *United Africa Company Statistical and Economic Review*, No. 4 (Sept. 1949).

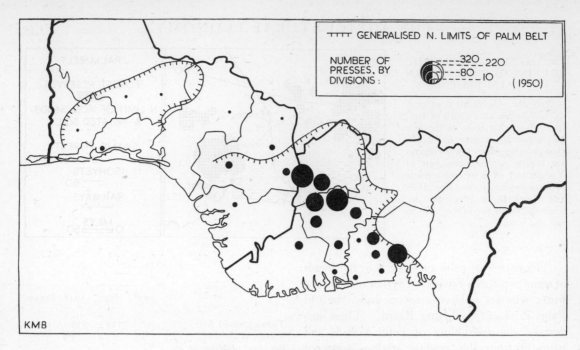

FIG. 105. PALM PRESSES

The distribution of hand-presses used in the process of oil extraction emphasises the concentration of oil production for export in the Provinces of Onitsha, Owerri and Calabar. Production is negligible north of a line joining Enugu and Calabar, a line which may be taken as the boundary between the highly developed and closely settled Ibo territory and the less developed "pioneer fringe" to the east.

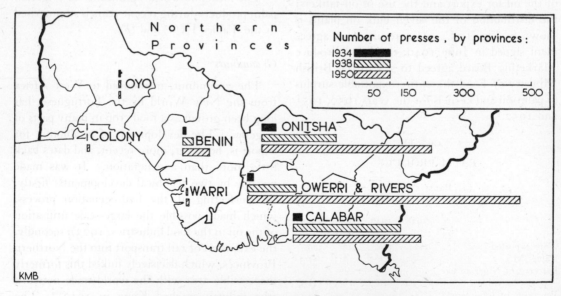

FIG. 106. HAND-PRESSES IN THE PALM BELT 1934–50

The simple hand-press gives an oil extraction rate of 65% as compared with 55% by traditional hand methods of extraction. The increasing use of such presses represents, therefore, a significant development in the palm-oil industry. Since 1934 the total number of presses in use has increased seventeenfold; the rate of expansion has been greatest in Owerri and Rivers Provinces (almost fiftyfold) and relatively insignificant in the Western Provinces.

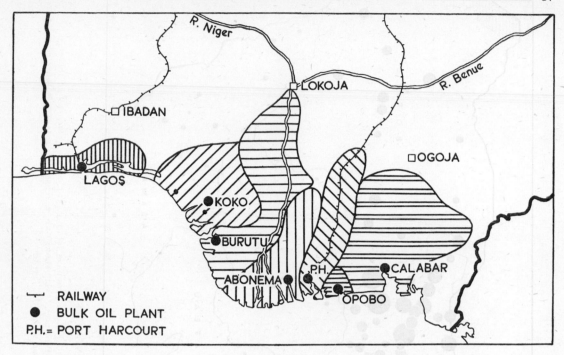

FIG. 107. BULK OIL PLANTS

Showing the seven bulk oil plants where the oil is stored in tanks before pumping into ocean or coastal tankers. By bulk handling wear and tear of casks is obviated and a considerable saving of time and expense effected. The areas tributary to each bulk oil plant are shown by hatching; note the influence of the Niger waterway and of the railway on the pattern of hinterlands.

followed these developments is summarised in the table below:

TABLE X

PRODUCTION OF GROUNDNUTS FOR EXPORT

5-YEAR AVERAGES

	000 tons
1910–14	8·2
1915–19	41·3
1920–24	44·3
1925–29	117·1
1930–34	188·8
1935–39	211·1
1940–44	181·9
1945–49	320·2

With the cessation of exports from the Indian sub-continent, Nigeria has recently emerged as the world's leading exporter of this crop. The importance of the crop in the Nigerian economy in recent years is summarised in the next table[1]:

TABLE XI
GROUNDNUTS IN THE NIGERIAN ECONOMY

	1938	1947	1948	1949
Tons exported (000)	180	256	245	355
Value (M.£)	1·3	6·3	6·8	12·0
Per cent. of Nigerian exports, by value	13·8	16·9	18·9	20·8
Per cent. of total world exports	9	38	28	40

Conditions in the Nigerian Sudan zone are well suited to the crop. The mean annual rainfall of between 25 and 40 inches, concentrated into the summer months, provides ideal

[1] Compiled from figures given in *Vegetable Oils and Oilseeds*, Commonwealth Economic Committee, London (1950).

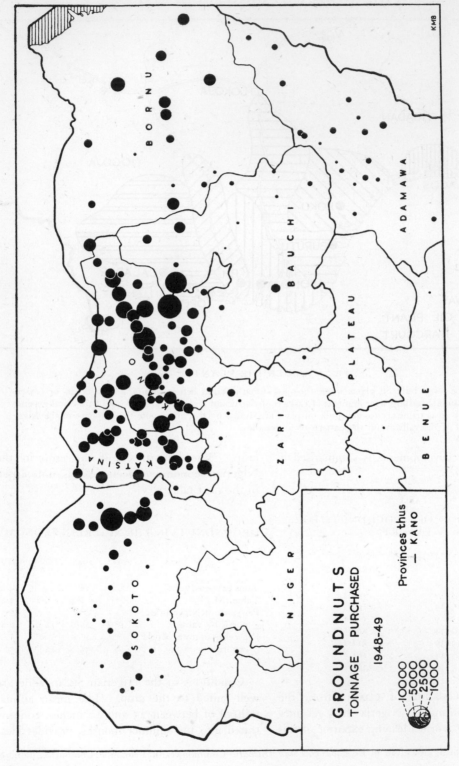

FIG. 108. GROUNDNUTS

Major concentration of production is on the light sandy soils of Kano and Katsina Provinces (cf. Fig. 22), with an extension of the main producing area along the railway and main roads into Sokoto and Bornu Provinces. Map shows only purchases for export and hence gives no indication of the very considerable volume of production for consumption within the Territory.

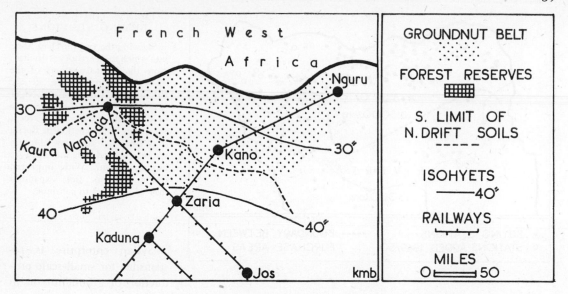

FIG. 109. THE GROUNDNUT BELT

Illustrating diagrammatically some of the factors which have produced the present pattern of production for export.   Note particularly the influence of the railway.

conditions for the crop; the generally light Northern Drift soils make for ease of harvesting and the crop, by reason of its nitrogen-fixing properties, helps to maintain soil fertility in an area where in the past distance from the sea has made the use of imported fertilisers uneconomic. It will be apparent from Fig. 109 that on its southern fringe the main groundnut belt extends on to the area of somewhat heavier Zaria-type soils, and here the normal "spreading" type of groundnut is replaced by an upright type which is easier to harvest on heavy land though slightly lower yielding than the "normal" variety.[1]

No data exists on the acreage under the crop. According to Turner,[2] the average yield of decorticated nuts is about 600 lb. per acre on the lighter soils and 500 lb. on the heavier soils, so that the export crop in recent years would represent the produce of approximately one and a quarter million acres.   Assuming that the average farmer cultivates one acre of groundnuts and that the average family unit consists of four people, we arrive at a figure of 5 million people dependent on groundnuts as their major cash crop.   This represents almost two-fifths of the population of the Northern Region, a proportion similar to the proportion of the Western Regions population estimated to depend on cocoa.

The general distribution of production for export is summarised in Fig. 108.   It will be evident that the main producing area is relatively clearly defined, and may be said to be contained within the quadrilateral Kaura Namoda–Zaria–Misau–Nguru.   The importance of accessibility in the evolution of this pattern needs no stressing (compare Fig. 110).   Outside this major groundnut belt, the crop is grown for export also in the Provinces of Bornu, Adamawa, Niger and Sokoto, but the aggregate production of these peripheral areas is not large,

[1] For a discussion of the importance of easy harvesting in the production of groundnuts see *Annual Report of the Department of Agriculture*, 1928, p. 8.
[2] "Economic Aspects of the Groundnut Industry in N. Nigeria" by R. Turner in *Empire Journal of Experimental Agriculture*, 1940.

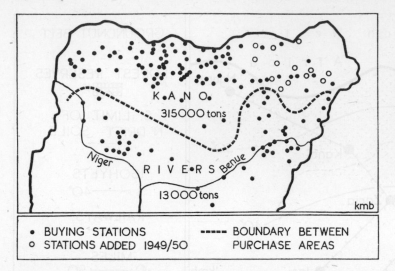

FIG. 110. GROUNDNUT BUYING STATIONS

Showing the two purchase areas into which the Territory is divided. Note the isolated outliers of the main producing region in the Provinces of Adamawa and Niger (where, however, the aggregate production is small) and the recent expansion of production in Bornu suggested by the new buying stations opened for the 1949–50 buying season. With improved communications this expansion may be expected to continue.

and in 1948–9 represented less than one-sixth of the total export production. With the greater proportion of the land suitable for groundnuts in the main producing area already under the crop, it is, however, clear that future expansion must largely be in these remoter areas. This centrifugal trend is illustrated by the development projects in the Provinces of Niger and Bornu, and by recent production figures. These latter show that, while all the major groundnut-growing areas increased their output over the period 1943–9, the rate of increase in Kano Province tended to lag, so that Kano's share of total output dropped from 56·6 to 49·5%.[1] No data is available on production for local consumption.

Syrian enterprise is responsible for small-scale production of groundnut oil in Kano City, and official development schemes provide for a wide scatter of groundnut mills throughout the North. At present, however, virtually the entire output is exported in the decorticated stage, and is processed abroad. Complete statistics on evacuation routes are not available, but the figures for groundnuts purchased by the United Africa Company (43% of the 1947–8 crop) provide a good index to the relative importance of the various routes. The percentages of the company's total purchases in 1947–8 evacuated by the various routes

FIG. 111. THE EXPANSION OF THE GROUNDNUT INDUSTRY

A doubling of the output between 1943–4 and 1948–9 has been accompanied by a marked expansion of output in the peripheral provinces of Katsina, Sokoto and Bornu.

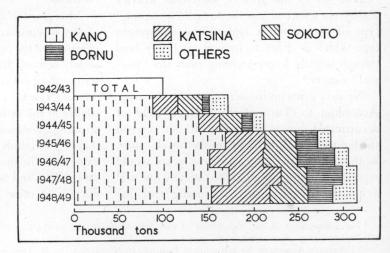

[1] *Minimum Prices for Groundnuts at Gazetted Buying Stations in the Kano Area*, Lagos (1950), p. 23.

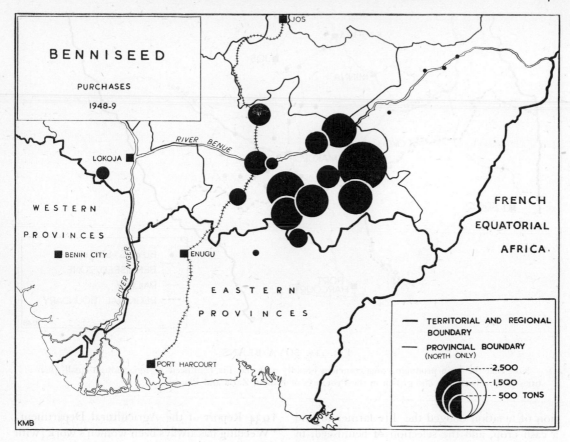

BENNISEED

PURCHASES

1948-9

JOS

RIVER BENUE

LOKOJA

WESTERN

PROVINCES

BENIN CITY

RIVER NIGER

ENUGU

EASTERN

PROVINCES

FRENCH

EQUATORIAL

AFRICA

PORT HARCOURT

KMB

— TERRITORIAL AND REGIONAL
BOUNDARY

— PROVINCIAL BOUNDARY
(NORTH ONLY)

-----2,500
----1,500
--- 500 TONS

FIG. 112. BENNISEED

Benniseed (sesame) is the major export crop of the Middle Belt and virtually the entire output comes from Tiv Division of Benue Province.

were as follows:

Western Railway . . 57·0
Eastern Railway . . 22·2
River . . . . 20·7
(Niger, 15·0; Benue, 5·7)

Of the total tonnage exported 81% is exported via Lagos, 13% via Port Harcourt and 5% via Burutu.

Minor Oil-yielding Crops

(a) *Benniseed:* Benniseed, or sesame seed, is, like groundnuts, an important source of edible oil. It is also used in the manufacture of

certain types of confectionery, and on a small scale in the manufacture of margarine and compound cooking fats. In Nigeria it is an excellent example of an "ethnically localised crop" (that is, a crop whose cultivation is virtually confined to one ethnic group), while its cultivation illustrates the influence which the human factors of custom and tradition may exert on the level of agricultural production.[1]

As Fig. 112 clearly shows, production of the crop is strongly localised in Benue Province, and here its cultivation is virtually a monopoly of the Tiv people. Production for export appears to have commenced when the introduc-

[1] On the early progress of benniseed production see the *Annual Reports of the Department of Agriculture*, esp. 1934 and 1936.

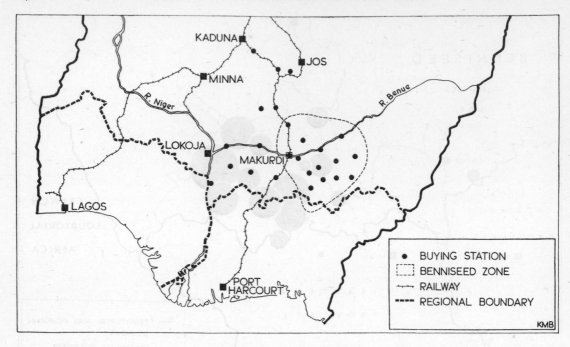

FIG. 113. SOYA BEANS

Note that the main producing area coincides broadly with the Tiv benniseed region, though small quantities of soya beans are also grown in the Provinces of Kabba, Zaria and Plateau.

tion of taxation obliged the Tiv farmer to find
a cash crop, and the selection of benniseed, in
preference to cotton which was advocated by
the Agricultural Department, was the result of
deliberate choice on his part.   The history of
the crop during the last twenty years shows
that the choice was the right one.   In the early
nineteen-thirties output was still relatively
small (2–3,000 tons); in 1937 it was over
11,000 tons, whilst in the last two years it has
been approximately 14,500 tons, worth between
£200,000 and £300,000.

The steady increase in export production
before World War II was due partly to an
extension of area, partly to better cultivation
techniques introduced by the Agricultural
Department, notably improved methods of
harvesting and the substitution of early for late
growing.   Yields, however, remain relatively
low, owing largely to the neglect of weeding
and thinning, a neglect which can be traced to
the influence of tribal custom.   To quote the

1934 Report of the Agricultural Department:
"Weeding has always been women's work [with
the Tiv] and the women weed the yam crop
efficiently, as is required by the old rules of the
tribe . . . they could not also undertake the
weeding of the newer crops.   It is below the
dignity of a man to do any weeding, and it is
contrary to tribal custom for him to do so.   So
the benniseed crop goes unweeded."

(b) *Soya Beans:* Soya beans are a comparatively new crop whose popularity has increased
strikingly in the last few years.   Production is
at present concentrated in the Middle Belt and
especially in Benue Province, though the crop
has also given good results on the heavier soils
of the Zaria area.   Table XII summarises
recent production trends for soya and benniseed.

Though the expansion of soya-bean production appears to have been in part at the expense
of benniseed, it should be stressed that the two
crops occupy quite different places in the
agricultural economy of the Middle Belt.

TABLE XII

EXPORTABLE SURPLUSES OF SOYA
AND BENNISEED

	Soya Beans	Benniseed
1946 . .	—	4,085
1947 . .	10	8,605
1948 . .	738	15,642
1949 . .	956	13,385
1950 . .	3,506	8,699
1951 (est.) .	6,000	9,000

Soya beans are normally planted on newly broken fallow or follow millet in July-August; benniseed, by contrast, is usually planted with the first rains on land previously occupied by corn or soyas, often when the rotation is nearing its end and the land is almost exhausted. There is thus little direct competition between the two crops. On the other hand, the fact that the farmer can make up his cash income by July-planted soyas means that he will no longer work overtime in April to get the maximum acreage under benniseed planted, and it is this quite natural attempt of the Middle Belt farmer to spread his labour more evenly through the farming year which accounts for the present recession of benniseed production.

Cotton

The cotton plant demands a rainfall of between 35 and 60 inches, with abundant sunshine during the growing period and a relatively dry period for harvest; it is moderately exacting as regards soil moisture conditions, and prefers a moisture-retentive yet well-drained loam or clay-loam soil. On climatic and soil grounds, therefore, a large part of the territory is suited to the crop, and, except on the sandy leached soils of the southern rain forest, cotton has a permanent place in the agricultural economy of most areas. It was formerly grown for export on a considerable scale in the dry-forest zone of south-western Nigeria, but as a result of the superior attractions of cocoa as an export crop and the ravages of fungoid and insect pests, export production in the South has dwindled to insignificant proportions. As late as 1925 the Yoruba Provinces were still producing a quarter of the country's export cotton, but in that year the decision of the British Cotton Growing Association to transfer their southernmost ginneries

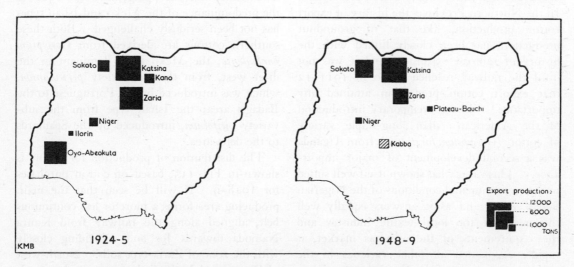

FIG. 114. SHIFTS IN EXPORT COTTON PRODUCTION IN 1924–5 TO 1948–9

Note the decline in production for export in the Yoruba Provinces where interest has shifted to cocoa and where the local textile industry now absorbs the entire production. In the Northern Provinces the centre of production has shifted north-west from the Zaria-Kano area towards Katsina and Sokoto. The hatched symbol in Kabba Province indicates ungraded Benue cotton.

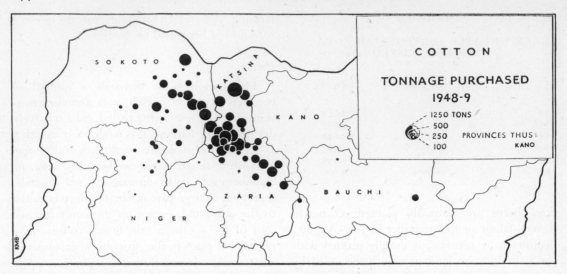

FIG. 115. COTTON PRODUCTION

The bulk of the Territory's cotton exports come from the Provinces of Zaria, Katsina and Sokoto, the limits of the export Cotton Belt being Kaura Namoda in the north-west and Soba in the south-east. Cotton is widely grown in Kano Province but the entire production is absorbed by the local textile industry. Note that the map shows only the "American cotton" area of the Northern Region and that the Lokoja area, producing the so-called "Ungraded Benue" cotton, falls outside the limits of the map. Production in the Lokoja area is, however, relatively small (3–5% of the total Nigerian export production).

at Abeokuta and Eruwa Road northwards to Dutsin Wai and Gusau was symptomatic of the decisive northward swing in cotton production. In the Northern Provinces the history of export cotton production, like that of groundnut production, has been closely linked with the history of railroad expansion, and it was not until the railway reached Kano in 1911–12 that export cotton production attained any importance.[1] The contemporary introduction of the American Allen long-staple variety of cotton (*Gossypium hirstutum*) from Uganda was a second development of major importance. This variety has shown itself well suited to the environmental conditions of the Nigerian Sudan zone, and as it answers equally well the needs of the local textile industry and the requirements of the overseas market, it rapidly supplanted all other varieties in the export cotton areas of the Northern Provinces.

In the forest regions of the south its susceptibility to disease has prevented its diffusion; it does not lend itself to mixed cropping, and in consequence the predominance of the Meko and Ishan types has not been seriously challenged. Both these southern cottons are derived from *Gossypium barbadense*; the Meko type, dominant in the drier west, from the sub-variety *peruvianum*, which was introduced by the Portuguese to the Badagri area; the Ishan type from the sub-variety *vitifolium*, introduced by the Spaniards to the delta area.[2]

The distribution of production for export is shown in Fig. 115, based on cotton purchases for 1948–9. It will be seen that the main producing area forms a more or less continuous belt, aligned along the railway from Kaura Namoda towards Jos and coinciding closely with the zone of Zaria-type soils. North-west of Funtua and Makarfi the cotton and ground-

[1] "Past, Present and Future of Cotton-growing in Nigeria" by P. H. Lamb in *Empire Cotton-Growing Review*, 1925.
[2] "The Dissemination of Cotton in Africa" by J. B. Hutchinson in *Empire Cotton-Growing Review*, 1949.

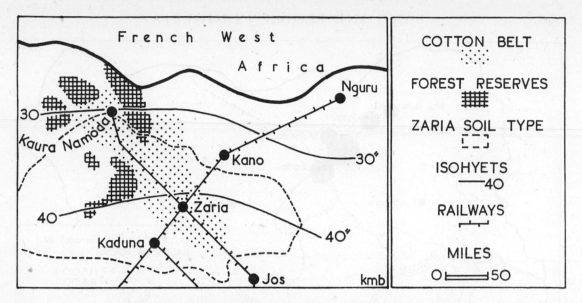

FIG. 116. THE GEOGRAPHIC SETTING OF THE COTTON BELT

Illustrating the concentration of production for export on the heavy Zaria-type soils and in close proximity to the Jos-Zaria-Kaura Namoda railway.

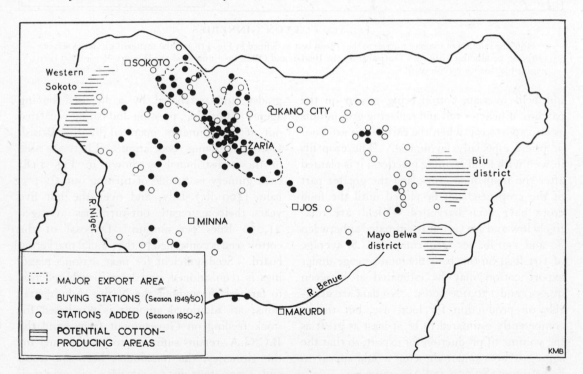

FIG. 117. THE EXPANSION OF COTTON PRODUCTION 1949–52

Since 1949 the number of cotton buying stations has increased from 91 to 158. This increase has been especially marked in the Bauchi area (a new ginnery is being constructed at Gombe to handle the Bauchi crop) and in parts of Sokoto Province. The most promising areas for future expansion appear to be the *fadama* zone of Western Sokoto and parts of Adamawa and S. Bornu, though before the potentialities of these areas can be fully realised, a great improvement in communications will be necessary (cf. Fig. 151).

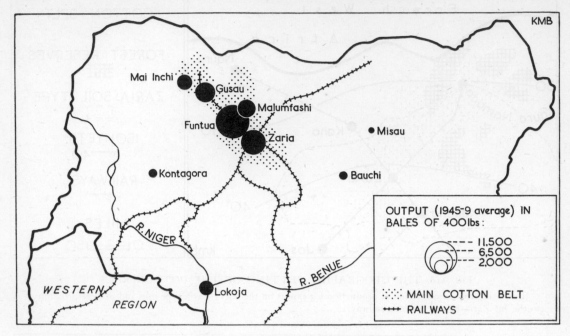

FIG. 118. COTTON GINNERIES

Note the relation of major ginneries to the cotton belt as defined in Fig. 116 and the scattered ginneries serving outlying producing districts. Output from the Ibadan and Oshogbo ginneries in the Western Region has been negligible during recent years.

nut belts overlap, cotton being grown on the patches of heavier soil and replacing groundnuts as an export crop when the early rains are poor or prices especially favourable. The crop fits in well with local farming practices; it is planted after the main food crops, and the greater part of the crop need not be picked until the food crops have been harvested. Yields are relatively low and are variously estimated at between 80 and 150 lb. per acre (compare U.S. average of 191 lb.); on this basis the total acreage under export cotton may be estimated at between 90,000 and 170,000 acres. No data are available on production for local use, but this is competently estimated to be at least as great as the volume of production for export, so that the aggregate area under the crop would appear to be between 180,000 and 340,000 acres.

All cotton intended for export must pass through an official cotton market, where it is graded and purchased by a licensed buying agent.[1] Ginning, pressing and baling is carried out at the ginneries operated by the British Cotton Growing Association. There are nine of these, distributed as shown in Fig. 118; each ginnery is capable of turning out 50–100 bales (400 lb.) daily, and over the last five years their aggregate out-turn has averaged 31,000 bales per annum. Disposal of the cotton seed is controlled by the official marketing board. Seed sufficient for next season's plantings is requisitioned, and later distributed free to farmers throughout the Native Administrations; an additional amount is purchased for stock feeding on Government farms, and the B.C.G.A. retains sufficient to provide fuel for the ginneries; the remainder, between 3,000 and 5,000 tons in recent years, is exported. This control of seed distribution, together with the prohibition on the cultivation of varieties

[1] R. Turner, "Economic Aspects of the Cotton Industry of N. Nigeria" in *Empire Journal of Experimental Agriculture*, 1948.

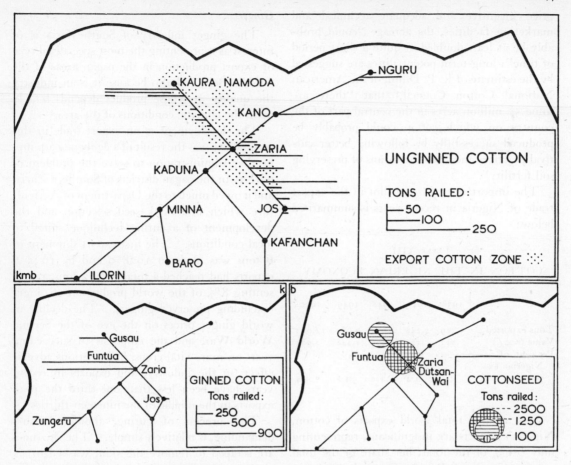

FIG. 119. MOVEMENT OF COTTON IN THE NORTHERN REGION

As in Fig. 153 length of horizontal lines is proportional to the tonnage railed out from each station.   Note the movement of unginned cotton from areas in Kano and Niger Provinces lying outside the main cotton belt; concentration of traffic in ginned cotton is at Funtua and Zaria (Zungeru handles the Kontagora output); a virtual monopoly of cottonseed traffic is enjoyed by Funtua and Gusau.

other than Allen in the so-called American cotton areas, has been of vital importance in maintaining the purity and high quality of the Allen long-staple variety in the Northern Provinces.

During recent years cotton prices in Nigeria have been maintained at a level below the world price, in order to divert attention to the production of food crops. It is, in consequence, difficult to draw any valid conclusions as to the future prospects of the crop from recent produc-

tion trends. It is probable that in the main cotton belt no great expansion of acreage is to be anticipated, and here any significant increase in output must come from higher yields; in this connection it is worth noting that new cotton strains selected from Allen have been shown to yield far more heavily than Allen. Outside the main cotton belt there are extensive areas in the pagan districts of the Middle Belt, whose potentialities have never been seriously tested. J. R. Mackie[1] has estimated that, given a

[1] J. R. Mackie, "Possibilities of Increased Production of Cotton in Nigeria" in *Empire Cotton-Growing Review*, 1948.

price incentive and adequate technical and marketing facilities, the acreage "could probably be at least doubled in quite a short period of time"; long-term potentialities are suggested by the estimate of R. P. Dunn, of the American National Cotton Council,[1] that "there are some 50 million acres in the central part of the country on which cotton could probably be produced successfully by following better cultival practices and scientific means of preserving soil fertility".

The importance of cotton lint in the export trade of Nigeria in recent years is summarised below:

TABLE XIII

COTTON IN THE NIGERIAN ECONOMY

	1938	1947	1948	1949	1950
Tons exported .	5,729	5,248	4,635	9,984	12,623
Value (000£) .	247	520	476	1,448	2,975
Per cent. of Nigerian exports . .	2·6	1·4	1·1	1·8	3·4

Seen against total world exports of cotton, Nigeria's exports are insignificant, representing only 0·1% of the total; her share of the total cotton exports of British Tropical Africa is, however, of the order of 10%.

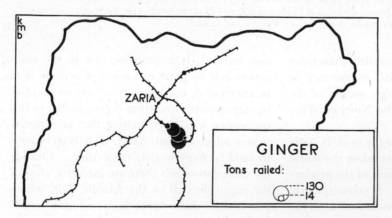

GINGER

Tons railed:

---- 130
---- 14

Ginger

The ginger industry of South Zaria is of interest as representing the most specialised type of export production in the pagan areas of the Middle Belt, and also because it is an industry the quality of whose product depends largely upon the climatic conditions of the area.[2]

The development of an export trade in this commodity was the result of a deliberate attempt by the Administration to solve the problem of poverty in the pagan districts of Southern Zaria, and it owed much to the Department of Agriculture which undertook seed selection and the development of a curing technique suited to local conditions. The first export shipment of 6 tons was made in 1928–9 and by 1935–6 exports had reached a total of 342 tons, representing 8% of the world production of ginger (excluding preserved ginger). The decline of world ginger prices on the eve of the Second World War, and the emphasis in succeeding years on more vital crops, had a serious adverse effect on the industry, and exports in recent years have been less than one-third the peak exports in the middle of the nineteen-thirties.

The process of curing, though labour-demanding, is relatively simple. The rhizomes are scraped to remove the skin, washed in six changes of water and dried in the sun; after drying, the ginger is again washed and dried, and this process is repeated until the desired colour is obtained. It has been found that rapid sun-drying in the strong sun of the Harmattan period "bleaches the ginger

FIG. 120. GINGER

Concentration of production in pagan districts of southern Zaria. For the importance of the climatic factor in the curing of the ginger see text.

[1] R. P. Dunn, *Cotton in French West Africa and Nigeria*, National Cotton Council, Memphis, Tennessee (1949).
[2] E. W. Momber, "Southern Zaria Ginger Industry" in *Farm and Forest*, Vol. VIII, No. 3 (1942), pp. 119–21. See also *Annual Reports of the Department of Agriculture*, esp. 1934 and 1937.

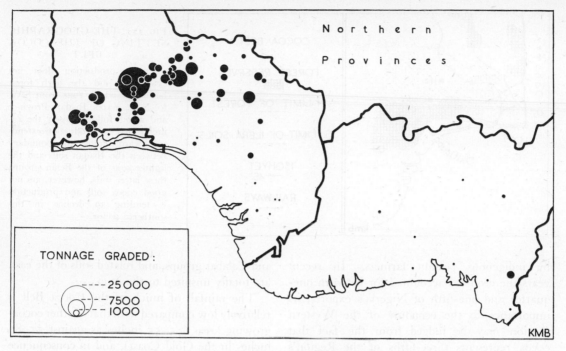

FIG. 121. COCOA PRODUCTION

Localisation of production in the dry forest zone and on the Ibadan soils of the Western Region; negligible importance of cocoa on the sandy soils of the east. Note the clearly defined character of the north-western boundary of the cocoa belt and compare with Fig. 122.

in a way which in many other climates can apparently only be attained by the use of sulphur fumes", and though small-scale production of sun-dried and kiln-dried ginger has been attempted in the south, the appearance of the product is far inferior to that of the northern ginger.

At the height of the expansion of the industry faulty curing threatened to ruin the reputation of the ginger on the English market, and, as it was impossible to supervise the 20,000 scattered producers, the area of production was restricted to the Kachia Jabas, and twelve central washing stations were set up under supervision. These control measures had the desired effect, and no further difficulties have arisen regarding the quality of the product.

Marketing is confined to Kachia market.

Here in 1949 82½ tons were purchased, of which 83% was classed as Grade I.

Cocoa

Like many other Nigerian crops, cocoa is not indigenous to the Territory, but was introduced from the New World, probably by way of Fernando Po. Tradition asserts that it reached Nigeria in 1874, having been introduced by a chief called "Squiss Bamego", who established a plantation in the vicinity of Bonny on the east of the Niger delta.[1] From Bonny its cultivation spread inland, and by the end of the next decade attempts at plantation production had been initiated by several European trading companies. These attempts proved abortive,[2] however, and as in the case of the Gold Coast the industry has been developed entirely

---

[1] *Tropical Agriculture*, Vol. XXIII, No. 9 (Sept. 1946), p. 172.

[2] The Onitsha and Abutshi plantations of the Royal Niger Company survived until 1900 when they were taken over by the Government of S. Nigeria.

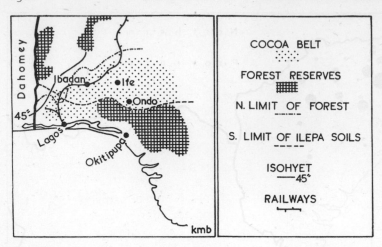

FIG. 122. THE GEOGRAPHIC SETTING OF THE COCOA BELT

Cocoa production does not extend beyond the high forest boundary which runs from S.W. to N.E. across Ibadan Province and which follows closely the 45-inch isohyet. Production extends southwards across the boundary between the Ibadan soils and the lighter soils of the Benin group; these latter soils, however, are not good cocoa soils and production is tending to decline in this southern sector.

by indigenous peasant farmers. In recent years the crop has accounted for between one-quarter and one-fifth of Nigeria's exports; its importance to the economy of the Western Region may be judged from the fact that cocoa represents three-fifths of the Region's exports; and directly supports two-fifths of the Region's population (excluding the very considerable number of middlemen and transport workers indirectly supported by the cocoa trade).

Cocoa is essentially a crop of the dry-forest zone of the Western Region[1]; here during the last thirty years it has replaced cotton as the major cash crop and today it dominates the economy of the Provinces of Ibadan, Abeokuta and Ondo, which contain 85% of Nigeria's cocoa land. Since it requires shade, high humidity and a moderately high rainfall, it is not grown in the open country of North-west Oyo, the northern edge of the dry forest, which follows closely the 45-inch isohyet, representing the limit of the Cocoa Belt in this direction. To the east, beyond the dry-forest zone, increasing rainfall, and subsequent prevalence of capsid, makes successful cultivation difficult, but the major limiting factor in Benin Province, and over much of the Eastern Region, is the soil factor. Little cocoa is grown outside the region of Ibadan soils (Fig. 22), and the Benin

and Calabar groups, and related soils of the east, are totally unsuited to the crop.

The rainfall of much of the Cocoa Belt is relatively low compared with that of other cocoa-growing areas (45–55 inches as against 55–80 inches in the Gold Coast), and in consequence soil moisture conditions are of critical importance. The very distinctive succession of soils on hill slopes in the Ibadan soil belt has been described elsewhere (p. 38), and this has exercised a vital influence on the pattern of successful cocoa production; throughout the Cocoa Belt the crop finds its optimum conditions on the sedentary Ilepa clays of the ridge tops or on the transported clay loams of the upper slopes, and makes only poor growth on the hungrier concretionary or sandy soils of the lower slopes. Unfavourable soil moisture conditions would also appear responsible for the decline of cocoa cultivation on the light soils in the extreme south-west (Agege type); here the last twenty-five years has witnessed a gradual swing over from cocoa to kola-nut production.

Cultivation methods are relatively "extensive". The crop is sown on cleared forest land, sharing its living space during the first three to four years with food crops. After some four years the young trees form a relatively closed canopy, and henceforth cultivation is restricted to an occasional cutlassing of weeds and under-

[1] J. West, "The Future of Cocoa in Oyo Province" in *Farm and Forest*, Vol. II, No. 3 (1941), p. 141.

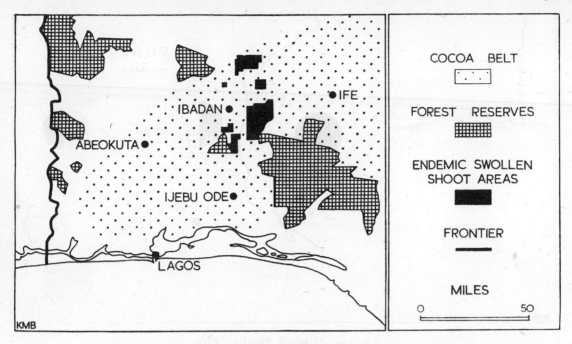

FIG. 123. SWOLLEN SHOOT DISEASE IN IBADAN PROVINCE

Swollen shoot disease has been present in Nigeria since 1944, and in 1950 the infected area covered some 245 square miles, containing an estimated total of 25 million cocoa trees, and running transversely across the heart of the Cocoa Belt. The future of the Nigerian cocoa industry depends in large measure upon the success of attempts to confine the disease to this endemic area and prevent the spread of the disease to the important producing districts around Ife, Abeokuta and Ijebu.

growth. The trees are spaced more closely than in other producing areas, but this does not appear to have any adverse effect, for yields are stated to be well above the West Indian average. Today the acreage under the crop is estimated at 600,000; this is divided between some 330,000 growers, so that the average holding consists of some 1·8 acres of cocoa, though the average holding tends to be below this figure in the westernmost sector of the Cocoa Belt. Final data on the age composition of the country's cocoa plantings are not available, but preliminary sampling suggests that the bulk of the trees are old; in Ibadan Province only 14% of the cocoa is under ten years of age; in Abeokuta Province 14%, and while the proportion of young trees is very much higher in the east, the total acreages involved in provinces such as Benin or Ogoja are negligible.

For long, Nigerian cocoa enjoyed an enviable immunity from disease, but today the situation is far less happy. "Black pod" disease is estimated to have destroyed 30% of the 1947 crop, while in the last five years the spread of the virus disease "swollen shoot" has struck at the foundations of the prosperity of the Cocoa Belt. The existence of swollen shoot in Nigeria was confirmed in the middle of the nineteen-forties; today the endemic area covers an area of 245 square miles in the heart of the Cocoa Belt, with a cocoa tree population of 25 million producing one-ninth of the total Nigerian crop.[1] Control measures involve the sealing-off of the affected area and the cutting out of the diseased trees, but the carrying out of rapid and effective counter-measures has been impeded by the opposition of many growers to the cutting-out policy.

[1] *Cocoa Conference* 1950. Cocoa, Chocolate and Confectionery Alliance, Ltd. (London), p. 14.

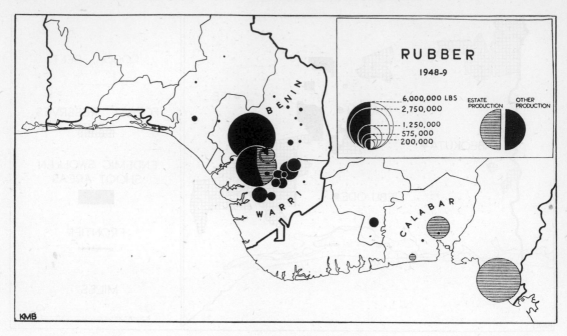

FIG. 124. RUBBER PRODUCTION

Major centre of production in Warri Province and in south Benin; secondary centres of production in
Provinces of Calabar and Cameroons.   Plantation production is more important in the rubber industry than in
any other branch of agricultural production; even so, as can be seen from the map, the greater proportion of the
Territory's output comes from small peasant holdings.

With the exception of the Cameroons crop and a small quantity exported through Sapele, the entire crop is exported through Lagos. The railway plays a negligible role in the evacuation of the crop to port; most of the production of Ibadan, Abeokuta and Ijebu is transported by lorry directly to Lagos, while part of Ondo's crop is evacuated by road to Okitipupa and thence by lighter to Lagos.

The 1948 exports were 91,450 tons, representing 15·2% of the world's cocoa exports.

Rubber

The early development of the Nigerian rubber industry was based on the tapping of indigenous rubber-bearing plants, notably the tree *Funtumia elastica* and the vines *Landolphia* and *Clitandra*. This early industry underwent striking fluctuations; thus the value of rubber exports was £2,371,892 in 1895, but dropped

to £131,000 five years later, recovering to £311,691 in 1910. Reckless tapping rapidly depleted the Territory's wild rubber resources, and under the impetus of the high prices then prevailing and with the active encouragement of the Forest Department, increasing attention was given to the possibilities of plantation production. During the decade preceding the First World War extensive communal plantings of *Funtumia* were made; these were especially numerous in the Benin area where, by 1910, some 700 villages had established plantations containing an aggregate of one and a quarter million trees.[1] At the same time several companies were formed to exploit *Funtumia* and *Landolphia* on plantation lines, but achieved no great measure of success owing to the low yields of these sources of rubber. The Para rubber tree (*Hevea brasiliensis*), upon which the world's natural rubber industry today is based, was

[1] E. D. Morel, *Nigeria: its Peoples and its Problems*, London (1912), pp. 69–70.

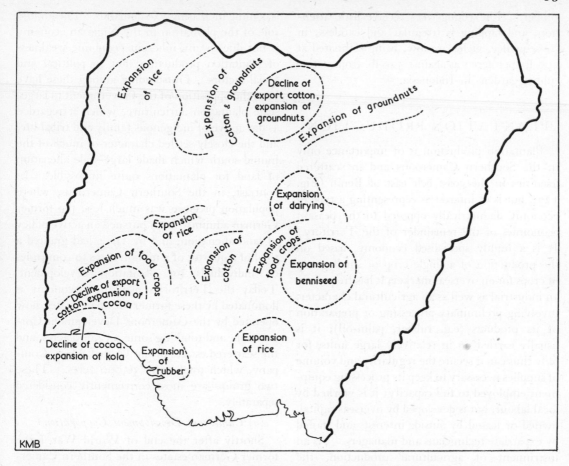

FIG. 125. SOME CHANGES IN THE AGRICULTURAL PATTERN OF THE TERRITORY
DURING THE LAST THIRTY YEARS

Note especially the decline of cotton cultivation and the northward shift of cocoa production in the Yoruba
Provinces; the decline of export cotton production and the expansion of groundnut production in Kano
Province and northern Zaria; the expansion of groundnut production in the outlying provinces of Sokoto
and Bornu; and the development of food crops in parts of the Middle Belt. Only crops produced for sale
are shown.

introduced experimentally into the Lagos area
in 1895, and commercial production was
initiated ten years later, when a large European
trading company established an extensive plantation in the Sapele area. Today, *Hevea* has
almost entirely supplanted *Funtumia* as a source
of rubber in Nigeria.

Before the Second World War the world
rubber situation precluded any large-scale
development of the industry and output remained stationary at a level of about 3,000 tons.
The loss of South-east Asia encouraged expan-

sion of plantation production, and a renewed
exploitation of the country's wild rubber
resources and output rose to a peak of 11,000
tons, dropping in the post-war period to some
7,000 tons worth, in 1948, £710,000.

Hevea will flourish on relatively poor soils,
and as Fig. 124 shows, most of the present-day
output comes from the Benin and Calabar soils
of south-central Nigeria. One quarter of the
output comes from six large estates, most of the
remainder coming from small growers who
interplant their yams and other crops with

rubber. The young trees receive little attention, and tapping is irregular and careless; in consequence, yields are low, being estimated at 200 lb. per acre[1] as against 520 lb. from native rubber gardens in Indonesia.

PLANTATION PRODUCTION

Plantation production is of importance only in the Southern Cameroons and in scattered localities in the coast belt east of Benin (Fig. 127), but is of interest as representing a type of economy diametrically opposed to the peasant economies of the remainder of the Territory.[2] It is a highly specialised economy, based on the production of a single crop or small group of crops for an overseas market; it has frequently an industrial as well as an agricultural character, involving preliminary processing or preparation of its products (e.g. rubber, palm-oil); it is usually carried on in relatively large units, for only thus can it secure the regularity and volume of supplies necessary to keep its processing equipment employed to full capacity; it is worked by local labour, but is developed by overseas capital, owned or leased by outside interests and staffed by expatriate technicians and managers. As an instrument of agricultural production, the plantation has many advantages over the small peasant holding. It enjoys easier access to the money market, and is in a much stronger position to carry out systematic research into problems of production, and to apply the results of that research. It is in a position to take advantage of each new technological improvement, and enjoys the advantages of division of labour and specialisation with all the opportunities for large-scale and skilled management. As far as trade is concerned, the plantation system can provide the regularity of supply and the uniformity of product which the world market is coming increasingly to demand. The limited role of the plantation in the Nigerian economy is not due to any inherent economic weakness of plantation production, but to political and social factors. Outstanding among these have been the opposition of the Government to large-scale plantation agriculture, which it regarded as disruptive of indigenous family and tribal life, and the closely settled character of much of the humid south which made large-scale alienation of land for plantations quite impossible. In contrast, in the Southern Cameroons, where population pressure was much less, the former German administration pursued an active policy of land alienation, and by 1914 had granted a total of a quarter of a million acres to companies or individuals for plantation development. Today the Territory's plantation economy is dominated by these former German estates, now operated by the Cameroons Development Corporation, and totalling some 253,000 acres, and the scattered estates of the United Africa Company, which total some 36,000 acres. These two groups are most conveniently considered separately.

(a) Cameroons Development Corporation [3]

Shortly after the end of World War I the former German estates in the Southern Cameroons were put up for auction; few were, however, sold, and in 1924 the properties were again put on the market, when all the estates then unsold were repurchased by their former German owners; by 1939 all estates, with one exception, had passed into German hands. At the outbreak of World War II, the estates were vested in the Custodian of Enemy Property, and at the conclusion of hostilities the Nigerian Government expressed the desire that they should not revert to private ownership, but should be held and administered "for the use and common benefit of the inhabitants of the

[1] T. R. Lamb, "The Benin Rubber Industry" in *Farm and Forest*, Vol. V, No. 2 (1944), pp. 35-7.

[2] For a general discussion of peasant and plantation production see Sir A. Pim, *Colonial Agricultural Production*, London. There is a comparison between the plantation economy of the Congo and the peasant economy of Nigeria in *United Africa Company Statistical and Economic Review*, No. 9 (March 1952).

[3] For the Cameroons Plantations see *Annual Report of the Cameroons Development Corporation* and *Report . . . on the Administration of the Cameroons under United Kingdom Trusteeship*, Colonial No. 276, London (1951).

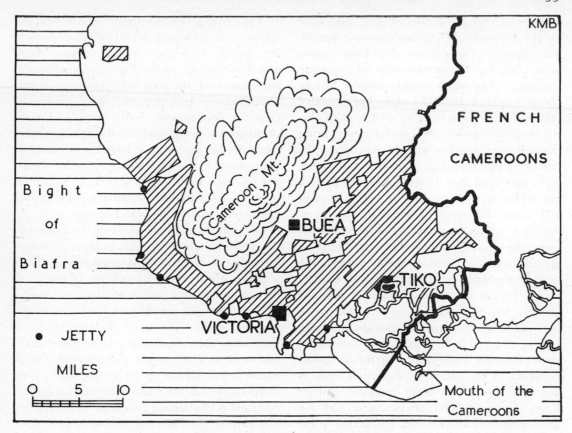

FIG. 126. THE CAMEROONS PLANTATION ZONE

Major concentration of plantation land is on the relatively level Tiko Plain and along the west coast plain. With the exception of the Likomba plantation (referred to in the text) the entire area is operated by the Cameroons Development Corporation. The Tombel Plantation is not shown; it lies close to the international frontier to the north-east of the area shown on the map.

British Cameroons". This was implemented in 1946, when the estates were purchased by the Nigerian Government and leased to the Cameroons Development Corporation, a statutory corporation which operates on a commercial basis and whose surplus profits are utilised for the benefit of the peoples of the Cameroons in such manner as the Governor may determine.

The main block of plantations extends in a semi-circle around the southern slopes of Cameroon Mountain and across the Tiko plain; smaller isolated estate areas are located in coastal areas to the north-west and north-east of the main block. The total area of land held by the Corporation is slightly over a quarter of a million acres, of which one-fifth is cultivated.

In addition, the Likomba estate (15,600 acres) is operated by Messrs. Elders & Fyffes, Ltd., in accordance with a tripartite agreement between the Government of Nigeria, the company and the Corporation. The major crops grown by the Corporation are as follows (in acres):

TABLE XIV

MAJOR CROPS ON THE HOLDINGS OF THE C.D.C.

	Mature	Immature
Bananas . .	18,058	2,467
Oil palm . .	15,476	491
Rubber . .	11,315	3,608
Cocoa . .	2,156	—

Bananas, initially developed on a large scale by the Germans during the inter-war period, today dominate the economy of the Corporation, accounting for almost two-thirds of the estate revenue. The major concentration of banana plantations is on the Tiko plain, but an active policy of developing outlying estates, chiefly on the west coast and in the Tombel area, is being pursued; such a policy will not only spread the risk of damage from hurricanes (which in spring 1950 destroyed over 2½ million banana plants), but will relieve the pressure on the Tiko plain and allow fallowing of some of the more depleted sections. 1949 banana shipments from the Corporation's estates amounted to approximately 3 million stems, representing 57% of the shipments from the British Cameroons. Production of dried bananas declined from 1,366,286 lb. in 1947 to 28,252 in 1950, but has recently shown a marked recovery (1951, 573,216 lb.). The bulk of this output comes from the Tombel estate on the north-east periphery of the plantation zone; this estate is dependent on the seasonally navigable Mungo River for evacuation of products, and the development of dried banana production is due to the fact that green bananas can be exported only during the high-water season.

The acreage under rubber is considerably less than the acreage under oil palms; nevertheless, rubber is second only to bananas as a source of revenue, accounting for approximately one-quarter of the total sales revenue of the Corporation. It is regarded as a promising crop for development in the area, and new plantings are being made at the rate of some 750 acres per annum; it is hoped to double this figure when staff and labour are available. Output has risen from 925 tons in 1949 to 1,606 tons in 1951, and will expand rapidly as the young plantations come into bearing.

Oil palms occupy one-third of the Corporation's planted area, but palm produce accounts for only one-tenth of its sales revenue. This is due partly to the inaccessibility of many of the palm areas, and also to the fact that many of the plantations are old and have a relatively low tree density per acre. Rehabilitation of some of the older plantations is being undertaken and a new 4,500 acres plantation is being established at Idenau on the West coast. The Corporation has three small oil-mills in operation, and is establishing two larger mills (1,000 tons capacity) at Bota and Mokundange. Exports of palm produce have shown a steady upward trend, palm-oil exports rising from

TABLE XV

AGRICULTURAL PRODUCTION ON THE C.D.C. ESTATES

	1947	1948	1949	1950	1951
Bananas (shipments: stems)					
Total, British Cameroons .	1,281,330	4,078,408	5,137,600	4,680,419	5,773,208
C.D.C. Estates . .	673,713	2,268,818	2,927,539	2,666,775	3,609,906
Dried Bananas: lb. . .	1,366,286	417,492	112,224	28,252	573,216
Palm-oil: tons . .	1,321	1,483	1,589	2,077	2,463
Palm Kernels: tons . .	788	842	666	1,157	1,265
Rubber: tons . .	1,314	1,335	925	1,324	1,606
Cocoa: lb. . .	—	40,854	255,770	194,040	186,480
Pepper: lb. . .	2,240	2,977	4,943	2,260	3,360
Tea: lb. . . .	26,208	1,738	—	—	—
Butter: lb. . .	6,528	5,935	5,441	4,827	8,438
Milk: gallons . .	15,590	19,205	19,238	15,272	24,870

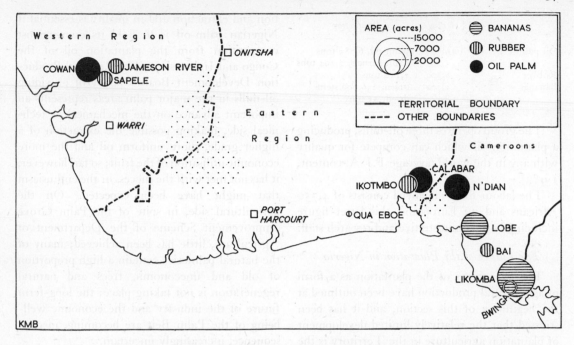

FIG. 127. DISTRIBUTION OF MAJOR EUROPEAN-OPERATED PLANTATIONS

Marked concentration in the less closely settled sectors of the humid coast belt. The stippled areas indicate area of potential plantation development. Cameroons Development Corporation lands are not included.

1,589 tons in 1949 to 2,463 tons in 1951 and palm-kernel exports from 666 tons to 1,265 tons over the same period.

Cocoa is of minor importance, and production since 1949 has shown a downward trend. In spite of rehabilitation measures, yields in the old plantations have continued to drop, and, to quote the official annual report, "there are, as yet, insufficient indications of this crop being economic, even at the present high prices, on the older plantations".

Minor crops include pepper and tea, though harvesting of the latter crop ceased after 1948 as being unprofitable (1947 production 26,000 lb.). In addition, vegetables and a growing output of milk and butter are produced for local consumption on Buea Farms.

The total labour force employed (1950) totalled 19,000 Africans and 141 Europeans. Details of the production of various crops on

the Corporation's estates are summarised in Table XV.

(b) Other Plantations

With the exception of a small group of African-owned rubber plantations in the Benin–Warri area, the only other estates are those of the United Africa Company.[1] These total 36,550 acres, of which 30,100 are planted and consist, geographically, of three groups, a group around Sapele (10,500 acres), a group around Calabar (9,750 acres) and a group in the Southern Cameroons (16,300 acres). Of the total, 16,300 acres are held freehold, these being ex-German properties in the Cameroons, and the remainder leasehold.

The acreage and production of various crops (1949–50) were as follows:

[1] Details of the United Africa Company's holdings are given in *U.A.C. Statistical and Economic Review No. 9.*

	Acreage	Production
Oil palms . .	19,600	palm-oil, 6,785 tons palm kernels, 2,294 tons
Rubber . .	8,800	1,150 tons
Bananas . .	1,700	green, 256,000 stems dried, 85 tons

The group operates three oil-mills, producing a plantation oil which can compete for quality with any in the world (average F.F.A. content, 1·9%).

The labour force employed consists of 4,750 Africans and 23 Europeans, this latter figure including both administrative and research staff.

(c) The Future of the Plantation in Nigeria

The advantages of the plantation as a form of agricultural production have been outlined at the beginning of this section, and it has been stressed that the relatively limited development of plantation agriculture in the Territory is the result of deliberate Government policy. Past plantation development in other areas was only too often associated with exploitation of the tropical peoples and with the disruption of indigenous social and economic life, and even though modern development in Nigeria has shown clearly that this exploitation and disruption are not inherent in the system, the old suspicions die hard. Moreover, present world trends, and more especially the adjustment of relations between the white and coloured peoples of the globe, are tending to create a psychological climate unfavourable to the extension in the tropics of large-scale expatriate-managed plantations. Nevertheless, it is becoming increasingly clear that, if Nigeria is to retain its position in the world market for perennial tree products, some method must be found of infusing into the existing system of indigenous-controlled production the agricultural and economic advantages of plantation agriculture. This is especially urgent in the case of the palm industry, where an improvement in methods of produc-

tion and extraction and in quality is essential if Nigerian palm-oil is to hold its own against competition from the plantation oil of the Congo and Indonesia. The Regional Production Development Board's policy of providing oil-mills in the major palm areas represents an important advance on the mechanical or technical side, making possible the extraction of a higher grade, more uniform oil and the more economic utilisation of the fruit; so far, however, it has not met with the success or the enthusiasm that might have been expected. On the agricultural side, in spite of the Palm Grove Improvement Scheme of the Department of Agriculture, little has been achieved; many of the natural palmeries contain a high proportion of old and uneconomic trees and natural regeneration is not taking place; the long-term future of the industry and the economic well-being of the Palm Belt are becoming, in consequence, increasingly uncertain.

In the light of these circumstances, and with the example of the commercial palm and rubber plantations of the coastal belt before them, it is not surprising that the Regional Production Development Boards should have shown a growing interest in the possibilities of plantation production.[1] This interest is expressed in the decision of the Eastern Regional Production Development Board "to undertake, either directly or through agencies, large-scale schemes of production, using wherever possible plantation methods. . . ." With this end in view the Eastern Regional Board (which has a majority of African members and is thus in a stronger position than a foreign *entrepreneur* would be) has agreed to the establishment of a large (12,000 acre) palm plantation and a similar-scale rubber plantation in the thinly peopled area of the Oban Hills, and of smaller plantations of oil palms, coconut palms, coffee and cashew nuts at other points in the region. A somewhat similar large-scale rubber plantation is reported from the Western Region. The

[1] See *Annual Report of the Eastern Region Production Development Board*; *Annual Report of the Western Region Production Development Board*; for a tripartite scheme of development see "The Future of the Nigerian Oil Industry" in *African Affairs*, Vol. 47, No. 186 (Jan. 1948).

smaller plantations are of a size for which land can be found in all but the most heavily peopled areas, and by the group development of five or more plantations within a radius of some 30 miles the overhead costs can be reduced to a minimum; at the same time their size makes them suitable as models which can be copied by villages as part of their community development programme.

As a result of these decisions, plantation agriculture, for long rejected in favour of small-scale peasant production, has at last been officially accepted as a legitimate form of agricultural development for the more thinly peopled sectors of the humid forest lands of the south. If, however, it is to make an effective contribution to the solution of the Territory's agricultural and economic problems, a very considerable expansion of the projected acreage is essential. The crying need for such large-scale development was stressed by one of the larger West African trading groups as long ago as 1944, and concrete suggestions as to areas suitable for such development were put forward, together with a scheme of tripartite plantation development analogous to the highly successful Gezira Scheme in the Anglo-Egyptian Sudan.[1] Within the framework of such a scheme the basic peasant pattern is preserved and the cultivator is closely associated with and has a personal interest in the development from its earliest stages; under West African conditions it would appear to hold out at least as great a promise as existing schemes based on dual partnership between the Development Board and a commercial agency.

NEW WAYS FOR OLD IN NIGERIAN PEASANT FARMING

Recent political developments in Africa, and more especially the growing racial tensions, have tended to divert attention from the more funda-mental economic problems which are arising as a result of the growing instability of African peasant agriculture.[2] The causes of this lack of stability vary from territory to territory but two are outstanding: the gradual growth of population as a result of improving health conditions, and the expansion of cash cropping to meet the growing demand of urban populations, to meet the urgent world demand for tropical products, especially vegetable oils, and to supply the revenue basic to all social and political progress. The results of these trends is an expansion of the cultivated area, a reduction in the length of the regenerative fallow period and a gradual decline in the level of soil fertility, leading, in extreme cases, to actual physical destruction of the soil by erosion. Nowhere are these developments more clearly to be seen than in Nigeria, where some of the densest agglomerations of rural population and some of the most specialised crop economies in Africa are to be found, and here, in recent years, the funds provided by the Colonial Development and Welfare Act and by the more recently constituted Regional Production Development Boards have made possible a new and fruitful series of experiments designed to solve this problem of agricultural instability and to integrate modern methods of crop production and processing into the traditional systems of peasant agriculture. Because of the extremely patchy distribution of population and the existence of considerable areas of virtually uninhabited bush, it was inevitable that experiments in planned population redistribution and internal colonisation should be an important feature of the Territory's agricultural development programme.

Classification of these development projects is difficult since many are multi-purpose projects; the following grouping, however, offers a convenient basis for discussions:

---

[1] Involving a partnership between the Government (supplying land, part of the capital and general supervision), the peasant (supplying his agricultural skill and labour) and a commercial company (supplying commercial and technical skill for the management of the plantation, processing and, if needed, marketing).

[2] On the breakdown of indigenous systems of cultivation in the continent see J. P. Harroy, *Afrique: Terre qui Meurt*, Brussels (1949).

(1) Schemes of planned resettlement.

(2) Schemes of large-scale mechanised cultivation.

(3) Co-operative farming schemes involving some degree of mechanisation.

(4) Schemes of integrated rural development.

(5) Livestock production schemes.

(6) Plantation development schemes.

(7) Irrigation schemes.

The account which follows does not claim to be exhaustive; rather is it intended to give a general picture of the scope of some of the more significant schemes undertaken in recent years.

Schemes of Planned Resettlement [1]

It has been pointed out in an earlier section (p. 62) that one of the most important factors behind the present-day population pattern of Nigeria has been the historical factor, notably past slave-raiding and internal wars, which depopulated vast areas of fertile land and brought about a defensive concentration of population in and around the walled cities of the Sudan zone, in the shelter of the southern rain forest and on the boulder-littered hill-tops of the Middle Belt and Cameroons. With the establishment of British control, the importance of the security factor has declined and the old pattern of population is breaking down: settlers are moving out from the northern towns and establishing farms in the empty bush beyond, the pagan farmers of the Middle Belt are moving down from their hill settlements into the more fertile lowlands, the Ibo are diffusing as farmers or as white-collar workers throughout the length and breadth of the South. Such a redistribution of population was inevitable once old pressures were relaxed, but it has given rise to a multitude of problems: problems of land tenure and administration, problems of disease control resulting from increased man/tsetse contact in newly settled bush and, last but not least, problems of land use arising from the replace-

ment of old conservational systems of farming by uncontrolled shifting cultivation destructive of both soil and vegetation. It is against this background that the growing official interest in schemes of controlled population redistribution and planned land settlement should be viewed.

In a valuable discussion of land settlement in the Nigerian Middle Belt, E. O. W. Hunt has pointed out that there exist in Nigeria two main schools of thought regarding settlement. The first is based on the conviction: "You cannot help men permanently by doing for them what they could and should do for themselves", and in settlement schemes thus motivated only the absolute minimum (construction of roads, provision of water supplies and of food during first season) is done for the settler, who himself clears his land and builds his house and store; rapid results are not to be expected, but progress is sure and the settler has the pride of achievement and the satisfaction of starting his new life unburdened by debt. The second school of thought is termed by Hunt the "Kontagora school"; here the emphasis is on heavy capitalisation which makes possible rapid results and high profits so that the settler can discharge his initial debt within a few years. The land is cleared by machinery or paid labour, villages laid out and built, and selected farmers are presented with a house, cleared farm, and implements and trained animals; they can thus start work immediately.

The first approach is represented by the Shendam Agricultural Development and Resettlement Scheme, aiming at the control of downhill migration of pagan farmers and the agricultural development of the thinly peopled Shendam district of Plateau Province.[2] "Its main objects are to limit the shifting cultivation being practised by migrating tribesmen from the exhausted land in the hill tracts, and by instruction in sound farming methods to raise the standard of living of the indigenous

---

[1] The background to settlement schemes in Nigeria is given by E. O. W. Hunt, *An Experiment in Land Settlement*, Kaduna (1951).

[2] On the Shendam Settlement see E. O. W. Hunt, *op. cit.*; *Annual Report of the Northern Regional Production Development Board* 1950–1, Kaduna (1951).

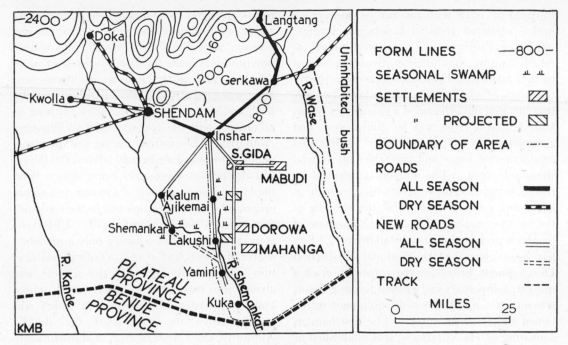

FIG. 128. THE SHENDAM SETTLEMENT

A scheme of planned resettlement, with the aim of controlling the migration of tribes from the southern edge of the Jos Plateau (Fig. 52) by creating planned villages across the line of advance. The scheme has included the creation of a new road system linking up with the Jos road and the creation of a water outlet to the Benue. The Shemankar area is the scene of a small-scale experiment in mechanised rice production.

population, and to increase the production of export crops and also food crops for the expanding urban centre of the Plateau." The project aims at controlling population movements by the progressive establishment of groups of villages, to which migrants can be directed, across the main line of advance. These villages are established by communal self-help and will accommodate between forty and seventy settlers with their families, each settler receiving about twenty acres of land, of which it is proposed one-third will be used for food crops and two-thirds for cash crops. Each settlement has its own grazing land and communal forest area, on the basis of forty acres per settler. Sleeping sickness is a problem, but health in the interim period is being watched over by the Sleeping Sickness Service, and of the two main vectors, *Glossina tachinoides* can probably be controlled by clearing and *G. morsitans* will retreat as game are driven back by settlement. Cropping

is based on a system of rotation and manuring drawn up by the Agricultural Officer, and erosion control is ensured by grass strips along the contour. Small areas of *fadama* (seasonal swamp) offer potentialities for rice-growing, and almost one-quarter of the crop area of Sabon Gida village, the first village established, was under rice in 1949; larger scale production, using machinery, is being developed in the Shemankar valley, on the western boundary of the settlement area. Improvement of communications has been an essential part of the scheme; the road link with the Jos area has been improved, internal roads opened up and the development of a water outlet to the Benue River is in hand. By October 1951, 284 settler families had been established and some 2,300 acres were under cultivation.

The "Kontagora school" of land settlement gets its name from the Kontagora Native Authority Land Settlement Scheme, which was initiated in 1948 with the aim of opening up under-populated areas in Kontagora Emirate in Niger Province.[1] The project aimed at establishing by 1954 fifteen settlements, each of twenty farmers. Holdings will average thirty-five acres, of which half will be fallow; they will be cultivated with the aid of a plough and cattle, and the main crops will be guinea corn and groundnuts, with the possibility of irrigated production of sugar and vegetables on alluvial streamside land. The scheme is financed by the Kontagora Native Authority, which is advancing £250 per settler for the clearing of the land by paid labour and for the purchase of livestock and equipment; in addition, £8,600 has been given by the Regional Production Development Board for the construction of a market, a dispensary and a mixed farming depot, where cattle will be trained, equipment maintained and fertiliser stored. The first hamlet, consisting of Hausa farmers, was established in 1949, and was followed in 1950 by the establishment of two settler groups of pagan Kamberi farmers.

In contrast to these schemes, developed in areas of open savana woodland and based on cultivation of annual crops, is the Bamenda–Cross River–Calabar (B.C.C.) scheme, a project of planned settlement based on perennial tree crops in the southern forest zone.[2] The scheme was designed to test the possibilities of planned redistribution of population between the over-populated areas of Iboland and the empty forest country in eastern Calabar Province. The main settlement, at Kwa Falls, consisted of some 5,900 acres, divided into an eastern and a western area, and was to accommodate 200 families; its economy was to be based on a 1,000-acre plantation of oil palms and on the cultivation of the basic food crops. Each settler was to receive seventeen acres of land: two acres for his house and compound, ten acres for food crops and five acres of oil palms, the latter to be maintained by the settler and leased to him when the palms had reached bearing, after the fourth year. In addition, provision was made for cash advances, of up to £60, to assist settlers to establish themselves. Rent was fixed at 5% of the capital value of the land, and settlers were expected to cultivate in accordance with the instructions of the Planning Authority. The initial clearing and the planting of palms was done by paid labour, this labour and the settlers themselves being drawn from the labour gangs, mainly of Owerri or Calabar origin, who had been employed in the construction of the Calabar–Mamfe road. Unfortunately, the scheme has achieved only a moderate degree of success, and in 1950 a radical modification was decided upon and the scheme was divided into two parts: an eastern area, where some 115 settlers are established, which will remain under the control of the B.C.C. Authority, and a western area, of approximately 3,000 acres, which was leased to the Eastern Regional Production Development Board for development as a palm-oil plantation (it includes 650 acres of land, the Massagha Swamp, used as an experimental rice area). The number of settlers in the eastern area is to be stabilised at its present level, and the economy of the reduced settlement scheme is to be strengthened by the development of 500 acres of surplus land as a palm plantation. The total cost of establishing a settler, exclusive of advances, has been £240. The reasons for the limited success of the project are complex: they include rising costs during the last few years; inadequate supervision; the failure of the settlers to maintain the palms, whose maintenance thus became a charge on the authority; and the undiluted opportunism of many settlers "anxious to get rich quickly and . . . keen to stay in the scheme only so long as cash advances were made to them".

It is probably in this matter of peasant attitudes that the explanation for the contrasts

---

[1] On the Kontagora Farm Hamlets Scheme: *Annual Report of the Northern Regional Production Development Board* 1950–1.

[2] On the B.C.C. Scheme: *Second Annual Report of the Eastern Regional Production Development Board*, London and Enugu (1951); *idem Third Annual Report* (1952).

in success between the Northern Region schemes and the B.C.C. scheme should be sought. It is true that perennial tree crops do not represent as satisfactory an economic basis for pioneer settlement as do annual crops and that little use can be made of mechanisation in the high-forest country of the south; even more important, however, is the get-rich-quick attitude, which is so widespread among some of the southern peoples and which may well prove a major obstacle to long-term agricultural development plans in the south. In this connection it is perhaps not without significance that the Southern Regional Production Development Boards are showing a growing interest in the plantation system as a method of opening up under-developed areas.

Schemes of Large-scale Mechanised Cultivation [1]

The development of mechanised cultivation, which has revolutionised agriculture in the temperate zone, and especially in the pioneer fringe areas of North America and Australia, is widely regarded as a solution to many of the problems today facing African agriculture. The African peasant, according to this viewpoint, can pass directly from his traditional hand techniques to the techniques of mechanised farming, by-passing the intermediate stage of animal-powered cultivation through which the Western World has passed. The argument is attractive, for mechanisation would appear to have many advantages in an African environment. If practicable, mechanisation would make possible a great increase in productivity per worker, enabling vast tracts of at present thinly peopled and under-developed country to produce large surpluses for export, and this relatively cheaply. It would make the peasant farmer more mobile, enabling him to cover a larger acreage in a given time or a given acreage

in a shorter time than by traditional hand methods. The increased speed of cultivation and harvesting is particularly important in areas such as the savana lands, which, as a result of rainfall conditions, have a limited growing season, and would make possible expansion of cropping into areas at present climatically marginal; at the same time, it would enable the farmer to overcome climatic hazards in the shape of delayed planting, whether due to excessive rain or late arrival of the rains.

These are important considerations, and their validity has been demonstrated in climatically marginal areas in both the New World and Australia; at the same time, it should be emphasised that mechanisation in a territory such as Nigeria raises problems quite different from those encountered in temperate regions. These problems fall into three broad groups—technical engineering problems, agricultural problems and problems of land tenure and human attitudes.

On the technical side the problems have been summarised in the Western Regional Production Development Board's Report for 1951–2: "Experience in the use of tractor-drawn implements is lacking throughout the whole of the tropics. Few implements have been designed specifically for the cultivation of tropical food-crops, and certainly none for two of the main staples of the region—cassava and yams. There is little doubt, however, that engineering skill is capable of devising suitable types of implements and tractors required for a wide range of annual crops, and that some degree of mechanisation is possible for the cultivation of biennials. On the purely engineering side of mechanisation success, therefore, will largely depend the efficiency of the organisation responsible for the maintenance and servicing of the machines and equipment. Whilst alive to the sales side of mechanical equipment, private enterprise

[1] On the problems of mechanised cultivation: *Report of a Survey of Problems in the Mechanisation of Agriculture in Tropical African Colonies*, London (1950), also *Annual Report of the Western Regional Production Development Board 1951–2*; on the Sokoto Rice Scheme see *N. R. Production Development Board Report 1950–1* and *Annual Report on the Agricultural Department*; the Niger Agricultural Project is outlined in *Commonwealth Survey*, Oct. 13th, 1950, and progress is summarised in *Colonial Development Corporation: Report and Accounts for 1951*.

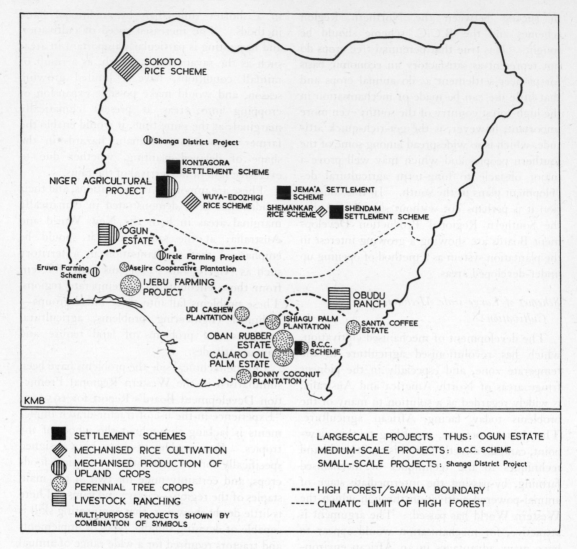

SETTLEMENT SCHEMES

MECHANISED RICE CULTIVATION

MECHANISED PRODUCTION OF UPLAND CROPS

PERENNIAL TREE CROPS

LIVESTOCK RANCHING

MULTI-PURPOSE PROJECTS SHOWN BY COMBINATION OF SYMBOLS

LARGE-SCALE PROJECTS THUS: OGUN ESTATE

MEDIUM-SCALE PROJECTS: B.C.C. SCHEME

SMALL-SCALE PROJECTS: Shanga District Project

----- HIGH FOREST/SAVANA BOUNDARY

- - - - CLIMATIC LIMIT OF HIGH FOREST

FIG. 129. AGRICULTURAL DEVELOPMENT SCHEMES

Broad contrast between the southern forest region where the schemes are based on the development of perennial tree crop production and the savana region of the north where the schemes are concerned with the production of annual crops and planned resettlement. Note the absence of development in the Territory's most extensive pioneer area—the Province of Bornu.

appears indifferent to the need for an adequate repair service and is unlikely to provide a service network such as that employed by farmers in the United Kingdom. The required organisation will represent a very substantial expenditure of capital, and until a network of repair facilities exists throughout the country there can be little hope of rapid expansion or for the individual

operator to embark successfully upon tractor cultivation."

Equally important is the fertility problem. Mechanised cultivation means open and permanent cultivation, and demands clearing of the forest or savana vegetation and stumping of the land. It thus becomes essential to devise some method of restoring and maintaining soil fertility in place of the traditional regenerative bush fallow. Grass fallows, as used in East Africa and as projected at Mokwa, may meet this need, especially if supplemented with artificial fertilisers, but until further long-term experiments have been carried out, no final answer is possible. The use of farmyard manure has been shown to be an answer to the problem of maintaining soil nutrient status under widely contrasting conditions in Nigeria, but unfortunately over much of the Territory tsetse infestation rules out large-scale keeping of cattle and hence the use of animal manure.

Thirdly, there are the human and economic problems. Large and compact holdings are an essential prerequisite to mechanised agriculture, and in this connection the traditional Nigerian pattern of small scattered holdings is a major obstacle to development. Consolidation of holdings under some form of group farming is essential, but how far such an agricultural revolution is likely to be acceptable to the peasant farmer, and how far such a system would be workable in view of the very patchy distribution of good land in areas such as the Middle Belt, have yet to be demonstrated. On this aspect the pilot schemes of small-scale co-operative mechanised farming in the Western Region should yield much needed data. The problem is less acute in newly settled regions, though the question of peasant attitudes to co-operative or group farming is still important. Finally if mechanised agriculture is to represent an advance on the traditional systems of farming, its productivity must be sufficient not only to cover operational costs, interest and depreciation, but to yield also a substantial surplus over the older methods; here again careful long-term investigations are essential to work out the economics of the system.

A wide range of experimental schemes and pilot projects has been initiated. Experimental work on the mechanisation of upland crops is being carried on at a group of small tractor unit farms operated by the Department of Agriculture. These are distributed so as to cover a wide range of savana environments and, though

no final conclusions can yet be drawn, experience to date has shown that the problems to be faced are many and formidable, and that "it would be unwise to be too optimistic concerning the scope for development in this direction".

More promising results have been achieved with mechanised cultivation for rice on the fertile *fadamas* of the Northern Region. In Sokoto Province the use of tractors and heavy implements has made possible the cultivation of considerable areas which in the past have been left uncultivated because of the labour involved in hand cultivation of the heavy clay soils. Heavy D7 Caterpillar tractors have proved necessary to cope with the ploughing, and in spite of difficulties the 1951–2 target of 25,000 acres was achieved and an expansion to 40,000 acres is looked forward to with confidence. The land is pooled for ploughing, and subsequently redistributed for sowing under a Native Authority Settlement Scheme; much of the land was formerly used as seasonal grazing by the Fulani, and its cultivation has created a minor problem of some delicacy. The small-scale scheme of mechanised rice cultivation at Shemankar (1952 acreage, 2,000) has been referred to above. This scheme differs from the Sokoto scheme in two respects: firstly, soils are less heavy and medium-powered tractors have proved adequate; secondly, it is opening up what was virtually an empty area, and one of the major limiting factors to expansion is labour; for this reason its fortunes will be closely bound up with those of the adjoining Shendam Settlement Scheme.

Mechanisation and planned settlement are the keynotes of the Niger Agricultural Project at Mokwa in Niger Province. This project aims at the development of 65,000 acres of empty savana country under a system of tenant mixed farming, and is managed by an operating company in which the Nigerian Government and the Colonial Development Corporation hold equal shares. The project is spread over seven years and will establish ten villages, each consisting of eighty forty-eight-acre peasant holdings. Mechanised equipment is being used in clearing and will be available to the settlers, and the ultimate aim is to establish a large cultivated area, cropped on scientific lines but where each peasant can retain his village community life. By January 1952 some 7,000 acres had been cleared (at a cost of £12 8s. per acre), and the first village—Ndyako—had been established. 1,800 acres were cropped, mainly with groundnuts or Bambarra groundnuts, but yields were low and the project showed a loss on the first season's operations; this was not unexpected in this initial stage. Details of rotations are not yet finalised, though a six-year three-course rotation of cereals, oil-seeds and grass leys has been planned, and livestock will be integrated into the system. Co-operation between settlers and management has been good, and the scheme has been hailed as "from every point of view— political, social, agricultural and economical— one of the most interesting and satisfactory of the Corporation's projects".

Co-operative Farming Schemes involving some Degree of Mechanisation

Experiments in mechanical cultivation on a co-operative basis and within the framework of an established village group are being undertaken by the Regional Production Development Board at New Eruwa, in Abeokuta Province and at Irele in Ondo Province.

The Eruwa Mechanised Farming Scheme was initiated by the Department of Agriculture in 1951, and taken over by the Production Development Board in 1952; it comprises some 500 acres of open savana woodland; soils are light and sandy, and to minimise erosion the land is being developed on a basis of contour strips, alternate strips only being used for cropping in the initial stages. The work of clearing is not heavy (about twenty man-days per acre) and some 200 acres have been cultivated with tractor-drawn equipment; the main crop in the initial stage is maize to be followed by a green-manure crop, while experimental acreages of yams, groundnuts and guinea corn have been established. One-fifth of the area is being set aside for pineapples, which should prove a valuable cash crop in view of the development of the local canning industry.

At Irele a group of 100 farmers belonging to two villages agreed to clear and stump 400 acres which, it was proposed, should be farmed with the aid of mechanical equipment provided by the Production Development Board. The machinery was to be used for breaking the land and for the initial cultivation; the land was then to be subdivided into individual plots and subsequent cultivation was to be by hand. The early enthusiasm shown by the villagers waned rapidly when the amount of labour involved in clearing became apparent, and in spite of subsequent modification of the scheme the results have been disappointing and the farmers have shown little desire to abandon their traditional methods. This is undoubtedly due in part to local environmental conditions; the clearing and stumping of the dense virgin bush demands on the average 100 man-days per acre and, in the words of the Regional Production Board's Report: "It is difficult for the native farmer to appreciate the purpose behind such an operation when he knows that he can prepare his farm by the native method for as little as twenty man-days per acre"; in addition, soils are very patchy and many are of marginal value, and under these conditions the traditional system of bush fallowing, with its pattern of scattered holdings following selectively the patches of more fertile soil, represents a more satisfactory adjustment to local conditions.

These two schemes, and especially the Irele scheme, have illustrated clearly some of the problems of mechanisation in the areas of dense vegetation and close settlement typical of much of the south; they serve, too, to underline the environmental advantages enjoyed by parts of the north, and more especially the Sudan zone, with its more open vegetation and more homogeneous soil conditions.

Schemes of Integrated Rural Development

Possibly the most striking demonstration of the potentialities of planned development on a regional scale is the Tennessee Valley Scheme in the Eastern United States; here a carefully integrated scheme of agricultural improvement, reafforestation, flood control and hydro-electric development revolutionised the economy of what was one of the most backward regions in the United States and opened the way to a fuller life for the Valley's $4\frac{1}{2}$ million people.[1] The lessons of the T.V.A. are particularly relevant in many parts of Africa today, where governments are faced with the same problems of wasting soil and vegetation assets, unused power resources and rural poverty; it is, however, a striking comment on the lack of imagination and the narrowness of outlook of the various colonial administrations that these lessons should have been so long ignored. Against this background the recent announcement of a scheme of planned regional development for the upper basin of the Ogun River in Oyo Province takes on a new significance; it represents not merely an important step in the development of the Western Region, it is indicative also of a new and more constructive approach to the development of the savana lands of Africa.

The Ogun River project "links together the possibilities of hydro-electric power and a land usage scheme employing improved cropping and stock-keeping methods. . . . Should the possibilities prove to be up to expectations, a large part of the country within 60 miles of the dam site should be provided with electric power. . . ." The investigation of the power potentialities of the Amaka Gorge is still in progress; in the meantime, the agricultural development of the 26,000 acres selected as a project area is proceeding. Experimental development will be along two lines: on the one hand, mechanised production of food crops; on the other, livestock production on the open-range system. If these prove successful it is proposed to weld the two into a balanced system of mixed farming. The area consists of open savana woodland with light sandy soils unsuited to continuous cropping; a system of fallowing

will, therefore, be essential and the land is being cultivated in strips aligned along the contour, strips being alternately under fallow and crop. Some 1,750 acres are in various stages of clearing, and for 1952 400 acres will be sown with early maize to be followed, as at Eruwa, by a green-manure crop (*mucuna*); the rotation tentatively adopted is maize followed by *mucuna* for three years, followed by three years of fallow. A smaller area has been set aside for experimental cultivation of other food and cash crops and for testing alternative rotations. The savana grasslands of the area are superior in both quality and length of grazing season to the grasslands of the Sudan zone, and would appear, superficially at least, well suited to livestock ranching. The area is tsetse-infested, but the indigenous dwarf shorthorn is resistant to trypanosomiasis, and the major limiting factor to the expansion of livestock numbers in the past appears to have been rinderpest. New techniques of rinderpest immunisation applicable to the dwarf shorthorn seem likely to overcome this menace, and the way will then be open for a considerable expansion of the livestock industry in these savana areas. The Ogun Estate has a significant role to play in the provision of foundation herds vital to this expansion and in the establishment of mixed farming techniques suited to local conditions, and these developments, linked with the harnessing of the Ogun River for power, may well revolutionise the rural economy of what is today one of the backwaters of the Western Region.

Livestock Production Schemes

One of the major dietary deficiencies among the people of the Middle Belt and the south is lack of protein, and it was, therefore, inevitable that schemes of livestock production should receive a high priority among development projects. The expansion of livestock numbers in Oyo Province alluded to in the preceding paragraph is important not only from the soil fertility

---

[1] On the Tennessee Valley Authority see D. E. Lilienthal, *T.V.A.*, London (1944); the Ogun Scheme is outlined in *Speech and Annual Statement presented by H.E. the Governor to the Legislative Council*, 1951, Lagos (1951), and in *Annual Report of the Western Regional Production Development Board 1951–2*.

angle, but also from the nutritional angle, since it would provide an important supply of animal protein within easy access of the urban markets of Yorubaland. In the Eastern Region the economics of livestock production to meet the needs of the great concentration of population in Iboland are being investigated on a pilot ranch at Obudu in Ogoja Province.[1] Here, on the flanks of the Cameroons highlands, wide expanses of high-level tsetse-free grasslands have long been used by the nomad Fulani, and here the Eastern Regional Production Development Board has established a 20,000-acre ranch with the intention of running some 4,000 head of cattle, together with flocks of sheep and herds of pigs. Cattle have been purchased from the French Cameroons, and a small Montbeliard herd is being built up; the latter, however, have suffered heavy casualties as a result of disease. Local sheep have not done well, but a small flock of imported Cheviots is flourishing. Forty miles of road have been constructed, and it is intended that this should link up with the Bamenda–Mamfe road system, thus opening up large areas of under-developed country. The contribution of this pilot scheme to the meat supply of the East will not be large; it is, however, stressed that the carcase weight of the Obudu cattle will be twice that of the emaciated beasts trekked into the region from the North or from the French Cameroons, while the scheme, if successful, will provide a pattern for large-scale development of commercial ranching in the Cameroons grasslands.

Plantation Development Schemes [2]

The agricultural development of Nigeria during the past half-century has been based on peasant production, and the role of plantation agriculture has been small. The results achieved in the case of annual crops, such as groundnuts, cotton and benniseed, have been striking; in the case of perennial tree crops, however, it is becoming increasingly doubtful whether, in a normal market, peasant production will be able to compete with the higher quality and more efficiently produced plantation product. This is particularly so in the case of palm products, a commodity on which some four million farmers are totally dependent, and which in the future may expect to have to face sharp competition from plantation-produced oil from the Congo and from Indonesia. The policy of the Eastern and Western Regional Production Development Boards in initiating schemes of plantation development to increase the output of both cash crops and food crops, to introduce new cash crops and to improve the quality and quantity of palm products indicates a growing but dangerously belated awareness of the limitations of peasant methods in the production of tropical perennials. These new plantation projects fall into three broad groups:

(1) Schemes of large-scale plantation development, usually in thinly populated areas, operated either directly or through the agency of a commercial firm.
(2) Small-scale plantations, which could be dispersed in groups in all save the most closely settled areas, and which would make available to surrounding villages not only modern processing facilities but also high-grade seed, and which would ultimately be taken over by the local villages.
(3) Co-operative development, on plantation lines, of existing areas of perennial tree crops.

In the Eastern Region two major plantation enterprises are to be developed on the edge of the Oban Forest Reserve in Calabar Province. The first of these, the Calaro Oil Palm Estate, comprises an area of 12,500 acres, and is being developed on the basis of partnership between the Eastern Regional Production Development Board and the Colonial Development Corporation; the second, the Oban Rubber Plantation, will comprise a similar area, and is to be devel-

---

[1] On the Obudu ranch: *Annual Report of the Eastern Regional Production Development Board 1951–2.*
[2] On plantation development see footnote on p. 158.

oped jointly by the Production Development Board and a commercial rubber firm. The area in which they are being established is very thinly peopled, and the plantations will provide regular employment for a considerable labour force drawn from the over-populated areas of Iboland. In the Western Region the Ijebu Farming Project represents an interesting example of large-scale mixed plantation development, comprising an area of 13,000 acres and, like the Calabar schemes, is located in what was formerly a Forest Reserve. It is to be developed as an estate for the cultivation of oil palms, citrus, cocoa and rubber, and is intended to be taken over ultimately by African interests. In contrast to some of the schemes in the Northern Region, there is at present no intention of establishing settlers, and during the initial stages the plantation is being worked by paid labour recruited locally or in the Eastern and Northern Regions. Soil survey has shown that some 3,500 acres are suitable for cocoa, 3,000 acres for citrus and 5,000 acres for oil palms, rubber, coco-nuts and "awusa" nut (*Tetracarpidium conophorum;* yielding a quick-drying oil used in paint-making). The citrus acreage will be adequate to maintain a modern canning factory, and the plantation will thus play an important role in the development of new industries. At the same time, the plantation will be able to supply improved planting material to farmers wishing to extend their plantings, and will provide "a large-scale demonstration of efficient plantation management and techniques evolved to suit local conditions".

The establishment in the Eastern Region of groups of smaller oil-palm plantations, providing processing facilities and acting as models for village plantation development, has been hindered by the difficulty of obtaining land; in view of the critical need to replace existing groves of over-age wild palms by improved plantings, this delay is particularly unfortunate. It is hoped to establish a 1,200-acre palm plantation at Ishiagu in Ogoja Province, but at the time of writing no progress had been achieved in the main Palm Belt. Other small-scale plantation schemes include the establishment of cashew plantations (the nut is the only natural source of phenol, as well as being used in the confectionery trade) on the bad-lands of the Udi area; a 1,000-acre pilot plantation of coco-nuts at Bonny in Rivers Province, and a 1,200-acre plantation of *arabica* coffee at Santa in Bamenda Province; this latter will provide a model for local coffee-growers, who will also be able to utilise the services of the plantation's factory for the processing of their crop.

In addition to initiating development projects, the Production Development Boards are giving active support to schemes of agricultural development on a community or co-operative basis. Thus, at Asejire, near Ibadan, fifteen farmers pooled the land and formed a Co-operative Farming Society for the purpose of developing oil-palm plantations in co-operation with the Western Regional Production Board, and this example has been followed by four other groups in the neighbourhood, the combined acreage of the societies amounting to over 200 acres planted with oil palms and with citrus on the better soils. In the Provinces of Benin and Delta, where, at the beginning of the century, communal rubber plantations had a short-lived success, negotiations are proceeding with the object of establishing communal plantations of rubber and oil palms. This pattern of development combines the social advantages of peasant production with the technical advantages of the plantation system, and would appear to have a promising future in the perennial tree-crop regions of the south.

Irrigation Schemes [1]

An expansion of the area under irrigation in the sub-humid areas of the Middle Belt and the Sudan zone would make possible a considerable expansion in the production of specialised crops, such as rice, cane and vegetables, and, by making

[1] Irrigation in Niger Province is dealt with in *Annual Report on the Agricultural Department* 1949–50 and 1950–1; the Chad Project is outlined in *Nigerian Citizen* (Zaria), April 21st, 1950.

possible dry-season cropping, would help to even out the highly seasonal pattern of farming activities typical of most of the savana region. Environmental conditions and the absence of basic topographical, climatological and hydrological data are, however, serious obstacles to any large-scale development in the immediate future, though a promising small-scale scheme is being undertaken in Niger Province and a reconnaissance of potentialities has been made. The Niger Province development is situated in the valley of the Kaduna River in the Wuya-Edozhigi area, and is a pilot scheme covering some 2,500 acres; "approximately 1,500 acres of land on which rice cannot be cultivated at

present will be made available for rice; sufficient water should be available for the dry season irrigation of up to 1,000 acres". In the same area recent investigations on the Gbako River above Badeggi suggest that a scheme ten times this size may be possible. Outside this area major interest has centred on the development of small-scale village schemes, though reconnaissance work has drawn attention to the possibilities of a major scheme in the Lake Chad area; this scheme would involve dyking of the dry-season shore-line of the lake, and the utilisation of the pent-up water for the dry-season irrigation of an area which might run into hundreds of thousands of acres.

CHAPTER IV

FOREST RESOURCES

The Forest Area

In a Territory such as Nigeria, where the area under continuous cultivation is negligible and where agriculture is based on the system of bush fallowing, it is virtually impossible to draw a clear-cut division between farm land and forest. In general terms, however, the position would appear to be somewhat as follows: officially demarcated forest reserves total approximately 27,000 square miles, or some 7% of the area of the Territory; agricultural lands, including land under cultivation and land under fallow, may be tentatively estimated at 230,000 square miles, or 60% of the total area; the residual area, some 115,000 square miles or 33% of the Territory, consists of "waste lands", mainly savana woodlands; these latter are communally owned and at present used largely for

hunting, though ultimately, as population pressure increases, they will be increasingly taken up for agriculture.[1]

Fig. 130 shows the general distribution on a provincial basis of the total area under forest, including uncultivated wasteland. It will be evident that this category of land attains its maximum importance in three major zones: a southern zone, extending from the thinly peopled area of Borgu in the west to Ogoja in the east, with a southern extension across the forest country of Benin; a central zone, comprising Zaria Province; and thirdly, in the extreme north-east, the thinly peopled Province of Bornu. The lowest proportion of "forest" land is found in Plateau Province and in the closely settled areas of Kano and the western Yoruba Provinces.

A more reliable index to the distribution of economic forest is, however, given by the distribution of Forest Reserves. As noted above, in 1949 these occupied 7% of the area of Nigeria; their detailed distribution is shown in Fig. 131, while the proportion of the

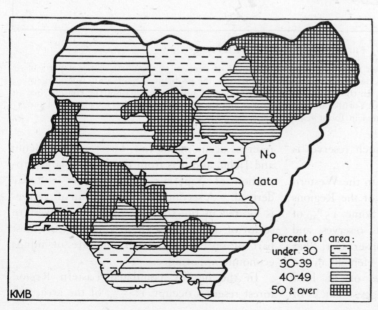

Percent of area:
under 30
30-39
40-49
50 & over

KMB

No data

FIG. 130. FOREST AREA

For definition see text. Note the thinly forested character of the Cocoa Belt, Jos Plateau and the Provinces of Kano and Katsina, and the high proportion of the total area under forest in Bornu, parts of the Middle Belt and the Provinces of Ondo and Ijebu.

[1] For the pre-war position see *Fifth British Empire Forestry Conference, London* (1947): *Statement prepared by the Nigerian Forest Authority*, Lagos (1947), pp. 4–5.

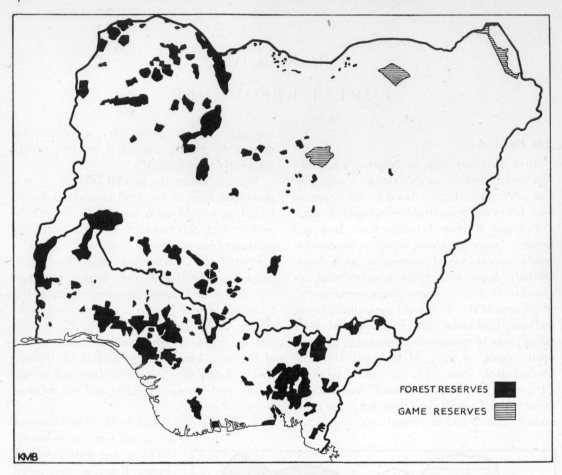

FIG. 131. FOREST RESERVES

Relatively little progress has been made with the establishment of reserves in the north-east and parts of the Middle Belt, but in these areas, owing to low population pressure, the problem of reservation is less urgent than in the closely settled south. In this latter area the distribution of reserves emphasises the contrast (see Fig. 35) between the closely settled Yoruba and Ibo territories and the peripheral area, less closely settled and with a high proportion of their area in forest reserves.

area of each Province under such reserves is shown in Fig. 132.[1]

Reservation is most complete in the Western Region, which was the earliest of the Regions to receive forestry attention. Some 15% of the regional area is set aside as reserves, and forestry, to quote the Chief Conservator, "has assumed its place as a profitable element in the permanent economic structure of at least part of the Region".[2] The biggest blocks of

reserves occur in the rain-forest zone of Benin and Ijebu, and it is from these that a large proportion of Nigeria's export timber is today derived. A second important group of reserves is located in the thinly peopled north-western sector of the Region; these consist for the most part of savana woodlands and are of minor economic importance.

In the heavily populated Eastern Region forest reserves occupy 10·5% of the area, and

[1] Based on *Annual Report on the Forest Administration of Nigeria*, 1941.
[2] *Annual Report on the Forest Administration of Nigeria*, 1948–9, p. 2.

FIG. 132. FOREST RESERVES
AS A PERCENTAGE OF
THE TOTAL AREA

Relative importance of the reserves is greatest in the Western
Region, in the thinly peopled
eastern sector of the Eastern Region and in Sokoto Province.

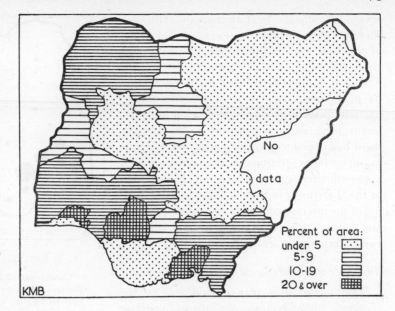

Percent of area:
under 5
5-9
10-19
20 & over

this figure, low though it is,
is considered to represent the
practical limit of reservation.
From the forester's point
of view the Eastern Region
falls into two clearly defined
zones: a western zone, comprising the Provinces of
Onitsha, Rivers and Owerri,
and an eastern zone com-
prising the Provinces of Cala-
bar and Ogoja and the Cameroons.[1] In the
western zone the heavy pressure of population
and resultant scarcity of agricultural land make
reservation virtually impossible and forestry is
of negligible importance. The eastern sector,
in contrast, contains extensive areas of very
thinly populated rain forest, and the establishment of reserves on a large scale has been possible, especially in the basin of the Cross River
and in Eastern Ogoja. It is unfortunate that
the bulk of these eastern forests are of limited
economic value and, except in certain favoured
areas, such as the Ikom–Obubra area, offer no
great prospects for the development of commercial timber production.

In the savana zone of the Northern Region
the process of establishing a Forest Estate is still
in its initial stage; only 5·5% of the Region is
set aside as reserves, and of this the greater
proportion is in the north-western Province of
Sokoto and in the peripheral Provinces of Kabba
and Ilorin. The development of the northern
savanas presents problems quite different from
those of the southern high forest; export production is ruled out by distance from the sea
and by the absence of commercially valuable

timbers, and the major problem is the development of these degraded, fire-scarred woodlands
as a source of fuel and constructional timbers
for the region's rapidly growing population.

Unfortunately, this programme is fraught
with difficulties.[2] The areas of sparsely inhabited savana woodlands which offer greatest
potentialities as forest reserves play a vital role
in the grazing economy of the northern peoples;
a compromise between the forester and the
grazier is essential, for unless these grazing
rights are recognised, approval for a reserve
would rarely be forthcoming from the Native
Administration. At the same time such
reserves, especially where a large game population is present, are often reservoirs of *Glossina
morsitans*, and as such have in the past been
regarded with considerable misgivings by the
Tsetse Control authorities. Recent discussions
between the latter and the Forest Department
have led to a working agreement on the need
for limiting the size of reserves (to 100 square
miles), and for some measure of game control
in the larger reserves. Finally, uncontrolled
migration (see page 78) in certain areas has
been accompanied by wholesale destruction of

[1] *Annual Report on the Forest Administration of Nigeria*, 1948–9, p. 3.
[2] *Annual Report on the Forest Administration of Nigeria*, 1949–50, pp. 6–7, and 29–30.

savana woodlands by farming, and although there is a growing appreciation in official circles of the vital role of the Forest Reserve in the rural economy, it is unfortunate that in the Shendam Settlement Scheme forest reservation has not commenced and that the Administration has put forward proposals to develop as settlements large areas which the Forest Department had hoped to set aside as reserves. These examples focus attention on the crying need for a co-ordinated approach to rural development in the Territory; only by a judicious harmonising of the interests of farmer and grazier, forester and medical man can a healthy and balanced rural economy be achieved.

The Role of Forests in the Nigerian Economy

The forest areas play a vital role in the economic life of Nigeria, not only as important contributors to the Territory's export output, but also as a source of many of the necessities of everyday existence. Timber exports, which before the Second World War represented only 0·8% of the total exports, have increased steadily in volume and in relative importance; in 1948 they exceeded £1,000,000 for the first time, representing 3% by value of the Territory's exports. In the internal economy of the country the forest areas are of major importance as a source of fuel, and in addition furnish a wide range of foodstuffs and of raw materials for peasant industries. They supply material for rope, twine, fibre bags, fishing-nets and mats; oils and fats for cooking and lighting and charcoal for metal working; materials for house building and food-wrapping; dyestuffs and a vast profusion of native drugs and medicines; honey, foodplants, edible snails and a variety of small game. It is quite impossible to assess the aggregate financial value of these sylvan products; they are, indeed, to be numbered among the essentials of daily life, and their progressive depletion in the overcrowded and overcultivated districts of the country leads to a

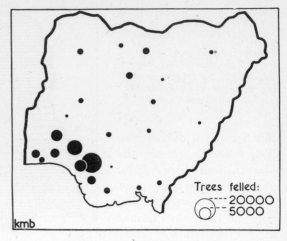

FIG. 133. TOTAL FELLINGS

Concentration of lumber production is in the Western Region; negligible production in the Eastern Region and in the Middle Belt.

general impoverishment of the whole peasant economy.[1]

A broad picture of the output of timber in the Territory is given in Fig. 133 and Table XVI.[2]

The dominating position of the Western Region in the forest economy of the Territory needs no stressing; it accounts for virtually the entire log output, for seven-tenths of the sawn-timber and four-fifths of the total value of timber produced; together with the Colony the

TABLE XVI

TIMBER OUTPUT 1948

(Figures denote solid cubic feet)

	Nigeria	As % of Total for Territory			
		West	East	North	Colony
Logs . .	9,840,486	97·9	0·6	—	1·4
Sawn Timber	839,315	69·8	13·7	15·6	0·9
Firewood .	8,751,536	23·8	3·3	72·9	—
Equivalent in round timber	25,804,936	65·7	4·0	28·3	2·0
Value (£) .	450,262	79·0	5·7	11·8	3·6

[1] J. H. Mackay, "Perspective in Land Use Planning", *Farm and Forest*, Vol. V, No. 3 (1944), p. 100.
[2] Compiled from *Annual Report on the Forest Administration of Nigeria*, 1948–9.

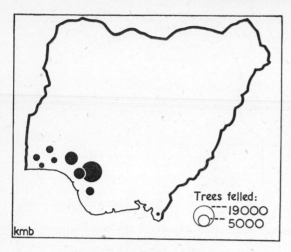

FIG. 134. EXPORT LUMBER
PRODUCTION

Virtually the entire output of export lumber comes from the Western Region where there is a notable concentration of production in the provinces of Benin and Ondo.

Region produces 99·5% of the country's export lumber. The greatest contribution to this output is made by the rain forests of Benin and adjoining Provinces; in 1948–9 Benin Province alone accounted for two-fifths of the Territory's total fellings and for three-fifths of the export fellings, while the three Provinces of Benin, Ijebu and Ondo together accounted for three-fifths of all fellings and for four-fifths of the export production. This great development in the Western Provinces has been favoured by the ease of water access [1] to the main lumber areas and by the relative wealth of economic species in the western rain forest; in both these respects the Region enjoys marked advantages over the Eastern Region. Expansion has been rapid during recent years—the output from the Benin N.A. Reserves increased 2½ times between 1946–7 and 1949–50, and this has been made possible by fuller utilisation of the forest and by improved handling techniques. Intensive felling, linked with full-scale natural regeneration operations, is tending to take the place of the selective felling of a few species; lumber exports, in consequence, are becoming more diversified in character, and the contribution of the six major tree species to total export output has dropped from 81·8% in 1945–6 to 57·5% in 1948–9. Improved timber roads and rafting techniques and the wider use of machinery, especially tractors, have simplified the process of extraction, while the growing maturity of the timber industry in the West is indicated by the establishment of large-scale manufacture of plywood and veneers at Sapele on the southern margin of the Benin rain forest.

The primary forest industries show, as might be expected, a marked degree of concentration in the south-western provinces; in 1948–9 the Western Region and Colony accounted for 98% of the value of out-turn of these industries and for 96% of the employment. The African Timber and Plywood Co.'s plywood factory and saw-mill at Sapele dominates the industry in the Western Region, while in the Colony the largest single unit is the P.W.D. saw-mills at Ijora. There are, in addition, a dozen smaller mills in operation in the south-west, as well as a number of small concerns which operate sporadically and a large number of pit-sawyers; no complete statistics are available regarding the latter, though it is stated that in the Lagos area alone there are about 150 saw-pits with a total production of some 90,000 cubic feet a year.[2] Recorded production in the other Regions is small.

Firewood and Miscellaneous Forest Products

As is shown in Table XVII, recent years have witnessed a rapid and striking increase in the export lumber production of the Territory. It must, however, be emphasised that the export lumber industry is very highly localised, and that over much of the Territory the major role of the forest area is that of a source of domestic fuel, while its major contribution to the export economy consists of minor forest products, such

---

[1] Though the very high prices obtaining for timber have made possible a greater use of road transport in the last year or so; see *Annual Report on the Forest Administration of Nigeria*, 1949–50, p. 14.
[2] *Annual Report on the Forest Administration of Nigeria*, 1948–9, p. 20.

as gums, fibres or skins. A brief examination of these subsidiary branches of production is essential if the country's forest economy is to be seen in correct perspective.[1]

(a) *Firewood:* Throughout the Territory, and in both expatriate and indigenous households, wood is the chief, often the only, form of fuel. Reliable data on total consumption are, in the very nature of things, quite impossible to obtain, though working estimates may be made from sample surveys of fuel consumption in various areas. These suggest an average *per capita* consumption of 0·75 cords per annum,[2] with figures rising above this in certain urban areas (Lokoja, 1·5), and dropping somewhat in areas where considerable quantities of cornstalks are used as a fuel (Zaria, 0·4). On the basis of a *per capita* consumption of 0·75 cords and working with prewar population data, Mackay[3] estimated the total Nigerian consumption of firewood at 14–15 million cords, worth, at 1940–1 price levels, between £3,500,000 and £4,000,000. For comparison, the total value of lumber exported in 1940 was £218,000, and, as has been seen, it was not until the height of the postwar timber boom that exports exceeded £1,000,000.

On the basis of estimated consumption and known yields under various silvicultural conditions, it is possible to assess, at least approximately, the area required to safeguard the Territory's rural fuel supply. With regular working on a fifteen-year rotation, it has been found possible to obtain a yield of 7·5 cords per acre in the savana zone of the north.[4] On this basis, some 34,000 square miles of fuel

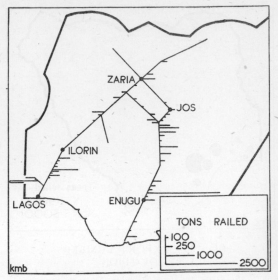

FIG. 135. TIMBER RAILINGS
(Port termini excluded)

A considerable volume of timber, mainly firewood and pitprops, is handled by the Nigerian railway. Note the large tonnages railed out from stations between the mining centre of Enugu and the Plateau tinfields.

reserves are necessary to safeguard the fuel supplies of the Northern Region's present population; this represents almost one-ninth of the regional area, and may be compared with the figure of 16,000 square miles actually reserved by 1950.[5]

(b) *Fibres:* A wide range of fibres is obtained; three examples of contrasting types are listed. *Piassava:* This is obtained from the ribs of the leaf sheaths and the lower part of the petiole of the wine palm (*Raphia vinifera*), typical of the freshwater swamps of the south. The fibre is

---

[1] Based in part upon reports on *Minor Forest Products* and *Firewood* by J. H. Mackay (1941), consulted in the headquarters of the Northern Region Forest Administration, Kaduna.

[2] T. A. M. Nash, *The Anchau Rural Development and Settlement Scheme*, London (1948), p. 10; see also the fuller analysis "Fuel Consumption in relation to Minimum Temperatures" in *Farm and Forest*, Vol. II, No. 1 (1941), pp. 34–6.

A "cord" is a stacked heap of timber 4 feet by 4 feet by 8 feet; its weight varies according to nature and dryness of wood, a typical cord of savana fuel weighing *c*. 1 ton. In heating value a ton of heavy hardwoods is about the equivalent of a ton of coal.

[3] J. H. Mackay, *op. cit.*; D. K. Rosevear, however, estimates fuel consumption at 50,000,000 tons per annum, *Nigeria Handbook* (1953), p. 193.

[4] This can probably be taken as a reasonable average for the Territory as a whole for although in the South cassia and teak will yield 25 cords per acre on a ten-year rotation, this is balanced by very much lower yields in the poorer savana areas of the North, e.g. Zaria 1·5–4 cords per acre.

[5] *Annual Report on the Forest Administration of Nigeria*, 1949–50, p. 44.

obtained by a process of retting, followed by beating and combing, and is exported on a small scale for use in the manufacture of brooms and mats. *Baobab bark:* The baobab, which is widely distributed throughout Northern Nigeria, yields a tough and durable bast fibre, which is used locally in the manufacture of card, rope and crude cloth. The hard outer bark of the tree is first removed, and the soft inner bark stripped off in sheets, which are beaten to remove the non-fibrous material and then sundried. As in the case of the cork oak, the bark grows again; for regrowth the optimum period would appear to be of the order of seven years, though in some districts the minimum period between strippings is as little as two years. *Yoruba soft canes:* These (notably the type *Sarcophrynium*) are used for mat-making, especially in the Ekiti district of Ondo Province, the stems being split into strips, scraped to remove pith and dried in the sun.

(*c*) *Rubber-yielding Plants:* The early attempts at exploitation of the Territory's indigenous rubber-yielding plants have been referred to above; present-day production of wild rubber is insignificant (average exports 1945–9 were only £9,500), but two types merit brief mention.[1] *Niger gutta* ("flake rubber" or "red Kano rubber") is the coagulated latex of *Ficus platyphylla*, a tree widely distributed throughout the Sudan zone; it has a low caoutchouc and high resin content, but attracted some attention before World War II as a possible substitute for chicle or jelutong in the manufacture of chewing-gum. A small-scale export actually developed in 1938, but was short-lived. *Funtumia rubber* is produced from *Funtumia elastica*, which is of interest as the only truly indigenous rubber tree. The tree grows wild in Kabba and Benue Province, but attempts at plantation cultivation at the beginning of the century broke down as a result of low yields (about 60 lb. per acre).

(*d*) *Vegetable Gums:* Though small quantities of gum copal have been produced in the past, the trade in vegetable gums is today dominated by gum arabic, and in 1948 some 700 tons of gum arabic, worth £40,000, were exported from Nigeria. The greater part of this export was derived, as Fig. 137 shows, from the Province of Bornu, and the figure includes a considerable tonnage (estimated in prewar days at 70% of the total Bornu output) purchased by the trading companies in the adjoining French Niger Territory.

The gum consists of an exudation from various species of acacia, the highest quality gum being derived from the *Acacia senegal*. Gum formation appears to be due to some process of infection following wounding of the tree by insects or grazing animals, and a considerable proportion of the Bornu output consists of such natural exudations. Careful tapping will, however, stimulate gum exudation,[2] and during the nineteen-thirties attempts were made, through propaganda and demonstrations, to encourage a more thorough exploitation of the province's gum resources.[3] Progress was, however, slow, and though the foundations of the industry have been laid, the superior attractions of crop production (especially groundnuts) make it doubtful whether any great expansion can be anticipated.

(*e*) *Shea Nuts:* The shea nut is the fruit of the shea butter tree (*Butryrospermum parkii*), which is a characteristic tree of the savanas of the Guinea and Southern Sudan zones. The nuts are embedded in a fleshy outer layer or mesocarp, but have a brittle shell which is easily removed when dry; the kernels contain 45–55% by weight of fat, and are exported on a small scale for the manufacture of soap, candles and edible fats. They are also widely used for the production of shea butter, which takes the place of palm-oil and groundnut oil in the domestic economy of the Middle Belt. Methods of

[1] For a list of some of the trees and plants from which rubber was extracted during the early years of the rubber trade see G. C. Dudgeon, *The Agricultural and Forest Products of British West Africa*, London (1922), pp. 128–9.

[2] Yields per tree are stated to vary from 0·1 lb. to 0·49 lb. with 0·25 lb. as a reasonable average.

[3] K. R. Macdonald, "The Gum Arabic Industry in Bornu Province" in *Farm and Forest*, Vol. II, No. 1 (1941).

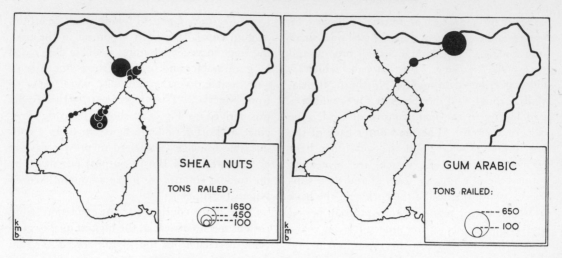

FIGS. 136 and 137. MINOR FOREST PRODUCTS

Shea nuts are collected for export in two major areas—the Middle Belt to the east of Bida, and in the vicinity of Zaria; gum arabic collection is typical of the savana zone of Bornu, the gum being railed out via Nguru.

preparation vary; the most common practice in the north is to boil the nuts, which are then cracked and the kernels extracted; these are roasted and reduced by pounding to a fine oily paste, from which the shea butter is extracted by boiling and skimming.[1] These methods give a relatively low extraction rate (25–27%), and the butter has a highly variable free-fatty acid content, due usually to faulty storage and subsequent germination of the kernels.

Though statistics are lacking, the export of shea nuts appears to have been of major importance in the early development of the Northern Region, and in his annual report for 1905–6 the High Commissioner stated: "The shea-nut export trade . . . formerly constituted the staple of Northern Nigeria".[2] The decline in production has been due partly to the fact that many Middle Belt peoples who formerly relied upon the collection of sylvan produce for their living now find crop production for the internal market more lucrative.

Exports in recent years have reached 15,000 tons per annum, and have been derived chiefly from eastern Niger Province and from Zaria Province.

Recent trends in the export trade in some of these commodities are summarised in the table below[3]; statistics for timber exports are added for comparative purposes:

TABLE XVII

EXPORTS OF MINOR FOREST PRODUCTS
(£000)

	1935	1937	1940	1946	1950
Piassava	5·8	9·8	11·8	102·4	146·5
Wild Rubber	0·5	1·4	2·1	13·4	1·0
Gum Arabic	10·6	9·9	30·8	146·8	62·1
Shea nuts	10·7	83·4	60·8	45·1	53·4
Miscellaneous[4]	30·0	110·0	108·0	202·0	244·0
Timber	156·0	201·0	218·0		1,059·0
M.F.P. as % total	27	52	49		32

[1] The various methods used by different tribes are described by F. R. Irvine, *Textbook of West African Agriculture*, London (1944), pp. 202–5.

[2] Quoted by G. C. Dudgeon, *op. cit.*, pp. 131–2.

[3] Based on *Annual Reports on the Forest Administration of Nigeria* and *Annual Trade Reports*.

[4] Including bees-wax, reptile skins, other skins, kapok floss and other gums.

CHAPTER V

MINING AND INDUSTRY

MINERAL PRODUCTION

Nigeria possesses a number of minerals of economic interest, but so far there is little evidence to suggest that these resources are likely to ensure the country an important place in world markets for any appreciable time. By far the most important of its present mineral products are the ores of tin and its associated minerals, but the proved resources of the tin-fields suggest that it will become increasingly difficult for output to be maintained at past levels, and it is probable both that tonnage will fall and that costs will increase considerably in the near future. Other minerals in international demand occur in insufficient quantity to place Nigeria high in a list of producers.

It is possible that development of mining activity in Nigeria will turn increasingly towards the establishment and satisfaction of internal demand rather than towards overseas trade. Coal may be included among the "domestic" minerals, although production has from the beginning included tonnage for export to other parts of West Africa.

The small-scale use of local mineral resources antedated the arrival of Europeans in Nigeria. The working of iron ores, not yet touched in Nigeria by the techniques of Western civilisation, may still be seen today in a number of localities. The first Europeans to enter the Northern Provinces found a trade in "straw tin" already in existence. The bronze used in the well-known art of Ife and Benin may have resulted from the early Portuguese contacts or may have originated locally. In the Eastern Region the lead-zinc occurrences of Ogoja Province show extensive early working, thought to date from the Portuguese trading era. Lead ores are still produced in a few areas in the Northern Region for use as a cosmetic. Salts of various forms have been worked in many places. It is probable that gold was also mined to some extent.

Early in the present century the Niger Company was granted certain rights with regard to minerals. Although the Company no longer engaged directly in mining, it drew half the mineral royalties over much of the Northern Provinces until this share was purchased by the Government in 1949 for one million pounds. In recent years the half-share had amounted to as much as £250,000 per annum.

It is of interest to note that the stimulated production of recent years has been partly due to marked increases in world metal prices which have led to renewed attention being given to some abandoned workings. The Mines Department Report for the year 1950–1 gives percentage increases of metal prices at March 31st, 1951, over average prices in 1939 as zinc 963%, lead 789% and tin 543%.[1]

Mineral production since 1910 is shown in Fig. 138.

The present position with regard to individual minerals can be summarised as follows.

Coal and Lignite

The occurrences of coal and lignite are shown approximately in Fig. 139. The map should, however, be treated with reserve, in that many of the deposits recorded are very thin and of no more than local economic interest.

Lignite deposits were first discovered in Southern Nigeria early in the present century, and those of the Western Region remain the most important of the Nigerian reserves. They

[1] Geological Survey of Nigeria, *Annual Report* 1945, p. 26.

occur in a broad belt across the country, particularly in Benin Province, but also extending east of the Niger into Onitsha and Owerri Provinces. Lignites also outcrop in Sokoto Province and in the Gongola valley, but these are of little economic significance. Lignites have been reported in south Abeokuta Province,[1, 2] but recent investigations have failed to locate the original occurrences.[3] The most promising lignite deposits are in eastern Benin Province, in places running in seams of a total of 35 feet in thickness in a zone 60 feet thick. East of the Niger they lie among soft sands, which tend to cave in and would make underground mining hazardous; while the overburden is sometimes over 200 feet deep and therefore renders open-cast working impracticable. Tests on the lignites suggest that their development may be for the production of carbon products rather than as a fuel, but possible underground burning for the production of electricity is not yet ruled out.[2] They may also be of value, even where the seams are too thin for large-scale economic exploitation, for use with associated clays in brick-making.

Black sub-bituminous coal was first discovered on the Enugu–Udi scarp in 1909, and five seams have been identified. Of these the most important is the No. 3 seam, which averages 5 feet in thickness; mining was commenced in 1915, and Port Harcourt and the railway to Enugu were built to provide an outlet. (Northbound freight on the railway includes pitprops from the coastal mangroves.) The seams on the scarp lie in the Lower Coal Measures of the Upper Cretaceous, and their situation at the base of the scarp can be recognised from Fig. 50. The Lower Coal Measures outcrop along the length of the scarp running approximately north–south through Enugu, and may be traced round towards the country east of the Niger–Benue confluence. The geological details of the escarpment have been described on pp. 4 and 6. Not all the outcrops are of economic value, but thick seams have been identified on the Nsukka–Idoma border and in Kabba Province.

Mining of the Upper Coal Measures has not yet been attempted. These beds lie west of the scarp, and reference has been made to them in the section on geology. They run from the Anambra syncline southwards, thick seams occurring in Onitsha Province, but in quality they are inferior to the coals of the Lower Coal Measures.

Coals occur in other parts of the country, as in Benin Province and the Gongola valley, but only as thin seams of no more than local significance.

The Nigerian coal does not compare in quality with most industrial coals in other parts of the world. It can, nevertheless, be used as a steam-raising coal (the Nigerian Railway is the largest consumer), and appears to have possibilities for gas manufacture. Carbonisation tests reveal a high yield of tars and oils, and it may be put to industrial use along these lines. Investigations are proceeding on its suitability for the manufacture of plastics and for the production of chemicals by distillation.

[1] Geological Survey of Nigeria, *Occasional Paper No. 1* (1925): R. C. Wilson, "Brown Coal in Nigeria", pp. 16–18.
[2] *Colonial Geology and Mineral Resources*, Vol. I (1950), "The Coal and Lignite Resources of Nigeria", p. 268.
[3] Geological Survey of Nigeria, *Annual Report* 1948, p. 3.

FIG. 138. MINERAL PRODUCTION 1910–50   *opposite*

Annual production of the leading minerals is shown: details are in the text. It should be noted that different scales are used for different minerals.

Coal is the mineral produced in greatest quantity, but tin is the most valuable: the tinfields are important in world markets, but dwindling reserves make their future problematical. Nigeria is the chief world producer of columbite. Gold output is negligible.

Future production of lead and zinc may show some increase, but it must be remembered that world production figures for these metals are high. Uranium ores exist but have not yet been worked, and their possible production is under investigation.

MINERAL PRODUCTION
1910 – 1951

Various vertical scales

1949 Figure includes 1st quarter
of 1950

1950 Figure includes 1950-51

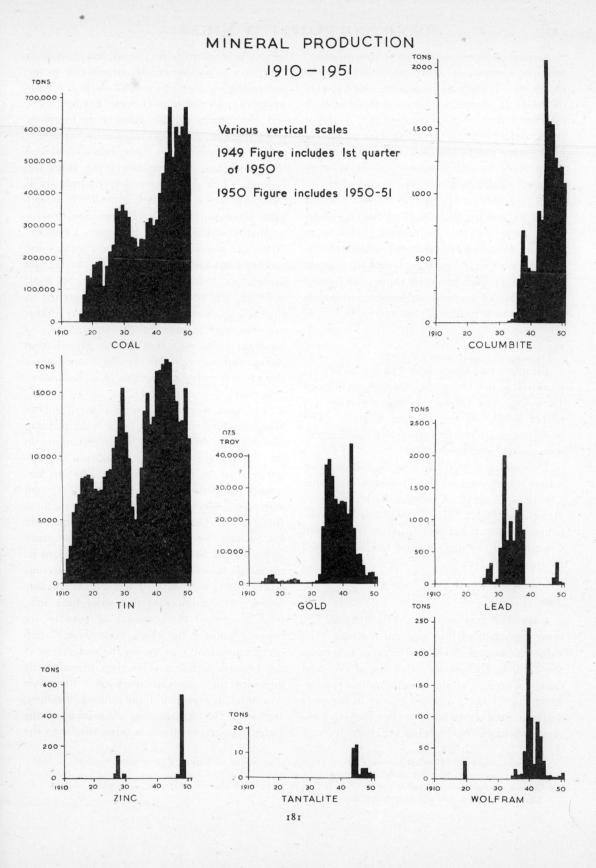

Annual coal production is now over 600,000 tons per annum, of which about one-sixth is exported. Exports in the past have been largely to the Gold Coast, but labour difficulties have interfered with regular production in recent years, and as a result the West African market has to some extent been lost; attempts are now being made to sell Nigerian coal in Western Europe. Estimated reserves were given in 1948 as only 16½ million tons,[1,2] which would suggest the desirability of evolving long-term plans for the coal-mining industry in relation to estimated domestic requirements. More recent investigations, however, indicate that reserves may be much above this figure,[3] and capable of meeting national requirements for a very long time.

Oil

Bitumen has long been known in several localities in the Colony and in the provinces of Ijebu-Ode and Ondo. It has also been reported locally in the Eastern Region. The occurrences are not extensive, and really represent impregnated sandstones.

Prospecting for oil has been carried out over a number of years in the Provinces of Ogoja, Onitsha, Owerri, Calabar, Rivers, Delta, Benin and Ondo. Results have not been published, but a start has been made on test wells in Owerri, and the first of these has been drilled to over 7,000 feet.[4]

Tin

Cassiterite (tin ore) is at present by far the most important of the Nigerian minerals. In value the annual production exceeds five times the combined totals for other metal ores and coal. Totals of annual production vary, averaging some 17,000 tons per annum in the years 1940–4; production lessened after the war. Increased prices in overseas markets have recently

given a new incentive for output, but production continues to decline slowly, largely due to the decreasing yield of the ground worked. Estimates of reserves in 1951 were 127,000 tons, and the future of the industry is therefore problematical.

The ore produced is from both alluvial and lode workings, the majority being from the former. The cassiterite is derived from small lodes and veins associated with the Younger Granites, mainly of the Jos Plateau area, or with pegmatite dykes in the Basement Complex. Attention was first directed to the Plateau some seventy years ago by the trade in thin metal bars known as "straw tin", produced by local smelting, and mining by Europeans started in the early years of the twentieth century. Mining was later assisted by the construction of the light railway (2 foot 6 inch gauge) from Zaria, and subsequently by the extension of the 3 foot 6 inch gauge system from Kafanchan (Fig. 151).

The early workings were all alluvial, the ore being obtained in the first instance by panning of the stream deposits, and the largest mines on the Plateau are still based on alluvial deposits rather than on lode workings. The ore was washed out of the Younger Granites into stream alluvium, which in a few places, such as Bukuru and Dorowa, is in sufficient quantity for mining by large machinery. In many localities the early stream valleys were filled by the earlier lava flows of the Plateau, now decomposed to the soft clays of the Fluvio-volcanic Series. Occurrences of this series have long been recognised as significant of possible ore deposits beneath the clays, even though such occurrences may now lie on the watersheds of the present surface. The clays present little difficulty for open-cast working. The later lava flows also resulted in the infilling of valleys, and with the approaching exhaustion of the easier deposits attention is being turned to the

---

[1] *Colonial Geology and Mineral Resources*, Vol. I (1950), "The Coal and Lignite Resources of Nigeria", p. 268.
[2] Mines Department, Nigeria, *Annual Report* 1948, p. 10.
[3] *Colonial Geology and Mineral Resources*, Vol. V (1955), p. 80, cites reserves as at least 150 million tons.
[4] The first deep test well was abandoned at 11,228 feet.

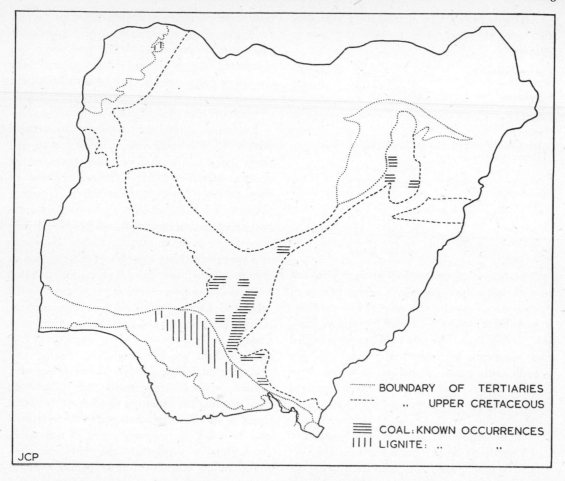

FIG. 139. COAL AND LIGNITE

Known occurrences are shown but not all are of economic value. The main coalfield of the Enugu-Nsukka area and the chief lignite deposits across the lower Niger stand out clearly.

The Nigerian coal and lignite deposits occur in the Upper Cretaceous and Tertiary beds respectively. The provisional boundaries of these beds are shown, as some indication of areas in which other deposits may be found; the former extent of the beds is, however, not always clear and isolated occurrences of coal or lignite may be found in outliers outside the boundaries shown.

possibilities of working the "deep leads" beneath the basalts by underground methods. Identification of deposits in the buried channels is not easy, and geophysical methods of prospecting have been tried in recent years. The cost of winning the sub-basalt ore will necessarily be much higher than that of exploiting the surface alluvium or the basal beds of the Fluvio-volcanic Series. It appears possible that the future may see the larger companies engaged on under-ground mining, with private operators continuing to work surface deposits of small extent, or in rocky valleys, where mechanical aids would be uneconomic or impracticable.

Lodes are worked in some places, as at Ropp and in the Liruein–Kano Hills, but most of the tinstone appears to have derived from small veins now eroded away. Payable alluvial deposits are rarely far from the Younger Granites.

Methods of winning the ore vary considerably. In the year 1950–1 production was as follows[1]:

Electro-mechanical		39% (of *yardage*)
Draglines .	.	10½% @ 9½d. per cubic yard
Dredges .	.	6½% @ 4½d.
Gravel pumps .	.	20% @ 1s. 5½d.
Shovels .	.	2% @ 5d.
Hydraulic		9½%
Ground sluicing .		5½% @ 9½d.
Hydro-turbine gravel		
pumps .	.	½% @ 11d.
Monitors and elevators		3½% @ 10½d.
Direct labour		51½%
Opencast hand		
paddocks .	.	23½% @ 1s. 4½d.
Tributing .	.	28% @ 1s. 6½d.
Underground pillar		
and stall .	.	⅛% @ 5s. 0½d.

The figures quoted are for yardage of ground moved, and are not necessarily representative of comparative costs for ore won. For example, it may be profitable to dredge ground yielding less than ½ lb. of ore per cubic yard, provided that the depth and extent of ground available is sufficiently great. Tributors, of whom more is said below, will tend to ignore ground yielding under 2 lb. of cassiterite per cubic yard.

The average yield of all ground worked in 1948 was 1·01 lb. per cubic yard; for the year 1949–50 this figure fell to 0·88 lb., and for the following year to 0·76 lb. Costs by mechanical methods vary considerably, however, depending not only on average yield of ground but also on the age of the equipment, since new machinery is now so expensive that depreciation, reckoned in terms of the life of the equipment and in terms of the proved reserves to be exploited by that equipment, may offset the whole of the profits if the ground yield of ore is low. Future large-scale mechanisation seems unlikely, in that unless substantial new reserves are discovered, the available ore may be insufficient to keep new machines fully employed to the end of their estimated working life, while the changing political scene may bring the imposi-

tion of new conditions during the same period, or might result in difficulty over renewal of leases due to expire before the machinery has completed the working of the areas.[2] On the other hand, labour costs rise steadily, and if equipment costs could be lowered some degree of mechanisation would probably be adopted.

Reference should be made to the tribute system of labour employment, which has applied particularly to the smaller leases managed by private operators. More than one-third of the total labour force of the minefields is tribute labour. In the past the northern labourers have preferred this system, which is virtually one of free-lance working. Either the whole or a part of the lease may have been assigned to tribute labour, and in this area the tributor worked where he wished, either singly or with others to form a small team. The tributor sells to the operator the ore he has gained at a fixed price per pound. The operator or his agent weighs the ore produced, making any necessary adjustment by check weighing of a known volume (frequently the ubiquitous cigarette-tin) for detection of adulteration with ilmenite or other minerals. Streak tests may also be used, or magnetic tests if necessary; although some cassiterite on the Plateau has been found to be magnetic. The operator builds the camp in which the tributors live, and has a certain number of salaried staff, such as camp managers, headmen, storekeepers and watchmen, and, in remoter areas, butcher and possibly magajiya. Salaried labour may also be employed directly on planned working of the lease, or for construction and maintenance of leats, sluice-boxes, etc. One result of this system has been that tributors have tended to work the richer parts of the ground, throwing tailings on to the parts with lower yield, and have then moved on to another lease when these richer areas have been worked-out, leaving low-grade ground not only unworked but often covered with waste dumps. Many small leases have therefore been

[1] Mines Department, Nigeria, *Annual Report 1950–1*, p. 8.
[2] Mines Department, Nigeria, *Annual Report 1946*, p. 11.

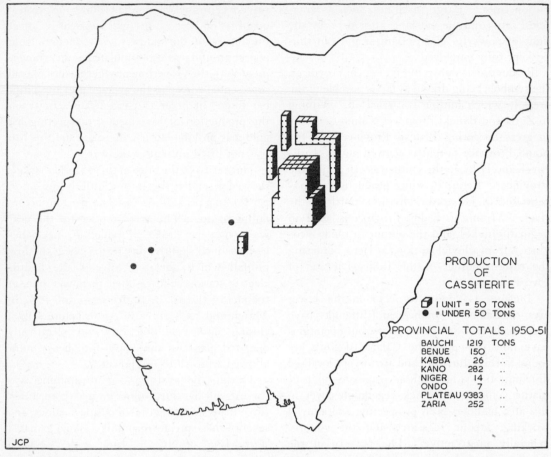

FIG. 140. TIN

Output of cassiterite (tin ore) is shown by Provinces, symbols being placed as nearly as possible in those areas of the Provinces where the mineral is mined. It will be seen that practically the whole of the output is from the area of the Jos Plateau and the neighbouring districts.

Working out of the easily mined alluvial deposits is likely to lead to a steady decrease in production during the next ten years, and the future of the industry is uncertain.

abandoned after the extraction of much less ore than could have been obtained by systematic operation. The system has also sometimes acted as an inducement to illicit trading of ore outside the lease on which it was mined.

Recent years, however, have seen the introduction of legislation requiring some degree of restoration of areas worked. This involves the removal and stacking of the topsoil, and the filling, draining and levelling of open-cast workings before the lease is surrendered. The Government is responsible for the replacement

of the topsoil. Restoration requirements are worked out for each new lease on its merits, since it is not intended to impose conditions which would render mining operations uneconomic.[1] It is clear that the coexistence of restoration and free tributing raises very great difficulties, and changes in the latter system may be necessary.

Most of the large machinery used on the Plateau is electrically driven. Reference is made on page 229 to hydro-electric power on the Plateau, and Fig. 166 illustrates the distri-

[1] Mines Department, Nigeria, *Annual Report* 1947, p. 6.

bution lines. Large machines, such as drag-lines, can continue working after dark by the light of powerful electric lamps, and can thus be kept fully employed.

Production is shown in Fig. 140, by provinces, the symbols being drawn as far as possible in the areas in which mining is carried on. Mining in Zaria and Bauchi Provinces is almost entirely in areas bordering Plateau Province, and the Kano Province output is centred on the Liru-ein–Kano Hills, in the south-western arm of the Province. Benue Province production is concentrated in Nasarawa Division, north of the river. Mining in Kabba Province is based on pegmatite dykes, and the output in Ondo Province is from alluvial working at Ijero, bordering the eastern border of the Ilesha Division of Oyo Province.

Tinstone is known to occur in the Uwet area of Calabar Province, and attempts have been made to work the deposits, but operations have now ceased. The Calabar deposits are found in thin alluvium, and are of very localised distribution. The tinstone originates in pegmatite veins. The thick vegetation cover in this area hampers both prospecting and alluvial working, labour is scarce and the country generally unattractive. The poverty of the deposits, coupled with these difficulties, makes working of the area uneconomic.

Prior to the outbreak of war in 1939 tin production was restricted under the quota system, world production being in excess of demand. The quota system was in abeyance during the war, when Malayan output ceased to be available, and the International Tin Agreement expired at the end of 1946.

The high Nigerian production of the later war years was due to a number of causes. No effort was spared to raise output to meet requirements, and whereas producers had previously met their quota by preserving a balance between the working of richer and poorer ground and so maintaining reserves, activity during the war was concentrated on ground yielding the greatest quantity of ore. This will necessarily affect the future of the industry. Production from poorer ground was also stimulated by an arrangement with the Government whereby prices paid represented costs plus the average previous profit per ton. In order to concentrate activity on the production of base metals, prospecting for gold was prohibited early in 1942, and this ban was not lifted until after the war.

During 1950 the price of tin in world markets showed a sudden rise from a little below £600 per ton to a peak of over £1,600 per ton, before falling again. The average price for the year was £933 per ton.[1] Production, nevertheless, declined slightly, one reason being the low rainfall which adversely affected the hydro-electric stations and resulted in power cuts at the end of the 1949–50 dry season of 50% in March and 75% in early April, before a final closing down of practically all electrically operated plant for nine days until heavy rains allowed a return to full power.[2]

During the year 1950–1 tin mining was carried on by thirty-nine limited companies, three firms under registered business names, and seventy-three private operators. Amalgamated Tin Mines of Nigeria, Ltd., with associated companies, produce approximately 50% of the total ore, and three other groups account for nearly 30%. Production for the year was 11,300 tons, and total output of cassiterite since the start of organised mining operations exceeds 400,000 tons. Annual totals are shown in Fig. 138.

Columbite

Nigeria is the chief world producer of columbite, the ore of niobium (or columbium), total output to the end of 1949 being 13,000 tons. The metal is used in the preparation of special steels for gas turbines.

Before the war there was a small demand from the United States, but even this ceased in

[1] Mines Department, Nigeria, *Annual Report* 1950–1, p. 5.
[2] Mines Department, Nigeria, *Annual Report* 1950–1, p. 12.

1938. In consequence there was no incentive to production, and much columbite, which is associated with cassiterite and is normally a by-product of tin-mining, was left on the waste dumps of the tin-mines. The war-time demand resulted in a peak output of over 2,000 tons in 1944, but this was largely the result of treatment of tailings, and production was regarded as unlikely to reach a similar figure again.[1] Early in 1953 columbite prices rose towards the unprecedented figure of £3,000 per ton, with a resulting new incentive to production, and columbite will understandably receive greater attention as long as its price remains above that of cassiterite. Output for the year 1950–1 was 900 tons, and estimated reserves at the end of that year were given as 9,800 tons.[2] Two companies work areas primarily for columbite, the remaining ore being obtained as a by-product.

The columbite occurs principally in the Younger Granite of the Plateau (Fig. 141), distributed throughout the granite as a primary constituent.[3, 4] It is worked from alluvial occurrences in the valleys of streams flowing off the granites, those in the Forum River Valley being probably the largest alluvial deposits in the world. The recent higher prices for columbite have resulted in attention being given to the possibility of working decomposed granite for primary columbite, but the content is very low and it is doubtful whether such working would be an economic proposition.[5]

Columbite also occurs in a number of localities in pegmatite dykes, usually in association with tantalite.

Possible reserves and future production will now, however, need revision in the light of 1952 reports on the radio-active granites. More detailed reference is made to them below, in the section on radio-active minerals, and it will be seen that large-scale working of the granites could raise output of niobium ore to a new height if suitable extraction methods can be developed.

Tantalite

This rare mineral occurs in pegmatite veins in association with columbite. The tantalite-columbite ratio varies widely not only in different localities, but also in any one vein.

Production was artificially stimulated during the war, 12 tons being produced in 1944 and 13 tons in 1945. The United States takes all the ore produced. Demand fell abruptly at the end of hostilities, and although the price offered is still high, output has almost ceased. In the year 1950–1 production was 1½ tons, bringing the total for Nigeria to 39 tons.

Tantalum is used in the manufacture of electrodes, and of tantalum carbide (one of the hardest materials known) for tools; it is also used in the production of special steels, particularly for surgical and dental instruments, being extremely resistant to corrosion. The latter property, coupled with the fact that tantalum is electrically neutral, has led to its increasing use for surgical plates and thread.

Wolfram

Wolfram (the ore of tungsten) is worked from small lodes in the tin-bearing veins. The stimulus to production, which resulted in an output of 240 tons in 1939, 98 in 1940 and 90 in 1942, did not survive the war, and in the five years 1945–9 inclusive a total of only 20 tons was produced. The total to the end of 1949 from Nigeria was 675 tons. Production for the year 1950–1 improved slightly to 10 tons.

Larger quantities of wolfram could possibly be produced if necessary, but prices remain low, and there is no inducement to separate the mineral as a by-product of tin working. Refer-

[1] Mines Department, Nigeria, *Annual Report* 1945, p. 10.
[2] Mines Department, Nigeria, *Annual Report* 1950–1, p. 12.
[3] Geological Survey of Nigeria, *Annual Report* 1945, p. 26.
[4] Geological Survey of Nigeria, *Occasional Paper, No.* 9 (1951): R. R. E. Jacobson, A. Cawley and W. N. Macleod "The Occurrence of Columbite in Nigeria".
[5] Mines Department, Nigeria, *Annual Report* 1950–1, p. 6.

ence has been made above to the tribute system of labour, and it is obviously impossible to expect tributors to work for wolfram while tin prices are so much higher.[1]

Gold

The main occurrences in Nigeria lie in the areas of Pre-Cambrian schists. Production was low until 1933, when it rose suddenly to 17,000 ounces troy, rising again to a little over 37,000 ounces in the following year. Output declined to some extent in succeeding years, averaging above 26,000 ounces for the years 1935–41, before reaching a high peak of nearly 44,000 ounces in 1942, when the Ife-Ilesha goldfield started production. Prohibition of further prospecting in that year caused a fall in production, and although the ban was partially raised after the end of hostilities gold production has become of less and less importance, and was only slightly above 2,000 ounces in the year 1950–1. Almost the whole output is taken by the Nigerian demand. (For comparative purposes it is worth noting that the annual gold production of the Union of South Africa is of the order of 12,000,000 ounces.) Total Nigerian production for the period 1914–51 is given as 365,000 ounces, but it is probable that this does not represent the whole of the gold mined. In spite of attempts at control, there is a certain amount of undeclared internal marketing, and during the war years there was considerable smuggling of gold to the Middle East, where the price per ounce in Egypt was £27 when the Nigerian figure was 8 guineas; control began to be effective in 1944.[2]

The Nigerian gold is principally alluvial, washed from quartz veins in the schist areas of the Basement Complex. In a few localities the ore is won directly from lodes. The Ife-Ilesha goldfield in the east of Oyo Province is now the chief producing area, but in the past leading areas have been in the Minna district of Niger Province and the Zamfara valley in south Sokoto Province. Ore is mined underground on a small scale in two places in Sokoto Province.

Most of the labour employed in gold-mining is on the tribute system, already described in connection with tin ore. Tributors tend to work individually in panning alluvial deposits, and in small teams on lodes, where a group may comprise four or five men engaged on quarrying the rock, two men on hand crushing, and one or two men on panning the resulting product. The tribute system has also been used underground to some extent, subject to close supervision by the operator to ensure safe development of galleries. Prohibition of tribute labour in the Ife-Ilesha field has recently resulted in a more systematic working in the area.

Silver-Lead-Zinc

Lead-zinc ores, partly argentiferous, occur as veins in the Cretaceous sedimentary rocks of Eastern Nigeria. One occurrence of galena is also known at Izom in Niger Province, where a quartz-sulphide vein runs through altered gneisses.

The main eastern occurrences are in the Abakaliki Division of Ogoja Province.[3] Large-scale exploitation of these veins appears to have taken place in the past, possibly as far back as the fifteenth century. European mining started in 1925, but operations ceased in 1930 when the price of lead fell to £11 per ton[4]; with a recovery in price levels activity was resumed in 1946–7, and large-scale operations were planned. The price of lead early in 1951 was £136 per ton and of zinc £151 per ton.[5]

The Ogoja activity has been centred on lodes in fractures across an anticlinal zone of the Lower Cretaceous shales. Galena and blende both occur, with variable quantities of marcasite,

---

[1] Mines Department, Nigeria, *Annual Report* 1948, p. 7.
[2] Mines Department, Nigeria, *Annual Report* 1944, p. 12.
[3] Geological Survey of Nigeria, *Annual Report* 1946, pp. 29–35.
[4] Mines Department, Nigeria, *Annual Report* 1948, p. 9.
[5] Mines Department, Nigeria, *Annual Report* 1950–1, p. 10.

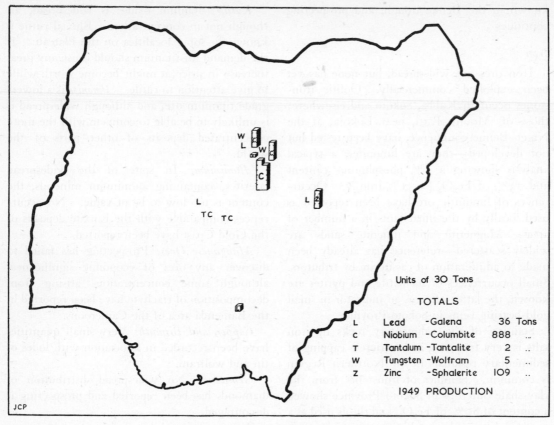

FIG. 141. OTHER BASE METALS

The distribution of columbite is seen to be similar to that of tin, previously shown. The lead–zinc offers a marked contrast.

siderite, quartz and chalcopyrite. Prospecting in 1947 suggested some 350,000 tons of lead-zinc ores.[1]

By 1953, however, it appeared unlikely that large-scale working would be developed in the near future.

Lead-zinc ores occur elsewhere, in the Cretaceous rocks of Eastern Nigeria. Attention has been given to a series of veins west of the railway in the extreme south-west of Ogoja Province, but investigation has not yet advanced to the stage of production.[2]

In the upper Benue valley other ore bodies are known, some of which were originally worked by the local people for internal trade, galena being powdered for use as a cosmetic (and usually mistranslated as antimony). Production has come mainly from Zurak,[3, 4] near the Jos Plateau–Adamawa provincial boundary, where mining was carried on by a company from 1931–7, and nearly 8,000 tons of galena extracted (giving 5,000 tons of lead and 900,000 ounces of silver). Work at Zurak was renewed in 1947, galena being worked underground, and sphalerite being taken from old dumps containing some 15,000 tons of mixed concentrates. Little ore was produced in the year 1950–1. Other occurrences are

[1] Mines Department, Nigeria, *Annual Report* 1947, p. 8.
[2] Mines Department, Nigeria, *Annual Report* 1949–50, p. 10.
[3] Geological Survey of Nigeria, *Annual Report* 1947, pp. 22–4.
[4] Geological Survey of Nigeria, *Annual Report* 1946, pp. 29–35.

known in the Benue trough, and prospecting continues.

Iron

Iron ores are widespread, but none has yet been exploited commercially. Oolitic iron-stones occur in Kabba, Sokoto and elsewhere; those of Mount Patti, near Lokoja, at the Niger–Benue confluence, have been tested but not developed—they are limonites, a typical analysis showing a 1% phosphorous content and 73% of Fe_2O_3 (=51% iron).[1,2] Occurrences of limonitic ore have been reported as used locally by the inhabitants in a number of areas. Magnetite and ilmenite sands are widely scattered—reference has already been made to adulteration of cassiterite by tributors. Small occurrences of hæmatite and pyrites are known, the latter often as an indicator in small gold-bearing veins in Sokoto Province.

Staining of the sedimentary rocks by iron salts is very frequent, and ferricrete capping of sedimentary residuals in the Northern Region is common. Samples of ironstones from the clay-shale outcrops in Sokoto Province showed a content of 80% of Fe_2O_3, and this is used as a good-quality ore by local smelters.

It would appear that the chief factors opposing the exploitation of Nigerian iron ores are the scattered nature of workable occurrences, and their distance from supplies of fuel and suitable fluxing material. Large amounts of iron carbonate have been recorded as occurring with the lead sulphides of the Eastern Region, and these might be developed as a by-product iron ore if the galena deposits are worked on a large scale.

Other Ores

Molybdenum occurs rarely in small quantity, normally in association with tin lodes.

Beryl and Tourmaline are found principally in quartz and pegmatite veins, but in insufficient quantity to have any economic significance.

Rutile (titanium oxide) is widespread, although not in concentration. Eluvial rutile is known in some localities on the Plateau. If the demand for titanium should cause any great increase in price, it might become worth while to give attention to rutile. *Ilmenite* is a lower-grade titanium ore, and although widespread it is unlikely to be able to compete with the more concentrated deposits of other parts of the world.

Aluminium: In spite of the widespread laterites, containing aluminium minerals, the content is too low to be of value. No occurrences comparable with the bauxite deposits of the Gold Coast have been reported.

Manganese Ores: Prospecting has failed to discover any ores of economic significance, although some concentrations arising from decomposition of trachyte have been reported in the Bamenda area of the Cameroons.

Copper and Bismuth: Very small quantities have been recorded in association with lodes of tin and wolfram.

Gemstones: No widespread distribution of diamonds has been reported and prospecting is discouraged.

Topaz is found locally on the plateau in greisen zones and in altered granites and porphyries, but is of no commercial importance.

The beryls referred to above are not of emerald quality.

Radio-active Minerals

Monazite has long been known, being first reported in the Calabar area early in the century, and monazite and thorite occur in the tin-field in association with tin and columbite. Such material has normally been rejected during ore-dressing, but prices have now been guaranteed for concentrates of fixed minimum percentages.[3] It may thus be worth while for mining companies to pay attention to these minerals as a by-product, and some small-scale export is possible.

[1] Geological Survey of Nigeria, *Annual Report* 1949–50, pp. 12–13.
[2] *Information in respect of Nigeria for the year* 1948 (Lagos 1950), p. 78.
[3] Mines Department, Nigeria, *Annual Report* 1949–50, p. 10.

Notice was published in 1952[1] of investigations carried out two years earlier into certain radio-active granites in the area of the Jos Plateau and the Liruein–Kano Hills. Of these rocks the most important appears to be an outcrop in the Kaffo Valley of the Liruei Hills, over an area of approximately 4,000 by 3,000 feet. Depth is unknown, but is not likely to be less than a few hundred feet. The granites contain pyrochlore, a source of niobium and uranium, and the report, using current market prices for these minerals against contents of 0·26% $(Nb, Ta)_2O_5$–0·012% U_3O_8 gives an estimated value of £5 2s. per ton to the Kaffo granite (equivalent to a gold ore of 8 dwt. per ton).

Methods of extraction of these minerals would require detailed study before any programme of economic exploitation, and official comment is at present guarded. The report indicates that 100% mineral recovery could not be attained, and to demonstrate the magnitude of operations required it cites annual output estimates such as:

	U_3O_8	$(Nb, Ta)_2O_5$
50% recovery		
3,000 tons per day milled	65 tons	1,420 tons
5,000 „ „ „	109 „	2,370 „
75% recovery		
3,000 tons per day milled	98 tons	2,130 tons
5,000 „ „ „	164 „	3,550 „

Problems of extraction, water supply and transport would presumably have to be overcome before any major development on this scale could be attempted. At present the nearest established transport service is 20 miles distant, in the form of the Bauchi Light Railway from Zaria; this line could not cope with any major increase in traffic and is, in any case, near the end of its useful life.

Mica

Muscovite mica occurs in sheets of economic size but of low quality in a few localities in the southern part of the country, such as in the western part of the Auchi Division of Benin Province. Small quantities were exported before the war, but no market at present exists for Nigerian mica.[2]

Phosphate

The Eocene beds of Abeokuta Province include some rock phosphate in the area east of Ifo Junction. The deposits average about 1 foot 6 inches in thickness, in places increasing to 4 feet thick. They are interbedded with clays.

Total reserves are unknown; they were originally stated probably to exceed one million tons, but are now known to be considerably less. Much of this lies beneath overburden up to 50 feet thick, but in some places the overburden is of a few feet only, and the phosphate could be extracted without difficulty. The deposits have not been mined.

Analyses of type area samples show a combined P_2O_5 and CaO content up to 70%; other samples show lower CaO values in favour of alumina. Iron and aluminium percentages were quoted in 1924 as making the deposits unsuitable for the manufacture of superphosphate, but some local agricultural use might be made of the raw material in a finely crushed state.[3]

Diatomite

Very extensive reserves of diatomite (principally amorphous silica) are known in the Chad basin. In a belt of 200 square miles of country north-west of Potiskum every well has passed into diatomite, usually about 100 feet below the surface, below a cover of drift and diatomaceous earth. In some cases spoil heaps from wells are almost entirely diatomite. The deposits outcrop some distance to the south-east of Potiskum, although it is thought that these may be Upper Cretaceous in age.[4]

[1] R. A. Mackay and K. E. Beer, *The Albite-Riebeckite Granites of Nigeria* (1952).
[2] Mines Department, Nigeria, *Annual Report*, 1946, p. 14.
[3] Geological Survey of Nigeria, *Bulletin No. 7* (1924): W. Russ, "The Phosphate Deposits of Abeokuta Province", p. 30.
[4] Geological Survey of Nigeria, *Bulletin No. 15* (1934): C. Raeburn and Brynmor Jones, "The Chad Basin Geology and Water Supply", p. 59.

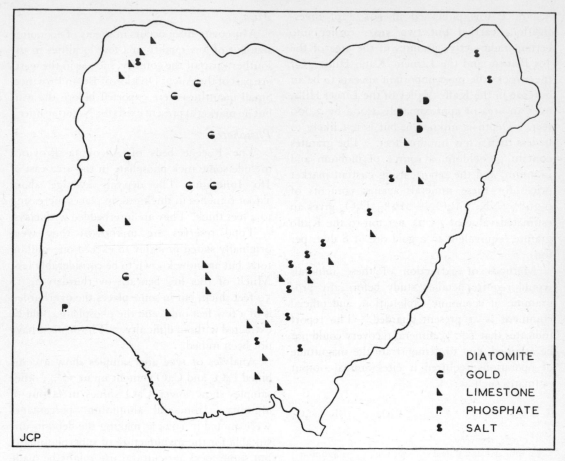

FIG. 142. OTHER MINERALS

The comparatively widespread occurrence of "domestic minerals" such as limestone is referred to in the text.

Locally the diatomite is used in fulling cotton and as a whitewash, but it has not been mined commercially. Diatomite can be used as an absorbent, for abrasive and polishing purposes, and as a high-temperature insulator—it can be combined with clay in the manufacture of refractory furnace bricks or roofing tiles. It may also be used in the making of glazes and pigments.

Kaolin

Kaolin occurs in small quantities in a number of places on the Basement Complex. It is not worked commercially. In Nigeria it is not infrequently misnamed "chalk".

Talc

This mineral is occasionally produced locally in small quantities from talc schists. The extent of such occurrences throughout the country is not known, and the mineral does not appear to have been investigated by mining interests. Quality varies, but grit-free material has been reported in western Kabba Province.

Salts

Nigerian salt supplies were never sufficient to meet local demands, and salt formed a major item of trade on the caravan routes coming into Kano. Supplies imported by sea have now largely supplanted the caravan products.

The Benue valley contains a number of brine springs in the Lower Cretaceous sediments. Some of the springs are warm, which may have some connection with the late volcanic activity of the region. Salt production on a small scale is a long-established local industry, which might be developed to some extent. Careful analysis of the salt would first be required: the Awe saltings on the north-east border of the Tiv Division of Benue Province may be a source of supply for the Tiv country, where goitre is prevalent, suggesting a low iodine content in the local product.

Northern Bornu shows a local industry based on four natural salts, these being common salt and three others known collectively as *kanwa*. These are produced by evaporation of small lakes which form during the rains. Kanwa is loosely translated as potash, but contains little or no potassium.

The common salt (*mongul*) contains some 69% of NaCl and 15% of Na_2SO_4. Red kanwa and white kanwa are both employed for cooking, the former also having medicinal uses, and both are added to drinking water for cattle; they contain approximately 20% of Na_2CO_3, 27% of Na_2SO_4 and 31% of $CaCO_3$. A second variety of white kanwa contains about 88% of Na_2SO_4 and is used only for tanning leather and for doctoring horse sores. All varieties as marketed show much variation in composition, possibly due to adulteration. The greater part of the salt deposits occur across the frontier in French territory.[1]

Other provinces show small quantities of salt, but of little importance. In Sokoto Province, gypsum occurs in the clay-shales and in the Mosasaurus division of the Rima Group, and might be developed for the manufacture of plaster of Paris and for minor local purposes; it is not in sufficient quantity to become a major export, and in any case transport to the coast would raise costs to too high a level.

Limestone

Limestones are widespread, but usually of no great thickness. The most promising occurrences are in the Eastern Region near Nkalagu[2] on the Enugu–Abakaliki road, where fourteen beds of limestone outcrop in a zone a mile wide in the Upper Cretaceous sequence, individual beds being from 3 feet to 15 feet in thickness. Large quantities of shale, also needed in the manufacture of cement, occur in the same sequence. Similar associations exist elsewhere, as in the lower Gongola area, but lack the proximity of coal supplies, which places the eastern deposits in a favourable position. The Nkalagu beds outcrop over at least 10 miles, with a dip of 6–9° W.N.W. First attention is likely to be given to this area.

Excellent limestones also occur in the west and north, notably in the north of Benin Province and north-west of Lokoja in Kabba Province. Samples of the latter rocks show a more or less constant calcium carbonate content of 98–99%. Both the limestones and nearby clays are suitable for cement manufacture. Reserves of limestone run to millions of tons. Fuel is the great problem, and early development is unlikely unless some use can be made of the lignites of the Western Region as a source of power.

Clays and Sands

Most parts of the country have supplies of clay suitable for production of bricks, tiles and coarse pottery. The clays may be sedimentary or alluvial, or the result of weathering of the crystalline Basement rocks.

Firebricks have been produced on a small scale from coal-measure clays at Enugu. Tests on these clays have shown them to be suitable for brick and tile production, and also for manufacture of fired drain-pipes. Use as a refractory material appears to be limited to relatively low temperatures. When finely ground the clays seem to be suitable for the manufacture of

---

[1] Geological Survey of Nigeria, *Bulletin No. 15* (1934), pp. 56–9.
[2] Geological Survey of Nigeria, *Annual Report* 1950–1, pp. 8–10. Supplementary data 1951–2, pp. 16, 18.

some types of medium-quality ceramic products.[1]

A ceramic factory has recently been started in the Lagos area, and there appears to be no reason why such industry catering for domestic needs should not develop in those parts of the country where fuel supplies are readily available.

Sands from the coalfield have also been tested for possible economic importance. The sand in its natural state is unsuitably graded for glass manufacture, but when screened to suitable grain size it could be used for the manufacture of common bottles. The Fe_2O_3 content appears low enough for the production of window-glass, but is the maximum permissible for the manufacture of high-class domestic glassware, and the development of the latter type of product is unlikely until more test work has been done and suitable techniques evolved.[2]

Roadstones and Building Stones

Laterite is commonly used for road surfacing. Such roads are sometimes tarred, but tarmacadam road metalling is unknown except in some of the major towns. With increasing development the country may require adequately metalled trunk roads, and many of the Basement granites and gneisses are suitable for such use. In a few areas Basement rocks or basalt are sometimes used as a loose top-dressing for road surfaces. The crystalline rocks already furnish ballast for the railway.

Rising standards of construction in the towns may also lead to an expansion of quarrying for building stones; rough-dressed granites have in some cases already given attractive results, and crystalline limestones might also be developed for building purposes. Construction in stone has, of course, to meet the competition of concrete, and both are beyond the resources of most of the people, for whom mud bricks and thatched roofs (or "pan" roofs in the towns) remain the essential building materials.

Rough stone is already used for major works such as facing dams and for coastal works; the breakwaters at Lagos required 2 million tons of granite from the Aro quarries near Abeokuta, 60 miles inland.

INDUSTRY[3]

(1) SMALL-SCALE CRAFT INDUSTRIES

Modern large-scale industry is as yet of very limited importance in the Nigerian economy. From this it should not be inferred that the Territory is negative industrially. Such is far from the case and, as in most tropical peasant communities, the aggregate volume of production and of employment accounted for by a wide diffusion of craft industries is very considerable. Especially in the remoter areas where European trade goods have not penetrated on a massive scale, almost every village has its craftsmen and women working up local raw materials into items of everyday needs, and utilising, along with these local raw materials, imported raw materials such as cotton yarn, and motor tyres, which are converted into sandals, and scrap iron which constitutes the basis of the blacksmiths' output. In the urban centres these local crafts are still important, though here they are complemented by forms of industrial activity which have developed as a result of the more specialised needs of urban society, such as motor engineering and cycle repairing, and by luxury crafts, such as brass founding, goldsmithing and photographic work. It is unfortunate that no adequate statistical material exists covering these forms of industrial activity, and the account given here must, of necessity, be largely descriptive. As a basis for discussion, it is convenient to adopt a broad grouping into the following categories:

(a) Textiles, including miscellaneous fibre industries.

(b) Woodworking.

[1] Colonial Geology and Mineral Resources, Vol. I (1950), "Fireclay from the Obwetti Colliery, Nigeria", p. 331.
[2] Colonial Geology and Mineral Resources, Vol. II (1951), "Glass Sand from Enugu, Nigeria", p. 36.
[3] Based in part on field observations by the writer; see also Report on the Department of Commerce and Industries by S. White (Kaduna 1951) for a discussion of industrial potentialities.

(c) Metalworking and small-scale engineer-
    ing.
(d) Leatherworking.
(e) Food-processing industries.
(f) Miscellaneous industries, including
    bricks, pottery and glass.

Textiles and Clothing

In spite of several decades of competition
from European factory-produced piece goods,
the cotton textile industry is still one of the most
flourishing and widely diffused Nigerian industries. In normal years, as has already been
stated, the Territory's exports of cotton lint
represent merely the surplus available after all
internal demands have been met, and in closely
settled areas such as Kano Province and in
remoter areas such as parts of Sokoto Province,
the demand from the local textile industry is so
heavy that no cotton is available for export. It
is unfortunately impossible to assess accurately
the volume of this internal demand, published
estimates varying between 30,000 bales (of
480 lb.) and over 100,000 bales.

Much of the local output comes from the
indigenous narrow loom which produces narrow strips, which are then sown together to
produce cloth of the desired width. The output of broad-loom cloth is relatively small, but
largely as a result of the efforts of the Department of Commerce and Industries is beginning
to expand rapidly; the recent establishment of
small-scale enterprises using the broad loom at
centres such as Benin City (p. 198) is a
significant development in this respect. At the
moment, shortage of yarn constitutes a serious
obstacle to increased production, but the introduction of improved methods of spinning at the
Department of Commerce and Industries Textile Centres, and the proposed establishment of
a cotton-spinning mill near Onitsha, should
go far to removing this bottleneck. For the
present, the shortage is being overcome by the
use of imported yarn (to the amount of 1

million pounds annually). The dyeing industry, which utilises both synthetic and vegetable
indigo dyes, is widely diffused throughout the
Mohammedan North and the Yoruba Provinces
of the Western Region.[1] There are striking
contrasts between these two areas. In the
north the industry is in the hands of the men
and the designs are woven in; in the south-west
it is carried on by the women, who produce a
wide and pleasing variety of designs by the
"tie-up" and *adire* (batik) methods.

The clothing industry uses both locally
woven cloth and imported textiles, and is very
widely distributed, almost every village of any
size having its tailor. In the bigger centres
tailors are the most widely diffused and
frequently the most numerous of all industrial
workers; a reconnaissance survey of Ibadan
referred to below gave a total of over 900
tailoring establishments, representing one-third
of all industrial units mapped.

The miscellaneous fibre industries—raphia
weaving, rope making and the manufacture of
mats and hats—may for convenience be included here. Ikot Ekpene in the Eastern
Region is the main centre of the raphia industry,
while rope, mats and hats are woven at several
centres in the Northern Region, notably Kano
City and Bida. Little statistical data exists on
the volume of production, though according to
the "Kano Survey" some £56,000 worth of
rope and mats are exported from Kano Province,
while in 1941 the Bida fibre industry is stated to
have produced some 66,000 hanks of twine,
372,000 yards of rope and over 7,000 bags,
worth in all £2,800.

Metal Industries

The traditional metal industries fall into two
main groups: the working of non-ferrous metals
such as brass, gold and silver, and the iron-
working and sheet-metal industries.

The former, like all luxury crafts, is concentrated in the main centres of population; it

---

[1] The popular assumption that indigo dyeing was introduced by the Fulani would help to explain this distribution.

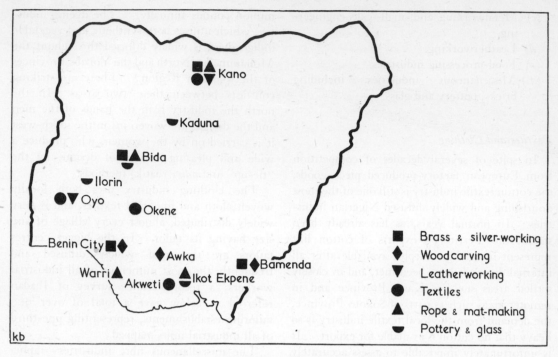

FIG. 143. HANDICRAFT INDUSTRIES

What might be termed "subsistence craft industries" catering for the needs of the immediate neighbourhood are to be found in most of the bigger centres of population.   This map shows some of the centres where
more specialised craft industries, catering for a wider market, have developed.

includes the production of jewellery and orna-
ments, the manufacture of brass and silver
hollow-ware and brass founding. Small-scale
manufacture of ear pendants, rings and neck-
laces of Nigerian gold and other precious or
semi-precious metals is found in most of the
towns; somewhat crude in technique, its products, nevertheless, find a ready market among
the urban population. The production of
hollow-ware—trays, bowls and the like—from
beaten brass or silver is a more specialised craft
and caters for a more restricted market. The
main centres of this industry are in the Northern
Provinces, notably Bida and Kano City, and
the itinerant Hausa trader plays an essential role
in the distribution of its products. Brass
founding by the *cire-perdue* method is practised in several of the bigger centres. Cast
ankle or arm bracelets of brass, nickel or Kano
silver are an attractive and distinctive product
of the Bida metal-working industry; they do

not, however, attain the degree of technical
perfection exhibited by the brass castings of
Benin City.   Here the industry has a long and
distinguished history, and the best of its products
—heads and figurines—rank among the outstanding achievements of Nigerian craftsman-
ship.

Iron working and associated metal industries
rely largely upon imported raw material in the
form of metal scrap, and since they cater for the
everyday needs of the rural community, they are
widely diffused. Hoes, knives, machetes and
other articles of domestic and agricultural use
make up the greater part of the Nigerian blacksmiths' output; while a small-scale sheet-metal
industry, producing lamps and such small
articles as medicine containers, is found in some
of the bigger centres. With the development
of modern methods of transport in recent years
many metal workers have adopted cycle- and
motor-repairing as a supplementary or even

major activity, and, though no great level of efficiency can be claimed for these small-scale engineering industries, they do provide a significant volume of employment. Even more important, in the long-term view, is the opportunity that these activities provide for a growing number of workers to acquire the rudiments of mechanical skill and aptitude, without which the future development of secondary industry would be impossible.

Woodworking Industries

These are particularly developed in the closely peopled districts of the south and fall into two broad groups: the first and most extensive branch producing domestic furniture based largely on European models; the second producing traditional objects, such as masks and figures. The former is widely distributed throughout all the large towns; in Ibadan, which may be taken as typical of the larger Yoruba centres, there are some 480 woodworking establishments (a number exceeded by tailoring establishments), many of which employed half a dozen or more workers. The traditional style of woodcarving is best represented in Benin City whose long-established woodworking industry using local ebony has received a new lease of life as the result of a growing European demand for its carved heads, statuettes, panels and book-ends. The co-operative woodworking establishment at Awka in Onitsha Province represents a synthesis of the two branches of the industry; European-style furniture is produced together with stools and other items of household equipment based on traditional Ibo designs.

Leather Goods

Apart from the preparation of cattle hides and goat- and sheep-skins for export, the leather-working industry is represented in most centres of population chiefly by sandalmakers. These utilise both hides and skins, and, increasingly in

recent years, old motor tyres for soleing; an approximate indication of their importance can be obtained from a survey of Ibadan which revealed a total of 190 sandalmakers and shoe repairers, representing 7% of the total number of industrial concerns mapped.

A more specialised branch of the leather-working industry is the manufacture of saddlery, scabbards, cushions, handbags and sandals from dyed goat- and sheep-skins. A wide range of local raw materials was formerly used in dyeing the tanned skins[1]—thus a bright red dye was obtained from pounded sorghum stalks, to which a solution of potash was added; a black dye from a mixture of honey and blacksmiths' slag, and a pale green dye from brass filings mixed with lime-juice, common salt and other ingredients; these local dyestuffs have, however, been increasingly superseded by imported chemical dyes. By the skilful introduction of pieces of differently coloured leather, elaborate and pleasing designs are produced. The main centres of this multi-coloured leather industry are Kano City and Oyo, while on a smaller scale it has been introduced into Lagos by Hausa craftsmen. Like the woodworking of Benin City, this branch of the leatherworking industry has benefited in recent years from a growing tourist-type demand from the European community.

Food-processing Industries

As might well be expected in a country whose economy is still dominantly agricultural, the processing and preparation of foodstuffs for market is a major branch of economic activity. Included under this heading are such diverse activities as preparation of "gari" from cassava, cornmilling, extraction of shea butter, expressing of oil from groundnuts and oil-palm fruit and the manufacture of sugar. It is only for these last two branches of industry that even approximate data are available.

Over nine-tenths of the Territory's palm-oil production is still carried on by hand methods,

[1] These dyed skins, formerly exported by caravan across the desert to the ports of the W. Mediterranean, are the "Morocco Leather" of commerce.

without the intervention of even the simplest machinery. These hand methods are not only excessively time-consuming (one authority estimates that to extract 1 ton of palm-oil by hand demands 200 hours of labour using the soft-oil method) but also give a very low extraction rate, estimated at not more than 55%. A marked improvement in efficiency is obtained by the use of simple hand-presses which handle up to $1\frac{1}{4}$ cwt. of fruit at a time, and which give an extraction rate of some 65%. The use of such presses has extended greatly in the Palm Belt during recent years, the number of presses increasing from 750 in 1938 to close on 1,600 in 1948–9; even so, barely one-tenth of Nigeria's palm-oil is produced by such presses, and the possibilities of extending this form of production are obviously very great. The rapid increase in the number of palm presses during recent years is shown graphically in Fig. 106.

The sugar industry has developed entirely within the last generation. As late as 1921 Dudgeon observed: "The preparation of sugar does not appear to be known in the country, and the sole use to which the plant is put seems to be the consumption of the green stalks by the inhabitants and their cattle". By 1949–50, however, 655 crushers, concentrated mainly in the Zaria–Katsina area, were producing a total of some 10,000 tons of sugar, and experiments had been initiated with a small power-operated

Top: Bow making, Maiduguri.
Centre: Canoe making, Okitipupa.

Bottom right: Rope making, Bida.
Bottom left: Broad-loom weaving, Benin.

crusher. Today, the sugar industry is an important and rapidly expanding element in the Northern Region's industrial pattern.

Miscellaneous Crafts

Outstanding among these are brickmaking, pottery and associated industries. These, owing to the difficulties of transporting bulky or fragile products, tend to cater largely for the immediate local market. Occasional exceptions are, however, found. Thus, the black pottery of Ilorin finds a market in many parts of the Western Region, while the pottery of Bamenda, Ikot Ekpene and the Gwari country enters on a small scale into local trade.

The Bida glass industry is unique in Nigeria, but may logically be included here. The craft, according to Nupe tradition, was brought from Egypt; it is today carried on in only one quarter of the town, and by a group which is one of the most highly organised and self-contained of all the Bida craft guilds. Both locally made glass and imported glass bottles are used as raw material; the products include multi-coloured glass bangles, rings and beads, and these find a ready market in almost every part of the Territory.

The Industrial Pattern of a Nigerian Town

No statistical data exists which would give a measure of the relative importance of the various

Bottom left: Woodcarving, Benin.
Bottom right: Glassworking, Bida.
Top: Tailoring, Bida.
Centre: Preparing patterned cloth for dyeing, Ibadan.

categories of industry discussed above. Nevertheless, a rough measure of the importance of the various groups in a southern city can be obtained from Table XVIII, which summarises the results of a preliminary count of industries in Ibadan carried out in 1949–50 under the direction of the writer. In interpreting this table, it must be emphasised that the figures cited refer to industrial establishments, and that these are of very uneven "employment capacity"; thus, the average tailoring establishment is a one-man business, while a carpenter's shop, a blacksmith's shop, a bakery or a printing establishment may employ half a dozen or more workers.

The total number of "industrial units" mapped was 2,700, distributed as follows:

TABLE XVIII
INDUSTRIAL UNITS IN IBADAN

Industry	% of all Industrial Units	Units per 10,000 Population
TEXTILES		
Tailoring	34·0	27·4
Weaving	3·4	2·8
Dyeing	13·5	10·9
METALS		
Engineering [1]	12·8	10·4
Blacksmiths	2·5	2·0
Tinsmiths	2·0	1·6
Brass-smiths	1·6	1·2
Goldsmiths	2·7	2·2
WOODWORKING		
Carpenters' shops [2]	17·7	14·3
OTHERS		
Leatherworking [3]	7·0	5·6
Pottery	0·5	0·2
Photo work	0·8	0·6
Food industries [4]	0·5	0·2
Miscellaneous [5]	0·7	0·5

The dominance of the textile trades is obvious, and this is typical of many southern towns; though in some centres (e.g. Oyo and Iseyin) the importance of spinning, weaving and dyeing is somewhat greater and that of tailoring proportionately less. The marked development of small-scale engineering (cycle and motor repairing) reflects the importance of Ibadan as a trading and traffic centre; so, too, does the relative insignificance of the pottery industry, for European pottery and enamelware and pottery railed south from Ilorin have tended to displace the local product. Perhaps the most outstanding features revealed by the table are the range of crafts practised and the large number of establishments in operation; these employ only the simplest equipment, are widely dispersed throughout the various quarters of the town (Fig. 146) and cater almost entirely for the local market. In all these respects they contrast sharply with the modern factory-type industry (as typified by the Nigerian Tobacco Company's factory and the newly established cannery), which in recent years has been grafted on to the age-old pattern of small-scale peasant handicrafts.

(2) MODERN FACTORY INDUSTRY [6]

The pattern of traditional handicraft industries sketched above is being rapidly modified by the expansion of modern factory-type industry in the Territory. To this expansion both private and Government enterprise are contributing. Development of new industries by local enterprise is encouraged by providing the intending industrialist with the technical advice and assistance of the Department of Commerce and Industries; financial aid for approved projects is provided by the Regional Development Boards. In addition, when private industry is not forthcoming, the Department of Commerce and Industries itself introduces new industries which for economic or social reasons

[1] Cycle repairing and motor engineering.
[2] Including one establishment producing carved calabashes.
[3] Mainly shoemaking with some tanning.
[4] Mainly bakeries and excluding preparation of cooked foods for sale.
[5] Mainly printing.
[6] See *Annual Reports of the Department of Commerce and Industries* and *Annual Reports of the Regional Production Development Boards*.

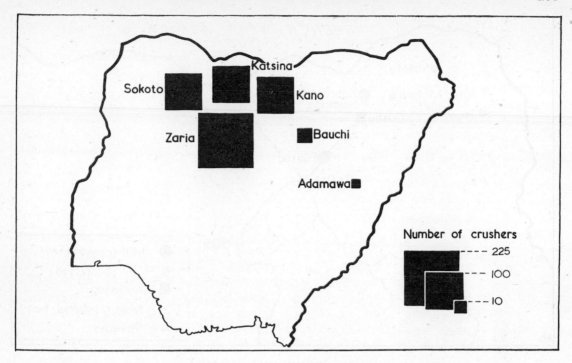

FIG. 144. THE SUGAR INDUSTRY

An example of a peasant processing industry developed with European encouragement during the last thirty years.   Concentration of the industry in the heart of the Northern Provinces.   For sugar production see Fig. 85.

it is considered desirable to establish, handing these over to local enterprise when their commercial success has been assured.   The role of the Department in shaping the Territory's new industrial pattern will be evident from the account that follows.

Food-processing Industries

In view of the dominantly agricultural character of the Nigerian economy, it is inevitable that food-processing industries should be of major importance.   These industries possess certain very marked social and economic advantages, for they can be conveniently carried on in small units widely dispersed throughout the raw-material producing regions, and their requirements in the form of capital investment and labour skill are relatively modest; they therefore make it possible to obtain the maximum diffusion of the benefits of industry at a very small cost.

These advantages are well illustrated by the Pioneer Palm-oil Mills which are being established by the Department of Commerce and Industries throughout the oil-palm areas of the south.   The advantages of the oil-mill over the traditional and hand-press methods of extraction are many: it gives a much higher extraction rate (it produces 40% more oil from a given quantity of fruit than the traditional hand method); it produces a higher quality and more uniform oil, and thus helps to overcome one of the main disadvantages of peasant as opposed to plantation methods of oil production; it reduces the amount of labour needed for oil extraction, and thus makes possible the harvesting of the considerable quantity of fruit formerly left to rot owing to labour shortage; finally, the introduction of mills into remote villages can play an important social role by bringing home to the peasant producer, and especially the younger generation, the advantages of mechanised pro-

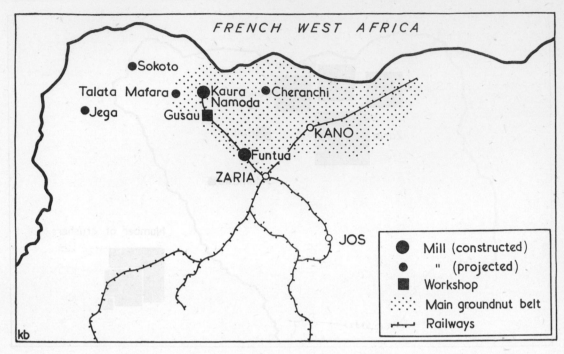

FIG. 145. GROUNDNUT OIL MILLS

Showing the pioneer groundnut oil mills established and projected in the western sector of the groundnut belt.   Only mills belonging to the Department of Commerce and Industries are shown; for mills established by Syrian enterprise see text.

duction.[1]   The present Pioneer Oil Mill programme provides for a total of 112 mills, of which 67 are to be established in the Eastern Region, 41 in the Western Region and 4 in the Northern Region (Kabba).   It is stated that the average output of a mill is some 350 tons of oil, so that the aggregate capacity of the mills projected will be 50,000 tons annually.   Since the mills can be operated economically only when there is an adequate density of palms, it may be necessary in certain cases to thicken up the groves near the mills by new plantings; this is being done in the vicinity of the Kabba mills. A comparable trend towards mechanised production is evident in the groundnut-oil industry of the Northern Provinces, though developments here are more recent and on a smaller scale.   Groundnut oil has long been produced by crude but effective hand methods throughout

the area, the oil and cake being consumed by the producer's household or sold locally.   Experiments with hand-press extraction were made by Katsina Native Administration in 1935, but were not followed up owing to the greater cost of production as compared with the traditional methods.   Large-scale mechanised production dates from 1942, when a Syrian industrialist established a mill at Kano; this has been enlarged several times, and three additional mills have been erected, again by Syrian enterprise, giving a combined production, when in full operation, of 10,000 tons of oil and 15,000 tons of cake.   In 1949 it was announced that a scheme for groundnut-oil production by the Department of Commerce and Industries along the lines of the Pioneer Palm-oil Mills scheme had been approved and that orders had been given for the purchase of six mills and a central

[1] See "The Processing, Storage and Transport of Nigerian Palm Oil" in *United Africa Company Statistical and Economic Review*, No. 13 (1954), and "Palm Oil Production in Nigeria", *ibid.*, No. 7 (1951).

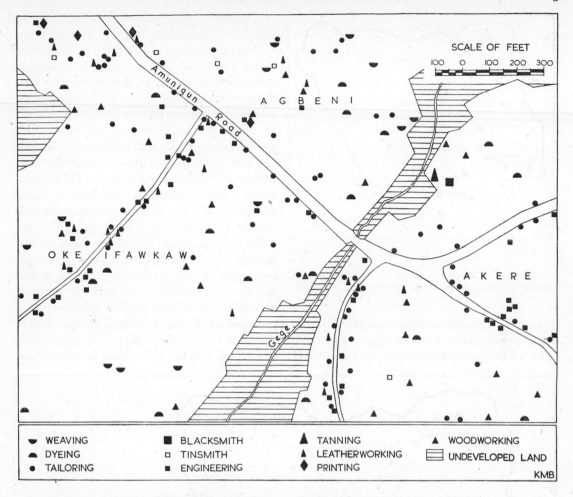

Scale of Feet
100   0   100   200   300

AGBENI

Amunigun Road

OKE IFAWKAW

Gege

AKERE

	WEAVING		BLACKSMITH		TANNING		WOODWORKING
	DYEING		TINSMITH		LEATHERWORKING		UNDEVELOPED LAND
	TAILORING		ENGINEERING		PRINTING		

KMB

FIG. 146. THE INDUSTRIAL PATTERN OF A NIGERIAN CITY

This sample map, based upon an industrial survey of Ibadan made in 1949–50, illustrates the wide diffusion of industries typical of the bigger Nigerian towns. Only in the case of engineering (i.e. cycle and motor repairing) is there any marked tendency to localisation along the major lines of communication. The textile industry, by contrast, is widely scattered on compounds away from the main roads. The larger symbols indicate industries employing larger groups of workers.

Note that the food industries (preparation of cooked foodstuffs for sale) are not shown.

workshop. After investigation, mill sites were selected in the Sokoto–Katsina area, grouped around a central workshop at Gusau. The mills at Funtua and Kaura Namoda were completed in 1951; construction of the remaining mills is postponed pending a re-examination of the whole scheme in the light of experience gained in operating the Funtua and Kaura Namoda units. Estimated capacity of the mills is 5–6 cwt. decorticated groundnuts per hour,

giving an annual output of 250 tons of oil and 350 tons of cake. The industry possesses all the advantages of the palm-oil industry, and at the same time could play a role of major importance in the development of the northern livestock industry by providing, in the form of groundnut cake, a cheap high-protein cattle feed.

In the Middle Belt food-processing industries are represented by the dairy industry of the Jos

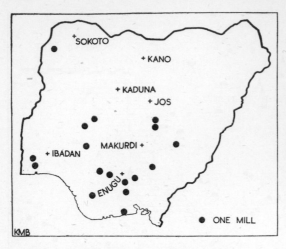

FIG. 147. RICE MILLS

Major concentration is in the south of the territory and notably in the developing rice-growing area of Ogoja.

Plateau. The general conditions of production have already been outlined (pp. 125, 127). The industry was taken over by the Department

of Commerce and Industries in 1948, and in 1949–50 it produced 273,500 lb. of butter, 81,200 lb. of cheese and 112,000 lb. of clarified butter fat. Recent years have witnessed a steady increase in output, and facilities for continuing this expansion and for improving the quality of the butter and cheese will be provided by the new dairy at Vom; this will include pasteurisation equipment, preheating and chilling vats, boilers, buttermakers, increased cold storage and canning machinery. Distribution under tropical conditions has been a major problem, and it would seem that the answer to this lies in canning, with refrigeration facilities at the main centres. Experiments with cheese-making have been carried on; these include the processing of new cheese types in cans and in tinfoil, and the effect of varying maturing periods on the staple Cheddar variety, which is produced at Vom; these experiments will be extended in the new dairy. A considerable unfulfilled demand still exists for butter and

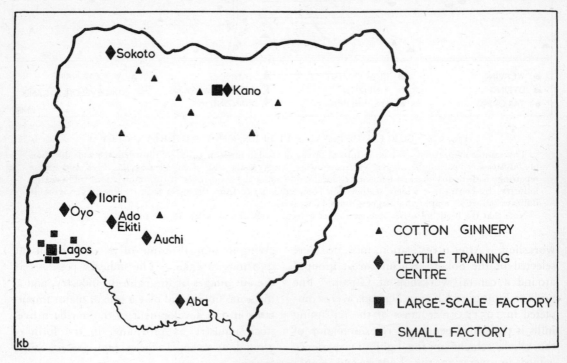

FIG. 148. THE TEXTILE INDUSTRY

Note the dominating role of Yoruba Provinces and the northern cotton belt. For textile factories see Fig. 149.

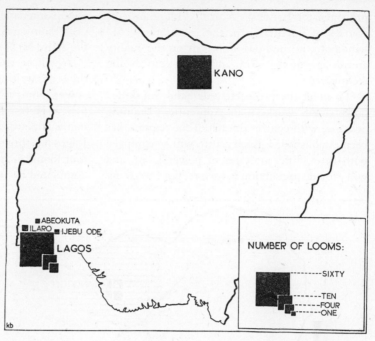

FIG. 149
TEXTILE FACTORIES
Concentration is in the Yoruba
Provinces with the beginnings of
a large-scale northern industry in
Kano City. Only factories in pro-
duction in 1951 are shown.

cheese, but the output of
clarified butter fat [1] has exceeded local demand, and an
export outlet is being sought.

The remaining food
processing industries are
concentrated in the south-
western sector of the country.
Lagos has miscellaneous
food-processing and pack-
aging industries, and a large-
scale modern brewery;
manufacture of fruit
squashes, utilising locally grown citrus fruit, is
carried on at Agege, on the outskirts of Lagos
and at Abeokuta; Ibadan has a newly erected
cannery and a large-scale tobacco factory. This
latter is operated by a subsidiary of the British-
American Tobacco Company and has encouraged the production, in Oyo and Zaria
Provinces, of Virginia tobacco; its output in
recent years has been 700 million cigarettes
per annum.

Textile Industries

The long tradition of textile working in
many parts of the Territory, the large and
increasing demand for cotton piece goods and
the fact that the Northern Region is a significant
producer of good-quality cotton have led to a
growing realisation of the potentialities of
modern large-scale spinning and weaving industries in Nigeria. Given adequate capital
and skilled labour (this latter depending largely
upon the provision of technical training facilities), there appears to be no major obstacle to
the development of the textile industry on a

scale sufficiently large to meet a considerable
proportion of the Territory's requirements of
cotton piece goods. Such a development will
not necessarily mean the extinction of the handweaving industry; as has been already indicated,
this small-scale industry has shown remarkable
vitality in the face of several decades of competition from imported textiles, and there is no
reason to anticipate any falling-off in the steady
demand for hand-woven local products. It is
significant in this respect that the textile-
development of the Department of Commerce
and Industries is based on the assumption that
the peasant handloom industry and large-scale
factory industry are complementary rather than
competitive lines of development.

The introduction of improved techniques in
the handweaving industry has been facilitated
by the establishment of Handloom Weaving
Training Centres at various points in the
country. Seven such centres are in operation
—at Ilorin, Kano and Sokoto in the Northern
Region, Ado Ekiti, Oyo and Auchi in the
Western and Aba in the Eastern; an eighth is

[1] This is produced from pure cream in areas too distant from the dairy to make transport possible; it is therefore
sterilised at the buying point.

projected for Benue Province.　These provide courses of instruction in the use of the broad handloom, in methods of improving the quality and design of the cloth and in modern dyeing techniques.

To meet the prospective demand for skilled power-loom workers an Apprentice Training Scheme, with centres in each of the regions, has been established.　Each centre will be equipped with three different types of power loom, and will provide instruction in the erection, servicing and maintenance of textile machinery.　Small-scale training along these lines commenced at the Minjibir Textile Centre, Kano, in 1949.

It will be evident from Fig. 149 that at the time of writing the major concentration of power looms is in the south-west of the Territory.　Here there are small-scale establishments at Ilaro, Abeokuta and Ijebu-Ode, while Lagos has three factories with a total of seventy-four looms.　In the latter centre the industry is dominated by the recently completed factory of

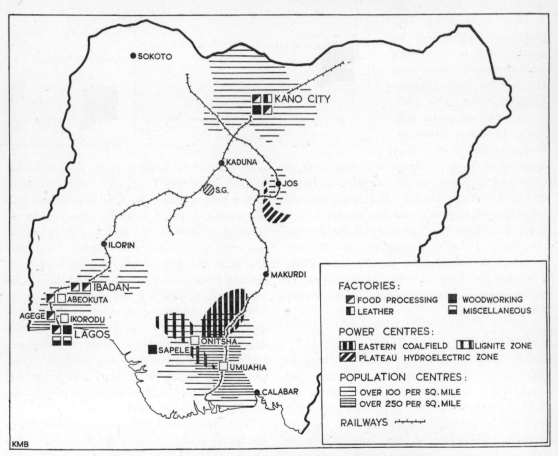

FIG. 150. FACTORY INDUSTRY (EXCLUDING TEXTILES)

Hollow symbols indicate projected factories.　Note the concentration in the Yoruba Provinces and the beginnings of a secondary concentration at Kano.　The two most promising areas for future industry are the Jos Plateau and the Ibo Provinces.　The former has a well-developed power network and a semi-skilled labour force and here industrialisation would help to solve the problem which the ultimate exhaustion of the Plateau tin ores will create; the area also enjoys the advantage of a central location and a relatively invigorating climate. In Iboland the power base is provided by the local coal and lignite deposits and potential lines of development include agricultural processing industries and plastics based on coal; a policy of industrialisation in this area would go some way towards relieving the critical pressure of population.　(S. G. = Shiroro Gorge.)

Messrs. J. F. Kamson at Mushin on the out-skirts of the city. The plant comprises sixty power looms, yarn preparation machinery and complete bleaching, dyeing and finishing equip-ment. When in full production it will have an annual output of 1,872,000 yards of cloth, manufactured from imported yarns. The Kano Citizens' Trading Company's factory at Kano has not been able to draw on the local power supply, and the company has had to install its own plant; otherwise the factory is almost a duplicate of the Kamson factory. In the case of all these developments financial assistance has been given by the Regional Development Boards, and advice on layout and purchase of machinery has been provided by the technical experts of the Department of Commerce and Industries.

Virtually the entire factory output of cloth, and a considerable proportion of the handloom industry, is dependent on the use of imported yarns. Considerable significance must there-fore be attached to the multi-purpose textile project at Onitsha. This will manufacture produce sacks (6 million annually) and will in addition have a cotton-spinning mill with an output of 2 million pounds of yarn annually. Such an output will go far towards meeting the needs of both the handloom weaver and the developing factory industry.

Miscellaneous Industries

In addition to the industries listed above, a small but growing range of miscellaneous industries is represented in the Territory. These do not in any way challenge the predominance of the food-processing and textile industries, nor, indeed, are they likely to do so in the immediate future, but they are of importance as introducing a welcome element of diversity into the country's industrial economy. They include the manufacture of soap and of metal cans, leatherworking and timber pro-cessing industries and the manufacture of pottery.

Small-scale manufacture of furniture is car-ried on at Lagos and Kano, but the outstanding enterprise in the woodworking group is the United Africa Company's plywood and veneer factory at Sapele on the southern margin of the rain forest. In 1949–50 this enterprise pro-duced for export some 8,000 tons of sawn timber, 6,170 tons of plywood and 1,342 tons of veneer. The pottery industry will be repre-sented by a large-scale plant under construction at Ikorodu, 25 miles east of Lagos. This will produce household pottery for the Nigerian market, utilising the most modern machinery and techniques; it is stated that its output will be sufficient to satisfy a quarter of Nigeria's present demand for imported pottery.

CHAPTER VI

TRANSPORT

RAILWAYS

Fig. 151 shows the distribution of railway lines and the dates of completion of the various sections.

The main-line system is on the 3-foot 6-inch gauge, and construction started in 1898 from Lagos northward to Abeokuta, reaching Ibadan in 1901 and Jebba in 1909.

In the Northern Provinces the first line was narrow gauge (2 feet 6 inches), opened in 1901 from Wushishi on the Kaduna River to Zungeru, the original capital of Northern Nigeria. This line was subsequently aban-

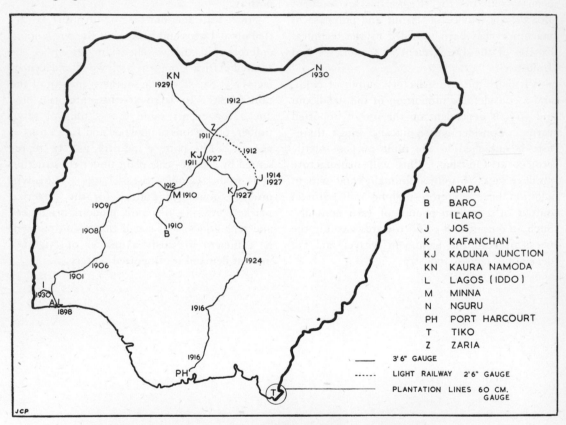

A	APAPA
B	BARO
I	ILARO
J	JOS
K	KAFANCHAN
KJ	KADUNA JUNCTION
KN	KAURA NAMODA
L	LAGOS (IDDO)
M	MINNA
N	NGURU
PH	PORT HARCOURT
T	TIKO
Z	ZARIA

—————— 3' 6" GAUGE

----------- LIGHT RAILWAY 2'6" GAUGE

PLANTATION LINES 60 CM. GAUGE

FIG. 151. RAILWAYS

The main railway system has developed from three separate centres, namely Lagos, Baro and Port Harcourt, and the gradual expansion and linking-up of these lines can be seen from the dates on the map. An extension from Nguru eastward to Maiduguri near Lake Chad, has been proposed, but no new lines appear likely to be constructed in the immediate future.

The main line system is on a narrow gauge of 3 feet 6 inches, and is as yet single-track throughout. The original line (the Bauchi Light Railway) from Zaria to Jos is on a 2 feet 6 inches gauge, and having reached the end of its useful life has an uncertain future. The Cameroons plantations are served by a private railway system of 60 cm. gauge, based on Tiko port.

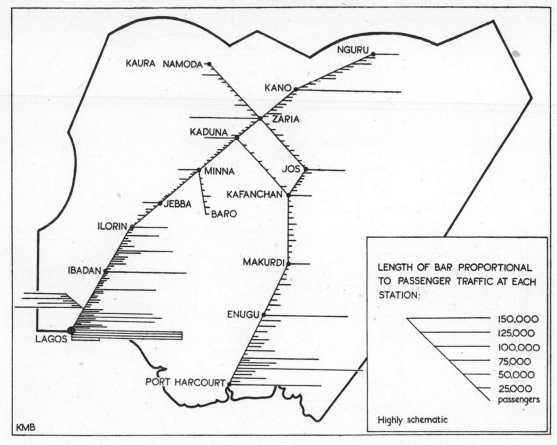

FIG. 152. PASSENGER MOVEMENT ON THE NIGERIAN RAILWAY

Note that outside the main towns passenger traffic in the Sudan zone is relatively small and does not compare with the traffic of the southern stations. This is in striking contrast to the state of affairs shown in Fig. 153.

doned after the development of Baro as the river port for the North, and the construction of a 3-foot 6-inch line from Baro to Minna and later to Kano, completed at the end of 1911. At the same time a line was finished from Jebba North to Minna, and in 1912 through rail communication was established from Kano to Lagos, utilising a steam train-ferry across the Niger at Jebba. Early in 1916 the ferry was withdrawn on the completion of the Jebba Bridge across the Niger; the section across the North Channel is 522 feet long, and that across the South Channel is 1,526 feet in length.

Meanwhile a 2-foot 6-inch gauge line had been built from Zaria south-eastward to the Jos Plateau, reaching Bukuru in 1914, to serve the tin-mines then developing on the Plateau. This is still known as the Bauchi Light Railway, although since the creation of Plateau Province it no longer touches Bauchi Province. For thirteen years it provided the only rail connection with the mines, and carried all the machinery originally required for the industry, no mean achievement in view of the gradients involved: in the 40 miles from Rahama to Jos it climbs some 1,500 feet. The line is now approaching the end of its useful life, and its future is uncertain.[1]

With the discovery of coal at Enugu, the eastern line was started to provide connection

[1] Nigerian Government Railway, *Annual Report*.

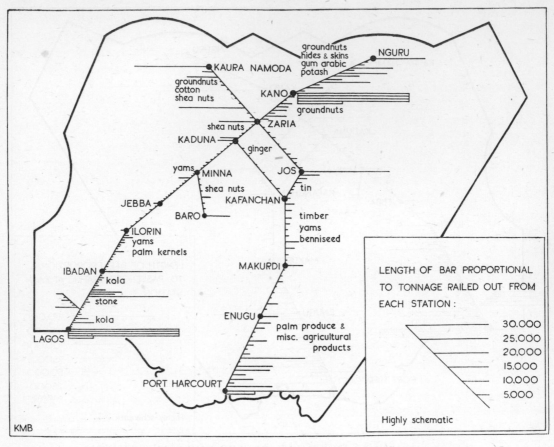

FIG. 153. TRAFFIC MOVEMENT ON THE NIGERIAN RAILWAY

Note the concentration of activity in the Cocoa Belt, the eastern Palm Belt, the Jos Plateau and, above all, in the groundnut and cotton-producing areas of the Sudan zone. The volume of traffic originating in the Middle Belt stations is relatively small. Some of the major commodities handled are indicated.

with the sea. The coastal terminus is at Port Harcourt, 40 miles up the Bonny River, where ocean-going vessels can lie alongside dry land. The railway reached Enugu in 1916, and construction northward was continued in 1922, reaching Makurdi on the Benue in 1924. A train-ferry at this point provided a through connection with the further extension to Kaduna, which was completed in 1927. This ferry was replaced by the great Benue Bridge, 2,624 feet in length, which was completed in 1932. The main line had meanwhile been extended in 1927 by a branch line from Kafanchan to Jos, rising some 2,600 feet in 78 miles, by the line northward from Zaria to Kaura Namoda in 1929,

and eastward from Kano to Nguru in 1930. No further extensions have taken place, although a line to Maiduguri to serve the Chad basin has been under consideration for many years; continuation of the line eastward from Nguru to Maiduguri has been contemplated, but the development of alternative forms of transport may be preferred. The railway operates road motor services from Gusau, on the Kaura Namoda line, to Sokoto, a distance of 136 miles.

The railway system is single-track throughout. Tunnelling has not been adopted, deep cuttings being preferred where necessary. On difficult sections gradients of the order of 1 in

80 are not uncommon, and average speeds are consequently low by European standards. Difficulties of construction and gradient have been considerable.[1] The railway reaches a maximum height of about 4,400 feet on the line from Kafanchan to Jos.

Traffic has increased steadily, and in the year 1950–1 the railway carried over $5\frac{1}{2}$ million passengers and $1\frac{1}{2}$ million tons of goods. Figs. 152 and 153 indicate passenger and goods traffic railed through individual stations and indicate two trends: firstly, the heavier passenger traffic of the south-west and south-east, and, secondly, an apparent predominance of *outward* goods traffic from the Northern Region, with the southern exception of Lagos. It should be noted, however, that coal traffic from Enugu is not included in the figures used in the construction of the map. The map is an indicator of rail traffic only, and not of goods moving in any area; road transport draws off much of the goods tonnage of the south-west and south-east.

The unusually heavy demands on the railway during the war years, and the difficulties of obtaining spare parts, put a considerable strain on working, but traffic has continued to increase. Notwithstanding the arrival of new loco-motives and rolling-stock and the relaying of long sections of track, the operating capacity of the railway remains fully stretched. The "pyramids" of Kano (groundnuts awaiting railing) reappear in each buying season, and any increase in crop production or checks to rail shipments are liable to result in the new crop being brought in before complete evacuation of the previous year's crop, and an expansion of carrying capacity would appear essential for the country's future development. Apart from the difficulties of the ratio between tonnage offering and tonnage capacity, the railway administration is faced with the ever-present possibility of "wash-outs" in the wet season. The effects of a break in the main line, inter-rupting traffic for one week, can be appreciated. Small culverts and bridges have sometimes proved inadequate under conditions of sudden flood, which is not surprising when it is realised that much of the line runs through virtually unmapped country, where accurate figures for rainfall totals and intensity, run-off and catch-ment areas are unknown.

ROAD TRANSPORT

The development of the road system of Nigeria is of recent date, the first main trunk road being constructed in 1905 from railhead at Ibadan northward to Oyo. Since that date the road network has extended rapidly, but many areas are still more than 30 miles from a motor road and very little of the total area of the country is within $1\frac{1}{2}$ miles of a road (Fig. 154).

Through trunk roads now run across many parts of the country, but the great rivers cause a canalisation of inter-regional road traffic through three points, namely the road-railway bridges at Jebba and Makurdi across the Niger and the Benue respectively, and the road ferry from Asaba to Onitsha across the Lower Niger. An additional ferry across the Lower Niger at Lokoja was established in 1952. In some other places roads come down to opposite banks of the rivers, but there is no method of ferrying vehicles across. Apart from the places named, the only other crossing is of the upper Benue near Yola, where vehicles can be ferried across to the road system of southern Adamawa. The term "ferry" should not be misunderstood: of the many ferries in the country only the Asaba–Onitsha and the Oron–Calabar are mechanically propelled, the remainder being pontoons poled or paddled across the rivers.

The original roads served as feeders to the railway system, and this is still largely true in the Northern Region. Comparatively close net-works occur only in the south-east and the south-west, principally serving areas of palm, cocoa and timber production, together with a small concentration in the tin-fields and an open network radiating from Kano. The develop-

[1] J. Stocker, *Nigerian Railway Jubilee* Lagos 1952).

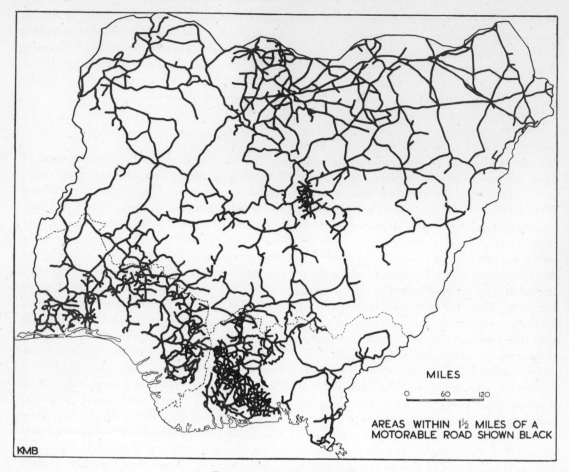

MILES

0   60   120

AREAS WITHIN 1½ MILES OF A
MOTORABLE ROAD SHOWN BLACK

KMB

FIG. 154. MOTOR ROADS

The road system (dry-season and all-season) is shown above.   The nuclei of the agricultural regions of the south and (to a lesser extent) Kano Province, are clear, and also the mining area of the Jos Plateau.   The Middle Belt stands out as an area of poor communications.   The scale of the map does not make clear the fact that, although roads may run down to opposite sides of the great rivers, the road system is divided into three parts by the Niger and Benue rivers.   Traffic crosses only by the bridges at Jebba and Makurdi, and by the ferry at Onitsha.   Dry-season roads deteriorate very rapidly if not fully maintained, and not all the roads shown on the map (1950) are now in existence, while other roads have been constructed since.

As the areas shown black represent not only the roads, but also the country within one and a half miles of a motorable road, it follows that over all the area shown white the movement of goods must be by animal or by headload (assisted by canoes and bicycles in some areas) and the importance to the country's trade of these primitive methods of transport may therefore be appreciated.

ment of the roads as an independent transport system is most noticeable in the south-west; here the roads compete directly with the railway, the most obvious commodity being heavy timber on the way to the coast at Lagos or at Okitipupa, whence it travels by water to Lagos. Fig. 155 shows the numbers of vehicles using some of the major "A" and "B" roads, and

although not a complete picture, it will serve to indicate the general pattern of road movement. Volume of traffic varies seasonally in some areas, but a steady general increase has frequently masked seasonal fluctuation, and the latter are not apparent in official traffic census figures over recent years.

It is not possible to determine passenger

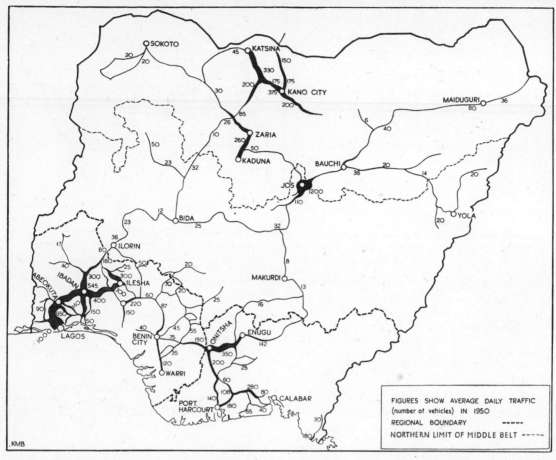

FIG. 155. TRAFFIC FLOW ON THE MAJOR ROADS OF THE TERRITORY

Thickness of line is proportional to the average daily traffic. Note the outstanding position of the four key economic areas of the Territory—the Cocoa Belt, the Palm Belt, the groundnut-cotton belt and the Plateau. The extremely tenuous character of the road links across the Middle Belt is emphasised by the map. An interesting light is thrown on the economic orientation of some of the "minority areas" (see page 96); thus, the main contacts of the Ilorin-Kabba area are with the West rather than the North, while the western Ibo area is oriented decisively towards the Eastern Region.

movement by road, but it is considerable. Long-distance motor coaches started running in 1952 from Lagos as far as Ilesha, 200 miles away, and by 1953 as far as Warri; but passenger travel in converted lorries—or in freight lorries—has been normal for many years and, although dusty and uncomfortable, is usually both cheaper and faster than a corresponding rail journey.

It is important to understand the quality of the road surfaces. Fig. 159 shows the extent of tarred roads in April 1951, and it should be realised that the roads shown had tarred surfaces and not tarmacadam. The tarred surface is normally wide enough for two private cars to pass, but if one or both vehicles should be of larger size use has to be made of the untarred margins. During the rains washing away of the margins may result in a drop of several inches at the edge of the tarred surface, and the constant passage of heavy lorries may rapidly result in a rough and broken edge and pothole development, with consequent danger to road users and rapid deterioration of vehicles.

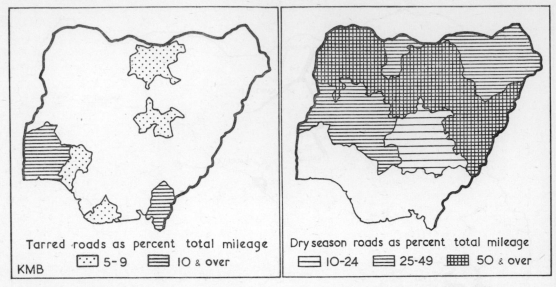

Tarred roads as percent total mileage
KMB   5-9   10 & over

Dry season roads as percent total mileage
10-24   25-49   50 & over

FIG. 156. TARRED ROADS AS A PER-
CENTAGE OF THE TOTAL MILEAGE

Tarred roads (see Fig. 159) are insignificant
outside the Yoruba Provinces and the Provinces
of Kano and Plateau. Note that in the case of
the Cameroons the total mileage of roads is very
small.

FIG. 157. DRY SEASON ROADS

While all the southern roads are, officially at
least, all-weather roads, over one-half of the
Northern Region's roads are dry-season tracks
and liable to seasonal interruption during the
rains.

The remaining roads are "dirt" or "laterite"
surfaced, variously called "all-season" or "dry-
season" roads, depending on the sum available
for maintenance. Such roads are inevitably
extremely dusty in the dry season and soft after
heavy rain in the wet season, and quality shows
wide variation.   Surfaces can be very good, but
are more commonly indifferent, one major
trouble being lateral corrugations which develop under heavy traffic, and which may persist
over long distances for months during the dry
season.   All roads are short-lived unless regularly maintained; a few years without attention
can result in a quite impassable track under tall
grass, studded with anthills and scarred by deep
gullies.

Such difficulties of road maintenance are, of
course, not peculiar to Nigeria, but are common
to most of Africa.   Distances involved are very
great (Lagos to Maiduguri is over 1,000 miles).
Local material is usually unable to sustain
heavy traffic.   A single storm can do extensive damage, particularly to culverts and bridges

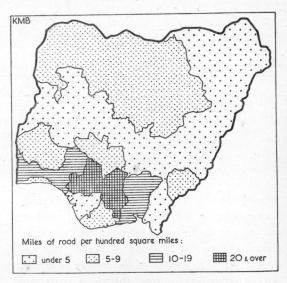

Miles of road per hundred square miles:
under 5   5-9   10-19   20 & over

FIG. 158. DENSITY OF THE ROAD
NETWORK

Note the high density in the Palm Belt and the
very low density in the Cameroons, in Bornu and
in the Middle Belt.   The average density for the
Territory is 7 miles per 100 square miles of area;
this is barely one-fortieth the density in a highly
developed area such as England and Wales.

FIG. 159. TARRED ROADS
Comparison with Fig. 154 reveals how little of the Nigerian
road system has other than a laterite surface (1950 data). It should
further be noted that the roads
shown on this map have a tarred
surface and not tarmacadam metalling. Reference is made in the text
to the effects of the road surface on
transport.

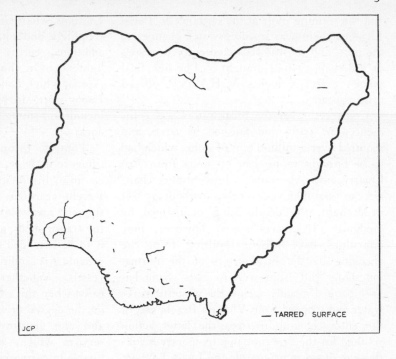

— TARRED SURFACE

inadequate in design owing to lack of data regarding maximum flood volumes. In addition, in the forested areas storms may result in road-blocks from fallen trees. Without capital expenditure on a scale beyond the capacity of the country, the majority of Nigerian roads must remain much as at present, and it is to the credit of the Public Works Department that, notwithstanding all the difficulties, existing road conditions are such that private motorists can travel up to 400 miles per day over the existing road system.

It must be stressed that the map of tarred roads represents the position as it was in 1951, and considerable additional surfacing has been completed since that date; as, for example, the greater part of the West–East trunk road from Ibadan to Enugu; improvements in the supply position have enabled some of this recent development to be carried out by mechanical methods, which give a higher standard of surface than was previously attainable.[1]

PORTS

Fig. 161 indicates import and export trade through the various Nigerian ocean ports. Fig. 160 shows individual port sites.

As with most West African ports, shallow water has been a constant difficulty with the ports of Nigeria. Even where, as at Port Harcourt, there is a good depth of water at the port, the seaward entrance is marked by a bar. Only at Victoria, on the open coast of the Cameroons, is the form of an obstructing bar absent, although the approach to Calabar, on the drowned estuary of the Cross River, shows some differences from those of the ports farther west. The existence of the coastal bars has been of fundamental importance in the history of Nigerian port development, in that ocean-going vessels were forced to lie off the open coast, until the major improvements of this century, with overside cargo handling into tenders, lighters or surfboats, with its attendant risks and disadvantages.

Lagos

Lagos is situated at the one point in the miles of coast eastward from the Dahomey frontier to the edge of the delta at which there is a break through the sandbanks which form the smooth outer coastline.

Until the construction of the breakwaters

[1] Public Works Department, Nigeria, *Annual Reports.*

and the training mole at the entrance to Lagos Lagoon, there was no deep-water channel to the port, and the bar restricted entry to vessels of less than 12-foot draught. The low tidal range (3 feet 3 inches M.H.W.S.)[1] offered little assistance.

Construction of the breakwaters was commenced in 1907 and finished in 1916, and required over 2 million tons of stone, which had to be brought more than 50 miles from Aro Quarry, near Abeokuta. The entrance channel can now take vessels of up to about 25 feet in draught, the depth being maintained by dredging. In recent years, however, new difficulties have arisen, resulting from the checking by the breakwaters of the normal longshore drift from west to east. Sand has been banked steadily against the western breakwater and stripped from Victoria Beach, east of the entrance, and in 1950 the latter action resulted for the first time in a temporary breakthrough of storm waves into the Lagos Lagoon, round the landward end of the east breakwater. Continued destruction of Victoria Beach will unquestionably lead to a permanent joining-up of sea and lagoon east of the present entrance, with serious results for the port, and some sort of control is obviously required; short groynes have proved ineffective, and pumping of sand from the west to the east side of the entrance is likely to be the most satisfactory solution.

The facilities of Lagos port are in two parts. On the east side of the lagoon are the islands of Lagos and Iddo, the latter carrying the railway terminus; a road bridge connects the two islands and a causeway joins Iddo to the mainland. The Ijora wharf on Iddo Island, approached by the western Apapa channel, is used principally for the unloading of coal brought by sea from Port Harcourt. The Customs wharf at Lagos accommodates three freighters, and adjacent mooring buoys provide additional berths for overside working into lighters. On the west side of the lagoon is Apapa, which handles the bulk of the traffic of Lagos port, is served by the railway, and includes oil-storage facilities and a small floating-dock.

Tonnage through the port of Lagos continues to increase, and available accommodation is now insufficient to meet requirements. Recent years have been marked by delays to shipping awaiting berths and by congestion in the transit sheds, and the main wharf at Apapa is to be extended southwards by 2,500 feet to provide five additional berths for ocean-going vessels. Whether or not the situation will be eased when this extension is completed depends on the degree to which overseas trade increases and the improvement of existing railway services which, as stated above, are already unable to carry existing freight.

Future development of the port must necessarily be on the Apapa side of the lagoon. Lagos Island is already overcrowded, but increasing areas may be made available for industrial use behind Apapa as reclamation of the swamps proceeds.

The overwhelming importance to Nigeria of Lagos Port is revealed by Fig. 161. Not only does two-thirds of the total volume of seaborne trade pass through it, but this total includes the largest quantities of palm products, cocoa, hides and skins, and groundnuts handled by any Nigerian port. If the economic development of Nigeria is to proceed unchecked, it is essential that every effort should be made to provide adequate and rapid handling facilities at the port of Lagos, and to ensure that the seaward channel is preserved.

[1] *Tide Tables* (Lagos).

FIG. 160. PORTS (*Map opposite*)

The sites of the major Nigerian ports are shown on the same scale in all cases.

In the bottom diagram the navigable channels for ocean-going vessels are dotted and the connecting waterways for river craft operating to the Niger and Benue river system are shown.

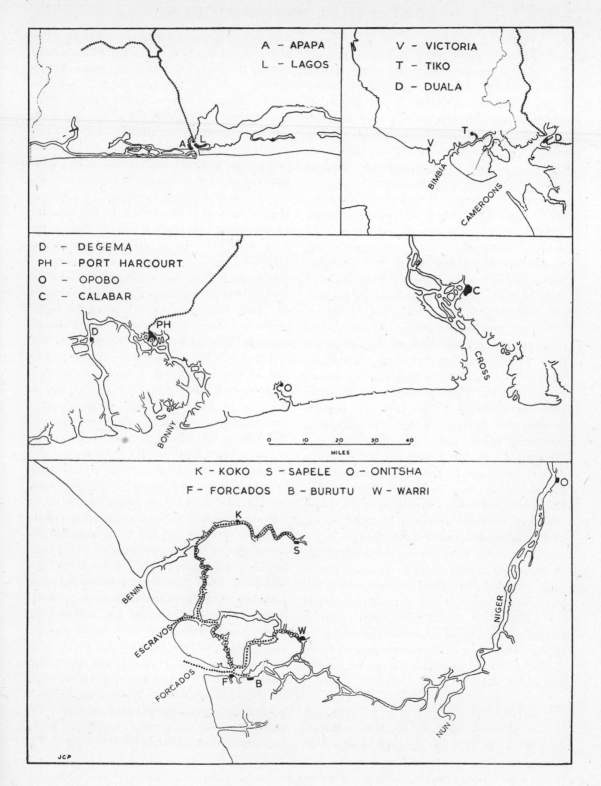

A – APAPA
L – LAGOS

V – VICTORIA
T – TIKO
D – DUALA

BIMBIA

CAMEROONS

D – DEGEMA
PH – PORT HARCOURT
O – OPOBO
C – CALABAR

C

PH

D

BONNY

O

CROSS

0   10   20   30   40
MILES

K – KOKO   S – SAPELE   O – ONITSHA
F – FORCADOS   B – BURUTU   W – WARRI

O

K

S

BENIN

ESCRAVOS

NIGER

W

FORCADOS

F   B

NUN

JCP

217

Port Harcourt

Second in importance to Lagos is Port Harcourt, the seaward terminal of the eastern railway, which lies on the estuary of the Bonny River. The latter has the Bonny Bar at its entrance, and although there is deep water in the Bonny River, the bends in the channel require careful navigation. Tidal rise (mean springs) is 6 feet 2 inches at Bonny Bar and 7 feet 11 inches at Port Harcourt.

Originally intended to serve as the outlet for the Enugu coalfield, the port now serves a much wider hinterland following the extension of the railway northwards. The construction of the branch line to Jos deflected to Port Harcourt the metal ores from the minesfield; development of the lead-zinc deposits of the Eastern Provinces will materially increase this class of export. The port also handles the largest quantity of palm produce passing through any port other than Lagos, together with an appreciable quantity of groundnuts. It is also the natural gateway to the Eastern Region for imported goods of all kinds. Like Lagos, it requires expansion of facilities to meet the increasing volume of traffic, and may well develop at a more rapid rate than Lagos. It is the obvious seaport for much of the Eastern Region and for much of the Northern Region. For those northern areas served equally by Lagos and Port Harcourt diversion of traffic to the latter could ease some of the congestion at the capital. There is, of course, the disadvantage of the longer passage to the open sea, and with high water at Port Harcourt two and a half hours later than at Bonny Bar, there is always the possibility of twenty-four hours' delay in reaching the open sea (assuming crossings of the bar by daylight only); but this may represent the loss of far less time than may be incurred by congestion at Lagos.

The Benin Ports

The ports of Sapele, Koko, Warri, Burutu and Forcados, although varying in character,

may be considered as one group in that they may all be approached by the same entrance channels, namely the Escravos River, opened to shipping in 1940, and the Forcados River. All three of the Benin, Escravos and Forcados Rivers have seaward bars, and the depth across the Benin entrance is insufficient for sea-going vessels. Both the Escravos and the Forcados bars are navigable at high water, with a mean tidal rise of 5 feet at springs and 4 feet at neaps, but even with maximum available depth it is not possible to load ocean vessels to full capacity. It is therefore customary for ships to sail in part cargo from these ports and to complete a full cargo at Lagos. In 1948 maximum depth of water over the bars was 13 feet at Forcados Bar and 14 feet at Escravos Bar. Some concern has been expressed over variations in depth across the bars, the Forcados depth having decreased from 21 feet to 13 feet between 1899 and 1947.[1] By 1949 the Forcados channel had improved slightly to a minimum depth of 11 feet, with H.W.O.N.T. at 15 feet, but the marking in 1950 of a new channel with a minimum depth of 10 feet across the Escravos Bar retains the advantages of the latter: the extra 1 foot of depth on Forcados Bar is offset by increased effective draught of vessels caused by rolling due to swell, which is on the beam at the Forcados entrance but passes directly up the Escravos channel. The consequent use of the Escravos entrance and the advantages and disadvantages of the two approaches is fully discussed in the article cited. It should be noted that these "bars" are large features not comparable with the narrow sand banks encountered on parts of the British coast: the Forcados Bar is over 3 miles wide where traversed by the shipping channel, and the Escravos Bar $\frac{3}{4}$ mile wide.

Navigation of the creek channels is no simple matter, as may be judged from Fig. 160 in which the deepwater routes are plotted, the channels being narrow and tortuous in the extreme. The passage between the Escravos and Benin Rivers includes a turn of 120° at the Fork. The

[1] United Africa Company, *Statistical and Economic Review*, No. 2 (Sept. 1948) and No. 6 (Sept. 1950).

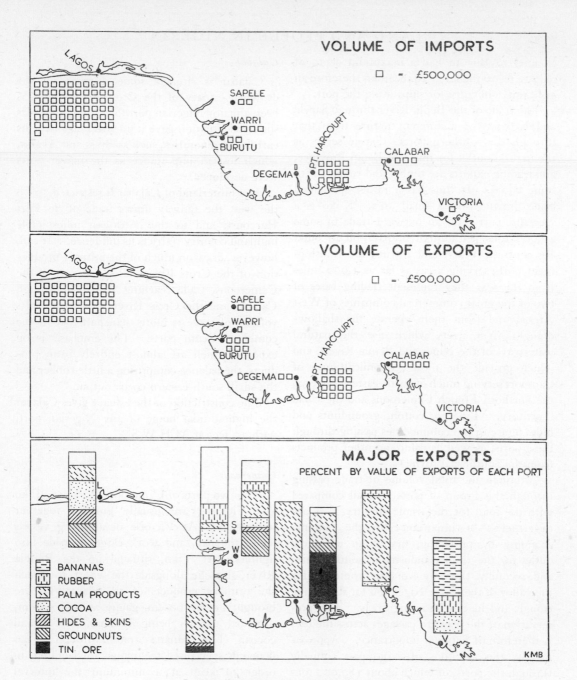

FIG. 161. THE TRADE OF NIGERIA'S PORTS 1948

Note the dominance of Lagos and, to a lesser extent, of Port Harcourt. In 1950 Lagos handled 73% of the import trade of the Territory and 56% of the export trade; for Port Harcourt the corresponding figures were 14% and 22%. Owing to their rail links with the interior these two ports monopolise the export trade of the Northern Region; thus, Lagos handles virtually the entire cotton export, nine-tenths of the export trade in hides and skins and two-thirds of the export trade in groundnuts; Port Harcourt is the outlet for all save a fraction of the Territory's tin. The remaining ports are concerned almost entirely with the exports of their immediate hinterlands, although a small proportion of the North's exports of hides and skins, groundnuts and cotton passes down the Niger, for export via Burutu. The total value of the Territory's imports in 1950 was £61,868,104, of exports £90,222,771.

channel to Burutu had a maximum depth of only 14 feet 6 inches in 1948, and is therefore an additional difficulty for ships using the port.

The trade of the Benin River through Sapele and Koko is of a different nature from that through the southern ports. Sapele serves as the natural outlet for much of Benin Province, and leading exports are timber and rubber, with some cocoa. It thus has a rather specialised trade drawn from a small area. Koko is a specialist port with an outward trade of some 10,000 tons per annum of palm-oil in bulk. By contrast, Warri and Burutu are transhipment ports serving areas as far as 1,000 miles from the sea; they represent trading bases of two of the great commercial companies of West Africa, and from them operate the shallow-draught river fleets which use the natural waterways of the Niger and Benue Rivers, and which provide the most economical form of transport serving much of north-eastern Nigeria, the northern French Cameroons and the Chad Territory. Tin ore, cotton, groundnuts and hides figure in the commodities passing through these ports, as well as palm and other products from the Southern Provinces.

Although the total volume of trade passing through this group of ports is small compared with the total for the whole country, they are nevertheless of importance in the national economy by providing, firstly, an economic outlet for the timber industry of south Benin, and, secondly, the only economic routeway for the valley of the lower Niger and for the Benue trough and its neighbouring areas. The preservation of the seaward passages across the bars is therefore of national importance. Approximately 280,000 tons of cargo pass annually through the ports, of which about 180,000 tons are shipped in ocean-going vessels and the balance is carried to Lagos in coastal vessels for export. The costs of transhipment in the latter case are borne by the whole of the trade passing through the Benin ports, but if all trade had to be moved by coastal vessels for transhipment at Lagos the costs might become prohibitive. In any case, timber is not suited to transhipment.

Calabar

Calabar is situated some distance up the drowned estuary of the Cross River, and has been a major Nigerian port for a long time. Its sheltered situation gave it an advantage over its early contemporaries, such as Brass and Akassa, which lost in importance as the newer ports were developed.

The hinterland of Calabar is restricted. To the west the railway draws trade off to Port Harcourt, and to the north-east inhospitable highland country restricts its influence. It can, however, draw on much of the primary production of the Cross River valley and part of the Cameroons, trade reaching Bamenda through Calabar and the Cross River to Mamfe. Its volume of trade is more than half that of the combined Benin ports. The emphasis is on exports, which are almost entirely palm products, the balance comprising a little rubber and the small south-eastern cocoa output.

The constriction of the estuary gives Calabar the highest tidal range of any Nigerian port, with 10 feet at M.H.W.S.

Cameroons

The two ports of Cameroons Province, Tiko and Victoria, are usually grouped together statistically. At Victoria ocean-going vessels lie in the bay, and work cargo overside into lighters. At Tiko, situated up the Bimbia River, ships lie alongside the wharf, to which the primary products of the plantations are brought by the 60-cm. gauge railway system, principal exports being bananas, rubber and cocoa. The banana trade through Tiko demands specialised techniques in handling, in order to keep at a minimum the interval between the cutting of the fruit stems and the closing of the ships' refrigerated holds, requiring a planned programme for the loading of each ship in a way not essential for vessels at other Nigerian ports. Distinction can be made between the types of vessel serving Tiko and Victoria: the latter are normally general freighters including the port as one of a series of calls along the Nigerian or West African coast, while the former are fast refrigerated ships running directly between Tiko and the port of discharge in Europe.

Apart from the refrigerated fruit carriers serving Tiko, ships built for the West African trade tend to show a number of particular points of design. These can be summarised as heavier equipment than is normal, in order to facilitate overside handling, and broad-beamed, flat-bottomed design calculated to give maximum carrying capacity on a low draught; the latter point applies particularly to vessels built to serve the Benin ports. Navigational aids are important on a coast with comparatively few shore stations, and the climate necessitates all passenger cabins having access to the ship's side. Ventilation of cargo space presents particular difficulties during passages to Europe during the months of the northern winter.

INLAND WATERWAYS

Inland water transport is an important factor in the economy of the country. It can be divided broadly into two main groups; firstly the coastal creek and river traffic, and, secondly, the traffic of the Niger–Benue river systems.

The sheltered waters of the coastal lagoons have provided an east–west routeway of fundamental importance. Canoes can travel from beyond the Dahomey frontier to the south-east of Nigeria without entering the open ocean, and powered launches now follow the same routes. No figures are available for this traffic, but the volume of goods moving to Lagos by water is considerable. For example, Okitipupa, on the creeks 100 miles east of Lagos, evacuates a significant quantity of palm produce and timber, and is the natural outlet for primary products for the greater part of Ondo Province.

Eastward from the lagoons, with their east–west routeways, lies the delta area with the radial pattern of distributaries joined by transverse creeks; the area between the two is marked by the occurrence of sudd, which greatly impedes water traffic and may bring even launches to a standstill, and open channels are maintained only by constant cutting. In the delta area the creeks provide the only natural routeways between settlements, and in some areas travelling canoe "shops" provide the only contact with the merchandise of other regions.

In the extreme south-east the creek pattern is less complete and the emphasis tends to north–south movement along the rivers to coastal outlets, such as Opobo and Calabar. Along the volcanic coast of the Cameroons there is no sheltered water and coastwise movement is largely by launch. The ferry connecting Calabar with Oron and the south-eastern road system is a special case of transport in the coastal creeks.

Trade movement along the great rivers is in rather a different category. There is, naturally, a considerable amount of canoe traffic very similar to that found in the creeks and lagoons, but there is in addition the highly organised traffic of the fleets of river craft operated by the large commercial companies, which operate from the Benin ports to beyond the Nigerian frontier. These river craft are specially designed to move considerable quantities with very little draught: the largest unit of the U.A.C. fleet (which at full strength will total twenty-six powered units and sixty-six barges with a total capacity of over 22,000 tons) is of 550 tons, 800 h.p., and has a loaded draught of only 7 feet 6 inches. Although recent experiments have been made with other forms of propulsion, most of the powered river craft are stern-wheel steamers capable of moving several loaded lighters in addition to their own cargo. An innovation is the Mississippi-type of stern-wheeler, which pushes its accompanying barges instead of towing them alongside; this method has advantages in rivers with constantly shifting sandbanks, by greatly reducing the chances of the powered craft grounding.[1]

The operational routing of the river steamers is controlled by the seasonal flooding of the rivers. The Niger high water allows naviga-

[1] *Nigeria*, No. 38 (1952) and No. 41 (1953).

tion at Lokoja from June to March, and steamers can be operated on the Niger as far as Jebba from August to February, as well as on the lower reaches of the Kaduna. As mentioned in the earlier section on railways, the first railway in the Northern Provinces connected with water transport at Wushishi on the Kaduna River, and Baro is still an important river port, open to shipping from July to March, and connected to the main railway system.

The arrival of the Benue flood permits extension of shipping eastward, reaching Makurdi in June and Yola in July. The smaller ships open the Benue season by laying fuel depots up the river, and with the arrival of the larger vessels are switched to working the tributary rivers, such as the Katsena Ala and the Gongola. The ultimate head of navigation on the Benue is Garua in French territory, open to shipping in August. With the fall in level of the Benue, shipping is withdrawn from Garua in September, from Yola in October and from Makurdi in November. At its confluence with the Niger, the Benue is obstructed by a bar which is covered by only 2 feet of water when the river is not in flood. Depth across this bar controls the size of ships operating on the Benue, and organisation of the season requires evacuation of the fleet from the Benue while the state of the bar permits.

Shipping can be worked to Onitsha throughout the year. The longest river journey, from Burutu to Garua, 986 miles, requires seventeen days on the upward journey and eleven days on the return journey.

As an indication of the type of traffic moved, one of the two large river fleets moved the following average annual tonnages in the years 1945–7:

TABLE XIX
RIVER TRAFFIC ON THE NIGER AND BENUE

Section	Upstream tons	Downstream tons
Lower Niger (Burutu–Lokoja section)	12,000	44,000
Middle Niger (Lokoja–Jebba and to North via Baro) .	9,000	20,000
Benue	18,000	25,000

Average figures for the fleet subsequently rose slightly, annual cargo for the fleet being 152,000 tons for the years 1946–9, with an annual average total of 59 million ton-miles.

Individual commodities moved during 1947 by this fleet on the river system as a whole were as follows:

TABLE XX
GOODS HANDLED ON THE NIGER AND BENUE

Imports	Tons	Exports	Tons
Salt . . .	19,000	Groundnuts .	35,000
Cement . .	4,000	Palm kernels .	26,000
Casks . . .	5,000	Palm-oil .	17,000
General merchandise	12,000	Cotton . .	7,000
		Benniseed	3,000
		Other products .	9,000

The allocation of shipping to the two rivers is dependent, not only on depth of water but also on rainfall distribution and the size of the harvest over much of the Northern Region. The latter factor obviously determines the tonnage to be moved, while the former affects not only crop production and river level but also the state of the northern roads which provide alternative evacuation routes. If roads deteriorate as a result of unusually heavy rain, it is desirable to transfer additional ships to the Benue service in order to move the crops, even if this reduces the facilities available between Lokoja and Jebba. The needs of the Niger valley can to some extent be met by the railway and road facilities of the area, but no comparable service exists for the Benue trough and its neighbouring areas; also the shipping season on the Niger continues after the closure of the Benue, thus permitting an end-of-season concentration of shipping on the Niger. It is, of course, obviously preferable to keep all sections adequately served for as long a period as possible, and in this connection limitations of the high-water period on the upper Benue must be borne in mind when planning development schemes in those parts of North-eastern Nigeria, or of French territory, which rely on the river for transport of freight. Individual ships can each make only two round trips per annum between Garua and the coast, and any large increase in tonnage offering at Garua requires a corresponding fleet expansion

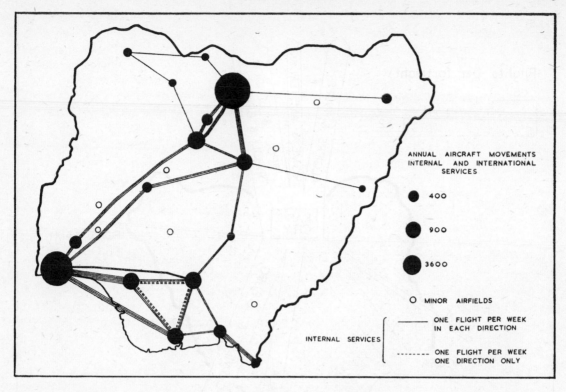

FIG. 162. INTERNAL AIR SERVICES

The network of internal routes flown by the West African Airways Corporation covers all the main centres of the country. The map includes international aircraft movements through the two main airports of Kano and Ikeja (Lagos).

A comparison with Fig. 151 explains why air fares between the S.W. and S.E. are cheaper than the corresponding rail fares. The slow train speeds also mean that air passages allow a very great saving in time even over comparatively short journeys.

Much of the internal letter mail is now carried by air, and the advantages both for mail and passenger traffic are particularly great in the case of services to Tiko, Yola and Maiduguri.

to evacuate produce in the months available; no "spread" of existing fleet capacity over a longer period is possible. In 1946, the U.A.C. fleet moved from Garua 9,000 tons of cotton, 1,700 tons of groundnuts, and 100 tons of general produce; any schemes for the expansion of the two main crops will, therefore, have repercussions on the capacity and organisation of the commercial fleets.

AIR SERVICES

Figs. 162 and 163 show aircraft routes and movements over Nigeria.

There are two large international airports in the country, at Kano and at Ikeja (Lagos Airport), serving transcontinental as well as internal traffic.[1] Kano is the more important for overseas services, lying as it does on the main routes from Western Europe to West, Central and South Africa. It is of interest to consider that the position of Kano for trans-Saharan transport is as significant for modern air traffic as it has been in the past for camel caravans. (The modern trans-Saharan 'bus route also passes through Kano, but is of no economic significance.) Lagos is less well situated for

[1] Department of Civil Aviation, Nigeria, *Annual Reports*.

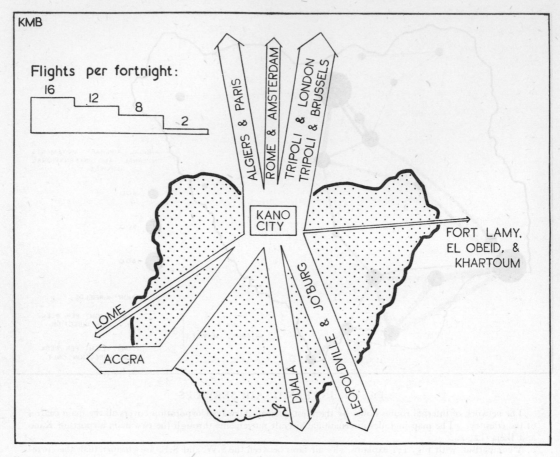

FIG. 163. INTERNATIONAL AIR SERVICES

The position of Kano as an international air centre is apparent, lying as it does on the major routes from Europe to South Africa, and Europe to West Africa and the minor route from West Africa to the Sudan.

It is interesting to reflect that Kano has been a trans-Saharan route centre for many centuries, and is still a departure point for camel caravans, as well as for the modern Trans-Saharan coach.

Ikeja (Lagos airport) is principally a terminal point for major international services: with increasing air traffic between Europe and West Africa, the London–Kano–Lagos–Accra service has given place to separate services from London through Kano to Lagos and Accra. International services from Lagos to Accra (connecting for the U.S.A.–South Africa route) include both first and second-class services which continue farther west.

international services, and with the increased range of modern aircraft may be ignored by aircraft flying from Accra to Kano or from Accra to Leopoldville and beyond; Accra lies on the air route from South Africa to North America.

Internal air services, operated by the West African Airways Corporation, formed in 1947,

are based on Lagos Airport, and provide a network serving most of the important centres in the country.[1] In view of the distances involved and the absence of fast road or rail communications, these passenger services are of great internal importance. In addition these aircraft carry much of the internal mail, and at a basic postal rate of $1\frac{1}{2}$d. per letter provide one of the

[1] *Nigeria*, No. 38 (1952) and No. 41 (1953).

fastest and cheapest postal services in the world.[1]

Second-class services are being developed, and with rising economic standards are being increasingly used. Such services now operate both westward to the Gold Coast and eastward to the Sudan, as well as on certain internal routes; the institution of cheap rates for air passages to Khartoum has opened up a new method of travel for Mahommedan members of the population who wish to make the pilgrimage to Mecca, as well as providing the cheapest route to India and the Levant; reference is made elsewhere to the position taken by nationals of these latter areas in the commercial activity of West Africa.

It should be noted that over some of the southern routes the first-class fare is less by air than by train, while the first-class air fare to Europe is cheaper from some parts of the country than is the corresponding rail fare to Lagos and the sea passage onward. Even without consideration of the saving in time, passenger traffic is therefore ensured to some extent. Traffic on the internal services, which in the year 1948–9 showed 14,000 passengers and 1,125,000 miles operated, rose to 25,000 passengers and 1,900,000 miles by 1950–1. An estimate for the year 1951–2 gives over 40,000 passengers with a slight increase in mileage.

Reference should be made to two difficulties in connection with Nigerian air services. In the dry season Harmattan haze sometimes reduces visibility to a very low figure and impedes navigation; in the rains low cloud and line squalls may have similar effects.

OTHER TRANSPORT FORMS

The wheel was not indigenous in West Africa, and before the impact of outside influences the customary methods of transporting goods were by head-porterage or, in the north, by donkey or camel. Away from the roads (Fig. 154) these forms still prevail, although now assisted slightly by the bicycle. Head-porterage moves the greater part of Nigerian trade at some stage, and the effect of this on the nation's economy and standards of life must be borne in mind. Assuming that the average carrier requires 1s. 6d. to move a 50-lb. load over a day's march of 20 miles, cost of transport represents approximately 3s. 4d. per ton mile, which is an exceedingly heavy charge for the country to bear. (On this figure head-porterage is roughly six times more costly than road transport.) If standards of life are to be raised appreciably, the development of cheaper forms of transport is essential. Any marked increase in daily wage for carriers may bring transport costs to an uneconomic level, and so reduce production in the more remote localities and retard any rise in the general standard of living.

[1] The internal rate for letters was increased to 2d. in 1954.

BIBLIOGRAPHY

Department of Civil Aviation, Nigeria, *Annual Reports.*
Nigeria, No. 38 (1952); No. 41 (1953).
Nigerian Government Railway, *Annual Reports.*
Public Works Department, Nigeria, *Annual Reports.*
Stocker, J., *Nigerian Railway Jubilee*, P.R.O., Lagos, 1952.
Tide Tables, Government Printer, Lagos.
United Africa Company, Statistical and Economic Review, No. 2, Sept. 1948; No. 6, Sept. 1950.

CHAPTER VII

PUBLIC AND SOCIAL SERVICES

WATER SUPPLY

Towns with water supplies are shown in Fig. 164. Only Lagos can be regarded as having a sizeable supply, and even there restrictions on consumption towards the end of the dry season are not unknown. In some of the smaller supply schemes water is laid on to Government quarters only.

In the towns, as distinct from the Government reservations, water is usually laid on to communal standpipes for general use. Piped supplies generally enjoy a popularity not so readily extended to the taxation necessary for their provision. It is not uncommon for such supplies to lead to wastage—social conscience has not yet advanced to the point where bystanders feel moved to turn off taps left running at full volume—but such misuse should decrease with the growth of a sense of public responsibility and the wider knowledge of the working of a water supply system.

The piped-water supply schemes in Nigeria aim at providing an easier source of supply than wells, and at reducing the transmission of diseases which is common with unimproved local wells. The piped water is not completely pure by Western standards, and it is desirable both to boil and to filter it before use; but it represents a great advance on the original sources of supply.

The fact that few schemes are as yet provided in the Northern Region deserves notice, in view of the shorter wet season in the North and the consequent earlier drying-out of river supplies. It must, however, be remembered that the map cannot show the distribution of wells of modern type, in the construction of which particular attention has been paid to the northern areas. Deep wells are not a new

feature, but with the disappearance of the slave status the tapping of deep supplies has become dependent on modern techniques and Government assistance. Particular reference was made in the section on geology to the depth of water supplies in Bornu. Wells must remain the source of supply for many areas of the North, where old-age geomorphological forms provide few suitable sites for large-capacity reservoirs, and where evaporation losses from barrage schemes of wide area and shallow depth would be very great. It is important that there should be a water-supply staff sufficiently large for well construction to provide supplies for an increasing population in addition to replacing old wells now collapsing. In areas where water supplies are at depth, a moderate-sized village may be dependent on a single deep well, and if this is of local non-permanent construction, its collapse may force the migration of the whole community.

Government-designed wells are not only permanent in construction but are designed to avoid pollution: simple devices such as outward-sloping concrete surrounds prevent contamination by guinea-worm sufferers. In areas where purdah is still strictly observed, householders have been encouraged to fit similar surrounds, at a low cost, to the private wells in their compounds.

In many areas, however, supplies of very doubtful quality are still drawn from streams or water-holes, with resulting prevalence of infections such as guinea-worm and bilharzia, to which reference is made in the section on disease, and much propaganda of a practical nature is required to convince the people of the need for better-ordered arrangements for water supply and sanitation.

Artesian water supplies are not reported.

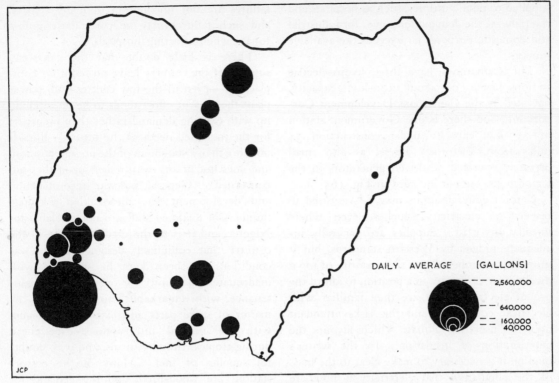

FIG. 164. WATER SUPPLY UNDERTAKINGS

Piped water supply schemes (1950) are shown. Most of the southern Nigerian centres enjoy such supplies, but it will be seen that capacity is very limited in many places, and supply is in some centres restricted to government buildings. Only Lagos has a considerable supply capacity, but the demand is high and restrictions not uncommon. Costs in some centres are very high, and are nowhere inexpensive.

Few centres in the Northern Region possess piped water supplies; in the extreme north, however, the emphasis has been on provision of deep wells, which cannot be shown on the map for reasons given in the text.

It should be noted that piped water is superior to normal well or stream supplies, but is not pure by European standards.

Sub-artesian streams are known in the vicinity of the Oji River, east of Onitsha, but exploitation of the deep supplies is not required in this area, as normal sources are adequate.

ELECTRICITY

Fig. 165 shows major electricity undertakings in Nigeria, and it will be at once appreciated that only a very small minority of the population enjoys the benefits of electric power.

Excluding the Plateau area, Lagos is in an outstanding position, by Nigerian standards, with power available not only for moderate domestic use but also for services such as street

lighting in some areas and for industrial employment.

In the Eastern Region the largest installation is at Enugu, serving parts of the town but principally the coal-mines, while 35% of the output of Kano, the largest northern installation, is required for the water-pumping plant.

The remaining centres can be regarded as having partial electric services only. In the case of the small stations it is not uncommon for only the Government areas to be supplied with power, and even an installation such as that of Ibadan cannot be regarded as adequate for the needs of the town; street lighting is necessarily very restricted, and after allowing for power supplied to public utilities, such as hospitals and the railway, the demand for power for industrial and domestic purposes far exceeds the available supply.

The Cameroons have three hydro-electric stations, each of about 400-kw. capacity, operated by the Cameroons Development Corporation, and there is one Government station of 750-kw. capacity under construction 34 miles from Victoria. These, as also small privately operated oil-driven generators in the Cameroons, are not included in Fig. 165.

Certain generalisations may be ventured in respect of electricity supplies, even where installations exist. Supplies are generally inadequate judged by Western standards, but it must be remembered that the majority of town dwellers are not as yet in a position to afford the use of electricity, nor are they familiar with electrical equipment and the risks attendant upon its use in a climate which favours the deterioration of insulation. In the writer's opinion it is necessary to make clear to the mass of the population that electricity is nowhere free, but has to be paid for in the same way as other forms of lighting. It must also be ensured that when the ability of a larger population group to afford the use of electricity makes its introduction possible, the risks of accident are minimised by adequate propaganda; fatal accidents occur now, even with individuals accustomed to working with electrical appliances.

Inadequate supplies are, however, an industrial concern as well as a domestic issue. Apart from larger projects for the equipment of new domestic industry, a minor item such as lack of power for the efficient servicing of vehicles, to quote one example, can have far more serious repercussions in Nigeria than in some other parts of the world; mention has been made of heavy wear and tear of vehicles on African roads. Another example would be insufficient power to operate X-ray equipment in some centres; this needs no elaboration. One further point remains to be mentioned, and that is the unreliability of such supplies as exist; power failures are not uncommon in many centres, and such failures may be particularly unfortunate when affecting hospitals.

There is little doubt that the electricity supplies of the country leave no room for complacency—even in the few centres with power plant the present effort tends to be on catching up with existing demand rather than preparing for the increased needs of the future. This is no more than a statement of the present position, and does not in any way reflect upon the staff concerned. General postwar reconstruction and development has meant that adequate numbers of qualified staff are not available for Nigeria, and it is to the credit of those in the country that equipment designed for prewar conditions has been kept in operation with inadequate opportunity for overhaul and maintenance, with remarkable improvisation in the matter of spare parts and expanding demand, with the normal interruptions experienced during tropical thunderstorms, and with doubtful supplies of fuel. Many of the power-stations are wood-fired, and the demand for wood fuel has increased very greatly in some localities, with a resulting ever-widening area from which supplies have to be drawn. The need for new equipment has been realised and orders placed, but general world conditions involve long delays before delivery can be expected.

Data relevant to existing installations may indicate the extent of former activity. Lagos Power Station was started in 1896, but was not followed by stations elsewhere until the period 1923–38, which saw the completion of Government undertakings at Port Harcourt and Kaduna, and of N.A. undertakings at Abeokuta, Kano and Katsina. Calabar, Warri and Zaria were added in 1938–9, and Ibadan in 1940. The dates will emphasise the effect of the war in restricting development at a time when expansion of services had achieved considerable momentum. In 1951 all Government and N.A. undertakings were transferred to the newly formed Nigerian Electricity Corporation.

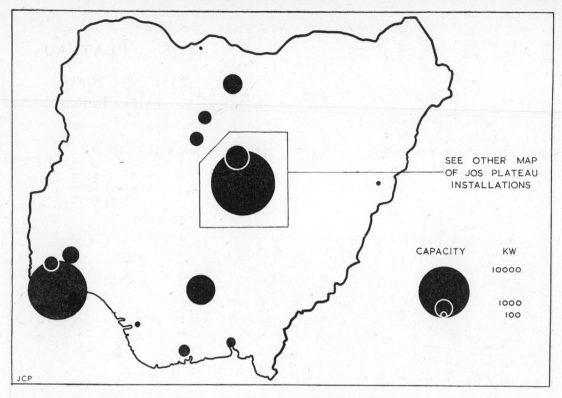

SEE OTHER MAP
OF JOS PLATEAU
INSTALLATIONS

CAPACITY   KW

10000

1000
100

JCP

Fig. 165. ELECTRICITY UNDERTAKINGS

Power stations existing in 1950 are shown. The small number of centres supplied with electricity is at once revealed, and also the inadequacy of production capacity. That capacity is low even at the centres shown is apparent from a comparison of the map with that of population centres (Fig. 42).

No mention has yet been made of the power supplies of the Jos Plateau. These are shown in Fig. 166, and the system is operated by a private company and not by the Electricity Corporation. The Plateau installations, taken as one group, are the largest in the country, and comprise four hydro-electric stations. Of these the three largest lie on the Kurra River where it passes over the western escarpment, and, situated one above the other, make triple use of the water available. Dams on the high plateau on the Kurra and its tributary, the Tenti, give reserves of water, which are normally adequate to carry through the dry season. Power is carried at 33,000 volts across the open plateau by overhead cables.

The power developed supplies the towns of Jos and Bukuru, and most of the larger mining centres. Reference to electrical equipment has been made in the section on tin-mining. Supply has been kept ahead of demand, this process being helped by the suitability of the Kurra River for the three-tier development. Any further expansion would require construction of new storage barrages elsewhere on the Plateau, as well as the installation of the actual generating plant.

The Plateau system is of great importance in the future planning of Nigerian industrial development. It has been stated earlier that the tin-field is a rapidly wasting asset, and that in a little more than a decade the tin-mining industry may cease to be of great significance. No announcement of policy regarding the future of the Plateau has yet been made, but it is suggested that this region might well be given

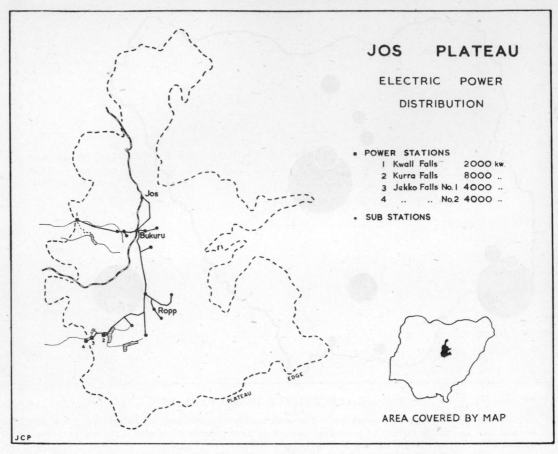

FIG. 166. THE JOS PLATEAU HYDRO-ELECTRIC NETWORK

A private company operates four hydro-electric stations on the Plateau, and the distribution lines carrying power to the mining centres are shown. The possibility of further expansion of power installations on the Plateau, and the development of the area as an industrial centre, is discussed in the text.

first priority for industrial development. The power is already available, more could be developed if required, and the Plateau now has a labour force which is, at least in part, accustomed to the handling of machinery and which could be diverted to new industry as mining employment declines. The retention of such a labour force as a single entity would be to the good of the country, whereas with gradual dispersal accompanying the working-out of the minesfield the benefit of accumulated experience would be lost. This point is introduced here because of suggested Government hydro-electric schemes, such as on the Ogun River in Oyo Province and at the Shiroro Gorge of the

Kaduna River in Niger Province. Such developments may well prove to be desirable in due course, but neither would appear to hold such early industrial promise as the Jos Plateau area.

If the Kaffo River area should be developed for the working of the radio-active granites, as mentioned on p. 191, an increased demand for electric power would certainly follow, and would involve the extension of the transmission lines northward to the Liruein–Kano Hills, and probably the erection of new generating stations. There should be no difficulty in finding suitable sites for the latter, as use could be made of rivers like the Sha, where they

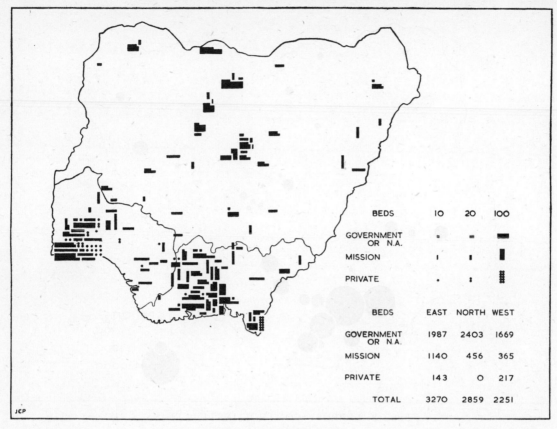

BEDS	10	20	100
GOVERNMENT OR N.A.			
MISSION			
PRIVATE			

BEDS	EAST	NORTH	WEST
GOVERNMENT OR N.A.	1987	2403	1669
MISSION	1140	456	365
PRIVATE	143	0	217
TOTAL	3270	2859	2251

FIG. 167. HOSPITALS

Hospital facilities (1952) are shown in the map. The greatly superior position of the East is noteworthy, and the part played by mission hospitals is greater than in any other region. The West shows a fair number of hospitals. Although there is some hospital provision in all parts of both East and West, the concentration of hospital provision in the Ibo and southern Yoruba areas respectively is very marked.

There is little to choose between the Middle Belt and the rest of the North, apart from the mining area and the larger towns of the latter. Bearing in mind the distances involved and the poor communications network, it may be said that hospital accommodation is not attainable for the majority of the Northern people, and the dispensary is the highest standard of medical service which may (or may not) be within reach. Point is added to this by a study of the disease maps showing the numbers of cases which may be expected during the frequent epidemics.

Population totals for the three Regions should be read against hospital accommodation, when it is seen that accommodation in the concentrated areas of the East and West is about six times greater than the average for the North. Even in the best areas, however, the figure for available beds per head of the population is below the level normally regarded as adequate.

descend the scarp, with suitable conservation on the high-plateau surface.

For the benefit of those unacquainted with African conditions, it may be mentioned that in the absence of electric lighting use is made of oil lamps in some form: wicks floating in palm-oil constitute the common illumination of many of the southern night markets. For those who

can afford it, kerosene is the common lighting fuel, used either in "hurricane" or in pressure-vapour lamps.

MEDICAL SERVICES

Medical officers in Nigeria have always been relatively few in number, and have frequently

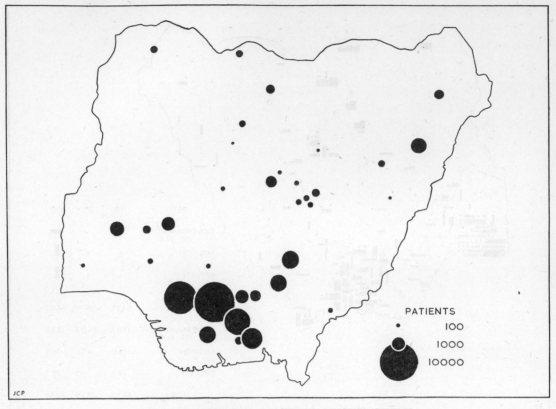

FIG. 168. LEPROSY CONTROL INSTITUTIONS

The great concentration in the East is very marked. For distribution of the disease see p. 44.

been responsible for very large areas; the 1952 total of 175 Government medical officers for the whole country presents a doctor/population ratio which is very low by European standards, even when due allowance is made for doctors in private practice or in Mission or other organisations. Fig. 167, showing hospital facilities in the country, gives an indication of the important part played by non-Government medical services. It must be remembered that doctors in Nigeria are faced with a number of unusual problems and duties; for example, much is still unknown about the diseases of West Africa, while duties in branches such as the Sleeping Sickness Service may involve qualified doctors in tasks such as the mapping of rivers and streams. The possible scope of such extra-medical activities has been documented in the case of the Anchau Corridor.

It is clear that there is room for a great increase in the number of qualified doctors in the country. The Medical Faculty of University College, Ibadan, will, it is hoped, be in a position to train many more Nigerians than could have obtained accommodation in medical schools overseas, but even this can provide no immediate great increase in numbers of medical practitioners, the period of training being seven years and the average annual intake at present being of the order of twenty-five students. For the near future it therefore appears that fully trained doctors will be in short supply.

Other grades of medical workers also show shortages, particularly in the case of fully trained nurses. Government has recently established a training centre for nurses at Ibadan, but the remarks above regarding time and numbers will also apply here, and it is necessary to take a long-term view rather than to hope for an immediate increase in numbers of qualified staff. Some reference should be made to the staff of Government dispensaries, who, with limited training, are not infrequently called upon to carry out unusually difficult tasks; in working under epidemic conditions such staff have sometimes earned high praise.

Hospital distribution is shown in Fig. 167, from which several points can be made, particularly the relatively low provision of facilities in the North, in regard to population numbers, and the generally low number of beds in the country as a whole. An approximate average figure of one hospital bed to every 3,000 people is very low, and in the Northern Region the figure is about 1 to 6,000. With regard to Mission activity in the North, the position is similar to that of secondary schools (see below). It should further be noted that the equipment available in the hospitals would in many cases be considered inadequate by modern standards; reference is made elsewhere (p. 228) to the distribution of electricity supplies and to difficulties to be faced when these are inadequate or absent, and comparison of Fig. 167 with Figs. 164 and 165 will reveal the number of hospitals which are located in centres lacking both electricity and piped-water supplies.

Fig. 168 shows Leprosy Control Institutions, which are not hospitals in the ordinary sense, patients normally living in special villages or, when these centres are full, in their own homes. Hospital beds in leprosy institutions are included in Fig. 167.

Little can be said about dental facilities except that they are barely significant. The total number of Government dentists in 1952 was 7, not all of whom would be in the country at any one time on account of leave arrangements.

EDUCATION

Much has been written about education in Africa, including Nigeria, and it is not proposed to do more here than to outline the present position.

Nigeria can now show all stages of education from the primary school to the technical college and the university. As in other countries, the function of Government is not so much the provision of schools as the advising and inspection of schools run by local authorities or other bodies. The great weight of teaching in the Southern Provinces has been borne by the various missions, although lately there has been an increase in the number of schools which are privately owned or which are managed by organisations such as the various tribal unions of recent growth. In the North, teaching was largely restricted to the Koranic schools, and the agreements reached early in the century between the ruling Emirs and the British excluded Christian Missions from the emirates; the subsequent admission of the Missions into the North has not brought the Region educational facilities in any way comparable with those of the East and West where educational work by the Missions is of long standing. This is true of primary education, and is even more striking in the case of secondary education (Fig. 169). This disparity between the northern and southern parts of the country, reinforcing differences of tribe and religion, can have serious repercussions on the future of the country; with the policy of "Nigerianisation" of the Civil Service in full swing, it necessarily means that even in the Northern Region many senior positions will be filled by men from Southern Nigeria in the absence of qualified northerners.

Interchange of men and ideas between the various Regions is in no way objectionable, and is, on the contrary, a desirable practice if the people of the country are to develop a sense of the unity of Nigeria over and above their tribal backgrounds, but over the coming years, during which the country will be feeling its way towards an autonomous national identity, the one-way tendency in senior (and junior) appointments may cause suspicion among the uneducated population, and may damage the ideal of Nigerian unity before it has a chance of developing. It is difficult to see how educational facilities in the North could have been expanded during the

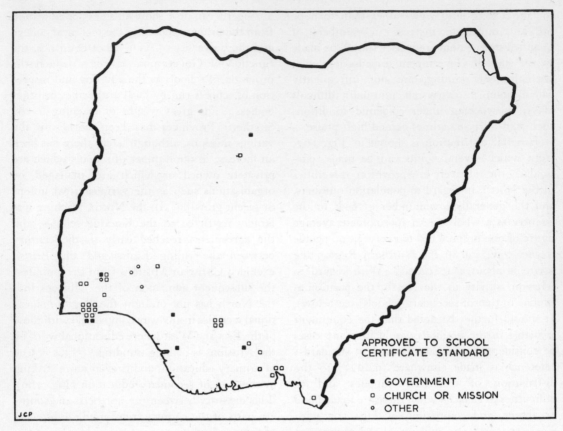

FIG. 169. SECONDARY SCHOOLS

The map shows schools approved to School Certificate standard in 1950. Other institutions engaged in secondary school work, but failing to meet all requirements for official approval, are not shown, but the distribution pattern is approximately the same.

The East and West, while being far from generously provided for, can show a moderate spread of secondary schools, although there is again a localised concentration in the same areas noted in Fig. 167 as best provided with hospitals. Opportunity for obtaining secondary education in the North is almost non-existent; for a population of nearly 17 millions there is shown as approved one mission school for girls and one government school for boys. Attention is given in the text to the urgency of rectifying this position in the interest of ensuring the development of a sense of national unity and of equal partnership among the Nigerian people in their rapid advance towards political autonomy.

first half of this century while preserving the ban on Mission activity resulting from the religious principles of the northern peoples; wider provision of schools by Government would have required diversion of considerable funds from other fields of development and would have involved a major change in the function of the Government Education Department as defined at the beginning of this section. The statement frequently made that the northerner is not interested in education compared with the southern Nigerian is an unfair generalisation, in the writer's opinion, and savours overmuch of the phrase that what is never known is not missed. The southern Nigerian can see the benefits of school education without difficulty, but it is perhaps unreasonable to expect enthusiasm for secondary education from a northerner whose nearest secondary school may be as much as 500 miles away, and who, if he is aware of it at all, knows that in the North only 1 schoolboy for every 20,000 people can hope for a place as far as the School Certificate Examination. It is suggested that a large-scale expansion of school facilities in the North should be of the greatest priority, not in any spirit of regional partisanship, but because it is considered doubtful whether any real sense of Nigerian unity can be achieved while the opportunities for advancement are so disproportionate in different parts of the country.

In order to obtain official approval schools need, among other requirements, to show varying proportions of qualified staff at different levels. Standards of qualification are still low: even secondary schools, with a requisite number of graduates on the staff, may have some junior teaching entrusted to staff whose own highest qualification is the School Certificate. This situation will persist for some years until the number of Nigerian graduates from Ibadan or overseas is large enough to supply the needs of the teaching profession.

As the result of an earlier Commission, a University College was established at Ibadan at the end of 1947. Over a million pounds for cost of buildings was provided from the Colonial Development and Welfare Fund, and a further capital sum of over two million pounds has been assigned by the Nigerian Government for the construction of a teaching hospital, but the University College is an autonomous institution. Under a Special Relationship with the University of London, Ibadan students take degrees of the latter university; in many subjects syllabuses have been modified in order to lay particular emphasis on Africa and African conditions. Existing faculties are those of Arts, Science, Medicine, and Agriculture and Veterinary Science. Student numbers are limited by the absence of much higher secondary education, and annual intake for the next few years is unlikely to be much above the 100–120 range.

The Nigerian College of Arts, Science and Technology is being established in three parts, at Ibadan, Zaria and Enugu. This is intended to provide higher training of non-university character, along lines similar to the Polytechnic institutions of the United Kingdom. A number of Government departments have maintained their own professional schools for a number of years in order to provide necessary training for their junior technical grades; such courses have, in some cases, included general education to the level of the Intermediate Examination in Science, and some of these departmental schools have produced junior staff of high quality. Normal practice allows better students to continue to a degree or to a professional qualification suitable for senior appointment, such additional training being taken either immediately after the first course or after a period of some years of satisfactory work and experience in the service of the department concerned.

The existence of forms of higher education should not disguise the fact that educational facilities are greatly inadequate at the lower levels. In 1944 it was estimated that 350,000 children below the age of 16 were attending school, and although numbers have risen considerably since that year the estimated number of children within this age range is $7\frac{3}{4}$ millions. The recommendation that a four-year primary course should be provided for all children would necessitate the employment of large numbers of uncertificated teachers. A four-year age group represents some $1\frac{3}{4}$ million children and would require some 60,000 teachers: a recent estimate [1] gave primary teachers in 1950 as approximately 17,000 in the East, with nearly 900 secondary teachers, and 4,500 in the North, with just over 100 secondary teachers. These figures reveal the scale of present available staff, and the disparity between East and North (remembering also that the northern population total greatly exceeds that of the eastern): they include, of course, staff teaching at levels above the four-year primary course, so that the staff required for the recommended scheme would be largely in addition to the present totals. Such great increases in numerical strength can be attained

[1] *West African Review* (1952), p. 734.

only with uncertificated teachers, but it would appear that this condition must be accepted if even so slight a beginning of general education is to be achieved.

In considering general education of this type, certain factors need to be noted. Firstly, the widespread employment of uncertificated teachers would need careful supervision, past experience having shown that in some private schools operated as business concerns an uncertificated teacher may do more harm than good. Some selective process would obviously be required, and the salaries offered, although necessarily low in view of the numbers involved in relation to the economic state of the country, would have to be sufficient to attract individuals in competition with other forms of employment. Secondly, repercussions on the social system would have to be faced. In a country where child labour forms an integrated part of the family economy, a four-year withdrawal of each child for its primary education would possibly have serious effects, and might result in an initial lowering of the standard of living. Such a scheme would therefore have to be carried through in the face of considerable opposition, accentuated by the very understandable reluctance of the older uneducated generations to risk the possible scorn of youth or a subsequent revolt against the authority of the senior members of the tribe or family.

Mass education campaigns might to some extent combat opposition by the older people, but such campaigns may themselves face the conservative outlook that it is unseemly for elder members to be instructed by younger men. Schemes such as those tried on the Gold Coast, suitably followed up to consolidate progress made, would appear to be suitable for Nigerian conditions also.

Teacher-training does not, perhaps, at present receive the attention due to it. There are various reasons for this, including the consideration of time required in relation to the urgent demand for staff with or without such training. The Education Department has in the past organised some very successful courses to prepare selected elementary teachers for secondary school work, and similar courses for both primary and secondary teachers might well be developed on a larger scale. The University College might be able to train graduate teachers, and the Nigerian College to train teachers with a lower academic qualification, but any programme of general primary education might require training courses on a scale beyond the capacity of either of these institutions. The expressed intention of the Regional Governments in the West and East is the provision of compulsory primary education as soon as possible. Some of the difficulties involved have been outlined, and it remains to be seen how far and how fast this desirable principle can be put into effect during the next decade.

POSTAL AND SIMILAR COMMUNICATIONS

Internal postal rates (at a basic charge of $1\frac{1}{2}d$. per letter) are very low considering the distances involved and, with much of the letter mail being carried by the internal air services, Nigeria can claim to possess one of the cheapest services in the world. It is hoped that these low rates will be maintained, since individual incomes at present are probably too low for the existing volume of mail to be preserved with higher rates, and it would be most unfortunate in a country with a low standard of literacy to discourage what is for many people the sole manifestation of such literacy.[1]

The popularity of letter-writing among that part of the population which can read and write should not mask the fact that the postal services mean nothing to the great majority. Fig. 170, showing distribution of post offices, is included to illustrate the remoteness of most areas from any sort of post office. Provision of a close network of post offices would not in itself encourage a drive for literacy, but the absence of such facilities may act as a discouragement in any area where a mass education campaign has taken place.

The map of Telegraph and Telephone

[1] The internal letter rate was increased to $2d.$ in 1954.

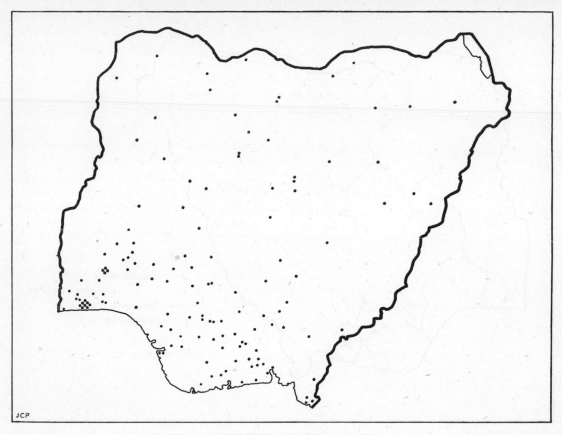

FIG. 170. POST OFFICES

Distribution must be related to distance, and reference is made in the text to the provision of postal facilities in relation to mass education campaigns.

Services (Fig. 171) emphasises the restricted influence mentioned above. A study of the map reveals the development along the railway system and of subsequent "tributary" expansion. Until very recently the telephone system was split into a number of separate regional parts, with the result that telephonic communication was possible, for example, between Makurdi and the North but not between Makurdi and Enugu. A nation-wide system is now being developed with the aid of radio-telephone connection, a method preferable to the laying of long land lines which are difficult to maintain and repair, and which are always liable to damage during the severe storms of the wet season.

Radio-diffusion services are operated at a number of the larger centres, incorporating both overseas broadcasts and programmes through Nigerian studios, partly in the local languages, and including local music and other features. These services are very popular, and can be of far greater interest and value to the people than normal overseas broadcasts, while the service charges are within the means of people who would be unable to afford the purchase of wireless sets. Nigerian wireless broadcasting is in process of serious development, and after a considerable period of experimental work may shortly emerge as a full service for West African listeners.

MAPS

The systematic mapping of Nigeria is far from completion. The national framework,

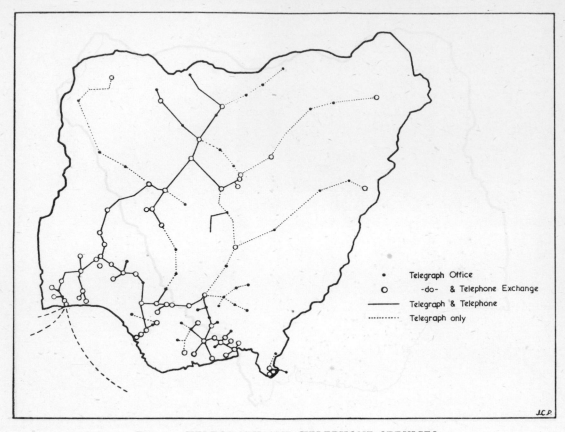

FIG. 171. TELEGRAPH AND TELEPHONE SERVICES

Services shown are those based on land lines, and the separation of the various telephone systems can be seen. Introduction of radio-telephone services has now united these systems, with a consequent great improvement in national communications. Many administrative centres, however, still rely on telegraph and postal services only.

as yet unfinished, consists of primary triangulation chains in the Northern Provinces, with the exception of the N.E. where the flat terrain of much of the Chad basin is unsuitable for triangulation. Although some of the triangulation chains extend into the Western and Eastern Provinces, recourse has had to be made to framework traverses in much of the area of high forest.

The only complete series of maps covering the whole country is on the scale of 1 : 500,000 and comprises 15 sheets. They are of variable accuracy, depending on sources of information, being in some areas compiled from 1 : 125,000 survey sheets and in others compiled from sources such as administrative divisional sketch-

maps which may be in error by a number of miles. In the latter case, for example, a series of villages along a divisional boundary may appear twice, in parallel disposition some distance apart and with variations in the spelling of names.

Parts of the country, approximately one-eighth of the total area (Fig. 172), are covered by topographical sheets on a scale of 1 : 125,000, which is adequate for most purposes in this type of terrain, but some of the Western Region sheets on this scale have not been revised for forty years. It is most unfortunate that survey services have tended in the past to be regarded as among the most suitable for reduction in times of financial economy. Field staff reached

FIG. 172. MAP COVERAGE

"Incomplete sheets" are un-contoured line maps produced from aerial photographs.

Sheets produced by the Kano Native Administration are not shown.

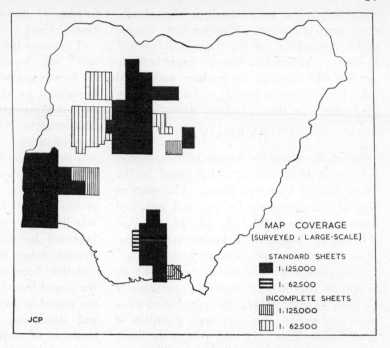

MAP COVERAGE
(SURVEYED : LARGE-SCALE)

STANDARD SHEETS
■ 1:125,000
▤ 1: 62,500
INCOMPLETE SHEETS
▥ 1:125,000
▥ 1: 62,500

JCP

a maximum in 1930, when establishment was approximately twice that of the present day, and retrenchment of nearly two-thirds of the field staff during the depression of the early thirties has, in the last decade, resulted in difficulties of recruitment, both from overseas and from Nigeria, men with the requisite educational background preferring a more congenial and more secure career among the many alternative forms of public service now open to them.

As has been stated in earlier sections, lack of maps has frequently led to a waste of money and effort which probably more than offsets the past decreased expenditure on survey services, and it is to be regretted that a large-scale mapping programme was not undertaken during the years of the financial depression, when labour and carrier rates were at a minimum and salaries low.

The general rise in cost of men and materials would make a large-scale programme expensive at the present day, even if staff could be obtained. One result of this (many of the British colonies can show a similar record with regard to surveys) has been the establishment by the Colonial Office of a central Directorate of Colonial Surveys, and the use of Royal Air Force squadrons for aerial surveys of colonial territories. Such surveys have been carried out in Nigeria since the war, where suitable conditions for photography normally exist during October and November (see p. 225 for reference to atmospheric clarity), and recent years have seen the production by the central organisation of

line maps on a scale of 1 : 62,500 of areas of Nigeria produced from such photographs: such maps are as yet uncontoured and show few names, but are greatly preferable to no maps at all. Further detail could be added if survey staff were available for work on the ground. This mapping programme will necessarily require a number of years, the effective annual season being short. Some air photography is carried out locally with a small chartered aircraft, but this kind of work cannot be organised economically for large-scale topographic mapping, and is normally concerned with individual projects for which photographs are required by other Government departments.

In 1954 map series on scales of 1 : 50,000 and 1 : 100,000 were started, and it is intended that these will become the national map scales. Large-scale plans can be obtained for most of the large towns, and specialised maps on various scales also exist.

An accurate map cover for most, if not all, of the country might be regarded as a necessarily early stage in development planning. Although development in many areas over the next few years cannot be suspended until maps are available, it is to be hoped that the value to the country of a large-scale mapping programme will be appreciated and that requisite action will be taken. Meanwhile more use might be made of available material to produce provisional maps for areas which have as yet no maps of any kind other than the 1 : 500,000 sheets.

CURRENCY

Standard coinage for Nigeria is that common for British West Africa, and is issued by the West African Currency Board. The notes in general circulation are for 20s. and 10s., and coins are 2s., 1s., 6d., 3d., 1d., $\frac{1}{2}d.$ and $\frac{1}{10}d.$ The last of these coins is known as the *anini*. West African currency is at par with sterling.

The anini was introduced in 1908, and is an important coin in local marketing, particularly in bush villages, where the preparation of a meal may require only very small quantities of some commodities. In such villages the florin may be refused by the vendor: the shilling may frequently involve recourse to a money-changer, and 10 pennies may be regarded by both parties as a fair and just return for a shilling. This is a factor to be considered when paying labour in the bush, and may involve the transport of a considerable weight of metal.

Some reference should be made to earlier forms of currency. The use of cowrie shells disappeared with the development of trade, large bulk for small value making them impracticable as a currency. Maria Theresa dollars, formerly common currency from Abyssinia westwards across the Sudan, have now almost disappeared; occasional specimens can still be obtained in the great northern markets. British coinage, with the aforementioned addition of the anini, was legal currency until the formation of the West African Currency Board in 1912.

The most interesting of the former "coinages" was the manilla. The exact origin of the form is unknown, but it appears to have been introduced by the Portuguese in the earliest days of West African trading, and survived in South-eastern Nigeria until 1949. Manillas were of various types, of which the commonest was the okpoho manilla, a metal rod of horseshoe shape, splayed at the ends, $2\frac{1}{4}$ inches in diameter and 3 ounces in weight. Until the prohibition of further import in 1902, the manillas were manufactured in Europe and imported by the trading firms as required. Manilla values fluctuated with seasonal trade, variations being of the order of 108 okpohos to the pound from October to March and 103 to the pound in June and July. Increased trade and decreasing manilla numbers following cessation of imports caused a steady rise in value of the manilla, and they were redeemed by Government at 80 okpohos to the pound in 1948–9, when their further use as a currency was prohibited. As this figure was above the maximum seasonal value yet reached, and the prohibition included the retention of more than 200 manillas by any individual (a figure allowing their continued use in ceremonial), it is probable that the great majority were redeemed. A total of more than 32 million manillas was received at a redemption figure of a little over £400,000; after sale of the manillas as scrap metal overseas, the cost to Government was nearly £250,000, which is not an unduly high figure for the withdrawal from a moderately conservative community of a currency form which had been in use for some four hundred years.

BIBLIOGRAPHY

Annual Reports of the following Nigerian Government Departments: Education, Geological Survey, Medical, Posts and Telegraphs, Public Works, Survey.
Electricity Corporation of Nigeria, *Annual Reports*.
Gray, R. F. A., "Manillas", *The Nigerian Field*, Vol. XVI, 1951, pp. 52–66.
Nigerian Government. Memorandum on Educational Policy in Nigeria, 1948.
United Africa Company, Statistical and Economic Review, No. 3, March 1949; No. 4, Sept. 1949 (on currency).

CHAPTER VIII

THE FUTURE

Economically, no less than politically, Nigeria has reached a critical stage in its development.

Its population, like that of many other African territories, appears to be entering a period of rapid expansion and unless a substantial expansion of the agricultural output is achieved the peasant farmer will find it increasingly difficult to provide both the basic foodstuffs required within Nigeria itself and the very considerable volume of export crops upon which the Territory's prosperity is coming increasingly to depend. Such an expansion of output might be achieved either by an increase in crop area or by improved cultivation techniques giving higher unit-area yields. It will be clear from the discussion of the population pattern that this pattern is immature and that scope exists for planned internal colonisation in both the empty areas of the Middle Belt and in the south-eastern and north-eastern sectors of the Territory. Some account of existing land settlement schemes in various parts of the country has already been given. It will be apparent from these accounts that the technical and social problems to be solved are considerable, and that any scheme of population redistribution will depend for its success upon social factors no less than upon technical factors: upon the overcoming of the peasants deep-seated land attachment, which impedes migration, and upon the harmonising of the interests of the immigrant group with those of already established groups (e.g. the Fulani in the Sokoto Rice area), no less than upon water supply extension, the building of new lines of communications or the eradication of the tsetse fly. The greatest prospects for expansion of output per unit area would appear to lie along three lines of development: the use of machinery in carefully selected areas, a wide use of fertil-

isers in placement spacings and an expansion of mixed farming. A promising start has been made in all these directions, but progress is slow; thus it is over two decades since mixed farming was introduced in the North, yet the number of mixed farmers in Kano Province is still less than 1 per cent. of the total number of farmers in the province. Further, as has been stressed in an earlier section, the integration of mechanised farming into the traditional peasant system raises a multitude of technical, sociological and agricultural problems, and a full assessment of the potentialities of mechanisation under Nigerian conditions can be made only in the light of the experience provided by pilot projects such as the Niger Agricultural Project or the Sokoto Rice Scheme. At the same time, it should be emphasised that all agricultural improvement schemes hinge ultimately upon the efficiency of the individual peasant, and in this connection the problems of disease and illiteracy are fundamental; in the expansion of agricultural productivity the role of the doctor and the educationist is no less vital than that of the agriculturist or engineer. There is no doubt that, given time, the productivity of Nigerian peasant agriculture can be greatly increased; but time is short and population growth is rapid.

Scarcely less important than the overall food problem are what may be termed the local problems. The spread of swollen-shoot disease in the Cocoa Belt threatens the whole economy of the Western Region, yet the conservatism of many members of the cocoa-farming community has impeded the carrying-out of rapid and drastic counter-measures designed to check the disease, and this same conservatism, together with the dangerous export-crop mentality typical of Nigerian agriculture as a whole, may be a major obstacle in achieving that diversification of cropping which alone can ensure the agricultural stability of the Cocoa Belt. In the Eastern Region the peasant-produced palm-oil may expect to meet increasing competition from the plantation-grown and factory-processed oil of the Congo and South-east Asia, and the local opposition to more effective methods of extraction by oil-mills and the failure to replace the ageing groves of wild palms by improved plantings are jeopardising the whole future of the Nigerian palm-oil industry. Existing schemes of plantation development may have an important educative function, but on the scale projected do little more than touch the fringe of the problem of production. These examples suggest clearly the importance of social and educational factors, as opposed to purely economic factors, and emphasise the point that while the policy of development through an indigenous peasantry is undoubtedly sound in theory, it is courting disaster to base ambitious schemes of economic development on a largely illiterate peasantry; without education there is only the illusion of progress.

The scanty development of modern industry in the Territory has been indicated; nevertheless, a substantial expansion of industry would do much to relieve the pressure on the land in congested districts, and would reduce the vulnerability and unbalance of the present economy. In such an expansion of industry the water-power resources of the Middle Belt (and especially of the Jos Plateau) and the coal resources of the Ibo Provinces will be locational factors of major importance. There is a wide range of secondary industries offering promising fields for local African enterprise, especially if electric power becomes more widely available: cassava processing, fruit canning and fruit juice bottling, the manufacture of leather goods and textiles, bricks, tiles and pottery, the extraction and processing of vegetable oils, industries based on wood and plastics. These smaller-scale industries possess marked social and economic advantages, for they can be carried on in small units widely dispersed throughout the raw material-producing regions, and their requirements in the form of capital investment and labour skills are relatively modest; they therefore make it possible to obtain the maximum diffusion of the benefits of industry at a very small cost. In the past it has been fashionable to attribute the low level of industrial development in the Territory to the policy of the imperial power, but this criticism has been deprived of whatever scanty foundation of fact which it may have possessed by the development policy of the Government during the last few years, and today it is increasingly apparent that some of the major obstacles to industrialisation are to be found in the attitudes and abilities of Nigerians themselves. Only too frequently the local businessman hesitates to invest in new industries, preferring the quicker returns to be obtained from commodity trading; further, it is undoubtedly true that the number of individuals with the initiative, skill and tenacity which new industrial development demands is small. This does not imply any reflection on the innate ability of the Nigerian entrepreneur or worker; it does, however, emphasise the point made earlier regarding the primacy of education, and it lends support to the view expressed by Mackay: "It is idle to think in terms of West African development *solely* by African enterprise for many years to come. In theory it would keep more wealth within the country; in practice it would be very much less efficient and less rewarding. There must be a period of transition." It is during this transition period, and in projects such as the Niger Agricultural Project, the Shendam Settlement Scheme and the Pioneer Oil Mills Scheme, and, above all, in the diffusion of the education basic to all development that Black and White have the opportunity to work out a new and rewarding pattern of co-operation in Nigeria.

APPENDIX I

CLIMATIC DATA

Station	Latitude	Longitude	Altitude (approx.)
Bamenda . . .	05° 56′ N.	10° 09′ E.	5,000 feet
Bauchi	10 18	09 50	1,940
Benin	06 19	05 37	258
Debundscha . . .	04 07	08 58	30
Enugu	06 27	07 29	763
Forcados . . .	05 22	05 26	10
Ibadan	07 26	03 54	748
Ikeja (Lagos Airport) .	06 35	03 20	132
Ilorin . . .	08 26	04 30	1,200
Jos	09 52	08 54	4,233
Kaduna . . .	10 36	07 27	2,118
Kano	12 02	08 32	1,561
Maiduguri . . .	11 51	13 05	1,160
Minna	09 37	06 32	853
Nguru . . .	12 51	10 28	1,100
Port Harcourt . .	04 51	07 01	67
Sokoto . . .	13 01	05 16	1,150
Victoria . . .	04 00	09 13	10
Wamba . . .	08 57	08 36	1,300
Warri	05 31	05 44	20
Yelwa	10 50	04 45	800
Yola	09 10	12 29	575

Mean Monthly Rainfall (inches)

Station	No. of Years	Jan.	Feb.	Mar.	Apr.	May	June	July	Aug.	Sept.	Oct.	Nov.	Dec.	Year
Bamenda . .	26	1·1	2·2	5·9	8·0	9·3	12·8	16·0	15·1	18·8	10·4	3·1	1·1	103·8
Bauchi . .	33	0·0	0·0	0·2	1·4	3·5	5·9	9·1	14·5	7·1	1·5	0·0	0·0	43·2
Benin . .	44	0·8	1·3	3·6	6·6	8·2	12·0	12·3	8·1	11·9	9·4	3·0	0·6	77·8
Debundscha .	25	9·2	10·1	21·9	19·1	30·9	47·0	55·8	53·8	61·3	45·0	25·5	14·4	394·1
Enugu . .	33	0·7	1·1	2·6	5·9	10·4	11·4	7·6	6·7	12·8	9·8	2·1	0·5	71·5
Forcados . .	37	1·9	3·5	7·1	10·7	16·0	23·3	25·4	14·3	23·3	16·3	6·2	2·2	150·2
Ibadan . .	46	0·4	0·9	3·5	5·5	5·9	7·5	6·3	3·4	7·0	6·1	1·6	0·4	48·4
Ikeja . .	47	1·1	1·6	3·8	5·6	10·8	18·1	11·1	2·7	5·5	8·1	2·7	1·0	72·0
Ilorin . .	35	0·2	0·7	2·3	3·9	6·6	7·6	5·3	5·4	9·6	6·4	1·2	0·3	49·5
Jos . .	29	0·1	0·1	1·0	3·5	7·9	9·1	12·9	11·6	8·4	1·6	0·1	0·1	56·4
Kaduna . .	35	0·0	0·1	0·5	2·7	5·8	7·0	8·6	12·3	11·0	3·0	0·2	0·0	51·2
Kano . .	46	0·0	0·0	0·1	0·4	2·5	4·4	8·0	12·4	5·0	0·5	0·0	0·0	33·3
Maiduguri .	34	0·0	0·0	0·0	0·3	1·6	2·7	6·9	8·8	4·1	0·8	0·0	0·0	25·2
Minna . .	35	0·0	0·2	0·7	2·4	5·9	7·4	7·9	11·0	11·9	5·7	0·2	0·0	53·3
Nguru . .	9	0·0	0·0	0·0	0·1	1·1	1·4	4·6	9·9	4·1	0·1	0·0	0·0	21·3
Port Harcourt .	37	1·2	2·3	5·0	7·5	9·9	13·3	12·8	12·3	15·5	10·7	5·5	1·8	97·8
Sokoto . .	35	0·0	0·0	0·0	0·4	2·0	3·5	5·8	9·3	5·7	0·5	0·0	0·0	27·3
Victoria . .	28	1·7	2·7	6·1	8·5	13·1	25·0	38·2	31·2	16·7	10·0	4·1	1·3	158·6
Wamba . .	22	0·0	0·3	1·3	2·8	5·9	7·8	13·3	15·7	12·9	5·0	0·7	0·0	65·8
Warri . .	44	1·5	2·1	5·4	9·1	10·9	15·1	17·3	11·7	16·9	12·5	4·5	1·4	108·4
Yelwa . .	13	0·0	0·0	0·1	1·0	4·0	4·7	6·0	10·4	8·7	3·2	0·0	0·0	38·1
Yola . .	35	0·0	0·0	0·3	1·9	4·9	6·2	6·8	7·7	7·8	3·2	0·2	0·0	39·0

Monthly Means of Daily Maximum Temperatures (1943–7)

(° F.)

	Jan.	Feb.	Mar.	Apr.	May	June	July	Aug.	Sept.	Oct.	Nov.	Dec.	Year
Bauchi	87·8	91·1	95·5	98·1	94·8	89·6	84·5	82·1	84·3	88·9	91·2	89·2	89·8
Benin	88·0	90·9	91·2	90·4	88·3	85·4	82·1	81·8	83·0	85·4	88·7	88·7	87·0
Enugu	89·7	92·1	92·7	91·1	88·1	85·1	82·9	83·0	84·5	86·5	89·2	89·3	87·8
Ibadan	91·2	93·5	93·9	92·4	88·8	85·6	82·2	82·1	84·7	86·7	89·5	90·3	88·5
Ikeja	90·5	91·0	91·5	90·2	87·9	84·2	82·2	81·7	83·9	85·7	89·3	89·3	87·3
Ilorin	93·4	95·5	96·6	95·9	91·3	87·5	83·9	82·7	84·8	87·5	91·3	93·1	90·3
Jos	82·1	85·6	87·2	88·5	85·0	80·9	76·4	74·9	78·6	82·2	83·4	82·4	82·2
Kaduna	88·8	91·0	93·7	95·7	91·5	86·0	81·7	79·9	83·6	87·9	90·5	89·4	88·3
Kano	85·6	89·9	95·7	100·8	99·3	94·5	87·2	85·1	88·0	93·5	92·5	87·1	91·6
Maiduguri	88·9	92·9	98·2	104·1	102·1	97·4	89·4	85·6	89·4	95·3	95·1	90·3	94·0
Minna	94·9	96·8	97·8	97·7	92·6	86·9	83·9	82·3	84·7	88·1	93·2	94·6	91·1
Nguru	87·8	91·8	98·0	103·6	101·7	100·2	92·3	87·3	91·0	97·0	95·8	90·2	94·7
Port Harcourt	88·7	90·6	90·3	89·3	87·7	85·3	82·9	83·7	84·4	85·6	87·3	88·2	87·0
Sokoto	91·6	95·5	100·7	104·9	102·8	97·6	90·7	86·3	89·4	96·1	97·7	92·6	95·5
Victoria	85·6	86·8	86·8	86·5	85·5	82·7	79·4	79·7	81·1	82·9	84·5	85·1	83·9
Warri	88·4	90·8	91·1	90·8	88·6	86·1	82·6	83·1	83·9	86·0	88·8	88·6	87·4
Yelwa	94·8	99·0	102·0	102·6	97·1	90·7	87·3	84·2	87·0	91·2	96·4	95·9	94·0
Yola	95·1	98·4	102·0	103·0	96·9	90·5	87·4	86·2	87·2	91·1	96·9	96·0	94·2

Monthly Means of Daily Minimum Temperatures (1943–7)

(° F.)

	Jan.	Feb.	Mar.	Apr.	May	June	July	Aug.	Sept.	Oct.	Nov.	Dec.	Year
Bauchi	59·0	62·7	68·4	72·7	72·0	69·4	67·9	67·5	67·3	67·5	63·0	59·7	66·4
Benin	70·7	71·9	72·9	72·9	72·3	71·4	70·6	69·6	71·0	70·8	71·7	70·9	71·4
Enugu	72·2	73·3	75·0	74·8	72·9	71·6	71·5	71·1	70·8	71·0	72·6	72·1	72·4
Ibadan	69·2	70·5	72·7	72·5	71·9	71·0	70·0	70·0	70·0	69·7	69·9	69·2	70·5
Ikeja	69·8	72·6	73·1	71·7	72·1	71·2	70·0	69·7	70·5	71·0	71·7	70·9	71·2
Ilorin	67·5	68·2	73·4	73·3	73·1	71·4	70·9	70·1	70·4	70·1	69·5	66·5	70·4
Jos	57·0	59·3	64·1	66·3	65·4	63·4	62·7	62·3	62·2	62·2	60·3	57·2	61·9
Kaduna	58·9	62·8	67·2	71·2	71·2	68·1	67·4	67·9	66·7	66·1	59·5	57·1	63·3
Kano	56·1	59·5	65·9	72·4	74·6	73·9	71·1	69·6	69·4	68·1	61·6	56·9	66·6
Maiduguri	54·7	58·0	64·9	71·1	75·4	74·8	72·7	71·2	70·9	68·5	59·6	55·4	66·4
Minna	66·6	71·5	73·6	75·4	73·4	71·1	70·4	70·5	69·6	69·6	66·5	65·5	70·3
Nguru	53·8	57·8	63·6	69·3	72·6	74·3	73·1	71·4	70·9	66·5	59·1	54·7	65·6
Port Harcourt	72·7	73·5	74·5	74·5	73·8	73·4	72·7	72·2	72·7	72·7	73·1	73·1	73·3
Sokoto	59·6	62·9	70·2	76·2	78·6	76·4	72·5	72·1	71·6	70·5	64·3	59·8	69·6
Victoria	70·8	71·3	72·7	72·4	72·1	72·2	71·6	71·5	71·6	71·3	71·5	71·4	71·7
Warri	71·4	72·1	73·7	73·9	73·1	72·4	72·0	73·2	71·9	71·9	72·4	72·0	72·4
Yelwa	58·7	65·6	72·6	77·7	77·0	73·2	72·5	71·9	71·1	70·7	62·4	56·8	69·2
Yola	65·2	69·4	75·5	78·8	76·1	73·4	72·4	72·5	71·5	71·9	67·5	65·1	71·6

Mean Relative Humidity (1943–7)
(%)

06.00 G.M.T.

	Jan.	Feb.	Mar.	Apr.	May	June	July	Aug.	Sept.	Oct.	Nov.	Dec.	Year
Bauchi	28	25	27	47	72	84	90	94	93	86	54	38	61
Benin	96	94	95	95	96	96	96	97	97	97	96	97	96
Enugu	82	80	86	88	91	92	92	91	93	93	91	83	89
Ibadan	94	92	95	95	96	97	97	97	97	98	97	96	96
Ikeja	98	97	98	98	98	98	97	97	97	98	98	98	98
Ilorin	79	77	81	86	86	86	90	89	91	91	89	83	86
Jos	33	40	45	66	83	92	95	97	96	86	51	40	69
Kaduna	36	35	45	61	81	91	94	95	95	92	71	51	71
Kano	37	33	31	42	63	74	88	94	92	80	48	43	60
Maiduguri	48	41	34	32	53	73	87	94	93	83	60	56	63
Minna	40	44	53	73	84	91	93	94	94	93	77	53	74
Nguru	35	31	25	30	49	68	81	92	92	75	44	41	55
Port Harcourt	94	95	95	95	95	95	95	95	95	96	96	95	95
Sokoto	28	31	23	33	56	71	81	90	90	82	47	38	56
Victoria	93	93	92	93	94	96	96	96	96	96	94	94	95
Warri	99	98	98	98	95	98	98	99	99	99	99	99	98
Yelwa	55	47	50	61	76	88	91	95	96	95	91	78	77
Yola	35	33	34	55	76	87	90	92	93	91	71	47	67

12.00 G.M.T.

	Jan.	Feb.	Mar.	Apr.	May	June	July	Aug.	Sept.	Oct.	Nov.	Dec.	Year
Bauchi	10	9	10	18	34	50	62	69	64	45	17	13	33
Benin	63	57	61	66	71	74	79	78	79	74	67	65	69
Enugu	46	46	54	62	69	73	75	73	73	70	58	50	62
Ibadan	51	49	54	60	67	74	78	78	75	70	63	56	65
Ikeja	62	64	65	73	78	82	79	78	77	77	70	69	73
Ilorin	39	39	39	47	57	65	69	72	68	66	50	43	55
Jos	14	17	18	24	46	62	71	76	63	45	21	17	39
Kaduna	15	17	20	30	50	64	72	77	68	53	23	17	42
Kano	13	12	12	19	32	46	60	71	61	36	15	12	32
Maiduguri	17	13	11	12	25	40	60	69	59	37	18	20	32
Minna	24	29	33	44	56	68	73	77	72	65	40	28	52
Nguru	15	12	10	13	22	36	53	68	58	29	16	16	29
Port Harcourt	65	60	67	70	73	76	78	75	75	76	71	69	71
Sokoto	12	16	10	17	29	41	55	68	63	41	16	17	32
Victoria	76	74	76	77	79	83	88	86	85	82	80	77	80
Warri	70	65	68	70	73	78	82	79	81	78	71	71	74
Yelwa	14	18	22	33	48	62	68	77	72	63	34	21	41
Yola	16	15	17	26	39	61	66	68	69	60	29	19	40

APPENDIX II

POPULATION OF NIGERIA BY REGIONS
AND PROVINCES, 1931 AND 1952-3

Region and Province	1931 Census (a)	1952-3 Census (b)
	Thousands	*Thousands*
TOTAL NIGERIA . . .	19,930	31,180
Northern Region . . .	11,434	16,840
Western Region . . .	3,855	6,369
Eastern Region . . .	4,641	7,971
NORTHERN REGION		
Adamawa	602	1,181
Bauchi	1,075	1,424
Benue	1,037	1,468
Bornu	1,068	1,596
Ilorin (d) . . .	520	531
Kabba	478	664
Kano	2,354	3,398
Katsina (c) . . .	870	1,483
Niger	535	716
Plateau	540	893
Sokoto	1,885	2,680
Zaria	470	806
WESTERN REGION		
Abeokuta	435	630
Benin	485	901
Colony	325	510
Delta (Warri) . . .	501	590
Ibadan (c) . . .	990	1,661
Ijebu	306	348
Ondo	466	946
Oyo	347	783
EASTERN REGION		
Bamenda (c) . . .	200	429
Calabar	900	1,541
Cameroons . . .	175	324
Ogoja	708	1,082
Onitsha	1,108	1,768
Owerri	1,175	2,080
Rivers (c) . . .	375	747

NOTES.

1. All figures include non-African population.

2. (a) These figures have been approximately adjusted on the basis of the size of the areas transferred and the densities of population in the Provinces concerned.
   (b) Figures for the Eastern Region are still subject to revision.
   (c) Provinces created since 1931.
   (d) Under-counted by at least 100,000 in 1952.

3. The phenomenal increase in the population of some Provinces between 1931 and 1952-3 must be attributed in part to an under-estimate of the 1931 population.

INDEX

PLACE NAMES

GENERAL